INTRODUCTION TO LITERARY CONTEXT

American Poetry of the 20th Century

INTRODUCTION TO LITERARY CONTEXT

American Poetry of the 20th Century

SALEM PRESS

A Division of EBSCO Information Services, Inc.
Ipswich, Massachusetts

GREY HOUSE PUBLISHING

Publisher's Cataloging-In-Publication Data

Introduction to literary context. American poetry of the 20th century / [edited by Salem Press].—[First edition].

   pages; cm

  Includes bibliographical references and index.
  ISBN: 978-1-61925-713-9

  1. American poetry—20th century—History and criticism. I. Salem Press. II. Title: American poetry of the 20th century III. Title: American poetry of the twentieth century

PS323.5 .I587 2014
811.509

First Printing

CONTENTS

PUBLISHER'S NOTE

Introduction to Literary Context: American Poetry of the 20th Century is the newest title in Salem's *Introduction to Literary Context* series. Other titles in this series include *American Post-Modernist Novels, American Short Fiction, English Literature, World Literature,* and *Plays.*

This series is designed to introduce students to the world's greatest works of literature – including novels, short fiction, novellas, plays, and poems – not only placing them in the historical, societal, scientific and religious context of their time, but illuminating key concepts and vocabulary that students are likely to encounter. A great starting point from which to embark on further research, *Introduction to Literary Context* is a perfect foundation for *Critical Insights,* Salem's acclaimed series of critical analysis written to deepen the basic understanding of literature via close reading and original criticism. Both series – *Introduction to Literary Context* and *Critical Insights* – cover authors, works and themes that are addressed in core reading lists at the undergraduate level.

SCOPE AND COVERAGE

American Poetry of the 20th Century covers 34 poems written by American poets who represent a variety of ages, life styles, and political beliefs, including those whose work has been banned, burned, and revered. Their work is based on personal experiences and struggles, as well as societal issues of the time.

With in depth analysis of works by the likes of Edgar Allen Poe, Allen Ginsberg, Sylvia Plath, and Langston Hughes, *Introduction to Literary Context: American Poetry of the 20th Century* offers students the tools to grasp more firmly and dig deeper into the meanings of not only the works covered here, but literature as it has been created around the world.

ORGANIZATION AND FORMAT

The essays in *American Poetry of the 20th Century* appear alphabetical by title of the work. Each is 6-8 pages in length and includes the following sections:

- Content Synopsis – summarizes the poem, describing the main points and prominent characters in concise language.
- Historical Context – describes the relevance of the moods, attitudes and conditions that existed during the time period that the poem was written.
- Societal Context – describes the role of society in relation to the content of the poem, from the acceptance of traditional gender roles to dealing with mental illness.
- Religious Context – explains how religion – of the author specifically, or a group generally, influenced the poem.
- Scientific & Technological Context – analyzes to what extent scientific and/or technological progress has affected the writing of the poem.
- Biographical Context – offers biographical details of the poet's life, which often helps students to make sense of the work.
- Discussion Questions – a list of 8 – 10 thoughtful questions that are designed to develop stimulating and productive classroom discussions.
- Essay Ideas – a valuable list of ideas that will encourage students to explore themes, writing techniques, and character traits.
- Works Cited

Introduction to Literary Context: American Poetry of the 20th Century ends with a general Bibliography and subject Index.

ABOUT THIS VOLUME

Poetry was the dominant form of creative writing for several centuries and was one of the barometers used to measure a civilization's artistic merit, as poets often reflected a people's social conscience. Alas, that has all but faded from view in the 21st century (some scholars will argue the songwriters have become the poets of our age). Poetry comes in all shapes and sizes—there are ballads, odes, sonnets, poems of only a few words to book-length Goliaths and can rhyme or be presented in free verse. One size does not fit all, but there's enough variety in the works presented here to please a wide array of tastes.

Reading poetry can be daunting to the inexperienced but as the numerous works in this collection illustrate, simple analysis of the imagery presented by the poet often can unlock the work's true meaning and greatly enrich the reading experience. Poems that on the surface differ greatly in construction and form with no visible similarities on closer inspection can reveal themselves to be quite alike in theme and emotion. Several of the works in this collection concern the ailments that plagued the world, i.e., the disintegration of society, gender inequality, and racism to name a few. Some are general commentaries on humanity while others are personal reflections of the author's singular experiences.

Poetry should be read in the same fashion as a novel; the author is presenting characters and situations for the reader to discover, and like in prose, a first-person narrator should not be construed as being the author—one should not read *Stopping by Woods on a Snowy Evening* while picturing Robert Frost mounted on a horseback watching snow falling on another's' field. Some of these poems, however, *are* personal reflections: Allen Ginsberg's *Howl* is the poet directly expressing his feelings.

American Roots

Edgar Allan Poe's *The Raven* was published in *The American Review* in 1845, immediately catapulting the 36-year-old Poe from relative obscurity to national fame in a matter of weeks. *The Raven* subsequently was republished in numerous international newspapers, periodicals, and poetry anthologies, generating not only fame but adequate financial success to allow Poe to write full time without supplementing his income through other means. A fortunate occurrence, since in his brief life Poe became one of our nation's most influential writers.

Poe's biography is an inventory of failures and disappointments. After an aborted military career, including enrollment at West Point, Poe journeyed down other career paths but met a dead end at every turn. When writing *The Raven*, Poe purposely designed it to appeal equally to critics and lay readers. Poe languished in obscurity—and poverty—and needed a hit to grant him admission into the ranks of popular American literature's inner circle *and* put money in his pocket. The 18-stanza poem had substance for scholars to chew on while its amazing rhyme scheme dazzled and delighted working-class readers. The poem also features a man mourning for the loss of "Lenore," the love of his life, an experience shared by many. The heartbroken first-person narrator is home alone on a "bleak December" night with only his books for company—a familiar image to many critics that surely would meet their approval.

While the man seeks solace in his texts, a visitor wraps at his door, which is opened to reveal not a fellow human but a raven. Poe sets an eerie almost supernatural tone to the opening of the poem with "midnight dreary," "bleak December," "fantastic terrors," and "rustling curtains" in the early stanzas. He introduces the human and spiritual elements and the addition of the raven brings the symbol of nature for the perfect triumvirate. The use of a black bird also encompasses all three symbols: ravens and crows feature in mythology as bringers of prophecy (both evil and divine); as birds they are within the realm of nature, but their ability to speak, however, elevates them to more of a human scale than another animal could, e.g., a black cat, which Poe utilizes in his fiction, also is traditionally associated with witches and dark magic but its inability to speak limits its use as a literary symbol. Poe chose wisely.

"Nevermore," the bird's single utterance, also is ambiguous. At its core, *The Raven* concerns a man lamenting for lost love, *but* is Lenore alive and simply has rejected him, is she dead and impossible to possess, or was the man's heart destroyed by her—alive or dead—to the point where he'll never love again? We don't know. After losing Lenore, the narrator has secluded himself, but a tapping at his door is met with excitement rather than fear or rejection. The creature at the door isn't human and perhaps not even a bird but a messenger from the dead (maybe Lenore herself). Poe could be construed as being a progenitor of American noir, as his characters seem doomed and without hope from the start.

Robert Frost's (1874–1963) *Stopping by Woods on a Snowy Evening* is a forward step in the development of American poetry. Although Frost's work isn't derivative of Poe's stylistically, they both incorporate nature imagery, but to vastly different ends. Again readers encounter a man alone on "the darkest evening of the year." But the darkness is not foreboding. The narrator is mounted on a horse watching snow fall and enjoying the simple beauty of the scene. The speaker believes he knows the woods' owner, which labels him a local man either in the past or present.

The traveler's origins are unknown. He could be returning from a long period away, perhaps a soldier returning from war, and remembers these woods from playing there as a child so they conjure the joys of home and family. The image is positive; the sight of the woods filling with snow generates joy. The woods are unspoiled, the snow is clean, and new life will come in spring. The rider, however, cannot linger; he has "promises to keep" and must attend to his responsibilities. The scene easily could be construed as melancholy—it's cold, dark, empty, the lone rider has only his "little horse" for companionship—but the emotion is positive. The silent rider is happy upon entering a familiar setting and expresses neither sorrow nor loneliness and will move forward in his life.

Frost's *Birches* interestingly employs many of the same images but with the opposite message. Here trees make the narrator long for the irresponsibility of boyhood. The poems share the lure of nostalgia but to different ends. The narrator desires not only the freedom of youth, but its solitude as well. He doesn't want to play baseball with other boys but wants to climb trees alone to commune with nature and ascend to the heavens. He appears to be a man whose life has gone astray. Perhaps he has not lived up to his responsibilities and desires to turn back time for a second chance at setting a straighter course. His longing to climb a tree to its snowy peak can be viewed as wanting to ascend to heaven to "leave earth awhile" and experience a metaphorical rebirth by bowing the tree limbs to return back to the ground to start life anew.

Society in Ruins

T. S. Eliot's *The Love Song of J. Alfred Prufrock* (1915) elevated the author to the Olympus of American artists. Eliot is among the modernists group of writers, but this work as well as his epic, *The Waste Land*, however, foreshadows the themes championed by the later post-modernist school. Eliot was heavily influenced by European writers, especially the French, in his use of symbols, making his work often difficult to interpret. Prufrock is an anxiety-riddled man seemingly reflecting on his life while in conversation with a woman he is wooing. He knows that he is not an attractive or desirable man; he is aging, his hair is thinning and has "seen the moment of [his] greatness flicker" and has been afraid. He already has had many women and has "measured out his life in coffee spoons" the mornings after, but in reflecting on his life he knows that he has misjudged and misunderstood many things, especially women, and doesn't want to rush the moment and make another error. Although he is attracted to women and polite society, he also has felt "pinned and wriggling on the wall" like an insect and he must put on a false front by preparing "a face to meet the faces that you meet." Prufrock's "love song" is satirical; it's not about love at all but a society that has become an obstacle course, especially in terms of gender relations.

Published in 1922, Eliot's *The Waste Land* is among the seminal works of American poetry and is to that form what James Joyce's *Ulysses* is to the novel. Eliot takes the idea of society gone astray presented in *Prufrock* to the extreme in this poem. Presented in five sections, the poem is more disjointed and difficult than *Prufrock*. The sense of societal decay that permeates *Prufrock* is extended beyond interactions between the sexes to envelop all of society. In the wake of the first world war, the world has become broken.

Allen Ginsberg's *Howl* is his signature work and arguably the most noted poem produced by the group of writers known as the Beats. The motivation of the Beat writers, which include Jack Kerouac, Gregory Corso, Gary Snyder, William Burroughs, and Lawrence Ferlinghetti, often has been misinterpreted and misunderstood. The Beats of the 1940s and 1950s often are viewed as a sort of vanguard for the hippies of the 1960s, but not so. While the hippies had a more revolutionary mindset bordering on anti-Americanism that demanded societal change often through violence, the Beats were the product of a tainted society. Ginsberg, Kerouac, and company, who were steeped in the

work of 19th century Goliaths like Whitman and Melville on up to modernists Proust and Hemingway, went in search of the America of their forefathers only to discover that it had vanished in the smoke of two world wars and the Depression. Their disillusionment manifested itself in alcohol and drugs. *Howl* sports many of the trappings of the post-modernist movement expressed in verse form but also adds heavy images of homosexuality and drug use, which was socially unacceptable at the time (not to mention illegal), another factor in the Beats often being misconstrued as deviants.

Like many Beat writers, Ginsberg's work is heavily autobiographical and incorporates his circle of friends into his works sometimes even using their actual names. Kerouac did this as well in the first draft of his signature novel, *On the Road* (fictional names later were introduced prior to publication).

Love and Death

Anne Sexton's *All My Pretty Ones* (1962) like Ginsberg's *Howl* is a first-person narrative that expresses the author's feelings. The poem is Sexton's admission of the trouble she experienced in coming to terms with her parents' deaths within a short period of each other (Sexton's mother and father both passed away in 1959). This poem finds the narrator examining her father's possessions soon after his demise, discarding the important items that were the keepsakes of his life but are meaningless to her. There are boxes of photos of long-gone relatives and friends and a scrapbook with news clippings recalling historic moments of the 20th century including Prohibition, the *Hindenburg* crashing, Herbert Hoover's presidential election, and war, none of which relate to her own life experiences.

These items could be the trappings of many lives, but as the narrator turns the pages of the book images from her lifetime—her sister, family dogs—appear and Sexton adds more personal notes in revealing that her father apparently had gone broke and that he planned to remarry very soon after his wife's death but she convinced him not to. The most startling admission is that her father was an alcoholic. In the fourth stanza, the narrator calls her father "my drunkard" and in the fifth refers to his "alcoholic tendency" noted in her mother's diary.

At first glance, the poem may seem a depressing inventory of human faults, but the piece ends on a positive note. After listing the man's numerous shortcomings, the narrator says she will "bend down my strange face to yours and forgive you." She understands and accepts that her father was a deeply flawed man but her love for him surpasses his human frailties.

Race, Religion, and Gender

Langston Hughes' *I, Too* (1926) is an assault on the blatant racism that afflicted society for centuries. Here, the narrator is "the darker brother," the black race. The use of the word brother is expertly chosen as it places the narrator on an equal level, which another word like "son" would not. The darker brother is hidden away when company—presumably white—comes to visit. The narrator does not fight his seclusion knowing that he will eat in solitude today but not tomorrow. His time is coming quickly when he will sit at the white table because, when they see that he will not be separated and they are forced to look at him, they will understand that he is equal and will be ashamed of their treatment of him and shuck the yoke of blind ignorance that has separated them.

He is not bitter because he believes with full confidence that his equality will be recognized. The poem's last line solidifies the point while mimicking the opening line to show progress. In the poem's first line, the narrator says "I, too, sing America," meaning that he praises and loves his country as much as others. In the closing line, "sing" is replaced with "am," an affirmation of equality. Hughes presents his declaration without

anger or resentment, stating it simply as fact that will become undeniably clear.

Claude McKay's *America* (1921) is a forerunner to Langston Hughes' *I, Too*. The narrator of this 14-line poem is a black man lamenting the prejudice that stares him in the face from every direction. Despite being fed the "bread of bitterness" and having the "tiger's tooth" of injustice sunk into his throat, the narrator expresses neither fear nor anger. Instead, he stands within America's "walls without a shred of terror, malice, not a word of jeer." Like Hughes' "dark brother," the narrator knows that he will triumph over time. Whereas Hughes' speaker will force others to accept him now, McKay's narrator understands that much time will have to pass before racial equality is achieved, and he must wait.

Marge Piercy's *My Mother's Body* (1985) echoes many of the identical emotions presented by Hughes and McKay years earlier only in regard to gender and the suppression of women. In this work a young woman physically feels the pain of her mother's death miles away while her father hears the crash of the woman's fall to the floor but ignores it and continues to nap while his wife lies in pain that's like "a knife tearing a bolt of silk." The poem's opening stanzas present the clear message of women's suffering. Like Hughes's "dark brother" in *I, Too*, women are treated like a minority. She extends the metaphor to include religion, describing the trappings of Chanukah—candles, latkes, a dreydle—while Christmas lights twinkle on palm trees in Florida. Like women are treated as inferior, so are Jews in a Christian-dominated society. Jews certainly know that it's the Christmas season, but are Christians equally aware that it's also Chanukah?

Piercy incorporates a series of images of laundry, dresses, curtains—all things associated with women—as metaphors for the female body. An angel folds up her dead mother like laundry/her mother's clothes hung on her body like window curtains. These unimportant items also can be put away, replaced by new, or simply discarded. Her mother's body, like her mother's mother and so on has been little else than a machine for giving birth. Whatever dreams they might have had beyond the prospects of motherhood never were allowed to come to fruition. The narrator, however, refuses to accept the fate of women past and is determined to break the cycle and live the life she desires, a life of equality and fulfilled dreams.

The narrator contends that in the past, a woman was just a mother and wife and when the physical possibility of child bearing ended she became an empty useless vessel. She will not allow that for herself and rebels against that mindset and will have what her mother and all women before her could not. She is a rebel *with* a cause. Although the poem relates the narrator's personal experience, Piercy gives the work a universal appeal by extending the sentiments beyond this particular mother and daughter to include all women.

Sylvia Plath composed the vitriolic *Daddy* shortly before committing suicide, and if this work epitomizes her state of mind it's not hard to imagine why she ended her life. Like Marge Piercy, Plath's narrator comes to terms with a parent's death. Plath, however, is as hateful and poisonous as Piercy is forgiving. Plath generally is considered a member of the confessional school of poets, but this work probably is not intended to be read as autobiographic—at least one hopes not. In portraying her father, the narrator employees the most nightmarish imagery possible.

In the poem's opening stanzas, the narrator claims to have wanted to kill the man but he died naturally first. He was German, and the poem is heavy with Nazi imagery while the daughter likens herself to a Polish Jew destined for the death camps in "Dachau, Auschwitz, Belsen." Plath also associates the father with the Luftwafe, and he is a "Panzer-man" in black "with a Meinkampf look" and a "love of the rack and the screw." Later in the poem, daddy is a vampire who drank the narrator's blood but now has "a stake in [his] fat black heart."

From the melancholy to hope to social decay to racial injustice to forgiveness, the poems discussed in this collection provide a vast array of themes presented in a variety of styles for a rich vein of study.

Michael Rogers
Freelance writer, editor, and photographer
Former Senior Editor, *Library Journal*

Acquainted with the Night

by Robert Frost

Content Synopsis

In "Acquainted with the Night," a solitary walker wanders a city that is empty of souls but full of menace. The speaker of the poem announces, at its beginning and end, "I have been one acquainted with the night." The word "acquainted" underscores the narrator's solitude, for he knows the night intimately in a way he does not know his fellow man. When he passes a night watchman, another walker in the city with whom the speaker might presumably have some bond, he confesses, "I dropped my eyes, unwilling to explain." Likewise, when he hears a voice in the distance, he stops in his tracks—only to realize that the voice is not meant, "To call me back or say goodbye." By detailing the many kinds of night-walks he has taken—walks out and back in the rain, walks down lanes and alleys, walks through the city center, where he can see "a luminary clock against the sky"—the narrator establishes the habitual nature of his behavior. He walks night after night. The night therefore emerges as the speaker's only real companion and the poem's only other fully developed character.

Just as he repeats his walks each night, so does he repeat the personal pronoun "I," as if each walk not only strengthens his acquaintanceship with the night, but with the confines of his own identity. Writing, "I have" nine times is a self-iterative act: it reflects the narrator's acute awareness of his own consciousness. This self-consciousness borders on the solipsistic, threatening to engulf the subject in

subjectivity. Indeed, everything the narrator sees or hears on his walks reinforces his sense of alienation. The poem's final image, of a "luminary clock" that proclaims "the time was neither wrong nor right," writes large this alienation. Time itself has no meaning for a man whom no one expects and whom no one awaits. Because the clock is "at an unearthly height," the speaker's loneliness takes on cosmological importance. The heavens themselves are indifferent to his plight. The poem's last line repeats its first, creating a closed circuit or a perfect circle. Form echoes and informs subject here, for the poem's doubling back on itself reflects the repetitive walks of its speaker and the solipsistic containment of his profound and paralyzing self-consciousness. Reader and speaker end the poem only to find themselves back at its beginning, setting out on another night-walk. The poem itself, like the city in which its subject walks, has become a prison of the mind.

The only promise of salvation is a grammatical one: the speaker says, "I have been one acquainted with the night." By casting the entire poem in the past perfect tense, he distinguishes himself as a narrator from himself as a walker in the city, and therefore may offer some hope that he is acquainted with the night no more.

Historical Context

Frost's poem is a densely allusive one, encoding within its rhyme scheme, imagery, and syntax references to other works of literature. The simplicity of the poem is deceptive: "Acquainted with the Night" is an example of the art that conceals art. As a peripatetic work—a poem having to do with the thoughts of a solitary walker—"Acquainted with the Night" engages with a great tradition of meditative verse.

The most explicit literary reference in Frost's poem is found in its terse rhyme scheme. Terse rhyme, or triple rhyme, is an interlocking pattern in which the central, unrhymed end-syllable in a rhyming triplet becomes the rhyming syllable in the subsequent triplet. We might represent this pattern as "a-b-a, b-c-b, c-d-c." In "Acquainted with the Night," the ending sounds of the first stanza are "night," "rain," and "light." The second stanza rhymes with the unrhymed, "rain": "lane," "beat," "explain." Terse rhyme is a tremendously powerful pattern of verse, for it creates a tension between the triplet, a-b-a, and the quatrain, a-b-a-b. Every triplet is incomplete, containing an unrhymed sound that pulls poet and reader forward into the next quatrain and triplet. Terse rhyme is therefore a very difficult rhyme scheme to write at any length, because it does not allow for unrhymed words: every end-syllable will rhyme with another, and every triplet is bound by rhyme to the one that precedes and follows it. Not surprisingly, then, the pattern is used rarely by English-language poets. Terse rhyme is an Italian form and one that lends itself more readily to the rhymes of a romance language than to that of a Germanic one. When an English or American does use terse rhyme, he or she does so as an implicit homage to the form's great master, Dante Alighieri. Alighieri, whose "Commedia" (popularly known as "The Divine Comedy"), is written entirely in lines of terse rhyme.

Yet there is a great irony to comparing the narrator of "Acquainted with the Night" to Dante the Pilgrim. Where Dante had both Virgil and his own faith to guide him through the Inferno, Frost's narrator is alone and faithless. At the end of the "Inferno," Dante says, "I saw the lovely things the heavens hold, / And we came out see once more the stars" (Canto 34: 138-9). Frost's narrator, on the other hand, sees a clock that "proclaimed the time was neither wrong nor right." Dante's stars represent fixity and cosmological order; Frost's clock speaks only to the random, arbitrary nature of the universe.

Shakespeare, too, gets a nod through Frost's prosody. The image of the clock suggests Hamlet's lament that, "The time is out of joint, oh cursed spite / That ever I was born to set it right" (I.v.211-2). Frost's one line collapses Shakespeare's two, retaining the rhyme ("right") but removing the duality of a wrong time and a right time. Hamlet will, by the end of his tragedy, set the time right again by avenging his father's death. Frost's speaker faces an irredeemable problem: the time is neither wrong nor right, and one therefore is incapable of effecting the sort of tragic reordering that Hamlet did. The speaker might share Hamlet's question, "To be or not to be," but he cannot share in his answer of heroic action.

"Acquainted with the Night" seems also indebted to two works by a more immediate poetic predecessor: T. S. Eliot's "The Love Song of J. Alfred Prufrock" and "The Waste Land." Like Prufrock, Frost's narrator wanders city streets that have become a labyrinthine trial. The repetition of the phrase "I have" at the beginning of half the poem's line might echo the rhetorical question that Prufrock repeats, "Shall I." Eliot's "The Waste Land" represents a fuller treatment of the modern city as a place of trial. Eliot juxtaposes images of modern London with those of a barren desert drawn from the books of Ezekiel and of Isaiah. Frost's choice of the word "acquainted" likewise echoes Isaiah, who speaks of "a man of sorrows, and acquainted with grief (Isaiah 53:3). Frost himself might have been uncomfortable being compared to Eliot, who, along with Joyce, Frost criticized as being too esoteric. Yet in drawing on the Bible, Dante, and Shakespeare to describe a city that has become a spiritual wasteland, Frost inevitably draws comparisons to Eliot.

Societal Context

The city and the social order portrayed in "Acquainted with the Night" seem designed to torture a man. The protagonist hears the voice of one person and sees another—the night watchman, whose duty compels him to be on the street at night—but these glimpses of humanity only reinforce his own alienation. Although he lives in a densely populated urban area, the man might as well be in a desert. In this respect, Frost's poem draws on the nineteenth-century tradition of American Naturalism, in which the industrialized city is routinely represented as a construct that degrades the individual. In works such as Crane's "Maggie: A Girl of the Streets," innocent people are broken and betrayed by the social and economic structures of the city.

One must also ask of a poem written in 1925, less than a decade after the Armistice, how the experience of World War I may have shaped the work and its protagonist. The speaker of "Acquainted with the Night" is haunted by something, and although there is no evidence within the poem to support the assertion, one might profitably read it alongside literary representations of shellshock. Has this protagonist witnessed the horrors of trench warfare? Such an experience might explain his insistence on simple declarative sentences, ("I have"), and his pattern of strictly reporting what he currently sees rather than delving into his memories or emotions. Walking and observing his surroundings may be a way of staving off the unbidden return of traumatic memories of the Great War.

Religious Context

As a poem of walking the city at night, "Acquainted with the Night" invokes and conflates two great Christian allegories: Augustine's "City of God" and St. John of the Cross's "Dark Night of the Soul." In Frost's 1927 collection West Running Brook, "Acquainted with the Night" appeared in a section of poems titled "Fiat Nox" (let there be night), an inversion of God's command in Genesis 1:3, "Fiat Lux" (Let there be light). The poem therefore invites a religious—and specifically, Christian—interpretation.

In "The City of God," St. Augustine writes, "two cities have been formed by two loves: the earthly by the love of self, even to the contempt of God; the heavenly by the love of God, even to the contempt of self. The former, in a word, glories in itself, the latter in the Lord" (XIV.28). Augustine's dichotomy long informed, and perhaps continues to inform, Western notions of urbanity. The city is sometimes still seen as a place of Godlessness, a Tower of Babel speaking to man's pride, or a Sodom speaking to his wickedness. Augustine's metaphor is powerful enough that the earthly city continues to invoke its heavenly counterpart.

The city of Frost's poem is clearly an earthly one, an industrial and financial center formed by "the love of self," rather than the love of God. Indeed, God is wholly absent from this city. The narrator looks up to the heavens and finds a sign not of God, but of man. It is a clock set "at an unearthly height" which proclaims, "The time was neither wrong nor right." In the heavenly city, one would look up and see the Throne of God. In a medieval city, one might look up to see the earthly vision of that throne: the towers of a cathedral. In the modern, industrialized city, one looks up to see the ticking hands of a clock, symbol of mechanization and efficiency.

Nevertheless, the setting of this poem involves not just a place but also a time: the night. The poem quite clearly invokes St. John of the Cross's "Dark Night of the Soul," in which the night comes to represent a form of spiritual darkness through which the peripatetic narrator must pass:

> One dark night,
> fired with love's urgent longings
> – ah, the sheer grace! –
> I went out unseen,
> my house being now all stilled.

Later, the poet will apostrophize, or address directly, the night itself, "O guiding night / O night more lovely than the dawn." Frost's narrator does not apostrophize the night, but like John of the Cross, he personifies it. In saying he has been "acquainted" with the night, the narrator ascribes to it a human quality. The night becomes a character with whom the narrator has a relationship. Reading "Acquainted with the Night" in light of "Dark Night of the Soul" may cast the poem in terms that are more hopeful. For St. John argues, in annotating his own poem, that one is gripped by darkness and despair only when one is approaching enlightenment, He writes, "Souls begin to enter this dark night . . . so that by passing through this state they might reach that of the perfect, which is the divine union of the soul with God" (1).

Scientific & Technological Context

An early review of Frost's "Collected Poems" (1930), complained:

> Frost cannot give us the sense of belonging in the industrial, scientific, Freudian world in which we find ourselves; That is why no one would think of maintaining that he is one of the great poets of the ages. To that extent the time is not right (Thompson 337).

Such a reading of Frost seems to miss the point entirely: it is not that Frost "cannot give us the sense of belonging in the industrial, scientific, Freudian world," it is that such a sense would be illusory. The industrial, scientific, Freudian world is an inherently alienating one, and Frost captures our sense of alienation rather than our sense of belonging. Nor does Frost draw the facile conclusion that if the industrial world is indifferent and alienating, then the natural world must be providential and inclusive. Rather, Frost sees a chilling indifference in industry and nature alike, with the implication that it is man himself who looks for and imposes patterns on the blank palette of his surroundings.

In this respect, Frost's poetry might serve as both a culmination of, and epitaph to, American and British Romanticism. Frost, like his nineteenth-century predecessors, faced what Mario D'Avanzo calls "the situation of confronting a valueless world and, out of their doubt and skepticism, finding it necessary to look at reality and impose some tentative value on it through imagination" (8). This imposition is as necessary in the woods as in the city. Frost's often-cited "two roads in a yellow wood" are nearly identical, for "the passing there had worn them really about the same." It is only in retrospect that the narrator of "The Road Not Taken," can assert that taking the path he did "has made all the difference." A random choice only later comes to be seen as providential or pre-ordained. That the poem is so often misidentified as "The Road Less Traveled" speaks to some generalized need to impose a morale on Frost's terrifyingly-indifferent conception of the cosmos.

The city of "Acquainted with the Night" writes large the arbitrary and indifferent nature of reality that one glimpses in "The Road Not Taken." Its deserted streets are a potent symbol of man and nature's indifference to the individual. The insistence of the narrator on his own self-identity is in part an act of defiance against a constructed, industrial world that has no place for him in its order. This pitting of the first-person confessional against an indifferent, industrialized world is central to Romanticism, for the movement's origins are bound with the Industrial Revolution. Science, industry, and the modern city were both foils and sources of inspiration for the Romantic poets. Wordsworth, for example, both laments that "little we see in nature that is ours" ("The World Is Too Much with Us") and marvels that "earth has not anything to show more fair" than London at dawn ("Upon Westminster Bridge"). The Romantic poet goes out into nature to rediscover his identity precisely because he is living in an age of scientific and technological advancement. While Frost begins writing more than a century after the time of Wordsworth and the other romantic poets, his first-person confessional poems nevertheless continue to explore distinctly-Romantic notions of the relationship between the individual and the natural and manmade orders.

Biographical Context

Although Frost is often thought of as a New England nature poet, he was born in San Francisco, where he spent the first eleven years of his life (1874-1885). Perhaps it is the rural setting of so many of his most famous poems, including "Mending Wall," "The Road Not Taken," and "Stopping by Woods on a Snowy Evening," that causes one to forget that Frost's childhood was an urban one. While Frost did live on farms or in small towns for much of his adult life, he periodically moved to large cities, including Boston, London, and Chicago. He was a student and later a teacher at Harvard (1897-1899; 1939-1943). In 1912, after living for over a decade on a New Hampshire farm, Frost and his family moved to London, where he began his career as a poet. In addition, for three years, from 1921-1923 and again from 1925 to 1926, Frost and his wife Elinor, lived in Ann Arbor while Frost taught at the University of Michigan. It was in Ann Arbor in 1925 that Frost wrote "Acquainted with the Night" (Cramer 94).

By 1925, the year he turned 50, Frost was well established as a poet. He had published four volumes of poetry—"A Boy's Will" (1913), "North of Boston" (1914), "Mountain Interval" (1916), "New Hampshire" (1924)—as well as "Selected Poems" (1923). Frost had been alternating between teaching at Amherst College and at teaching at the University of Michigan. In 1925, he and his wife Elinor moved back to Michigan. In the middle of the fall term, however, their daughter Marjorie became ill and Elinor moved back to Massachusetts to care for her. Frost was left alone in Ann Arbor. It was a period of loneliness and isolation for the poet. On a letter dated New Year's Eve, Frost complained, "What I want is a farm in New England once more" (305).

The situation of "Acquainted with the Night" therefore echoes Frost's personal situation at the time in which he composed the poem. It would be published two years later, first in The Virginia Quarterly and then in the collection "West Running Brook."

If poetry is, as Wordsworth defined it, "emotion recollected in tranquility," how might "Acquainted with the Night" be identified with an emotionally fraught period of Frost's life? Certainly, Frost knew, at various points in his life, the despair that grips the protagonist of his poem. His father died when he was eleven, and by 1925, when he wrote the poem, his mother and two of his own children had died. A third child, Marjorie, was gravely ill in the fall of 1925. On occasion, and in the face of despair, Frost had chosen the self-exile of the narrator of "Acquainted with the Night." When Elinor refused to marry him in 1894, saying she wanted to finish her college degree, Frost left Dartmouth and moved to the Dismal Swamp. When Elinor passed away in 1936, Frost again responded with self-exile, resigning from Amherst College, selling his house, and retreating to the country. The haunted wanderings of the poem's narrator are therefore consonant with the life of the itinerant poet.

John F. Kennedy, speaking at Frost's memorial service in Amherst on October 26, 1963—a mere month before the president's own death—quoted the first line of "Acquainted with the Night." Kennedy read the line as a summing up of Frost's life and ethos: "Because he knew the midnight as well as the high noon, because he understood the ordeal as well as the triumph of the human spirit, he gave his age strength with which to overcome despair" (Thompson 514). To understand "Acquainted with the Night" is to understand Frost.

Matthew J. Bolton, Ph.D.

Works Cited

Augustine. *City of God.* New York: Random House (Modern Library), 1994.

Cramer, Jeffrey S. *Robert Frost among his Poems: A Literary Companion to the Poet's Own Biographical Contexts and Associations.* Jefferson, North Carolina: McFarland & Company, 1996.

D'Avanzo, Mario L. *A Cloud of Other Poets: Robert Frost and the Romantics.* Lanham, Maryland: UP of America, 1991.

St. John of the Cross. *Dark Night of the Soul.* New York: Doubleday, 1959.

Thompson, Lawrence, and R. H. Winnick. *Robert Frost: A Biography.* New York: Holt, Reinhardt, and Winston, 1981.

Discussion Questions

1. What effects does repetition produce in this poem? Think about the repetition of the phrase "I have," which appears seven times, as well as the repetition of the first and last lines. What does repetition reveal about the narrator's state of mind? At what point does repetition denote obsession?

2. Consider the line, "I have stood still and stopped the sound of feet." How does this phrase reflect the narrator's state of mind—and specifically his relationship between his mind and his body?

3. How specifically and concretely can we diagnose the narrator's affliction? What is troubling him? Are his night walks a part of the problem or a part of the solution?

4. Misapprehension is a revealer of motivation. What does it mean that the narrator misapprehends the "interrupted cry"? What do his stopping and his subsequent realization that the cry is not meant "to call him back or say goodbye" reveal about his past?

5. Discuss the night as a character. What is the relationship between the narrator and the night? What are the connotations of the terms "acquainted" and "acquaintance" and how do they help to define this relationship?

6. The narrator says that when he passed the night watchman, he "dropped his eyes, unwilling to explain." Notice that he is not "unable" to explain his walking at night, but rather "unwilling" to do so. What explanation might he offer was he willing to explain?

7. Is "Acquainted with the Night" a religious poem? How does it raise and subvert religious themes and images?

8. How does this poem construct the modern city? Is its treatment of the city inherently anti-urban?

9. What is the path out of the labyrinth for this narrator? Is there evidence other than the use of the past tense that the narrator will eventually walk his way toward enlightenment or self-realization?

10. How legitimate is it to conflate the situation of the narrator of "Acquainted with the Night," and by extension, the situation of any literary character, with that of the poet?

Essay Ideas

1. Read selections from one of the source texts referred to in the essay above: Dante's "Commedia" (particularly the "Inferno" or the "Purgatorio"), Augustine's "City of God," St. John of the Cross's "Dark Night of the Soul," or Eliot's "The Love Song of J. Alfred Prufrock." How does this inform your reading of "Acquainted with the Night"? How does Frost both echo and subvert the form or theme of the earlier work?

2. Compare Frost's treatment of a man passing through a city at night with his famous treatment of a man passing through a natural setting at night, "Stopping by Woods on a Snowy Evening." How does the vision of the city contrast with that of the woods? Does the natural setting offer a form of release that the city does not? Compare the rhyme schemes of the two poems as well. How does Frost use repetition in relation to rhyme in both poems and is there a relationship between the poem's rhyme scheme and their issues of solitude?

3. Critics of both Chaucer and Dante often write about there being two Chaucers and two Dantes: the pilgrim on his way to Canterbury or through the Inferno, and the poet who reflects on that pilgrim's experiences. Chaucer the poet has a wisdom and perspective that his counterpart on the road to Canterbury lacks. Think about "Acquainted with the Night" from this dual perspective. How is the narrator as he relates the poem substantively different than the character who walks the night? What lines or phrases evoke the distance between the time at which the pilgrim walked the city and the time in which the poet reflected on these walks?

4. On a similar note, consider Wordsworth's dictum that poetry is "emotion recollected in tranquility." What evidence is there that the narrator of this poem has achieved some measure of tranquility?

5. Terse rhyme, like any rhyme scheme, is best understood through practice rather than through theory. Write a short poem in terse rhyme on a topic of your own choosing. Remember that the terse rhyme pattern is A-B-A, B-C-B, and so forth, and that you will need to find a way, as Frost did, to end this potentially infinite progression of unrhymed central syllables. Once you finish your poem, reflect on the process of writing it. What are the challenges and rewards of composing in this particular rhyme scheme?

6. Situate "Acquainted with the Night" within the context of the First World War and the post-war phenomenon of shell shock. Does the narrator exhibit any of the symptoms of shellshock? How might this poem be read in relation to the work of World War I Trench Poets such as Siegfried Sassoon or Wilfred Owen?

7. Unpack the symbolic resonances of a single line, image, or character. Consider the night watchman, the interrupted cry, or the luminary clock.

8. "Acquainted with the Night" is primarily composed of monosyllabic words. In the first and last line, for example, "acquainted" is the only polysyllabic word. Many lines are entirely monosyllabic. The poem's handful of polysyllabic words is therefore worth dwelling on. Use a good dictionary, such as the Oxford English Dictionary, to look up the etymology and definition of one of the poem's polysyllabic words: acquaint, watchman, unearthly, or luminary. How do the different valences, connotations, or alternative definitions of one of these words help to shed light on the poem as a whole?

9. Situate "Acquainted with the Night" within the larger context of a literary movement such as Romanticism, Naturalism, or Modernism. Compare the poem to representative works from the movement you have chosen. How does Frost invoke or subvert the conventions of this movement.

10. Track the passage of time in "Acquainted with the Night." How are time and its passage represented through reiteration, repetition, How does the image of the clock and the reference to the time "being neither wrong nor right"

All My Pretty Ones

by Anne Sexton

Content Synopsis

"All My Pretty Ones" (1962) is the second collection of poetry by Anne Sexton and continues the autobiographical vein established in her first collection, "To Bedlam" and "Part Way Back" (1960). The title of the collection alludes to a line in the play "Macbeth," which is quoted as an epigraph, in which the character Macduff laments that "All my pretty ones" have died. For Sexton, many of the poems in the collection were written in the midst of death-the deaths of three important members of her family: both her parents and her father-in-law.

The first poem in the collection, "The Truth the Dead Know" is identified as an elegy for Sexton's parents. In the poem, the speaker describes walking away from a funeral service; "tired of being brave" (line 4). In the second stanza, she is in Cape Cod with an unnamed other but still seems haunted by the funerals. The use of the word "touch," which repeats several times in the poem, emphasizes the physicality of their living bodies, in contrast to the dead who "lie without shoes/in their stone boats. They are more like stone/than the sea would be if it stopped" (13-15).

The second poem, "All My Pretty Ones," is directed towards the speaker's father, whose death (four months after her mother's) is a "jinx" that "rides us apart" (1). She is left having to sort through his things, "a gold key, your half of a woolen mill /twenty suits from Dunne's" (6-7).

Pictures of people she tries to identify, thinking they are of her grandfather, stop her. She regrets the opportunity she is lost to find out more about her family: "I'll never know what these faces are all about" (19). The next stanza lists clippings from newspapers kept in a scrapbook begun when she was born, then notes that the father had intended to marry a widow but that she had cried and prevented it. The next stanza juxtaposes pictures of memories of Sexton's parents' lives together, such as one where her father is standing by a kennel of dogs and one where he is "standing like a duke among groups of men" (38). The next line undercuts the image as "duke" by calling him a "drunkard" (39). The last stanza then moves into a reflection of her mother's journal, which records the father's alcoholism, a legacy the speaker wonders if she will continue: "My God, father, each Christmas Day/with your blood, will I drink down your glass/of wine?" (44-46), an image that also makes a connection to the religious sacrifice of drinking wine to symbolize the blood of Jesus. The poem ends with the speaker's acknowledgement that she is still alive and that she forgives him.

The lyrical poem "Young" recalls lying outside on the lawn at night as a "lonely kid/in a big house" (2-3) and looking up at her parents' windows. Out of the mother's window runs "a funnel/of yellow heat" (9-10) and her father's window is half shut, "an eye where sleepers pass" (12). The girl "thought God could really see" (21) her, conveying the idea that as a child one sees oneself as the center of the universe, a perspective that changes as one gets older.

"Lament," as the title indicates, is another elegy, alluding to the poet's father-in-law's car accident. The tone here is of one of regret for what she did not do, wondering if she "could have stopped it" (6). The images conveyed are ones of self-absorption: a Canada goose taking flight, a cat asleep, and the sun setting.

"To a Friend Whose Work Has Come to Triumph" is a reaction to the awarding of the Pulitzer Prize to Sexton's mentor, W. D. Snodgrass, for "Heart's Needle" in 1960 (Middlebrook 231). In the poem, Snodgrass's work is compared to Icarus, the mythological figure who tries to fly. In the myth, Icarus is the son of Daedalus, who comes up with the idea of putting wings on himself and his son in order to escape Crete. However, only Daedalus is successful because Icarus flies too close to the sun and falls to his death. Diane Middlebrook reads the poem as suggesting "a comparison between two types of poets: the Daedalus, whose know-how gains him practical advantages, and the Icarus, whose craziness carries him very high" (231). In the poem, the speaker admires Icarus "wondrously tunneling/into that hot eye & helix; while his sensible daddy goes straight into town" (11-14).

"The Starry Night" takes as its subject Vincent Van Gogh's famous painting by the same name, allying itself explicitly with the painting using a quote from Van Gogh as an epigraph. The speaker transcends the boundaries of viewer/spectacle in her cries that "This is how/I want to die" (11-12). The speaker expresses the effect the painting has on her as one of pure transcendence, where death comes like a "rushing beast of the night,/sucked up by that great dragon, to split/from my life with no flag/ no belly/no cry" (13-17).

In "Old Dwarf Heart," the heart of an old, fat, female dwarf operates as a metaphor for what resides in the speaker's heart. She exists, as a reminder of all she wants to hide, like "sores she holds/in her hands" (14-15). She is inextricably bound up with the speaker, who accepts her with a sense of resignation: "how patiently I untangle her wrists/like knots" (21-22).

"I Remember" presents a series of concrete, summery images as the speaker addresses a lover. Images like "the grass/ as tough as hemp" (3-4) and "we had worn our bare feet/ bare since the twentieth/ of June" (7-9) evoke a sense of comfort and solid familiarity between the speaker and listener. The repetition of "bare" evokes a sense of nakedness, of vulnerability but also of trust. The "bareness" is offset by the depiction of the speaker looking like "a puritan lady" (19), evoking a purity and innocence to their love. Their playful innocence is underscored by the image at the end of having separate doors, though the doors lead to each other.

"The Operation," the last poem in the first section of the collection, depicts the experience of a surgical procedure. Here Sexton "displaced her identification with her mother into extraordinary imagery, pairing surgical technologies and primitive terror" (Middlebrook 120). As Middlebrook explains, the poem was a response to Sexton's experience in surgery where she had an ovarian cyst as well as her appendix removed. The experience linked her to the experience of her mother's operation for breast cancer. This connection is explicitly established in the first three lines of the poem when, "After the sweet promise, /the summer's mild retreat/from mother's cancer" the speaker comes to the doctor's office and is told she might have cancer, too. The cancer works alongside the speaker's self as a metaphor, as both cancer and baby were "housed" by the mother's body (12). The speaker describes visiting her mother in the hospital, seeing beyond the lie that there was

"No reason to be afraid" (28) to the truth of her impending death, that "the historic thief/is loose in my house" (37-38). The second section continues the comparison of life to seasons begun in the first section, where the mother's death is associated with winter, and her dying is represented in a dead leaf the speaker kicks. For the speaker, now entering surgery, "Only the summer was sweet" (46). The image of the speaker, pre-operative, is one of a "shorn lamb," ready for slaughter (51); being caught by the nurse's flashlight evokes a picture of animal caught. The animal image is repeated in a later stanza when she waits in her hospital room "like a kennel of dogs/jumping against their fence" (66-67). The last stanza in the second section again draws a connection between cancer and the baby in the womb as she is given anesthesia, where she allies herself with women in labor and with babies being born, and, finally, where she calls to her mother. The final image is of her being lifted into a crib. In the third section the speaker's physical experience post-surgery is characterized by inertia and oppression, as the first stanza here has metaphors like the soul that "sinks now in flies and the brain/flops like a docked fish"(94-95). Ironically, she realizes her prognosis for life as she remembers her mother, "the sound of her/good morning, the odor of orange and jam" (113-114). The last stanza of the poem brings the speaker back to the ordinary yet valued details of life: mailing a letter, wearing pink bunny slippers, and getting back into the "game" with the final metaphor of her "stomach laced up like a football" (123).

Part Two of the book begins with a poem that seems to counteract the poems in the first book. "A Curse against Elegies" seems to be a direct counterpart to "The Truth the Dead Know." The speaker is now "tired of all the dead" who "refuse to listen" (3-4); she calls for the listener to "Take your foot out of the graveyard" (6). Here the tone is one of anger rather than mournfulness, anger for "the last empty fifth of booze and the thin-lipped preacher/

who refused to call" (9-14). While she is done with the dead, she exhorts the listener to "go ahead" (21) down to the graveyard and "talk back to your old bad dreams" (25). The implication here is that she is moving on with her life while the listener is not.

"The Abortion" recounts the speaker's experience of traveling out of state to terminate a pregnancy. The line in italics "Somebody who should have been born/is gone" acts like a refrain throughout the poem. The landscape here evokes a sense of guilt and sin, "its roads sunken in like a gray washboard /where, in truth, the ground cracks evilly / a dark socket from which the coal has poured" (9-11). While she expects the doctor who performs the procedure to be like Rumpelstiltskin, the fairy tale character who bargains with a girl to get her firstborn, he is not "at all, at all" (18). The speaker refuses to mince words about what she has done, coming out at the end with a direct, explicit description of what the abortion was: "this baby that I bleed" (27).

The epigraph of "With Mercy for the Greedy" provides the information that the poem is addressed to Ruth, "who urges me to make an appointment for the Sacrament of Confession" (p. 62). The speaker responds by describing the cross that she's received and talks of the ambivalence of her beliefs, that she tries "to believe/in The Cross" (11-12), likening it to a physical body with its "tender hips, its dark jawed face,/its solid neck, its brown sleep" (12-13). She wants to believe in Jesus, but he is "frozen to his bones like a chunk of beef"; in other words, he is not alive for her (16). Instead of confession, the poet explains, she uses poems, calling them work that has "mercy/for the greedy" (28-29).

The poem that follows, "For God While Sleeping" expands on the speaker's religious feelings, comparing a sleeping God to an old man "drooling blood and vinegar" (5) and whose "jaws gape" and "diaper sags" (12). He is little more than someone who rolls in his sleep "seasick/on your own breathing, poor old convict," conveying the idea that God is shut away, imprisoned, and dying from neglect (20-21).

"In the Deep Museum" takes on the voice of Jesus just after his crucifixion as he lies in the tomb. A rat comes to him and licks his sores. Jesus blesses "this other death," (29) his living death in the cave that lies "Under the rotting veins of its roots" (30). The rats are a way for him to "correct" the "flaws" of "The Cross" (35). The rats ingest the body of Jesus in order to convey him out of the tomb. Through the lowly rat, Jesus is resurrected.

In "Ghosts" repetition is used to reinforce the idea of living ghosts as beings requiring attention; women are "Not witches, but ghosts" (4); men are "Not devils, but ghosts" (11) and children are "Not angels, but ghosts" (16). These lines insist on seeing ghosts as more than just stereotypes or idealized images. Whatever they are, their images seem to haunt the speaker while she lies in bed, the women "moving their useless arms/like forsaken servants" (5-6), the man who "thumps barefoot, lurching" (12), and the children who wail "for Lucifer" (20).

"The Fortress" comprises the third section with the epigraph, "while taking a nap with Linda," refers to a moment with Sexton's daughter. Here the speaker talks to her daughter about all that she can do and all that she cannot do. She looks ahead to when her daughter will grow up and become a mother herself, and realizes "life is not in my hands" (31). She cannot "promise very much" (51) but she can lie with her and watch a pheasant dragging a feather, and laugh, making memories which "Time will not take away" (60). J. D. McClatchy observes that the "love [the speaker] leaves her child seems as fragile as innocence" ("Anne Sexton: Somehow to Endure" 269).

In Section 4, "Old" presents a speaker "tired of rubber sheets and tubes" (2). The speaker wants to hold on to memories of when she was younger, "walking/ and picking wild blueberries" (7-8).

She yells at someone to "Leave me alone!" (16) because she is dreaming. In a dream, "you are never eighty" (18).

"The Hangman" posits the speaker as a father talking of a son who is troublesome, who is "a stone to wear around" his mother's neck (20), who has been pulled back from death six times. Yet the father acknowledges their blood tie, one that does not necessarily prevent his death, and it did not prevent the deaths of nine sons killed by their father, in a Scandinavian tale.

The "you" in "Woman with Girdle" is a woman whose body betrays her age, yet who also has incredible capabilities, rising like "a city from the sea,/born long before Alexandria was,/straightaway from God you have come/into your redeeming skin" (25-28). Middlebrook notes that the poem has an "immanence of a goddess archetype in the imagery" (305).

"The House" depicts characters at a house with a "dreadful" family (6) in the 1940s. The characters in the house include a father who goes on a "monthly bender," or drinking binge (34), a mother who is "made all wrong" (42), a maid who "knows something is going on" (52), an aunt who knits and listens to the radio, a Filipino houseboy who looks like a "wise undertaker" (71), a milkman, and gardeners, "six at a time" (75). The speaker, recalling this in memory, takes refuge in the penthouse, "to slam the door on all the years/she'll have to live through" (94-95). Later she dreams either she's dead or back in that house that seems to be a source of oppression for her, the memory of which waits for her like a "machine" (110). According to Middlebrook, "The House" is one of the many poems that Sexton wrote in which she explored her complex relationship with her father. These poems attest to the theory that "For Sexton the artist, the developmentally layered and conflicted love of a girl for her father was a source of insight into the psychological and social complexity of living as a woman" (Middlebrook 58). This could explain one of the most emotionally charged lines in the poem, when the girl in the penthouse will "rip off her blouse" and wail "Father, father, I wish I were dead" (102-103).

In "Water," the speaker declares, in a metaphor for a relationship, "We are fishermen in a flat scene" (1). The poem explores the relationship of these fishermen to the water, one of love but also mystery: "Who knows what goes on in the halls below?" (10). It is a relationship more complex than one with a woman because it "calls to a man to empty him" (22) and ultimately one that will wear one out, dancing and singing all night. The poem suggests a deeper current from the superficial aspects of a love relationship between two sexes, a current that dives below the surface of gender differences.

The speaker in "Wallflower" calls to a friend to tell him or her "an old story" (2). The speaker is a wallflower, someone who sits by and watches the actors and stage play their parts while her "thighs press, knotting in their treasure" (15), a line which connotes a virgin keeping herself pure. The speaker feels out of place where s/he is, a place of "olives and radishes" and "blissful pastimes of the parlor" (26-27). The poem conveys the sense of a woman who now knows the truth of sex looking back on a time when she was innocent with a sense of ambivalence.

"Housewife" plays on the word with the first line: "Some women marry houses." This kind of "wife" is passive, waiting for the men to "enter by force, drawn back like Jonah/into their fleshy mothers" (7-8). This act of violence is in contrast to the woman, who "is her mother" (9), or in other words, is independent and owns herself instead of being owned by a house or husband.

"Doors, Doors, Doors" depicts three separate characters who live in the same building. The first is the old man, who is living out his last days in a pathetic state, in a tiny, cluttered room, with the telephone as his only luxury. The young go

by, and the alarm clock that "rings and unwinds them" can be a metaphor for the ticking by of their lives, a mortality that the old man reminds them of (1: 22). The seamstress laments that her son has decided to become a minister. She resigns herself to her fate: "I guess I'll get along" (2.21). The third is a young girl, who visits a young man in the building. She reveals that they are both married and are in a love affair with each other. She insists on their "need" for each other, exhorting her lover to tell them (the old man and the seamstress) that "need prevails" (3:19).

The fifth and last section of the book begins with the poem "Letter Written on a Ferry While Crossing Long Island Sound," the first of three love poems. This poem captures a moment in time, specifically, "2 o'clock on a Tuesday/ in August of 1960" (11-12) when, "although everything has happened / nothing has happened" (14-15). The speaker longs to see events that go beyond the earthly details she notices around her, like "the cement lifeboat that wears/its dirty canvas coat" (28-29). Instead, she longs to see a group of nuns fly up into the air, "four abreast/in the old-fashioned side stroke" (59-60). The nuns, her "dark girls" (66, 79, 86), stand in for the lighter-than-air emotions she is experiencing with her love for the listener. Their status as servants of God connect her to the "gauzy edge of paradise" (94) where they call back, "good news, good news" (95).

In "From the Garden," the speaker calls on her lover to join her in the garden, where she calls for him to "put away your good words/and your bad words" (14-15); to go beyond the limitations of language and savor the bodily pleasures of the garden where they will "eat my pleasant fruits," a line with decidedly sexual overtones (18).

In "Love Song for K. Owyne," the speaker reflects on a meeting between herself and her lover, from whom she is now separated, he in Ohio "among the hard fields of potatoes" (4), a line evoking harshness and the mundane. They have spent time together by the sea, living "in sin" (2). The guilt of the sin may explain the waves that "came running up the stairs/for me" (7-8), which she compares to the "nervous trees / in Birnam wood" (8-9) that "crept up upon Macbeth / to catch his charmed head" (9-10). The lovers had quarreled, growling "like lawyers" (16). When the morning comes, their attitudes change; he finds her fair. The last image mirrors the image of the lovers, "imported swans" an image that evokes both their grace and beauty and being transplanted from their homes (23).

"Flight" presents the speaker moving first through eager anticipation to see her lover, as she drives into Boston to the airport. After she parks she runs through the airport, "Wild for love" (37), only to be caught up by inertia when she finds the "flights were grounded" (41). Both the planes and gulls "sat, / heavy and rigid in a pool of glue" (42-43). The imagery here evokes not only a literal flight grounding but also the "grounding" of a love ending abruptly. This reading is borne out by the next line, "Knowing I would never find you" (44). As she drives away, she is as if an insect "sucked in" by the streetlights and with "nowhere else to go" (53-54). The ending image is one of smallness, passivity, and, ultimately, of despair.

In "For Eleanor Boylan Talking with God," the speaker witnesses a friend in her kitchen "motioning to God with her wet hands / glossy from the washing of egg plates" (7-8). For Boylan, God is her intimate, someone who is "as close as the ceiling" (12). The speaker reflects on her own relationship with God; evidently, it is not "casual but friendly" as Boylan's is (11). She does not think God has a face; she sees him as a "great resting jellyfish" (17). She cries to Boylan to talk to God for her, before Boylan dies, indicating that the speaker does not have her own relationship with him. This poem is a prime example of the deep religious ambivalence Sexton weaves through much of her work.

In "The Black Art," the speaker compares female and male writers. A female writer "feels too much" (1) and a male writer "knows too much" (9). A writer is a "spy" (7) and a "crook" (15). Women and men who are writers "love each other" (19) but never themselves. They have children who "leave in disgust" (23), with too much food left in "weird abundance" (25). The poem establishes differences in male and female poets, but observes that, ultimately, both will end up neglecting their children. Taken on a more metaphorical level, the poem could read as a cautionary one warning two poets against loving each other, since it may cause them to neglect their "children," a metaphor for their creative work.

The last poem of the collection is "Letter Written during a January Northeaster," a poem of unrequited love. The poem is split into days: it begins with Monday, then goes to Tuesday, then repeats Monday again four times. The repetition of the day conveys the idea of the speaker being stuck in time, waiting for word from her lover. Similarly, she seems to be stuck in an otherworld of a snowstorm, with no noise, "no smells, no shouts, or traffic" (16). In the first stanza the speaker refers to the dead, "gone for over a year," linking the poem to the very first one about her recently dead parents (4). Images of stasis and a desire to block out the outside world reappear over the next several stanzas, including that of "a child/tucked in under the woolens" (28). In the fifth stanza, the speaker admits, "It must be Friday by now" (56). She seems to be willing to come out of her fantasy world, asserting, and "Days don't freeze" (58). The last stanza asks directly, "where are your letters?" (70) She is left with the double image of her lover and her grandfather, "fading out like an old movie" (80), both gone but belonging to her "like lost baggage" (83). "Baggage" has the connotation of carrying within it parts of her; thus the ending image imparts a feeling that parts of herself are lost and will not return.

Historical Context

Anne Sexton is a key figure in American poetry. She is often coupled with Sylvia Plath, her contemporary, as representing a new phase of poetry by women that embraced formerly taboo subjects. She, Plath, and Adrienne Rich were "the beginning of an era," according to Carol Muske-Dukes (281). She is also often categorized as a "confessional" poet along with W. D. Snodgrass and Robert Lowell, both of whom were teachers and mentors for Sexton. Such poetry undoubtedly influenced greatly by the increasing popularity of the theories of Freud and of psychoanalytic analysis by the middle of the twentieth century.

Another important phenomenon for Sexton's emergence as a poet was the stirrings of feminist consciousness. Sexton wrote from the perspective of a 1960s housewife, at a time when American middle-class mores dictated that the primary role of a woman was of housewife and mother. "Housewife" speaks directly to the passivity that these mores enforced. The claiming of female experience—and especially female bodily experience—as appropriate subjects for poetry, such as in "The Abortion," was an activity that pre-figured and perhaps contributed to the second wave of the women's movement in the late 1960s and early 1970s. Sexton's friend and fellow poet Maxine Kumin declares that "Women poets in particular owe a debt to Anne Sexton, who broke new ground, shattered taboos, and endured a barrage of attacks along the way; . . ." (xxxiv).

Sexton is quoted as saying that she was "'not a political poet. I just do my thing and it's very personal'" (Middlebrook 297). While Sexton's poems do not explicitly comment on public or historical events, they do reveal the consciousness of a woman at a volatile period in American history. One of the slogans of the women's movement was the "personal is political," and the courage with which Sexton bared her soul to the public in her poetry was a quality that was embraced wholeheartedly.

"The Abortion" is an example of how personal events become political property, but also how political forces can shape personal experience. In 1960, Sexton had a pregnancy terminated; abortion was illegal at the time. In the poem, the speaker goes on a journey, presumably to have the abortion, repeating the refrain that "Somebody who should have been born/is gone." The speaker castigates herself, feeling guilty, ending with an attempt to be truthful to her feelings: "Or say what you meant, /you coward; this baby that I bleed" (26-27). Middlebrook reports that the next poem, "With Mercy for the Greedy" came out of Sexton's confession about the abortion to a friend, who then sent her a cross. While the poem explores abortion in a very personal way, its very existence, in making the illegal public, paved the way for very public discussions nearly a decade later.

Societal Context

The female experience for Sexton includes the stereotypical experiences of being a housewife and mother, but it also includes the pain and guilt of abortion and adultery. Jane McCabe notes that Sexton "was not and never claimed to be a feminist," but that many of her subjects touch upon issues "of primary interest to any feminist" (216-217). She notes that another critic, Suzanne Juhasz, identifies Sexton as "feminine," rather than feminist because through her poems she exhibits a clear female identity. A feminist poet by contrast "realizes and analyzes the political implications of being both female and a poet" (McCabe 220). For McCabe, Sexton's poems exemplify a feminine sensibility in poetry, as "in all her writing [she] insisted on an explicitly female persona" (223). Furthermore, they testify to the fact that "Women experience the world through different bodies than men. This is nowhere more clear than in Sexton's poetry" (McCabe 223).

However, a reading of "The Black Art" calls for a reconsideration of Sexton as a feminist poet, even if she was not self-identified as such. In this poem, Sexton compares the male poet to the female poet. While she marks the woman poet as different, contending with "cycles and children and islands" (line 3) in contrast with men's "erections and congresses and products" (11), both have "eyes full of terrible confessions" (21). When the male and female poets marry, their children will "leave in disgust" (23), leaving no one to "eat up" all the food in its "weird abundance" (25). The ending image of too much food implies that the poets are too busy working to eat or care for the children. Thus, the poem puts men and women on equal footing when it comes to their art.

Religious Context

Section Two of "All My Pretty Ones" features Sexton's religious poems. The epigraph, a quote from Guardini, is perhaps telling here: "I want no pallid humanitarianism—If Christ be not God, I want none of him; I will hack my way through existence alone" (Sexton, "All My Pretty Ones" 60). The quote sets the tone for her poems as explorations of a tentative sort of religious searching, a searching that never quite bears answers. This is especially prominent in the poems "With Mercy for the Greedy" and "For Eleanor Boylan Talking with God" (the latter actually appears in Section 5). Both of these poems are addressed to friends who have a stronger conviction than the speaker does. In the first poem, the speaker declares, "I detest my sins and I try to believe/in The Cross" ("With Mercy for the Greedy," 11-12), but finds her solace in poems, which provide "mercy/for the greedy" (28-29). In "For Eleanor Boylan Talking with God," the speaker stands in admiration for a friend's "casual but friendly" (11) conversations with God and calls on her friend to "tell him & helix; / Oh Eleanor, Eleanor / tell him before death uses you up" (24). While it is unclear what the speaker wants Eleanor to tell God, the effect of the lines, with the ellipses representing

an unspoken thought, conveys a message that the speaker is unsure about sending, perhaps because of her own ambivalence about God, and her own lack of a personal relationship with him.

By contrast, in "In the Deep Museum," the speaker is in actuality Jesus Christ, sealed in the tomb just after his crucifixion. Here the poem displays a sense of awe and admiration for the story of Christ, reborn through the lowly rats as they convey his body out of the tomb, the "hairy angels who take/my gift" (26-27). The use of rats in this poem is characteristic of Sexton, who included images of rats in several of her poems and whose favorite palindrome was "Rats Live on No Evil Star." 'Rat' was one of Sexton's metaphors for her sick self," according to Middlebrook (124). The inclusion of rats in this poem, as in "With Mercy for the Greedy," suggests the power of words and poetry to do redemptive work in place of religion.

Scientific & Technological Context

In "The Operation," Sexton records her experiences of having surgery to remove an ovarian cyst and her appendix. The poem attempts to lay claim to a woman's living body and mind in contrast to the distancing effects of medicine. The doctor's office is "white" and "sterile," giving the picture of hardness and coldness (4). The "almost mighty" doctor is seen as an authority figure (7), whose glove inside her is an "oily rape" (6). In the hospital, her body becomes "dumb," like "meat" (45). Her anonymity is underscored when she is shaven in the near-rhyming lines, "All that was special, all that was rare/is common here" (43-44) and again when the nurse blinds her with a flashlight "to see who I am" (52). Over and over again the poem emphasizes the passive nature of the patient in the hospital; the doctor decides he will operate; she lies like a "shorn lamb" (51); she is not allowed to drink or eat; she waits "like a kennel of dogs/jumping against their fence" (66-67). Still, she claims her body: "On the stretcher, citizen/and boss of my own body still," and gives herself over to "science and pitfalls" (69-71), a coupling of words that indicates the fallibility of medicine. In the third stanza, the speaker fully enters the position of patient, comparing herself to a child in a crib and to a senile woman. Her wearing of pink bunny slippers, shuffling around the hospital, reinforces this picture. The last lines connote the voice of a condescending nurse or doctor who allows her to leave, "run along, Anne, and run along now" (122).

More broadly, Sexton's work can be illuminated within the context of psychoanalysis. J. D. McClatchy points out that "all the contemporary poets central to confessionalism have undergone extensive psychotherapy, and while it would be foolish to account for their poetry by this experience, it would be careless to ignore its influence" ("Somehow to Endure" 249). Sigmund Freud, a doctor interested in mental illness and in the unconscious, developed psychoanalysis in the late nineteenth century, and gained popularity in the early decades of the 1900s. Through psychoanalysis, of which Sexton took part and was dependent on from the time she had a breakdown at the age of twenty-eight, a patient is encouraged to come to an understanding of "the crucial patterns" of a person's life (McClatchy, "Somehow to Endure" 249). Like narrative poetry such as that in confessionalism, psychotherapy's main mode is the narrative structure in which "the experiences still painfully central and the unaccountable gaps are endlessly recircled" (McClatchy 249-250). These experiences are "recircled" both in therapy and in poetry, where they appear in forms that directly correspond to the actual lived, experiences—; "forms that can include and reflect direct, personal experience; a human, rather than a disembodied voice; the dramatic presentation of the flux of time and personality; and the drive toward sincerity" (McClatchy 251). Thus, the rise of psychoanalysis is identified as a key factor in the development of confessional poetry.

Biographical Context

It is difficult to separate Sexton's self-representation in her poetry from the actual events of her life since she consciously wrote about herself and her life in many of her poems. In 1991, Diane Wood Middlebrook published Sexton's biography, which was written with the full support of Anne's daughter, Linda Gray Sexton, who provided Middlebrook with full access to her mother's personal writings. Linda also published her own memoir, "Searching for Mercy Street" (1994). The biography and memoir flesh out many of the topics and themes in Sexton's life. Anne Gray Harvey was born in 1928 in Newton, Massachusetts, a suburb of Boston. She was the youngest of three girls born to Ralph and Mary Harvey. The Harveys were "children of the Roaring Twenties: well-to-do, party-loving, and self-indulgent" (Middlebrook 4). Sexton's Sexton and her sisters called her Nana, and when Sexton was eleven, "Nana" moved into the Harvey household. A few years later, Nana's health deteriorated and she was put into a mental hospital. When Sexton herself experienced a mental breakdown at twenty-eight, she worried that she would end up spending her last days in a nursing home, which is where Nana lived until she was eighty-six. She also "believed that she had personally caused her great-aunt's breakdown" (Middlebrook 16).

After attending a junior college, Sexton married Alfred "Kayo" Sexton at the age of nineteen. She and Kayo lived in various places while he was in the military and then they settled in the suburbs of Boston, where they subsequently had two daughters. Sexton's own breakdown came shortly after the birth of her second daughter, Joy. She then entered therapy and was occasionally hospitalized, usually when she was on the brink of committing suicide. Finding poetry as an outlet was crucially important to Sexton, who "began writing poetry in an effort to master the intolerable feelings that brought her repeatedly to the brink of suicide. Suicide was so much part of Sexton's everyday life and art that she seems to have constructed her personal and artistic identity around it" (Berman 178).

Sexton's mother died in March 1959 from cancer; her father followed in June from a stroke. The following year, her father-in-law, George Sexton, died in a car accident. "All My Pretty Ones" takes as one of its main subjects the deaths of her parents ("The Truth the Dead Know" and "All My Pretty Ones," among others) and her father-in-law. Many of the poems that appear in the collection come out of her work in psychotherapy that explored a particularly complicated relationship with her father. In the biography, Middlebrook reports that Anne had talked about episodes of sexual abuse with her father. While Middlebrook notes that Sexton's symptoms and behavior throughout her life were consistent with those of a victim of sexual abuse, she is also careful to say that the inconsistencies in her descriptions raised questions about the validity of these accounts. Indeed, her therapist did not believe the episodes actually happened. (Middlebrook 56-58). Whatever the nature of her relationship with her father, Sexton's poetry was often preoccupied with it. In addition to the elegies mentioned above, the poems that explore this relationship include "Young," "Ghosts," "The House," and "Wallflower" in "All My Pretty Ones" (Middlebrook 58).

Another subject that appears often in the collection is that of romantic love and the complex nature of her many extra-marital affairs. Several of these poems coincide with, and are written out of, her affair with poet James Wright: "Letter Written on a Ferry Crossing Long Island Sound," "The Black Art," and "Letter Written During a January Northeaster" (Middlebrook 148-149). Section 5 is actually inscribed to Wright, whom she called "Comfort." Other poems in the collection illustrate major events in Sexton's life, such as "The Operation," which describes her own surgery. "The Fortress," describes a moment with her daughter Linda, and "The Abortion" and "With Mercy for the Greedy," came out of her own experience having an abortion in 1960, when Sexton thought the pregnancy might have been the result of an affair.

Sexton's next collection, "Live or Die" (1966), was awarded the Pulitzer Prize. Between the time that she published her first collection, "To Bedlam and Part Way Back" (1960), and her death, she published eight books of poetry and co-wrote three children's books (with Maxine Kumin). Sexton also received numerous grants and awards in her lifetime and wrote a play, "Mercy Street," which was produced in Boston. Following her divorce from her husband, Sexton committed suicide in 1974. Two more books of poetry were published after her death.

Alyssa Colton, Ph.D.

Works Cited

Berman, Jeffrey. *Surviving Literary Suicide*. Amherst: U of Massachusetts P, 1999.

Gunn, Thom. "Poems and Books of Poems." *Yale Review* 51.1 (Autumn 1963): 140-141. Excerpted in McClatchy, ed. 124-126.

Kumin, Maxine. "How It Was." *Sexton, The Complete Poems*. xix-xxxiv. Houghton Mifflin. New York.

McCabe, Jane. "'A Woman Who Writes,' A Feminist Approach to the Early Poetry of Anne Sexton." McClatchy, ed. 216-243.

McClatchy, J. D., ed. "Anne Sexton: The Artist and Her Critics." Bloomington and London: Indiana UP, 1978.

_____. *Anne Sexton: Somehow to Endure*. McClatchy, ed. 244-290.

Middlebrook, Diane Wood. *Anne Sexton: A Biography*. Boston: Houghton Mifflin, 1991.

Muske-Dukes, Carol. "Women and Poetry: Some Notes." *After Confession: Poetry as Autobiography*. Eds. Kate Sontag and David Graham. St. Paul: Graywolf Pr, 2001. 281-304.

Sexton, Anne. "All My Pretty Ones." 1962. Rpt. in *The Complete Poems*. 47-92.

_____. *The Complete Poems.* Boston: Houghton Mifflin, 1981.

_____. *No Evil Star: Selected Essays, Interviews, and Prose.* Ed. Steven E. Colburn. Ann Arbor: U of Michigan P, 1985.

_____. "With Harry Moore." *Talks with Authors.* Ed. Charles F. Madden. Carbondale: Southern Illinois UP, 1968. Rpt. in Sexton, "No Evil Star." 41-69.

For Further Study

Bixler, Francis. *Original Essays on the Poetry of Anne Sexton.* U of Central Arkansas P, 1988.

George, Diana Hume. "Oedipus Anne: The Poetry of Anne Sexton." Urbana: U of Illinois P, 1987.

Sexton, Linda Gray. *Searching for Mercy Street: My Journey Back to My Mother, Anne Sexton.* Boston: Little, Brown. 1994.

Discussion Questions

1. One interviewer has commented, "Through [Sexton's] personal quality we feel what has generally been described as universality" ("With Harry Moore" 52). Choose one or more of the poems from the collection and discuss how the use of the personal might be an example of this universality.

2. How is death understood in "The Truth the Dead Know?" Does this understanding of death change in subsequent elegies?

3. What is the speaker's attitude towards her father in "All My Pretty Ones"? What lines lead you to this reading?

4. What is the speaker saying about childhood in "Young"?

5. Do you think the comparison to Icarus is appropriate for "To a Friend Whose Work Has Come to Triumph"? What is the speaker's attitude here?

6. Read "The Starry Night" in conjunction with Van Gogh's painting. What ways of "reading" the painting does the poem offer?

7. Analyze the various poetic devices employed in "The Operation" (e.g. rhyme, rhythm, section separations). What purpose do they serve?

8. What is the speaker's attitude towards her abortion in "The Abortion"? What political stance do you think the speaker (or poet) would take on the right to an abortion?

9. Compare and contrast two of Sexton's "religious" poems and discuss how Christianity shapes the poet's worldview.

10. Discuss the use of nature imagery in "The Fortress."

11. Discuss the possible metaphorical significance of the three different people represented in "Doors, Doors, Doors."

12. Reread the poems in Section Five and discuss their commonalities and how they might correspond to the various phases of a romantic relationship.

Essay Ideas

1. Compare and contrast two poems from the collection with similar subjects or themes; for example, death, love, religion, sex, the body.

2. Analyze the use of poetic elements in one of Sexton's poems and explain how they reinforce the theme of the work.

3. Explain the uses of autobiography in poetry, using Sexton's work as an example of the differences between "confessional" and "autobiographical." Analyze debates over the uses of autobiographical material and whether or not it detracts from a work, citing specifically how this material makes Sexton's poetry effective or not.

4. Critic Jane McCabe has noted that we might look at Sexton as a "feminine" poet rather than a "feminist" poet. Write an essay in which you argue which kind of poet Sexton should be considered, using specific poems from the collection to support your thesis.

5. Examine one or two of Sexton's poems that are not explicitly autobiographical (many of the poems in Section 2, for example) and explain some of the concerns and themes repeated throughout these poems and how specific images reinforce these themes.

America

by Claude McKay

Content Synopsis

When Claude McKay quotes his poem "America" in his autobiography, "A Long Way from Home," he says it expresses his "bitterness, hate, and love" (135). This ambivalence toward the United States reflects his experiences as a black immigrant in a time of intense racial and social conflicts. The opening line of the poem personifies the nation as a nurturer, but one with a negative effect as she "feeds [the speaker] bread of bitterness." Then the second line shifts to the more threatening image of a tiger, sinking her tooth into the speaker's throat and "stealing [his] breath of life" (3). Yet he "confess[es]" that he loves the country, though he again shows conflict with the oxymoron "cultured hell" (4). America is "cultured," with much to offer to its people, but at a time of segregation and racial violence, it could be "hell" for African Americans and other victims of prejudice.

The next three lines use powerful water imagery of tides and floods to depict the "strength erect against her hate" (6) that the speaker receives both from America's "vigor," which is shown to be a powerful influence as it "flows like tides into [his] blood" (5), and from her "bigness," which " sweeps [his] being like a flood" (7). "Bigness" reflects the grandness of America's geography, but its vagueness allows the term to apply to many other qualities of America, from its architecture to its spirit. In any case, these favorable traits of "vigor" and "bigness" are shown to be virtually irresistible.

With line eight, the poem shifts imagery to depict a "rebel" confronting a king with no trace "Of terror, malice, not a word of jeer" (10). In other words, while the speaker's attitude towards America is not one of fear, neither does it involve anger or contempt, even though he refers to his place in America as "standing within her walls" (9), suggesting the constraints imposed by the dominant society.

The final four lines shift the focus from present to future to predict a mighty fall. The speaker does not sound happy to foresee the decline, for he uses "Darkly" to modify his "gaze into the days ahead" (11), where America's "might and granite wonders" are seen "sinking into the sand" (14). "Darkly" connotes the speaker's skin color or the lack of clarity of the image, perhaps with a direct allusion to I Corinthians 13:12: "For now we see through a glass darkly." However, it also implies sorrow at seeing the vision of a diminished America. The "granite wonders" might denote the public buildings of Washington or New York or other American cities, but the term also brings to mind other civilizations that have lost their glory throughout history, such as ancient Egypt, Greece, or Rome. Many critics have noted the allusion to Shelley's sonnet "Ozymandias," in which a traveler tells of finding ruins of a glorious civilization in the desert. In McKay's poem, the destruction is the result of "Time's unerring hand" (13), which suggests not only that the decline is inevitable, but also that it is deliberate and infallibly appropriate ("unerring"). It is as if "Time" has passed judgment on the country for its failure to fulfill its potential by allowing its entire people to partake of its opportunities, freely and equally.

Formal Qualities

Although "America" is a sonnet, McKay takes liberties with the sonnet form. The rhyme scheme fits the traditional English (or Shakespearean) sonnet, with alternating rhymes in each of the three quatrains and a closing couplet (ababcdcdefe-fgg). However, while the English sonnet generally employs strong punctuation and shifts in the imagery or idea after lines four, eight, and twelve, McKay chooses to make his shifts at the end of lines four, seven, and ten, with the most significant shift marked by the word "yet" at the beginning of line eight. In doing so, he sets up a logical structure that is more like the Italian (or Petrarchan) sonnet, which traditionally sets up one idea in the first eight lines and then comments on it in the last six lines. William J. Maxwell describes the structure as two "ingenious half-Petrarchan block[s]"; that is, each seven-line unit is divided into separate units of three or four lines, like a condensed Petrarchan sonnet, with the second seven lines constructed as a reversed reflection of the first.

Most of McKay's protest poems are sonnets, which leads to an odd dissonance between form and content. Such poems require the poet to adapt the content to fit the constraints of a form with a long European tradition, yet McKay's explosive messages seem to strain against the limitations of the form.

McKay has been criticized for inverting syntax, or disrupting the structure or logic of sentence structure, to meet the demands of the rhyme scheme and the iambic rhythmic pattern (Huggins 219); however, in "America," the only two phrases in which the word order is reversed seem designed for emphasis. By placing "erect" after the noun in line six, "Giving me strength erect against her hate,"

McKay allows the adjective to function almost as a verb, suggesting that the speaker's strength has been erected as a defensive weapon. By beginning the eleventh line with an adverbial phrase, "Darkly I gaze," the poet draws attention to the different possible functions of the word "darkly": to suggest the vision is itself dark or obscure, to suggest the speaker's regretful attitude towards his vision, or even to hint at his racial identity.

Historical Context

For a decade after the Civil War ended in 1865, many Blacks, both those formerly free and those who gained freedom from slavery as a result of the war, had reason to be hopeful that they might be accepted into American public and political life as social and political equals. Yet, with the end of Reconstruction in 1876, the rights that Negroes had gained began to be taken away, especially in the South. By the early 1900s, Jim Crow laws had institutionalized segregation and discrimination, and Negroes were terrorized by public lynchings of those who, in the eyes of the dominant white culture, had violated written and unwritten social codes intended to keep them "in their place."

Through the 1910s, life for many African Americans grew even more threatening and oppressive. Black men who went off to fight for their country in segregated units in World War I, a war "to make the world safe for democracy," returned in 1918 and 1919 to a country that often denied them democratic rights. The year 1919 is, by some measures, one of the worst for Negroes since the end of slavery. At least 76 Negroes were lynched, and the "Bloody Summer" of that year saw race riots in many American cities, during which mobs of whites rampaged through Negro neighborhoods, beating and shooting Negroes and burning their homes, businesses, and churches.

World War I had changed some Americans' views of their country. The war was widely unpopular and new laws that limited free speech, such as the Sedition Act of 1918, met opposition to the war. With the Russian Revolution of 1917, many American political and business leaders also found new ammunition in their opposition to socialism. The years following the war saw both violence caused by radicals, including bombings and attempted bombings aimed at public officials and institutions, and harsh prosecutions and often deportation of socialists deemed too subversive or dangerous. William J. Maxwell suggests that the images of the rebel and of destruction in "America" might "exploit a vivid contemporary fear of underground Red violence."

Societal Context

As the historical situation indicates, the years preceding McKay's writing of "America" were filled with divisions and controversies in American society. Racism is one social issue that cannot be overlooked. An indication of the degree to which racism was institutionalized in American culture was the widespread use of stereotyped images of the large, kerchief-headed Mammy or the slow-talking, watermelon-eating man with giant red lips against a black face. The minstrel theater had been popular for years, using such stereotypes for comic effect, and early movies distributed such racist humor even more widely. One of the most vivid and harmful examples of a serious use of racial stereotypes is D.W. Griffith's film "The Birth of a Nation." This blockbuster movie, set in the years of the Civil War and Reconstruction, depicts black characters as lazy, drunken, and lustful. The only force standing between the freed slaves and the total destruction of white culture, and especially the sanctity of white womanhood, is the Ku Klux Klan, which is consequently glorified in the film. Not surprisingly, it was around this time that the Klan was resurrected as a potent social and political force in many states.

In part because racism tended to be less institutionalized and violent in the cities of the North than it was in the South, the first two decades of the twentieth century saw a major migration of African Americans. The availability of jobs and the vibrant social life of cities such as Chicago, Detroit, and New York provided further incentives to leave the South. Consequently, places such as Harlem developed their own identities, with a substantial African American middle class that included professionals and business owners.

African American responses to racism took various forms. From the 1870s through the beginning of the twentieth century, Booker T. Washington had been widely seen as the spokesperson of the race, even though many African Americans disagreed with his program of encouraging education in agriculture and the trades while accepting unequal laws and educational opportunities and giving up the right of African Americans to vote. When W.E.B. DuBois published "The Souls of Black Folk" in 1905, an alternative voice emerged. DuBois called for greater self-assertion and self-determination in opposition to the Washington's goals of accommodation and assimilation. When the NAACP was organized in 1910, DuBois became editor of its publication, the *Crisis*, which he used to present his views and to publish works by Negro writers and artists, which in turn helped to fuel the Harlem Renaissance. When Marcus Garvey arrived from Jamaica in 1916, Harlem became the center for his United Negro Improvement Association, which won many followers by advocating economic independence for people of African descent and a return to Africa. As Nathan Huggins writes, Garvey's extreme ideas and style made the "self-conscious aggressiveness [of DuBois and James Weldon Johnson] seem conservative" (22).

Religious Context

Some critics have seen in the term "darkly," used in line 11, as an allusion to I Corinthians 13:12. However, if McKay intended to refer to the Bible, he did so only as a literary allusion; for he had been an atheist from the time he was an adolescent and read philosophical books in his brother's library. Shortly before he includes the text of "America" in his autobiography, McKay announces, "I am a pagan; I am not a Christian"; while he says this in the context of enjoying the "physical and sensual pleasures of life" (134), it reflects his lack of religious faith at the time. This was, after all, a time when many churches in the North, and virtually all in the South, were segregated, and some maintained racist doctrines. It was only in his last years that McKay became conventionally religious.

Scientific & Technological Context

While McKay showed little interest in science or technological developments, the image of "granite wonders" suggests the impressiveness of architecture in cities such as New York. McKay writes, in terms that illuminate his use of the word "bigness" in "America," "One loves in New York its baroque difference from other cities, the blind chaotic surging of bigness of expressions" ("A Long Way" 133). While "America" was written about a decade before the Empire State Building was erected, the skyscrapers of the early 1920s were tall enough to be impressive. McKay and some friends once crossed the Hudson River to see the city, which he described as "one solid massive mammoth mass of spiral steel and stone." Then he adds, "We stood there a long time drinking in the glory of the pyramids" (134). The comparison to the pyramids suggests the closing image of "America," with the "granite wonders" depicted "sinking in the sand" (12-14).

Biographical Context

While a reader should always be cautious about assuming that the poet is the speaker of the poem, "America" does appear to be an expression of McKay's own ambivalence toward the United States. Therefore, it is significant to note that he was an immigrant. McKay was born in 1890 in a rural, hilly region of Jamaica. His father was a relatively prosperous farmer. At the age of seven, he went to live with his brother, a teacher with a library of literature and philosophy that helped shape Claude's later ideas and art, especially his use of traditional verse forms. Later, McKay met a well-educated Englishman, Walter Jeckyll, who became his mentor. Jeckyll, who had published a collection of Jamaican folktales, broadened McKay's knowledge of European literature and encouraged him to publish poetry written in Jamaican dialect. Published in 1912, both "Songs of Jamaica" and "Constab Ballads" employ common people as speakers to express affection for friends and family and love of the country life.

It was not until McKay came to the United States that he experienced the intense racism to which he would respond in "America." Jamaica was not free from racism, but much of it was intraracial, with lighter-skinned Blacks looking down upon darker-skinned people, including McKay. When he stepped off the boat in Charleston, South Carolina, on his way to study at Tuskegee, McKay encountered a level of discrimination and hostility he could only have imagined before then. After a few months in Alabama, McKay moved to Kansas State College to study agriculture. Within two years, he left Manhattan, Kansas, to try a new life in the Manhattan of New York.

McKay tried to run a restaurant that failed, and he married a childhood sweetheart, Eulalie Imelda Edwards. Within six months, she returned to Jamaica, pregnant with a daughter that McKay would never see. Over the next few years, McKay worked a number of jobs, most notably as a waiter in a railway dining car. While the railroad took him across the country, he continued to consider Harlem his home.

He started submitting poems to magazines, publishing "Harlem Dancer" in "Seven Arts" in 1917, and "If We Must Die," a powerful call to fight back against racial violence, in "The Liberator" in 1919.

"The Liberator" was a socialist magazine managed by Max and Crystal Eastman, who hired McKay as an assistant editor. After spending some time in England, where he worked for another socialist publication and published a collection of poems, "Spring in New Hampshire and Other Poems" (notably omitting the militant "If We Must Die" on the advice of his editors), McKay returned to New York and "The Liberator."

At this point in his life, when McKay was writing many of his protest poems, the American socialist movement was a major influence, with its emphasis on conflicts caused by economic disparities and divisions between economic classes. Yet racism remained a more significant reality in his life, even around New York City. Immediately preceding his inclusion of "America" in "A Long Way from Home," McKay tells of a trip to New Jersey with two white friends to see the skyline of the city. Growing hungry, they tried to get a meal "at several hotels and restaurants," but were unsuccessful because they would not serve a black man. They finally had to settle for a meal served in the kitchen of a restaurant, where the workers ate (134). A few pages following the poem, McKay relates an event when he and a white illustrator went to review a play for "The Liberator," only to be told they could not sit in the front seats with other critics; instead, they sat in the balcony with other African Americans. When McKay wrote "America," then, he was viewing the nation from a number of perspectives: as an immigrant, a socialist, a failed business owner, a worker of low-paying jobs, and most significantly as someone who had experienced years of intense racism.

After publishing "Harlem Shadows" in 1922, McKay decided to visit Russia. Even though he later insisted he was never a Marxist, he participated in a conference of communists and socialists from around the world and he published articles in communist periodicals. He left Russia after a few months, but stayed overseas for twelve years, living primarily in France, Spain, and Morocco.

Often he was short on money, leading him to work menial jobs and to ask friends for financial assistance. Partly to make money, as well as to find a new medium through which to express his views on race and society, he turned to fiction, publishing three novels and a collection of short stories between 1928 and 1932, and in 1934 he finally returned to the United States.

In 1937, McKay published his autobiography, "A Long Way from Home," which includes sketches of many of the prominent people he knew and reflections on his beliefs. His political and religious views changed over the years, as he lost faith in socialism and, after suffering a stroke, he joined the Catholic Church. McKay died in Chicago in 1948.

Michael Schroeder, Ph.D.

Works Cited

Cooper, Wayne F. "Claude McKay: Rebel Sojourner in the Harlem Renaissance." Baton Rouge: Louisiana State UP, 1987.

Huggins, Nathan Irvin. "Harlem Renaissance." New York: Oxford UP, 1971.

Keller, James R. "'A Chafing Savage, Down the Decent Street': The Politics of Compromise in Claude McKay's Protest Sonnets." "African American Review" 28 (Fall 1994): 447-456. "Academic Search Premier." EBSCO. Gordon Library, Savannah State University.

Maxwell, William J. "On 'America.'" "Modern American Poetry." Compiled by William J. Maxwell, University of Illinois at Urbana-Champaign <http://www.english.uiuc.edu/maps/poets/m_r/mckay/america.htm>.

McKay, Claude. "America." "Poet's Corner." Ed. Nelson Miller <http://www.theotherpages.org/poems/mckay01.html>.

———. "A Long Way from Home." New York: Lee Furman, 1937. New York: Arno, 1969.

Tillery, Tyrone. "Claude McKay: A Black Poet's Struggle for Identity." Amherst: U of Mass. P, 1992.

Discussion Questions

1. The structure of the sentences and logic of "America" does not correspond to the traditional rhyme scheme of the sonnet. (See the discussion of formal qualities above.) Do you see this conflict as a strength or weakness in the poem? Why?

2. What is implied by the speaker's use of "confess" in line 3? Discuss some of the ways in which someone in the early 1920s might have seen America as a "cultured hell."

3. In what ways might the speaker be similar to a "rebel" who "fronts" (or confronts) a ruler against whom he is rebelling? What sorts of attitudes would you expect the rebel to feel in the situation?

4. Is it possible to gain strength from someone or something that hates you?

5. What are some of the connotations and denotations of the words "vigor" and "bigness" as they might apply to America?

6. What does the water imagery add to the poem? What is implied by the phrases "flows like tides into my blood" or "sweeps my being like a flood"?

7. Paraphrase the final four lines and discuss the suggestions of the image. Do you think McKay is suggesting that the "might and granite wonders" of America will literally be destroyed?

8. Do you believe that McKay is suggesting that decay or destruction is inevitable, or that it could be avoided if America changes its ways?

9. How would you characterize the overall tone of "America"? Does the poem sound angry? Regretful? Defiant? Condescending? Does the tone change in the course of the poem?

10. Most of McKay's poems are about traditional romantic topics such as love and nature, with poems on political or racial topics, such as "America," interspersed among them. Does the incongruity of such a forceful protest amid traditional poems about love and nature make it seem out of place, or is it more powerful for being atypical of most of McKay's poetry?

Essay Ideas

1. McKay writes, "I wrote a series of sonnets expressing my bitterness, hate, and love," yet "Some of them were quoted out of their context to prove that I hate America" ("A Long Way" 135). Using the poems "Baptism," "The White City," and "The White House" as well as "America," argue that McKay is not expressing hatred for the United States, but rather demonstrating affection for it while criticizing its worst traits.

2. Identify the uses of personification, metaphors, similes, and allusions in the poem and discuss their effectiveness. What suggestions do they add to the meaning? Do they create any confusion?

3. Claude McKay and Countee Cullen are known for using formal English and traditional poetic forms such as the sonnet in contrast to the colloquial language and open form used by Langston Hughes. Contrast some of the poems by the poets, such as those listed below, and write an essay in which you discuss the different effects achieved by the different forms and diction of McKay and Cullen, on one hand, and Hughes on the other.

4. Critics have noted echoes of several poems from British literature in "America," including Shakespeare's sonnets "When in Disgrace with Fortune" and "Nor Marble, nor Gilded Monuments" as well as Shelley's "Ozymandias" (Keller). Read those poems, and write an essay exploring some of the similarities in theme, wording, and imagery. Research the social and artistic history of the United States of the 1920s, and write a documented essay showing how the social conditions of the time might lead to an observer viewing the United States as a "cultured hell."

Robert Frost, pictured above, wrote "Birches," featured opposite. Three other works by Frost appear in this volume: "Acquainted with the Night," page 1; "The Road Not Taken," page 165; and "Stopping by Woods on a Snowy Evening," page 181. Photo: Library of Congress

Birches

by Robert Frost

Content Synopsis

Speaking directly to the reader, the poet begins by relating what he imagines when he looks at white birch trees in the midst of a field of other, straight-standing, dark, trees: how they have come to be bent in their great down-swooping arches because a boy has been swinging on them. Once this thought is out, however, the poet immediately returns, in the fourth line, to the world of factuality from his reverie. He explains the actual cause of their permanent stoop: ice storms and the weight of the glassy ice casing that encrusts and weighs them down. He then describes how the ice falls from the branches like clinking pieces of glass on the crust of the snow beneath the trees and notes that it appears, in his imagination as if the inner dome of heaven, an imaginary crystal sphere had fallen. After noting how the ice must be cleared away, he returns to the birch branches.

The pronoun "They" beginning the fourteenth line does not refer to the last-mentioned plural noun in line twelve, the "heaps of broken glass," but to the birch branches. This referential ambiguity reinforces the colloquial quality of the poet's language. The poet notes that once they have been bent, the birches stay bent and concludes his discourse on the phenomenon with a metaphor, comparing the bent branches throwing their foliage on the ground to girls on all fours tossing their hair over their heads for it to dry in the sun.

The use of metaphor apparently reminds him, at line twenty-one, that he is not intent on giving a disquisition on birch trees but using them to write a poem, to express the kind of truth derived from fancy rather than from facts.

He returns to his reverie, which he prefers to the facts, and embroiders a story about a solitary boy living too far away from a populated town to learn games like baseball, who plays by himself as he goes about his daily farm chores, primarily swinging on birch branches and causing their permanent arching. The poet thinks of it as a process of the boy's subduing his father's wishes. The poet thinks of the branches as stiff at first but that the boy conquers them by his swinging, softens them, and makes them hang limp. The swinging is described as a process of learning the right way to launch himself and to maintain his poise.

At line forty-two, the speaker turns back from metaphor and his mediation on branch swinging and recalls his own youth when he would swing on branches. He speaks about his longing to return to his youth, to the time before the stresses of life assault and pain him, which he conveys in the painful image of a twig having lashed across an open eye, reprising and revising the image of a swung and bent branch but in a new context.

This experience of life as a stab of pain brings the poet to confess that there are times, like a boy flying above the ground when swinging on a birch branch that he would like to get away from earth, but only for a while, so that the experience is not death but a transcendental joy. He expresses a desire to experience a realm beyond life that is a fundamental experience of being alive followed by its complement, the joyful experience of coming back to earth. Following the colloquial attitude of the poem, the poet returns from his transcendental reflections with the homespun phrase that ends the poem and shows him solidly a denizen of the earth.

Symbols & Motifs

The principal motif of the poem involves the act of bending the facts of the world to one's own needs, of taking the matter of the world and using it as the material whereby one can express oneself, of making one's own mark on the world and deflecting tradition so that it flows through the channel that one devises. For the boy, the authority that he challenges and bends to his own will is his father's as represented by his birches. For a poet the authority to be challenged is the authority of the precursor poets, as he bends tradition to his expressive needs. They are his father figures who have left him woods and trees that he must refashion and make his own through the exercise of his own vitality, bending the past to his practice and forming a new configuration.

Since this is a poem and its writer is a poet, it is reasonable, from the way Frost describes swinging on the branches to think that the description of swinging and of mastering its art can be read metaphorically as an individual learning the poet's craft through practice.

Historical Context

First published in *The Atlantic Monthly* magazine in August 1915, "Birches" stands somewhat outside history, set, as it is, in a peaceful wood. Only ice storms or an unexpected lashing of the eye by a wayward twig disturbs it, and by the transcendental ruminations of memory, longing, and melancholy,

far from the battlefields of Europe, where Frost had lived in England until the very year in which the poem first appeared. The war and the madness of governments, nations, and men are present only to the reader aware of their absence in the poem.

The poem also represents a historical movement in poetry away from the trappings that had defined poetry in the late nineteenth century. The poets of the early twentieth century, Frost one of the principals in this movement, shifted the diction of poetry away from the formality of late nineteenth-century decorum. They wrote verse freer of the constraints by which poetry had been defined in the preceding century. Rhyme, meter, and formal diction were made to give way to the looser rhythms and accents of colloquial and even common speech. Unlike his contemporaries, Ezra Pound and T.S. Eliot, rebellious in their own ways against the past, Frost did not demand great classical learning or familiarity with the body of western and eastern literature, philosophy, and anthropology in order to enter the world of his poetry. His was the poetry of an individual man as he experienced that part of the earth upon which he lived a life.

Societal Context

"Birches" is the poem of a solitary man, one who imagines a boy living on a farm away from any populous town. He is an isolated boy who must invent his own games, unable to learn social games, like baseball. . In the same way that it is outside history, it is outside society. Even as a grown-up, the speaker's society is his environment rather than any human community.

Religious Context

"Birches" celebrates an unformulated and informal religion of nature. In it, the poet conceives of swinging on birches as a means of achieving a state of transcendental exaltation. Swinging the body heavenward on their branches is an exercise that frees the spirit from the absolutes of gravity and permits a safe encounter with the anxious giddiness of death without abandoning the stability of rootedness in life.

Scientific & Technological Context

The poet contrasts truth or factuality, as in his disquisition on ice storms and their effects on birch trees, with poetry and imagination. Poetry and its essential component, imagination, as they are presented in "Birches" represent the mental technology for realizing truth that is not bound to or limited by factuality. Through the imagery of a boy swinging on birches, the poet comes to the needs of the soul to shuttle between the grounded and the transcendental realms of experience.

Biographical Context

Frost was one of the best-known American poets of the twentieth century. Many of his poems, like "Fire and Ice," "The Road Not Taken," "Mending Wall," Birches," "Death of A Hired Man," "Stopping by Woods on A Snowy Evening," and "Mending Wall," or phrases from them, have entered the mainstream of American culture and discourse. He was awarded the Pulitzer Prize for poetry four times. He often appeared on television programs and read an inaugural poem at the inauguration of John Kennedy.

Despite his apparently bucolic poetry, Frost lived a difficult life, enduring financial hardship and mental turmoil, as well as earning fame and success. He worked as a farmer, but rather unsuccessfully, and as a schoolteacher. As a poet, he was a gentleman farmer, working his land but not dependent upon it. He married Elinor White in 1894. In 1937, she was diagnosed with breast cancer and died of heart failure in 1938. Of their six children, their son committed suicide and their daughter suffered an emotional collapse. American as he was as a poet, Frost lived during the early years of the twentieth century, his formative years as a poet, in London.

Frost was born in San Francisco, California, on March 26, 1874. Frost's father was a teacher and newspaper editor, but he died when Frost was eleven, leaving his family penniless. Frost's mother moved the family, Frost and his younger sister, to New England, a part of the country with which Frost and his poetry were strongly associated. He was a founder of the Bread Loaf Writers' Conference at Middlebury College, in Vermont, in 1921. His mother died of cancer in 1900 and his sister died in a mental hospital in 1909.

Frost died on January 29, 1963 in Boston, Massachusetts.

Neil Heims, Ph.D.

Works Cited

Meyers, Jeffrey. *Robert Frost: A Biography*. Boston: Houghton Mifflin, 1996. Print.

Parini, Jay. *Robert Frost: A Life*. New York: H. Holt and Co., 1999. Print.

Discussion Questions

1. What do you think is the poet's sense of the relationship between sons and their fathers? Why? From what in the poem do you get that idea?

2. What is Frost's attitude toward youth? What is it toward adulthood? What is the difference?

3. Is the figure of swinging on birches an open symbol? What are all the things it can signify? What are its limits?

4. How important is solitude for the poet? What are his feelings about solitude? Is the poet a happy man?

5. How does Frost convey the greater cosmic world in a poem in which his focus seems to be only a forest of predominantly birch trees? What is the sense of the cosmos that he imparts?

6. Contrast the images used to convey the activities of boys and of girls? How do they differ? Do you feel that there is there a significance in this difference? What seems to be the relationship between boys and girls in the poem?

7. What is the significance of "the pathless wood" to which the poet refers?

8. What does "Birches" tell you about the poet's attitudes towards life and death?

9. In what way can "Birches" be said to be a poem about writing poetry?

10. Where does the poet of "Birches" locate himself in relation to the history of poetry? How does he accomplish this?

11. Can you think of examples from your own experience of situations and feelings comparable to the ones Frost describes in "Birches?" Discuss them and describe similarities, differences, and their effects on you.

Essay Ideas

1. Describe the poet's character.
2. Analyze the way the speaker thinks about things.
3. Discuss the poet's relation to nature.
4. Analyze the poem as an expression of the poet's desire for excitement and his sense of anxiety.
5. What does the diction of "Birches" tell you about the character of the speaker?

Daddy

by Sylvia Plath

Content Synopsis

"Daddy," one of Plath's most well-known poems, was written in the months before her suicide in 1963 and included in her 1965 collection "Ariel." Like many of the "Ariel" poems, it represents a stark world observed by a strained and haunted subject. The poem is dark in tone, and addresses such themes as anger and the Holocaust. Yet, the poem also depicts the speaker's transformation from victim to self-knowing subject, a narrative that parallels the evolution of Plath's own poetic voice.

The poem begins with an indictment of the "Daddy" of the title. The speaker tells her father "you do not do" (line 1), and states she has been confined "like a foot for thirty years" (3-4) inside the "black shoe" (2) of her father. In contrast to this opening image of entrapment, she claims, "Daddy, I have had to kill you" (6), but then reveals her father "died before I had time" (7). "I used to pray to recover you" (14), she says in the third stanza. Later, she admits a suicide attempt at twenty was an attempt to "get back, back, back to you" (59). These revelations, and the contradictory emotions they suggest, set the pattern of successive transformation that characterizes the poem. They also outline the speaker's situation. Although she is now an adult-aged thirty, as suggested by the opening stanza-she still suffers both the stifling authority of her father and the pain of his early death. This tension between resentment and sadness forms the context for the poem's main theme: the speaker's journey through horror and rage to self-individuation.

In the second stanza, the speaker characterizes her dead father as a colossal presence, his body "a bag full of god" and a giant "ghastly statue" (9) stretching across America from the "Frisco seal" (10) of San Francisco to the Atlantic. At the end of this stanza, Plath introduces the German and Holocaust imagery that dominate the speaker's presentation of her father. "Ach, du" (15), she says in German ("Oh, you.") The speaker reveals her father came from a Polish town with a common name: "So I never could tell / Where you put your foot, your root" (22-23), she says. The attempt to "recover" her father is frustrated even by his nebulous ancestry. However, it is also frustrated by his Germanic status, which she does not share: "I never could talk to you. / The tongue stuck in my jaw" (24-25), she says, "Ich, ich, ich, ich, / I could hardly speak. / I thought every German was you" (27-29).

This characterization of remote, foreign father and alienated daughter quickly resolves into a series of Holocaust images, beginning in the seventh stanza. Alluding to her father's German background, the speaker compares him to a Nazi. Her father's German language is "obscene," "an engine / Chuffing me off like a Jew" (30-32) to the concentration camps of "Dachau, Auschwitz, Belsen" (33). The speaker presents her father's culture as rendering the "snows of the Tyrol, the clear beer of Vienna; not very pure or true" (36-37). In this Nazi-made world, she is an outsider, a Jew, or one of the gypsies also persecuted by the Nazis: "With my gypsy ancestress and my weird luck / And my Taroc pack and my Taroc pack / I may be a bit of a Jew" (38-40). In turn, her father becomes a "panzer [tank] man;" not God after all "but a swastika / So black no sky could squeak through" (45-47). He gains a "neat moustache" like Hitler's and an "Aryan eye, bright blue" (43-44). This light coloring-blond hair and blue eyes, was prized by the Nazis as a sign of "true" German ethnicity, in contrast to the darker coloring of the Jewish people the "Final Solution" sought to purge. By developing this analogy; comparing Nazis and Jews to father and daughter, Plath stresses the speaker's belief that she, too, has been imprisoned, and that her identity as a person has been taken over and erased. Additionally, the darkness of the Holocaust imagery suggests the desperation of the speaker's situation, and hint at the trauma she must undergo to free herself from it.

In the tenth and eleventh stanzas, the speaker introduces the theme of masochism: "Every woman adores a Fascist, / The boot in the face, the brute / Brute heart of a brute like you" (48-50). She refers to a photograph she has of her father: "You stand at the blackboard, daddy, / In the picture I have of you" (51-52). She toys with the image of her father as a charming teacher, insisting that despite the cleft in his chin he is "no less a devil for that, no not / Any less the black man who / Bit my pretty red heart in two" (54-56). Here, we learn that the speaker was ten when her father died, and that ten years later she tried to commit suicide to be reunited with him, even if only in death: "I thought even the bones would do" (60). When this attempt failed, she "made a model" (64) of her father, finding a "man in black with a Meinkampf look / And a love of the rack and the screw" (65-66). She marries him, "And I said I do, I do" (67), perpetuating the cycle of victimization the poem has detailed.

This moment of looking back on her life, however, is also a moment of self-awareness. For the first time, the speaker hints at her own complicity in being victimized. The poem has served as a means of projecting anger onto her father, but also as a means of analyzing this seminal relationship. Once the speaker admits her attempts to "recover" her father have only been self-destructive, she can begin to exorcise him. This epiphany is only implicit, as Plath does not detail the speaker's change of perspective. Instead, the poem shifts direction dramatically. The line after "And I said I do, I do" (67) reads, "So daddy, I'm finally through" (68). The imagery that follows is of death and disconnect: a "black telephone," "off at the root," so "voices cannot worm through" (69-70); a vampire whose "fat black heart" (76) has been staked; and finally, villagers "dancing and stamping" (80) on the corpse of her father. The poem's last image suggests an analogy between villagers who have destroyed a vampire and are rejoicing over its death, and the daughter who has finally rid herself of her father.

Although these images are in keeping with the dark tones of the poem, their darkness is tempered with triumph rather than animosity and horror. The obscenity of the Holocaust motif has given way to the villagers and the speaker rejoicing over a longed-for death. The speaker's tone, at first tentative and later outraged, has muted into a relieved bitterness. "Daddy, you can lie back now" (75), she says calmly. The poem has acted as confession and therapy, allowing the speaker to address and resolve her anger through a series of metaphors about her relationship with her father. The underlying problem has been revealed to be not only the trauma of her father's death, but also more significantly the speaker's own lack of agency because of this trauma. This, too, is resolved through the poem's changing images, which allow the speaker to recognize her self-destructive behavior-her passive nature, the suicide attempt, and her problematic marriage, for example. By the end of the poem, the speaker has evolved from stuttering the word "I" in her father's language-"Ich, ich, ich, ich" (27)-to asserting herself through her own (poetic) language in the final line: "Daddy, daddy, you bastard, I'm through" (80).

Historical Context

Although first published in England, "Daddy" suggests an American perspective. The speaker distances herself from her German father, positioning him as an out-of-touch immigrant and herself as a first-generation citizen speaking English. Yet, the looming figure of the father, which spans the continental United States and even extends into the Atlantic, is also a metaphor of America's expanding global influence during and after World War II. Plath's own father died in 1940, and this incident in Plath's life would have been bound up with the events of war: news of the London blitz, the invasion of Pearl Harbor and America's entry into the hostilities, the dropping of the atom bomb, and the horrific revelation of the Nazis' Final Solution. By the mid-1950s, when Plath was again studying at Smith College after a suicide attempt, America was a changed place. Haunted by the traumas of the war, the country was also fostering an era of many changes: rapid technological development, the growth of consumer capitalism, the rise and global influence of American culture, and the social unrest that would spawn the civil rights movements of the 1960s. If post-war, postmodern America embodied the exhilarating opportunities of a new age, it also symbolized a profound malaise, a sense of progress undermined by lingering horrors of the recent past. Although "Daddy" is about the speaker's specific past-the death of her father-the poem's tension between stasis and change, and its representation of resurfacing traumas, reflect the America of the times.

Societal Context

"Daddy" also reflects many aspects of the social sphere in the mid-20th century. The generational tension in the poem anticipates the rebellious youth

cultures of the 1960s and 70s. The ethnic quality of this tension-the antagonism of the American daughter toward her German father-also reflects the social diversity of a country shaped by immigration, and hostility toward Germany after the war. The fact that the poem narrates a daughter's rebellion against her father is also significant, reflecting an atmosphere of increasing feminist awareness. In "Daddy," Plath associates the figure of the father with other figures of oppression-Hitler, a torturer, a vampire. The poem could be read as a harsh critique of patriarchal authority and women's relegation to passive roles. In this sense, "Daddy" and other poems in "Ariel" (see "Lady Lazarus," for example) offer visions of feminist rebellion and rewrite gender roles. This aspect of Plath's poetry has given rise to diverse feminist readings of her work, and to Plath's status as a feminist icon.

Psychology has played a similar role in the Plath myth and literary criticism. The poem's therapeutic function reflects a society deeply influenced by Freudian psychoanalysis, and invested in the question of mental health. Sigmund Freud, who devised psychoanalysis in the late nineteenth century, takes the view that all mental disturbances are rooted in the unconscious. Accordingly, treatment centers on discussion between the analyst and the patient and involves interpreting associations, memories, and dreams to uncover the unconscious desires or fears causing the patient's problems. In bringing these desires and fears into the open, the patient is able to free him- or herself from them. Freud's work had an enormous influence on Western conceptions of mental disorder, although psychoanalysis was not the only means used to treat mental disturbance in 1950s America. In-patient care, prescription of tranquilizers, and electroshock therapy were also common practice. Plath herself underwent different forms of therapy after a suicide attempt, an experience fictionalized in her novel "The Bell Jar" and explored in her poetry. Although the biographical context of Plath's work has sometimes unduly swayed critical judgment, it has also raised interesting questions about so-called "confessional" literature.

Religious Context

"Daddy" also reflects a postmodern skepticism about religion. The speaker characterizes her father as "a bag of god." (8) Omnipresent and omnipotent, he dominates his daughter's actual and emotional landscape. Yet, the speaker's attitude toward this God is one of derision rather than piety. She challenges his power and authority, revealing it problematic and unstable. She prays to recover him, but praying establishes neither spiritual connection nor personal fulfillment. Praying is not even an emotionally comforting gesture, but rather a crackling telephone with a dead connection. In this bleak world, even God himself is dead. By the end of the poem, the speaker has reduced her god-like father to a Nazi caricature, then to a slain vampire, and then to nothing-the dust beneath the villagers' feet. This skepticism about the father's power suggests skepticism about power more generally, including the power of the Christian god to which he is compared.

Scientific & Technological Context

References to science and technology in the poem generally concern the technology of German warfare. There is the "panzer man" (45) and "roller" (17) (or tank) that level Polish towns; there is "an engine, an engine / Chuffing me off like a Jew" (31-32), which refers to the trains used to transport prisoners to concentration camps; and there is also the "Luftwaffe" (42), or German air force, of the speaker's imagined Nazi father. All of these images allude specifically to the mechanics of violence and death, which heighten the reader's, and the speaker's, sense of the obscene. These images, like that of the telephone toward the end of the poem, also form a sharp contrast to Plath's nature imagery. "The waters off beautiful Nauset" (13) and the Austrian landscape have both been invaded and/or exploited by these other, negative forces. The ocean where the father's

head lies is "the freakish Atlantic" (11), and the Austrian Alps, under a fascist regime, are "not very pure or true" (37). At the end of the poem, however, the natural side of Plath's dichotomy triumphs over the mechanical one, as the rural villagers overcome the technological advances of the Nazi-vampire figure.

A less obvious but perhaps more significant appearance of science and technology in the poem concerns the image of the speaker's tongue "stuck in a barb wire snare" (26). Given the context of the Holocaust analogy at work, this image recalls the barbed wire of the concentration camps, the subjection of prisoners therein to "scientific experiments," and the pseudo-science behind the Nazi agenda of ethnic cleansing. This theme of science gone awry returns when the post-suicidal speaker remembers recovering from her suicide attempt: "But they pulled me out of the sack, / And they stuck me together with glue." This Frankenstein-like attempt at cure only causes the speaker to turn to her own destructive mechanics. In making "a model" (64) of her father in her husband, she merely submits again to "the rack and the screw" (66). Part of the malaise of the poem corresponds to its postmodern, post-war context: to an awareness that science and technology can be ineffective, or, with more disastrous consequences, overreaching.

Biographical Context

Sylvia Plath was born in 1932 in Massachusetts. Her mother was of Austrian descent and her father, who died when Plath was eight, was German-facts alluded to in "Daddy." A strong student and active writer, Plath won a partial scholarship to Smith College in 1950. Two years later, she won the "Mademoiselle" fiction contest. She was selected to work as a student guest editor at the magazine that summer. In 1953, she went to New York City for this purpose, but returned depressed. She attempted suicide at her home and was hospitalized, where she underwent psychiatric treatment (events also alluded to in "Daddy").

After recovering, Plath returned to a successful undergraduate career at Smith, eventually winning a Fulbright scholarship to study at Cambridge in 1955. There, she met the poet Ted Hughes, whom she married in 1956. In 1959, after two years teaching and writing in Massachusetts, the pair moved back to London.

In 1960, the birth of Plath's first child, Frieda, coincided with the publication of The Colossus, her first collection of poems. A year later, after a miscarriage, Plath and Hughes moved to Devon where Plath gave birth to a son, Nicholas. However, her marriage to Hughes deteriorated, in part due to Hughes's affair with aspiring poet Assia Wevill). (Wevill was the wife of Canadian poet David Wevill, and she began an affair with Hughes in 1961. Their affair continued after Plath's death, and resulted in the birth of their daughter, Shura, in 1965. Four years later, Wevill killed herself and Shura using a combination of sleeping pills and gas from the kitchen oven.) After separating in 1962, Plath moved back to London with the children. During the final months of her life, she completed the poems that would comprise "Ariel." In February 1963, she committed suicide by gassing herself.

Hughes, who later became poet laureate of England, collected and posthumously published Plath's "Winter Trees" and "Crossing the Water" (1971). He also edited Plath's "Collected Poems" (1981), which earned her the Pulitzer Prize. Hughes's own collection, "Birthday Letters," was addressed to Plath, and was published in 1998, the year of his death.

Jennifer Dunn

Works Cited

Alvarez, A. *The Savage God: A Study of Suicide.* Harmondsworth: Penguin, 1974.

Bronfen, Elisabeth. *Sylvia Plath.* Plymouth: Northcote, 1998.

Plath, Sylvia. *Ariel.* London: Faber, 1965.

Rose, Jacqueline. *The Haunting of Sylvia Plath.* London: Virago, 1991.

Steiner, George. "Dying Is an Art." *Language and Silence.* London: Faber, 1967. 324-31.

Wagner, Linda. *Critical Essays on Sylvia Plath.* Boston: G. K. Hall, 1984.

For Further Study

Banjeree, Jacqueline. "Grief and the Modern Writer." English: *The Journal of the College English Association*: 43 (1994). 17-36.

Broe, Mary Lynn. *Protean Poetic: The Poetry of Sylvia Plath.* Columbia: U of Missouri P, 1980.

Bronfen, Elisabeth. *Over her Dead Body: Death, Femininity, and the Aesthetic.* Manchester: Manchester UP, 1992.

Bundtzen, Lynda K. *Plath's Incarnations: Women and the Creative Process.* Ann Arbor: U of Michigan P, 1983.

Gilbert, Sandra M. and Susan Gubar. *The Madwoman in the Attic: The Woman Writer and the Nineteenth-Century Literary Imagination.* New Haven: Yale UP, 1979.

_____. *No Man's Land: The Place of the Woman Writer in the Twentieth Century.* New Haven: Yale UP, 1994.

Homans, Margaret. *Women Writers and Poetic Identity.* Princeton: Princeton UP, 1980.

Schwartz, Murray M. and Christopher Bollas. "The Absence at the Centre: Sylvia Plath and Suicide." *Sylvia Plath: New Views on the Poetry*, ed. Gary Lane. Baltimore: Johns Hopkins UP, 1979. 179-292.

Young, James E. *Writing and Rewriting the Holocaust: Narrative and the Consequences of Interpretation.* Bloomington: Indiana UP, 1988.

Discussion Questions

1. What do you think the final line means? Is the speaker really "through?"
2. What does the speaker mean when she says that the villagers "always knew it was you?" Why does Plath use this image of the community at the end of the poem?
3. Some critics have accused Plath of exploiting the Holocaust by using its imagery to her own ends. Do you agree?
4. "Confessional" poetry is sometimes seen as self-indulgent. Does "Daddy" depict a forceful poetic transformation, or adolescent solipsism? Why?
5. Is the poem dated? Do the issues raised-about family, war, and death-relate to the contemporary world?
6. Plath underwent therapy throughout her life. Do you think this poem acted as a kind of therapy? Do artists and writers resolve issues through their creative work? Does doing so make it less artistically valid?
7. Is this a particularly "female" poem? Could a man have written this to his mother wife, or father? Is gender a fundamental aspect of poetry or creative expression?
8. There has been controversy over Hughes's involvement in the publication of Plath's letters. Given the subject matter of "Daddy," what do you think about relatives or other poets editing a writer's work? What do you think about writers who "write back" to each other, as Hughes did in Birthday Letters?
9. There has been a "Plath myth" industry, of which the film Sylvia is a recent example. Discuss how real-life figures become mythologized and commercialized. How does the myth of Plath-or the Plath depicted in the movie-compare to the voice behind "Daddy?"
10. It is difficult to read Plath's work without thinking of her own life. Is it possible to read poetry in a non-biographical context? Do you think there are problems with relating the author's life to the characters they create? What is the difference between fiction and biography?

Essay Ideas

1. Compare "Daddy" to another poem in "Ariel." What are the differences and similarities? Compare motifs, form, and imagery, for example.
2. Compare "Daddy" to a poem from Plath's first collection, "The Colossus." In what ways is "Ariel" different?
3. How does the form of the poem-such as its rhymes and diction-relate to any of its themes?
4. Both Plath and Anne Sexton studied under Robert Lowell. Compare the three poets' work. Why do you think their poems are called "confessional poetry?" What are the consistencies and differences between their motifs and styles?
5. Death-as-rebirth and death-as-vengeance are frequent themes in Plath's poetry, and are often shown to be intertwined. What role do they play in this poem?

The Fish

by Elizabeth Bishop

Content Synopsis

"I caught a tremendous fish" (1) begins Elizabeth Bishop's poem of dense visual details, which narrates the story of this catch. Like many of her poems, "The Fish" creates a slightly altered world from the one we know, though the events of the poem are recognizable, even mundane. The descriptions, accurate and illuminating, of the caught fish, point towards an inner world at work that informs the perception of the speaker, giving it the images that quietly transcend the actual scene in odd, associative leaps.

Most of the poem is given over to descriptions of the fish, beginning with the outside and working in: "his brown skin hung in strips / like ancient wallpaper" (10-11) then "the coarse white flesh / packed in like feathers" (27-8). The poet thinks of the inner organs of the fish, "the dramatic reds and blacks / of his shiny entrails" (30-1). Looking into his eyes the poet is reminded of "tarnished tinfoil / seen through the lenses of old scratched isinglass" (38-9). Lastly, she sees the fish's jaw-"grim, wet, and weapon-like" (50)-and the multiple hooks and lines that the fish has broken in previous attempts to catch him. The poet feels an overwhelming sense of "victory" (66) at first, and then-strangely, perhaps-she lets the fish go.

While there is not much action to speak of in the poem, there is a sense of movement, which we could account for by calling it the movement of the observer's own mind. As the poet "stared and stared" (65) at the fish, his body (the fish is gendered male by the poet) takes on a life of its own, even as he lies slowly dying in "the little rented boat" (67). What drives the poem is not the dramatic action, which is nominal, but the action of observation, which repeatedly transforms the fish with simile: the fish's body is "like ancient wallpaper" (11), "like full-blown roses" (14), "like feathers" (28), "like a big peony" (33); the pieces of line are "like medals with their ribbons" and "a five-haired beard" (62-3). All of these images crowd and intersect with our actual vision of the fish, transmogrifying him into an impossibly complex organism who is half-fish, half-man, and-mathematics be damned-half-imagined being.

The concluding line of the poem is as plain as the opening one: "And I let the fish go" (76). However, just before she lets him go (perhaps even the cause for his release) she has visions of "rainbow, rainbow, rainbow" (75): a transcendent rainbow spreads through the sheen of oil in the "pool of bilge" (68) and seems to cover the boat, and implicitly, beyond it. This moment is brought on by the process of observation and comparisons the poet has made earlier, which seem to have excited the mind and eyes to the point that the rainbows overload them with sensory information, and the release of the fish is as necessary as letting go of an electrified fence.

Historical Context

Bishop wrote "The Fish" in late 1939 or early the next year, according to her letters written to Marianne Moore ("Letters" 79). She recounts a story of catching a parrotfish in a letter in January of 1939, while she was living in Key West, Florida. Here she vividly describes it to Moore: "They are ravishing fish-all iridescent, with a silver edge to each scale, and a real bill-like mouth just like turquoise; the eye is big and wild, and the eyeball is turquoise too-they are very humorous-looking fish" (Ibid). After Bishop sent her a draft of the poem, Moore replied that she found it "concentrated and valorous" ("Selected Letters of Marianne Moore" 397).

The poem appeared in "The Partisan Review" in 1940, and in Bishop's first book, "North & South," in 1946. "The Fish" was singled out by reviewers, especially the poet-critic Robert Lowell, who was to become a close friend of Bishop's. Lowell wrote to Bishop that the poem was "perhaps your best; I'm a fisherman myself, but all my fish become symbols, alas!" (Goldensohn 166). The peculiarity of the poem, then and now, lies in the refusal to make the fish an identifiable symbol; in refusing to be metaphor for Death, Forgiveness, Male/Female identity (and many more), the fish remains an enigmatic, though closely observed figure. As Bonnie Costello observes, "He remains a contradictory figure and returns to the flux he never entirely leaves" by reentering the ocean at the end of the poem (61).

Societal Context

"Elizabeth Bishop is spectacular in being unspectacular," wrote the poet Marianne Moore in a review of "North and South," Bishop's first book ("Complete Prose" 406). Indeed, Bishop's poems often are not spectacular, nor do they overwhelm with virtuosic cascades of language. However, today Bishop stands as perhaps the most celebrated mid-century American female poet. Moreover, she stands as the perhaps most relevant figure from that era, having survived the Modern, Formalist, Confessional, and Post-Modern eras with her reputation and admirers intact. During her lifetime, in comparison, esteem for her work was limited to a small number of admirers, her close friend and widely-acclaimed poet Robert Lowell among them. Today, Lowell, as well as other then-popular poets like Theodore Roethke, Weldon Kees, and John Berryman lags behind Bishop in anthologies and academic studies; her poems are more widely read than any female author save Emily Dickinson. In a prophetic moment, Lowell, who himself was America's premier poet at the time, wrote in a letter that Bishop's language and images seemed to "belong to a later century." This description has proved correct, as the 20th and 21st centuries have seen an incredible increase in the volume of study on her life and work.

In an article in "The New Criterion" Gioia speculates that Bishop's later ascendancy to her current reputation can partially be attributed to the academy's increased interest in marginalized and displaced voices. Bishop occupied an almost constant status as outsider, since she was often a stranger to her surroundings, living a peripatetic life from such a young age. Additionally, Bishop's status as a lesbian has encouraged study of her poems using ideas from gender studies and Queer theory. However, Gioia concludes, these factors are secondary to the poems themselves in making Bishop so popular. Comparing her to Keats, Gioia writes that Bishop possessed what Keats described as "negative capability," a term describing the poet's state of ambiguity and mystery. "She had a native genius for reflecting the rich complexity of experience without reducing it into abstraction or predetermined moral judgment," writes Gioia, echoing Moore's description. "She is inclusive by being artfully inconclusive" (8). "The Fish," with its refusal to symbolize any one particular meaning, is an apt demonstration of this inclusiveness: it has been read in multiple ways, yet has not suffered the death-by-paraphrase of many anthologized poems as a poem about something, and end up taught as being about only one thing.

Religious Context

It is difficult, in a symbol so charged with religion and mysticism as a fish, to deny religious associations in "The Fish." However, nowhere in her letters and notes does Bishop allude to this interpretation of the poem; the poem itself avoids images of religion. The symbol of the fish, of course, has long been identified with Christianity, but it is also a mystic figure from pre-Christian religions-a symbol of fertility, the feminine; a deeply shamanistic figure whose folklore history Bishop explores later in the poem "The Riverman," in "Questions of Travel."

Scientific & Technological Context

Bishop's interest in optics, the science of visual perception, was keen. In Key West she had worked in a factory making binocular lenses, and knew the intricacies of light refraction and reflection. "The Fish," with the "lenses / of old scratched isinglass" (39-40), as well as the ending rainbows, contains numerous references to this knowledge, as well as a knowledge of the fish's anatomy (isinglass is actually the clear, gelatinous material that comprises the fish's swim bladder). The ability of see farther and in more detail than with the normal human eye, which is the power of the binoculars, also is the power of Bishop's poem, which enlarges at the same time as it focuses on the visual appearance of the fish.

Biographical Context

"The Fish," as we can learn from Bishop's letters, is based on a "real" experience, yet the facts of it are largely irrelevant to the poem's focus. Although she maintained that one need not know the biography of a poet in order to appreciate the poem, Bishop's life certainly informs and enlarges the scope of her own poetry, which alludes obliquely, when it does at all, to biographical experiences.

From an early age, Bishop had to deal with loss and displacement. When she was five years old, her mother was committed to a sanitarium in Dartmouth, Nova Scotia, after a prolonged period of mental illness. Her father was already gone, having died when she was eight months old, so Bishop was left in the care of her mother's parents, who took her to the Nova Scotia town of Great Village. This age and landscape are described in "Sestina," and in the prose stories "Primer Class" and "In the Village" (*Collected Prose*). Bishop moved from Nova Scotia in 1917 to Worchester, Mass., to live with her father's parents, and then to her aunt's house a year later. At the age of eight, she had lived in four households with four different families. For Bishop, the themes of travel and loss became intertwined at a young age. As author Bonnie Costello notes, Bishop's poetry, despite domestic settings as in "Sestina," illustrates that "a house is no shelter from pain and loss" (199).

In 1930, Bishop enrolled at Vassar, where she majored in English Literature and co-founded the school's literary magazine, "Con Spirito" and served as the editor of the college yearbook. The most important event of her college life occurred in 1934, however, when she first met the poet Marianne Moore. The friendship between them lasted until Moore's death, and was instrumental in bringing Bishop to New York, where she moved after graduation. Moore wrote an introduction for the first publication Bishop received, a group of poems in the anthology "Trial Balances." Moreover, the two women discussed and criticized each other's work; Bishop was heavily influenced by the interplay between formal structure, rhyme, and rhythm that is a hallmark of Moore's work.

Bishop traveled extensively throughout her life. In the three years following her graduation she lived mostly in Paris, and took multiple trips throughout Europe, Morocco, and Florida, where she lived briefly in Key West. In 1942, on a trip through Mexico, Cuba, and Haiti, she met Lota de Macedo Soares, a Brazilian woman from a prominent family in Rio de Janeiro; in 1951 the two would begin living together in Brazil. By this time, Bishop was an acclaimed, if not wildly popular poet, having been offered a Guggenheim Fellowship in 1947, an appointment as Consultant in Poetry at the Library of Congress in 1949 (similar to the current position of Poet Laureate), and an award from the American Academy of Arts and Letters in 1950. However, she continued to have trouble with depression and alcoholism, problems that had not been helped by her lifestyle in New York. Her trip to Brazil was part of an around-the-world tour she hoped might be a welcome break from the pace and anxieties of the city-she later wrote to Lowell "I was miserably lonely there most of the time" (Goldensohn 9). However, upon arrival, Bishop had a violently allergic reaction to a cashew she ate, and was hospitalized for five days. Soares, who Bishop had planned to visit, invited her to extend her stay and recuperate her home, which was a meeting place for many Brazilian architects and writers. Bishop accepted and ended up staying for over a decade.

Bishop and Soares lived together intermittently in Rio, in Petropolis, and in a 17th century house in Ouro Preto, Brazil. At the beginning, Bishop's life in Brazil had a cathartic effect on her health and poetry; she began to confront her longstanding addiction to alcohol and her depression. As her career flourished, though, their relationship began to deteriorate. The publication of "Poems: North & South-A Cold Spring," which combined her first book with new poems, won the Pulitzer Prize in 1955. "Questions of Travel," her third collection, was also well received, and dealt with familiar themes of travel, displacement, and tourism: "Should we have stayed home and thought of here?" she asks in the title poem (14). However, there were significant strains in her relationship with Soares at this time, who was afflicted by her own problems with depression and anxiety relating to her job as a city planner. Bishop spent less and less time in Brazil, teaching instead at universities in the U.S. and coming back to Brazil intermittently. In September of 1967, while visiting Bishop in New York, Soares overdosed on sleeping pills in an apparent suicide.

After her partner's death, Bishop lived primarily in Boston, teaching at Harvard and writing the poems that would be published in *Geography III*. She continued to travel extensively (a partial list of places includes Yugoslavia, Ecuador, Norway, Sweden, and the Galapagos Islands), and in 1976 received the prestigious Books Abroad / Neustadt Award, the first American and first female recipient. On October 6, 1979 she died at home in Boston.

Andrew Allport

Works Cited

Bishop, Elizabeth. *The Complete Poems*. New York: Farrar, Straus, and Giroux, 1993.

_____. "*One Art: Letters*." Ed. Robert Giroux. New York: Farrar, Straus, and Giroux, 1994.

Costello, Bonnie. *Questions of Mastery*. Cambridge: Harvard UP, 1991.

Gioia, Dana. "From Coterie to Canon." *The New Criterion*. Vol. 22, No. 8. April 2004.

Goldensohn, Lorrie. *Elizabeth Bishop: The Biography of a Poetry*. New York: Columbia UP, 1992.

Moore, Marianne. *Complete Prose*. New York: Viking, 1986. 406-7.

Discussion Questions

1. The word "like" appears repeatedly in "The Fish." What effect does this have on the reader? Does it have different effects at different times?

2. The beginning of the poem begins in a consciously plain way: "I caught a tremendous fish" (1) and "He didn't fight. / He hadn't fought at all" (5-6). How does this plain narrative style affect the reader's perception of the story?

3. Describe the tone of the poem. Is there a shift is tone from the beginning to the end? What words/phrases highlight the poet's tone?

4. Unlike many of her renowned poems, Bishop wrote "The Fish" in a free verse that adheres, mostly, to three stress lines. But Bishop has clearly paid close attention to other formal elements of the poem, such as enjambments and rhyme. Where do these formal elements influence and shape the poem?

5. What happens at the end of the poem? What prompts all these rainbows? Are they symbols, or figments of imagination, or meant simply to describe the oil pooling in the boat?

6. Is the fish a symbol of death? Of wisdom? Christ? Does it have to be a symbol? Can it avoid being one?

7. Though the poet immediately calls the fish "he," the poem makes the fish's gender explicit by giving other details about him- what are these details, and why does the fish's gender matter in the poem?

8. The fishing story—"He was thiiiiis big"—is ubiquitous in American culture. Some of the fundamental functions of fishing stories are bragging, lying, exaggeration, and regret for "the one that got away." How does Bishop engage these tropes; how does she utilize/ subvert them?

9. Such a cluster of vivid images crowd the lines of "The Fish" that it is difficult, at times, to remember what is being described. What effect does this multitude of objects and comparisons have on the reader?

10. Compare this poem with another of Bishop's dealing with an encounter with nature.

Essay Ideas

1. Fish are a common theme for Bishop and Marianne Moore. Compare Bishop's "The Fish" with Marianne Moore's poem of the same name. When Bishop first sent Moore the poem, she wrote that she was "afraid it is very bad, if not like Robert Frost, perhaps like Ernest Hemingway!" ("Letters" 87). How do these two poems reflect the differences and similarities of the two? How do they illustrate Moore's influence and Bishop's resistance to it?

2. Compare "The Fish" with yet another fish poem, "The Drunken Fisherman" by Robert Lowell, who wrote in a letter to Bishop, "All my fish become symbols, alas!" What does the fish in Lowell's poem symbolize? What, if anything, does Bishop's fish symbolize? How do the two poets create these symbols?

3. "You'd just wish they'd keep some of these things to themselves," Bishop told "Time" in 1967 for their cover story on Robert Lowell, whose Confessional style included brutal truths about his own troubled life, even excerpts from his wife's anguished letters. In the ensuing 30 years, poetry, at least in the popular imagination, seems to mean something closer to the free verse confessions of Lowell and Sylvia Plath than Bishop's formal poem, "One Art." In what ways does Bishop keep things to herself in this poem? What clues-or even confessions-does she make to the reader in this poem?

4. Bishop's poems often use sea imagery in conjunction with man-made shapes. This juxtaposition is partially what seems to cause the "rainbows" at the end of "The Fish." Using another example from Bishop's work-"Seascape," "At the Fish-houses," "Florida" or others-examine the connections between Bishop's observation of the ocean and human life.

5. The personification of animals is a constant theme in Bishop's work. Using "The Man-Moth," "The Fish," "The Moose" or other poems, write an essay that explores the connections that Bishop finds between the animal world and the human. Why do you think the fish in "The Fish" is compared to so many different things, for example?

Her Kind

by Anne Sexton

Content Synopsis

In this poem, one of Sexton's most famous and admired; the speaker begins, appropriately enough, by emphasizing the word "I"—perhaps the key word in the entire work. This, after all, will be a poem of self-assertion, self-definition, and self-explanation. Paradoxically, however, the precise identity of the opening speaker is never made entirely clear, and indeed, there even seem to be several speakers in this work (perhaps as many as four). In the first line, however, none of this confusion or ambiguity is immediately apparent. Instead, the poem begins as a straightforward gothic (or even supernatural) lyric as the speaker identifies herself as "a possessed witch" (1). The poem thus opens in a way that seems to suggest that it is fanciful, not to be taken entirely seriously, and remote from real, present concerns. Even in responding to the first lines, questions begin to arise: what kind of "witch" (a word that receives especially strong metrical emphasis) does the speaker mean? Is this "witch" real or simply metaphorical? In what sense is this "witch" "possessed"? Is she evil? Is she satanic? Alternatively, are these possibilities merely fanciful and deliberately ironic? In what sense(s) has the speaker "gone out" (1)? By the end of the first line, then, Sexton has already aroused, in various ways, our sense of curiosity and has created an appropriate air of mystery and suspense.

Line 2 continues to create an atmosphere of mystery and ambiguity, first by describing the witch "haunting the black air," then by describing her as "braver at night." Even the word "haunting" is fundamentally ambiguous, since on the one hand it connotes the habit of frequenting a particular place as it implies frequenting such a place with a malign or troubling intent. The fact that the "air" that is haunted by this witch is described as "black" might reinforce the latter of these two interpretations, but then the witch herself is described as "braver at night" (2) suggesting that she is more vulnerable, more apprehensive, or less powerful during the day. The first half of line two suggests the power of this witch, but then the second half of the line limits or circumscribes that power. Once again, then, the tone of the poem is essentially mysterious or ambiguous. The witch can be simultaneously threatening and threatened, dangerous and sympathetic.

In the shift to line three, the witch seems more unambiguously evil as she dreams, but even the phrasing seems strangely qualified. After all, she confesses that she is merely "dreaming" evil, not doing it, and then the tone of the poem alters to the almost-comic when the speaker announces that she has "done [her] hitch"—phrasing that makes being a witch sound almost like performing temporary military service. The phrasing here seems almost briefly humorous, and then there is a shift back to the perspective of line two, as the witch describes herself hovering "over the plain houses, light by light" (4). The adjective "plain" suggests a contrast between these uninteresting homes and the mysterious witch herself, while the phrase "light by light" not only contrasts with the darkness emphasized earlier but suggests, perhaps, that the witch is alluding to the closely nestled homes found in suburban neighborhoods.

Whatever the case, the air of confusion and mystery remains: we have no idea who, exactly, this "witch" is, what her precise motives are, in what period she lives, or how seriously we are meant to take her. In the shift to line five, the tone of the work becomes even more ambiguous: the witch now describes herself as a "lonely thing, twelve-fingered, out of mind." The first phrase makes her sound sympathetic and almost pitiable (and thus counter-acts the reference to "evil" in line 3). The second phrase alludes to a physical deformity that can seem both unnatural and a reason for further sympathy. Yet, the third phrase"out of mind"--is especially ambiguous, since it can suggest that she is literally insane while also suggesting (in addition, or alternatively) that she is ignored or not even part of the consciousness of the people she might earlier have seemed to haunt. A witch who might previously have seemed somewhat dangerous now seems nearly off the communal radar. She may be "possessed," "haunting," and "dreaming evil," but no one seems to be taking much notice.

Finally, in line six, the identity of the witch as a "woman" is emphasized (twice), and yet even as this line stresses her womanhood, it qualifies that assertion: "A woman like that is not a woman, quite" (6). Thus, the poem's dominant tone of ambiguity continues, and now an even further uncertain element is introduced: "like that" implies the witch herself is no longer speaking—that a new speaker has unaccountably been introduced into the poem. Suddenly, then, we have both a new speaker and a new perspective, and this fact is emphasized in the shift to line seven: "I have been her kind." Who is this new "I"? In what sense has she been the witch's "kind"? No sooner, however, do we begin to ponder these questions than the poem goes off, in the second stanza, is another confusing and thought-provoking direction.

The ambiguity continues as the second stanza opens. It is natural for a reader to assume that the "I" who begins speaking in this second stanza is the same "I" who began speaking at the start of stanza one, and, for a moment, the imagery sustains this possibility. The speaker of stanza two mentions having inhabited "warm caves in the woods"—habitations that might indeed be fitting for a witch, although the adjective "warm" already implies an abode less dark and gloomy than one would expect of a sorceress who dreams of evil. By the time we reach lines nine and ten, in which the speaker mentions having filled those caves "with skillets, carvings, shelves / closets, silks, [and] innumerable goods," we can no longer be confident that the speaker is now the witch of stanza one. She seems, instead, almost the central figure in some benign domestic fairy tale, especially when she mentions having "fixed suppers for the worms and the elves" (11)—phrasing which is itself peculiar, especially when the speaker states, even more confusingly, that she has been "whining, rearranging the disaligned" (12). The behavior of a witch is archetypically familiar, and many of the details mentioned in stanza one (possession, haunting, activities at night, deformities, associations with evil) conform to those familiar patterns. In the second stanza, however, we are dealing with a new woman whose circumstances, motives, and identity are far less recognizable.

Indeed, the woman featured in stanza two is not given a simple or convenient label, such as "witch." She seems, in some ways, to resemble a modern suburban housewife, particularly in her emphasis on domestic activities and caring for others, but by the end of the stanza we are no more sure than we were at the beginning who or what, precisely, this woman is. Little wonder then, that the other speaker who enters in line thirteen says, "A woman like that is misunderstood." Others who populate her world presumably misunderstand such a woman, but she does not seem to be understood any better—if at all—by those who stand outside that world, including Sexton's readers. Thus, it is even more puzzling and ambiguous when the speaker of the final lines of the second stanza says of this puzzling woman, "I have been her kind" (14). What kind, exactly, is being examined now? Even more than in the first stanza, Sexton writes in a way that seems deliberately disorienting and confusing. The poem seems designed to be mystifying and unsettling; certainly, it has had this effect on many readers. There is something odd, strange, mystical, and mythical in the very phrasing of the poem, not only in the two female perspectives it has described so far.

Ambiguity and mystery become, if anything, even more pronounced in the third stanza. Now the speaker is an unidentified woman who has driven in a "cart" and who directly addresses the cart's unnamed, unidentified "driver" (15). The reference to a "cart" implies a pre-modern mode of transportation, and the suggestion of a pre-modern setting continues in the reference to "villages" in the next line (16). The fact that the speaker refers to waving her "nude arms" while passing these villages suggests, once more, a pre-modern sense of proper dress: bare arms would not typically, in the modern era, be described as "nude." Further details—such as the reference to "flames" biting the speaker's "thigh" and the reference to her "ribs" being "cracked" due to the winding of "wheels" (18-19)—also imply pre-modern forms of torture and punishment. Yet despite all these consistent details, we cannot be entirely sure who this woman is, or why she is being punished. Is she punished for adultery, fornication, or some other sexual sin (as the glancing use of the word "nude" may imply)?

Is she punished for alleged witchcraft, as all the pre-modern details may suggest? Is she a martyr of some sort, especially since she is said to be "not ashamed to die" (20)?

In some ways, the identity of the woman in the third stanza is even more uncertain than the identities of the women in the preceding two, and indeed, there seems to be increasing ambiguity stanzas as the poem progresses. We know, at least, that the woman in the first stanza identified herself as a "witch." We became less sure about what to call the speaker of the second stanza; and now the identity of the voice in the third stanza (as well as the precise nature of her apparent crime) is even less clear. This fact makes the final restatement of the poem's refrain, "I have been her kind" (21), seem all the more enigmatic. There is, indeed, a riddling quality to the entire poem, and the final line, while seeming to offer a clear, definite assertion, only helps enhance our sense of the poem's ultimate mystery. What "kind," precisely, does the speaker of the refrain have in mind? For that matter, who is the speaker of these refrains? Is it the poet herself? Is it some invented, symbolic speaker? In what ways, precisely, has the speaker been the same "kind" as all these other women? The poem, effectively enough, does not say; instead, it leaves us to ponder the various possibilities that it both vaguely and vividly suggests.

Historical Context

History plays an important role in Sexton's poem, especially in the first and third stanzas. Those stanzas explicitly remind us of periods in the actual human past when women were persecuted either as witches (as in stanza one) or as sexual transgressors, martyrs, or outlaws of some other kind (as in stanza three). Stanza 2, meanwhile, evokes a different kind of pre-modern, almost fairy-tale kind of mythology. The poem suggestively describes the various kinds of roles that women have freely adopted (or been forced or presumed to enact) in various periods of human history and/or in various aspects of the human imagination. The poem seems to suggest the relevance of those roles to the relevance of women's lives in the modern period, especially the period when Sexton's own poem was written. This was a period when women enjoyed far less freedom than they tend to enjoy today in modern Western nations. The poem seems to imply that modern women still have not completely escaped from many of the bonds and confining stereotypes that have bedeviled women throughout much of human history. Sexton's poem is a product of the period immediately preceding the rise of feminism in the late 1960s and early 1970s. The poem can be seen as a protest against the injustices and limitations of this pre-feminist period and as a precursor of the rise and triumph of feminism in the decades to follow.

Societal Context

In the interaction between the three main stanzas of this poem and each stanza's final refrain, "I have been her kind" (7, 14, 21), Sexton suggests the connection of the past to the present, particularly the relevance of the restrictions and stereotypes imposed on women in the past to the lives women were leading when the poem was written. Society, she seems to imply, has not changed as fundamentally for women as one might have hoped or presumed. Women, she arguably suggests, are still trapped in various stereotypical roles (witch, provider, and victim) that limit their options, but also provide them opportunities to display inner strength and resourcefulness in different ways. The speaker of the refrain seems to identify with these variously marginalized women. She recognizes the ways in which the limitations imposed on their lives have affected her own. At the same time, she draws certain strength from her ability to identify with them. To the extent that they have chosen or reveled in their outlaw, outsider status, she creates a common cause among them. Each time the

refrain is repeated, it conveys an element of sympathy, an element of empathy, but also an element of defiance and sisterhood. Little wonder, then, that this poem is often perceived as a founding text of modern feminism. The tone of each refrain is increasingly sympathetic and self-assertive, so that the final refrain ends by emphasizing the kind of pride and self-respect that many women were beginning to feel in Western society at the second half of the twentieth century.

Religious Context

Religion can be seen as playing a role in each of the poem's three stanzas, if only by implication. Stanza 1's various references to witches, possession, and evil, for instance, inevitably remind us of the roles supposed witches have often played in Christian cultures, especially during the so-called witch crazes of the sixteenth and seventeenth centuries. Witches have often been perceived as satanic figures and have been defined as opponents of orthodox Christianity. Christianity, in turn, has been one of the leading forces helping to promote patriarchy in the history of western culture. It hardly seems surprising, then, that Christians would historically regard supposedly powerful women (witches) as sources of threat to their religion and as proper objects of persecution and punishment, including death. Meanwhile, the woman featured in the second stanza of Sexton's poem also seems somehow associated with a kind of errant paganism, especially because of her close involvement with worms and elves. Finally, the woman featured in the third stanza seems either another witch (or a Christian woman regarded, like Joan of Arc, as a kind of witch by other Christians), or perhaps as a sexual transgressor and thus in any case deserving of religiously sanctioned punishment. Sexton's poem subtly reminds us, especially in stanzas one and three, that Christianity has often played a prominent role in the persecution of women in the history of western culture.

Scientific & Technological Context

Science and technology play little obvious role in this poem. Indeed, Sexton seems to have gone out of her way, in each of the poem's three stanzas, to conjure up a pre-modern (indeed almost primitive) atmosphere, as if to suggest that the troubles and limitations women have faced are ancient, not merely modern. Sexton herself knew the ways in which women were stereotyped and handicapped throughout most of the twentieth century, but her poem implies that the limits modern women faced were just the latest incarnations of limits women had faced during many earlier centuries.

Biographical Context

From a very early age, Anne Sexton (1928-1974) lived a mentally troubled life. Although born into a relatively privileged family, she seems to have never been entirely happy, and she became increasingly depressed the older she became. She committed suicide before her forty-eighth birthday, after more than a decade of a successful career as a poet. She began seriously writing poetry at the suggestion of a therapist in the 1950s, who thought that writing might help her cope with some of her inner demons. Sexton's own strong sense of being an outsider, of being set apart from conventional society, clearly seems reflected in "Her Kind." Sexton could never quite function successfully in the various standard roles (daughter, wife, and mother) she was expected to play. "Her Kind" reveals her power as an artist even as it implies her vulnerability as a human being.

Robert C. Evans, Ph.D.

Works Cited

George, Diana Hume. "Oedipus Anne." *Oedipus Anne: The Poetry of Anne Sexton.* U of Illinois P, 1987. 3-23. Print.

Johnson, Greg. "The Achievement of Anne Sexton." *The Hollins Critic.* 21.3 (1984): 1-13. Print.

Kester-Shelton, Pamela, ed. *Feminist Writers.* Detroit: St. James Press, 1996. Print.

Lombardo, Jeanne Belisle. "Woman as Witch in Anne Sexton's 'Her Kind.'" *Center for Future Consciousness.com.* Center for Future Consciousness, n.d. Web. 12 Sept. 2010. <http://www.centerforfutureconsciousness.com/pdf%5Ffiles/2008%5FEssays/Woman%20as%20Witch%20in%20Anne%20Sexton.pdf>.

McCabe, Jane. "A Woman Who Writes: A Feminist Approach to the Early Poetry of Anne Sexton." *Anne Sexton: The Artist and Her Critics.* Ed. J. D. McClatchy. Bloomington: Indiana UP, 1978. 216-43. Print.

Middlebrook, Diane Wood. *Anne Sexton: A Biography.* New York: Vintage Books, 1992. Print.

_____. "Poets of Weird Abundance." *Parnassus: Poetry in Review.* 12/13.1-2 (1985): 293-315. Print.

Pollard, Clare. "Her Kind: Anne Sexton, the Cold War, and the Idea of the Housewife." *Critical Quarterly.* 48.3 (Autumn 2006): 1-24. Print.

Sexton, Anne. "Her Kind." *Selected Poems of Anne Sexton.* Eds. Diane Wood Middlebrook and Diana Hume George. 1988. New York: Mariner Books, 2000. 18. Print.

Wagner, Linda W. "Anne Sexton: Overview." *Reference Guide to American Literature.* Ed. Jim Kamp. 3rd ed. Detroit: St. James Press, 1994. Print.

Wagner-Martin, Linda. "Anne Sexton's Life." *Modern American Poetry.* Department of English, University of Illinois at Urbana-Champaign, Feb. 2000. Web. 21 Sept. 2010. <http://www.english.illinois.edu/maps/poets/s%5Fz/sexton/sexton%5Flife.htm>.

Discussion Questions

1. Discuss the various possible meanings of the phrase "gone out" (1). What does this phrase imply about the witch's normal existence? In what various senses may this witch be "possessed"?

2. Scan the meter of line two. Which words receive the strongest metrical emphasis in that line? How does Sexton achieve such emphasis? What (if any) metrical pattern do you discern in this poem? If a regular pattern is lacking, why might Sexton have chosen to dispense with such a pattern? How might the lack of such a pattern contribute to the tone of the poem?

3. How does the phrase "done my hitch" (3) contribute to the complexity of the poem's phrasing? How would you characterize that phrasing? For example, is it formal, colloquial, or some mixture of both? Are there any touches of humor elsewhere in the poem? If so, why do you think Sexton included them?

4. Discuss some connotations of the word "thing" in line 5. What are some other nouns that Sexton could have used here, but how does the word "thing" contribute to the essential ambiguity of the poem?

5. What are some possible relations between the phrase "twelve-fingered" and the phrase "out of mind" (5)? For example, how does each phrase suggest a kind of deformity, but how do the kinds of deformity differ?

6. How do lines 9-11 contrast, by implication, with the entire first stanza? How do the motives and circumstances of the woman in the first stanza differ from the motives and circumstances of the woman in the second? Which of the two women would you rather be? Explain your response. What are the advantages and disadvantages of each woman's life?

7. Discuss the connotations of each of the nouns mentioned in lines 9-10. How does each noun help characterize the speaker? Is there perhaps a pun contained in the last adjective and noun of line 10? Discuss the structure of line 11. Why does Sexton arrange the line as she does? How is the structure surprising, and why might she want it to surprise?

8. Discuss the implications of the word "whining" (12). Why might the woman be "whining"? How might the rest of the line help explain the causes of her "whining"? How does the word "whining" almost sound like the behavior it describes?

9. Discuss the implications of the word "waved" in line 16. How does that verb help foreshadow the meaning stated in line 20? How does that verb help characterize the third woman?

10. What sound effect is used with special prominence in line 17? Where else is the same sound effect used, and how does this sound effect contribute to the music of the poem?

Essay Ideas

1. Read a biography of Sexton, try to determine the approximate date of this poem's composition, and then try to relate the meaning(s) of this poem to the circumstances of Sexton's life at the time she was writing the poem.

2. Discuss the progress of the poem, stanza-by-stanza. How does the woman of the first stanza differ from the woman of the third? How is the woman of the second stanza a kind of intermediary figure? How, perhaps, is each woman more confined than the one before her? In what other ways is there a distinct movement from one stanza to the next?

3. Why is there such a heavy emphasis in this poem on the fact that the main figures and commentator in each stanza are women, rather than men or human beings in general? What might this poem suggest about the situations of women throughout the centuries? Are women freer today than they were when this poem was first written?

4. How is the final stanza of the poem somewhat ominous? What might this stanza suggest about the ultimate fate of women? Is this a poem about women in general or only about certain kinds of women?

5. Do some research into the status of women in the United States in the late 1950s and early 1960s. How is this poem relevant to the kinds of lives women were leading then, and how is the poem indeed somewhat prophetic in view of developments in the late 1960s and early 1970s?

T S Eliot, pictured above, wrote "The Hollow Men," featured opposite. Three other works by Eliot appear in this volume: "The Love Song of J. Alfred Prufrock," page 89; "Old Possum's Book of Practical Cats," page 135; and "The Waste Land," page 215. Photo: National Portrait Gallery, Smithsonian Institution; partial gift of the National Portrait Commission and senior staff in memory of Donald P. Klopfer

The Hollow Men

by T. S. Eliot

Content Synopsis

The two epigraphs of T. S. Eliot's poem "The Hollow Men"—Mistah Kurtz—he dead" and "A Penny for the Old Guy"—provide the poem with a rich allusive context that guides the reader in apprehending the larger social and personal message the poem conveys. Both epigraphs have in common expressions of brutal disregard for fictional and historical characters of great determination and purpose: Mistah Kurtz, for example, is a reference to Joseph Conrad's "Heart of Darkness," in which Kurtz journeys into the wilds of Africa on a civilizing mission and instead becomes a mad despot of a group of natives. He is eventually "rescued" by the main protagonist, Marlow, but dies quickly after realizing—in a moment of clarity—the depravity to which he had sunk in Africa. His final words, "the horror, the horror" have become an epigraph in and of themselves, and function as a eulogy for the death of the civilized self. The second epigraph,

"A Penny for the Old Guy" is part of the ritual of Guy Fawkes' day, when an effigy of Guy Fawkes, a Catholic and one of the main actors in the Gunpowder Plot, is burned in celebration of the failure of his attempt to assassinate James I. The "Penny for the Old Guy" refrain is part of a tradition that involves carrying around a straw effigy of Fawkes in order to collect money. Through this childish mockery, Guy Fawkes, misguided but purposeful though he was, is reduced to a laughable, impotent target of collective contempt.

The first section of "The Hollow Men" personifies the personal and moral vacuousness embodied in both the effigy of Guy Fawkes and the dismissive remarks of the servant who announces Kurtz's death in Conrad's "Heart of Darkness." The personae of Eliot's poem announce themselves as the hollow men; saying "We are the Hollow Men / We are the Stuffed Men / Leaning Together/Headpiece filled with Straw/ Alas!" (lines 1-5). The robotic incantations of their credo of soullessness, of a self that refuses conviction, reverberate with the epigraphs that frame their self-presentation.

Another allusion is also connoted by the hollow men's self-presentation. Not only are these hollow men the straw men of conviction, they are also the poetic specters of Dante's "hollow men"—those who, in Dante's words, "lived with neither infamy nor praise. / Commingled are they with that worthless choir / of Angels who did not rebel, nor yet/were true to God, but sided with themselves" (Aligheri 35-8). Called cowards by Dante's guide in heaven, these convictionless men are accepted neither into heaven or into hell. They reside in a permanent purgatory of placelessness. They are recalled in Section III of Eliot's poem, "gathered on the beach of this tumid river" (60), and fruitlessly wait passage from their purgatory. Eliot's hollow men reside in a similar placelessness: convictionless, even their voices are robbed of the volume of authority, but rather are phantom whispers, saying nothing: "Our dried voices, when / We Whisper Together / Are quiet and meaningless/ As wind in dry grass / Or rats' feet over broken glass / In our dry cellar" (5-10). The final lines of this section ring with envy or those "who have crossed / With direct eyes, to death's other Kingdom" (13-5). The Hollow Men, as they themselves realize, will only be remembered not "as lost / Violent souls, but only / As the Hollow men / The Stuffed men" (16-8).

The second section of the poem abandons the collective "We" for the singular "I." This section presents an autobiography of hopelessness, told through memorial fragments signifying lost moments of emotional significance. Symbolically, this section reintroduces the specter of the "eyes" that seem to haunt the speaker; we have of course confronted these "eyes" in the first stanza, in the form of those who could, unlike the hollow men, cross to "death's other kingdom." In this section, the eyes appear as accusation—they are to be avoided as they remind the speaker of moments when a lived existence was perhaps possible: "Eyes I dare not meet in dreams / In death's dream kingdom / These do not appear" (19-21). Ironically, death's dream kingdom is transformed into a place of respite rather than torture in this section. The speaker is rescued from meaning in this space since death's dream kingdom is constituted of broken images that fail to signify anything. They connote rather than denote, "There [in death's dream kingdom] the eyes are / Sunlight on a broken column / There, is a tree swinging / And voices are / In the wind's singing / More distant and more solemn / Than a fading star" (22-8). For the reader, this section allows a smorgasbord of interpretation that ultimately mirrors the purposelessness that is the poem's credo. The image of sunlight on a broken column, for example, uneasily binds an overused symbol of hope (sunlight) with one of wreckage and destruction; similarly, a tree swinging, connotes both the play of leaves in the wind, and death by hanging. Like the vague remnants of memory the speaker alludes to above, he here renders himself as ultimately unseeable and unknowable through the use of disguise: "Let me be no nearer / In death's dream kingdom / Let me also wear/Such deliberate disguises / Rat's coat, Crowskin, crossed staves / In a field / Behaving as the wind behaves / No nearer—" (29-36). These disguises recall the epigraphs and allusions of the first stanza—the crowskin, for example, suggests a scarecrow (the Guy Fawkes effigy). The crossed staves—that of Dante's horde of empty men alluded to in "The Waste Land:" "So long a train of people, that I should never have believed death had undone so many" ("The Waste Land," ll. 62-64). Disguising himself, the speaker wishes to avoid a moment of self-knowledge, of confrontation with the self as vacuity: "No nearer— / Not that final meeting / In the twilight kingdom" (36-38). He wishes to behave as the wind behaves instead and thus to remain unfixable, unknowable, and ultimately uncatchable.

The third section provides topography of vacuity and purposelessness referenced in the autobiographical second section. Moving from a discussion of the self as hollow, disguised and unknowable, the poem projects this vacuity onto a landscape of inescapable infertility: "This is the dead land / This is cactus land/Here the stone images / Are raised, here they receive / The supplication of a dead man's hand / Under the twinkle of a fading star" (40-48).

Rhythmically, this section resembles the first section of the poem: it recalls the robotic incantation that first introduced the hollow men to the reader. In addition, symbolically, this section obliquely recalls the poem's opening: rather than the effigies of straw, we are here presented with stone images, broken statues commemorating past glories. These stone images also do not receive the respect of the living, but rather the despairing salute of pathos: "the supplication of a dead man's hand/Under the twinkle of a fading star" (43-44). The last paragraph of this section returns us to the persona of the second section. Here the qualitative emotion is one of despair, a yearning for connection that, in the first section, had been decisively rejected as an impossibility: "Is it like this / In death's other kingdom / Waking alone / At the hour when we are / Trembling with tenderness" (46-50). This humanization is, however, short-lived. While the persona momentarily wonders whether his personal torture will consist of "Waking alone/At the hour when we are/Trembling with tenderness" (47-50), he soon realizes that the "lips that would kiss" (50) will be denied emotional reciprocity but will rather "Form prayers to broken stone" (51).

The fourth section resurrects the "eyes" of the second section, but only in their explicit absence. Continuing thematically a topography of a hollow land, the poem reverts to the rhythmic incantation of the first section, focusing on the absent eyes: "The eyes are not here/There are no eyes here/In this valley of dying stars/In this hollow valley/This broken jaw of our lost kingdoms" (52-6). The mourning for sites of significance is most clear in these lines. Described as "this broken jaw of our lost kingdoms" (56) this poetic geography becomes a symbolic carpet covering that which is lost in a world without faith and without hope. The absent eyes nevertheless bear witness to the absence of purpose—they are both there and not there—accusing by and through their absence those who have constructed a wasteland of human dignity and

purpose. Once again, Dante's geography of hell is revisited as the hollow men here "grope together" (58) / In this last of meeting places…And avoid speech / Gathered on the beach of the tumid river" (57-60). The tumid river is none other than Acheron, the river by which Dante encounters those who "lived with neither infamy nor praise"—his hollow men, permanently residing in an inescapable netherworld—not in hell, not in heaven, forever placeless.

The last stanza of this section anticipates the final section of the poem. The eyes, absent in the first nine lines of this fourth section suddenly reappear as part of a symbol of religious salvation—the multifoliate rose which recalls Dante's vision of paradise in his work, "Paradiso." The center of the multifoliate rose is God, around which the saved in heaven arrange themselves and so resemble abundant rose petals. This multifoliate rose, a symbolic redaction of heaven, becomes a means of sight for the hollow men. They remain sightless "unless / The eyes reappear / As the perpetual star/Multifoliate rose / Of death's twilight kingdom / The hope only / Of empty men (61-7).

The fifth and final section of "The Hollow Men" begins with the recital of a nursery rhyme set apart from the other text by italics. It is a perversion of the mulberry bush rhyme. Eliot replaces the mulberry bush with a prickly pear, so that the rhyme is as follows: "Here we go round the prickly pear / Prickly pear prickly pear / Here we go round the prickly pear / At five o'clock in the morning" (68-72). The prickly pear suggests the topography of the hollow land of Section II. It is a fruit borne of harsh conditions and is in itself difficult to enjoy, covered with thorns that can prick if peeled. Although seemingly an image of hope, in this context, the child's game seems to mock both the speaker and the reader with the fruitlessness of memory. A sense of innocence does not emanate from the recitation of the child's game; rather it suggests a kind of mad despair—a perversion of a conventional symbol of play and enjoyment. The nursery rhyme is juxtaposed with fragments of the Lord's Prayer, which is itself continuously interrupted throughout the rest of the poem. The lines that precede the first articulation of the Lord 's Prayer prefigure these interruptions: presciently, they anticipate the impossibility of resolution or action—in life or in faith: "Between the idea / And the reality / Between the motion / And the act / Falls the Shadow" (72-6).

Typographically, the Lord's Prayer, like the nursery rhyme, appears in italics and is relegated to the margins of the page. Visually, this reinforces the sense of interruption and futility that is articulated by the speaker. After the italicized "For Thine is the Kingdom" (76), for example, comes another articulation of the impotence of action, "Between the conception / And the creation / Between the emotion / And the response/Falls the Shadow" (78-82). The "Shadow," capitalized, functions as an entity in these lines—a kind of disabling spirit that prevents the speaker from realizing emotional or spiritual fruition. It is the antithesis of the Lord's Prayer that may be seen as the figuration of vacuity: shadows, like hollow men, are projections of a thing rather than the thing itself; they are in this way as insubstantial as the straw men of the first stanza. This anti-credo eventually finds itself also in the margins of the page, positioned between articulations of the Lord's Prayer. If we just read the italicized portions, this duality becomes clear: "For Thine is the Kingdom/Life is very Long/For Thine is the Kingdom" (Section V).

By the end of Section V, the Lord's Prayer has been reduced to unintelligible fragments, again interrupted by similar fragments of the expressions of hopelessness we see earlier in both this section and the poem in general. The first three words of the prayer are all that remain, interspersed with the first two words of the italicized anti-prayer that followed the Lord's Prayer earlier in this section: "For Thine is/Life is/For Thine is the" (92-4). This syntactical redaction of both credos—that of faith

and that of cynicism—is followed by a strikingly cynical nursery-rhyme of hopelessness, the last lines of which have become, in their own right, an epigraph for both this poem and the modernist despair in general. It is presented in italics and so seems to displace typographically and philosophically the Lord's Prayer that precedes it: "This is the way the world ends/This is the way the world ends/This is the way the world ends/Not with a bang but a whimper" (95-9).

Historical Context

The cataclysmic political and social changes that resulted from World War I (The Great War, as it was called before World War II) provided the historical context for Eliot's work and world-view during the 1920s, a period where his first collection of poems, including "The Hollow Men" was published (1925). The Great War signaled the end of a social outlook that believed in the invulnerability of "civilization," defined loosely as a shared faith in human decency, chivalry, honor in battle, progress, and the benefits of scientific innovation. In fact, the technological innovations celebrated before the war only accentuated its brutality, giving birth to unimagined methods of mass human destruction, such as the machine gun, bombs, and chemical weapons. Such malevolent uses of the products of scientific innovation undermined the naive pre-war belief in "progress" as unquestionably positive, and the unmitigated horror of the new trench warfare emasculated previously held notions of chivalry and honor through battle. In an echo of the belief that the War fundamentally changed the character of Western civilization, Gertrude Stein would remark in characteristically pithy fashion, "after the war we had the twentieth century." "The Hollow Men's" final stanza, with its interruptions of the Lord's Prayer by echoes of personal despair, mirrors Eliot's assimilation of the dialectic of despair and hope that characterized the post-war Western view of human civilization.

The War facilitated the adoption of radical new political ideologies that reshaped much of Europe: this change was the most pronounced in Russia where in 1917, Vladimir Lenin and his Bolshevik party overthrew Czarist rule and instituted a communist / socialist regime that continued well into the twentieth century. By the 1920s, fascism was a rising force in both Italy and Germany and England itself was plagued by economic and social upheavals caused by successive changes in government, and by the growing strength of the union movement. Eliot was not immune to these influences from abroad: he admired the work of Charles Maurras, for example, who advocated an outlook that closely mirrored the key tenets of fascism. His doctrine advocated a return to a more feudal, monarchical social order in which the individual's freedoms were limited and society was rigidly hierarchical. Not surprisingly, during World War II, Maurras was a staunch supporter of Germany and became a member of the Nazi-controlled Vichy government in France. Although Eliot was no fascist, he nevertheless was deeply influenced by Maurras; this influence most clearly manifested itself in Eliot's later belief in a Christian society, constructed from and ordered by the core tenets of the Church of England.

Societal Context

Upon his arrival in London in 1914, Eliot came upon a literary establishment—ostensibly led by Ezra Pound—in a process of reevaluation and revolution; this revolution in both the aesthetic and social spheres is commonly referred to today as "modernism." While aesthetic revolutions are hardly unique—the history of English and American literature is nothing else than a survey of successive reinterpretations of the goals and purpose of the artist and his work—Eliot's "revolutionary" context was nevertheless remarkable for its sustained influence upon arts and letters to this day. Reacting against the aesthetics of romanticism and the related politics of complacency, modernism

was a vortex of competing ideologies and attitudes towards a host of interrelated, yet distinct "ideas of Western civilization:" the concept of the individual, the role of the artist, and the meaning of social engagement. While each school of modernism tended to announce a wholly original perspective, they nonetheless shared some key elements which defined them as "modernist," as unstable as this term is.

These elements were a deep suspicion of "social norms" and societal constructs, a belief in the ability of language to communicate emotion, a suspicion of the romanticization of the individual (a key tenet of romanticism) and a commitment to engaging in social critique through the arts. What distinguishes schools of modernist aesthetics is not so much ideology but methodology: while the Georgians employed the pastoral to signal their independence from Edwardian aesthetics and philosophies, the shortly lived Vorticists (offspring of the Imagists) promoted an aesthetics based in 20th century mechanization and technological innovation.

For Eliot, the Imagists were to prove the most significant school of modernist thought, although it would be a mistake to draw too clear a line of influence between his poetry and the imagist credo. As Pound himself remarked after reading "The Love Song of J. Alfred Prufrock," Eliot was a self-made modernist. Nonetheless, it is helpful to review Imagism in order to contextualize Eliot's work within the aesthetic that was most clearly in his particular social and cultural purview. Imagism, like other modernist movements, was a reaction against Romanticism's privileging of the artist's vision over expression. While Romanticism argued that the authenticity of a work of art could and should be measured by the sincerity of the emotion that inspired its creation, Imagism rejected this deification of the artist's emotional world for an aesthetic that communicated impressions and emotions in ways that were realizable universally—seeable and knowable to the reader and not just the writer.

The Imagist credo can best be understood as a dedication to a "direct treatment of the thing," a treatment that assiduously avoids any words that distracts from its clear presentation. As is indicated by their name, the Imagists' goal is to project an image, which Pound defined as "that which presents an intellectual and emotional complex in an instant of time" (Sharpe 40-41).

In Eliot's own thinking, Imagism was less a wholesale credo but a useful model for writing authentically. Thinking of his own poem "The Love Song of J. Alfred Prufrock," Eliot would describe Imagism as the ability to "replicate in its textual feeling, a pattern of human emotion." ("The Sacred Wood") In order to do so, he believed that the poet's language must at all times efface itself—the author's own struggle with language must not compromise what the poem aims to convey.

Although profoundly influenced by Imagism in regards to poetic style, the content of Eliot's writing was in part molded by his admiration by French writers of the late nineteenth and early twentieth century, such as Charles Baudelaire and Jules Laforgue. The theatricality of the "I" present in both these writers provided Eliot with a model for poetic personae most clearly seen in the "Preludes" and "The Love Song of J. Alfred Prufrock." The persona of Prufrock seems a directionless, emotionally disconnected consumer of the cultural pretenses that surround him. For Eliot, this poetic stance allowed him to launch perspicacious critiques of the meaningless social situations in which he frequently found himself both in England and in America. The signal phrase of this social dreariness and its representation in literature can be found in both "The Love Song of J. Alfred Prufrock" and "The Hollow Men." In the former, the construction is more humorous, consisting of a recurring rhyming couplet, "In the room the women come and go / speaking of Michelangelo ("Prufrock" ll. 35-7)." In the latter, this social dreariness devolves into a profound moral lassitude, present in the metronomic opening lines, "We are the hollow Men / We are the stuffed men / Leaning Together / Headpiece filled with straw. Alas" (1-4)!

Religious Context

To the shock of most of his contemporaries, T. S. Eliot became a convert and member of the High Anglican Church in England in 1927. Before this time, Eliot had been a dilettante in matters of religion. Faith had always been an important part of his world-view—he rejected the coldness of scientism for the metaphysics of F.M. Bradley as early as 1909 in his doctoral dissertation—but he had never espoused a particular religious outlook for himself. His most famous poem "The Waste Land" is dotted with religious references that encompass the Old and New Testaments of the Judeo-Christian Bible, as well as Hinduism and Buddhism. By 1927, however, Eliot was a firm Anglo-Catholic; his conversion marked the end of a long period of psychological struggle in regards to faith and purpose. "The Hollow Men's" ending section echoes this struggle when it intersperses portions of the Lord's Prayer with declarations of personal despair.

Eliot's post-conversion writing is theological in content than his previous work. The poems that comprise the "Four Quartets," for example may be read as a salvation-biography in verse. Similarly, one of his most famous plays, "Murder in the Cathedral" concerns the life and death of Thomas Becket, an Anglo-Catholic martyr, killed in 1170 by Henry II and later sainted by the Catholic Church.

Scientific & Technological Context

An important critique of science and scientific rationalism was published in 1925, the same year that "The Hollow Men" appeared in print. Alfred North Whitehead's "Science and the Modern World" was a wholesale indictment of the notion that scientific positivism provided the sole method of confidently understanding the natural and social worlds. Whitehead's text ushered in a new view of rationalism that would challenge and finally subvert the widely held belief that scientific rationalism, called by some detractors "scientism," was the only reliable methodology for the discovery of social and natural "truths." Eliot's own view conformed to Whitehead's—by 1925, he held scientism in contempt, and believed that it in fact produced despair rather than salvation. Writing after the "Great War," Eliot knew all too well the devastating effects of scientific innovation in technology. Instead of alleviating human suffering as 19th century scientism claimed scientific progress would necessarily do, these advances had instead facilitated mass destruction during the war.

Philosophically, Eliot was deeply suspicious of a world-view that rendered God and faith meaningless to human happiness. His own philosophical work for his PhD at Harvard had focused on a philosopher, F.H. Bradley, who espoused a philosophy based in feeling and emotion rather than cold, calculating "scientific" objectivity. Against the scientific method that tends to dissect the world into distinguishable and analyzable pieces, Bradley posited that all such fragmentation is an illusion and that the "real" is to be found in the "whole" or what he called the "Absolute"—an idealized convergence of social and natural forces ("The Sacred Wood"). He also claimed that apprehension of reality, as the Absolute was possible only through feeling and emotion, and not through traditional objective scientific methods. It was Bradley's "mysticism"—his privileging of intuition and the human soul—that attracted Eliot and would be a significant influence upon his own personal philosophy and later writings.

Biographical Context

Born in 1888 in St Louis, Missouri of a distinguished family whose ancestors hailed from Massachusetts, T. S. Eliot was the second son of Charlotte Stearns and Henry Ware Eliot. His father's family tree included such prominent members as the President of Harvard, Charles Ware Eliot and John Adams, John Quincy Adams and Rutherford B. Hayes. Although living in the Midwest because of Eliot's grandfather's move to St. Louis to found the first Unitarian church, Eliot and his family (particularly his mother) founded their American identity in their northeastern roots and in their historical, social, and familial connections to Massachusetts. Eliot himself returned for his undergraduate education to the Northeast by enrolling at Massachusetts' prestigious Milton Academy in 1905, followed by Harvard in 1906.

As a young man, Eliot was seemingly destined for a career in academia. This was in part due to his parents' desire that Eliot follow in the familial tradition of scholarship and university teaching. To that end, Eliot began and eventually completed a PhD in philosophy; his dissertation was a study of the philosophy of F.H. Bradley.

Although he completed his dissertation, Eliot was never at home psychologically or philosophically in academia: his real passion lay in writing and being a significant part of the growing literary scene in Europe, particularly England. His academic career was therefore punctuated by sojourns to Europe, some of which were initially intended to forward his studies in philosophy, but which inevitably resulted in a commitment to a life of letters in England's vibrant literary community.

Although abandoned by 1910, Eliot's academic career nevertheless provided abundant grist for his aesthetic mill. Eliot's early poetry is marked by an intellectualism that is doubtless traceable to his extensive studies in Latin, Greek, German and French as well as philosophy, Eastern religion and Western literature at Milton and Harvard. His academic education also provided an arena for his early sojourns into creative writing. *The Harvard Advocate* published his earliest poems and through this magazine, he formed one of the most influential friendships in his life with poet and writer, Conrad Aiken.

With the completion of "The Love Song of J. Alfred Prufrock" in 1911, Eliot definitively entered into what many biographers have identified as the second "phase" of his life—that of a pure commitment to modernist aesthetics and writing and his decision to relocate to Europe permanently. Although the latter seemed predestined—his Harvard career was punctuated with extended stays in France and England ostensibly legitimated by academic scholarships—his decision to relocate to Europe was underscored by his hasty and disastrous marriage in 1915 to the neurotic, if brilliant, Vivien Haigh-Wood, much to his parents' dismay. Eliot's self-imposed estrangement from both his parent's wishes and a promising academic career proved more difficult than he imagined. Without familial support, he was forced to sustain himself and a frequently ill wife. This state of affairs led Eliot to take alternatively disastrous positions as schoolmaster and then bank clerk, while at the same time trying to write, cope with his own and Vivien's ill health and supplement their paltry income with extensive but poorly paid lecturing at university extension programs. The bright spot in these weary years was his close association to some of the most important modernist writers of the time, and their unflagging support of his own aesthetic/poetic endeavors. The most famous and influential of his contemporaries was Ezra Pound, whom Eliot met through Conrad Aiken in 1914. Pound immediately recognized Eliot's work as groundbreaking; after reading Prufrock, he remarked that Eliot had invented a modernist aesthetic independently. Pound was instrumental in publishing "Prufrock" and other poems by Eliot and was a close advisor (along with Vivien Eliot) in the author's composition of "The Waste Land," perhaps the most important modernist literary production of the twentieth century.

"The Hollow Men" falls into this period of Eliot's life; the final form was an amalgamation of fragments composed over a three-year period, from 1922-1925." The Hollow Men" is perhaps Eliot's last gasp of modernist despair and disillusion before his conversion to Anglicanism in 1927. This conversion marks what biographers consider the last period of his life, which was characterized by several key events that would lead Eliot from desperation to emotional and religious salvation. First, Eliot left Vivien in 1932, literally escaping their marriage by fleeing to America for a series of lectures at Harvard. Eliot would return to England, but would never see Vivien again. Vivien was eventually institutionalized for mental illness; she died in a fire at the asylum in 1947. Eliot himself remarried in 1957 at the age of 69. His wife, Valerie Fletcher, had been his secretary at the publishing house, Faber and Faber where Eliot worked as a director after leaving banking in 1925. Artistically, in 1933, Eliot turned from poetry to drama, producing a body of verse-plays, quite popular during his lifetime but hardly performed today. He died on January 4, 1965, his obituary boasting, "Our age beyond any doubt has been . . . the age of Eliot."

Jennifer A. Rich

Works Cited

Behr, Caroline. *T. S. Eliot: A Chronology of his Life and Works.* New York: St. Martin's Press, 1983.

Cahill, Audrey. *T. S. Eliot and the Human Predicament.* Natal: U of Natal P, 1967.

Eliot, T. S., *The Collected Poems*: 1909-1962. New York: Harcourt, 1963.

Eliot, T. S., *The Sacred Wood, Essays on Poetry and Criticism.* New York: Bartleby.Com, 2000.

Gordon, Lyndall. *T. S. Eliot: An Imperfect Life.* New York: Norton, 1998.

Menand, Louis. *Discovering Modernism: T. S. Eliot and his Context.* Oxford: Oxford U P, 1987.

Schneider, Elisabeth. *T. S. Eliot: The Pattern in the Carpet.* Berkeley: U of California P, 1975.

Sharpe, Tony. *T. S. Eliot: A Literary Life.* New York: St. Martin's Press, 1991.

Discussion Questions

1. Who are the hollow men? What kind of people are they? What characteristics make them hollow?

2. What is the atmosphere evoked in the poem?

3. How does the poem's use of allusion invoke a particular atmosphere? Why does Eliot pick these particular allusions to Conrad, Dante and Guy Fawkes' day?

4. Discuss the topographical images of the poem. How do they evoke a wasteland?

5. What are some of the recurring symbols in the poem? Discuss the recurrence of one symbol, such as the eyes, in the poem. How does the symbol both mirror and challenge the poem's atmosphere? In considering the symbol of the eyes, for example, you might consider how they challenge the speaker's expressions of hopelessness.

6. Discuss the use of nursery rhymes in the last section of the poem. What is their purpose?

How do they contribute or detract from the overall atmosphere of the poem?

7. Consider the final nursery rhyme. How does its final line sum up the speaker's spiritual outlook?

8. Consider the incorporation of the Lord's Prayer in the poem. Why does Eliot choose to include this prayer? How does its inclusion challenge or support the emotional tenor of the poem?

9. Consider the use of interruption as a rhetorical device in the poem. Why does Eliot use this rhetorical device? What effect does it have on the reader?

10. Describe the range of emotions that the speaker undergoes during the course of the poem. How does the poem suggest hopefulness in the speaker? How does the poem suggest despair in the speaker?

Essay Ideas

1. Compare "The Hollow Men" to "The Wasteland." In what ways are the themes and symbolism similar in both poems? How do the poems compare in their use of allusion? How are they similar in their treatment of faith, hope, and love?

2. Research Dante's "Inferno," particularly Canto III where he describes the group of purposeless figures who were the basis of Eliot's hollow men. How does Eliot modify Dante's conception of these figures? Conversely, how does Eliot remain faithful to Dante's description? Make sure to explicate each allusive instance in the poem in detail.

3. In "Tradition and the Individual Talent" Eliot describes the artist as being a product of a long tradition in Western culture. He also, however, stresses that the artist must both incorporate and differentiate himself from this artistic lineage. Discuss how "the Hollow Men" exemplifies Eliot's artistic philosophy.

4. Discuss in detail how the form of the poem—its rhythm, its versification and its visual presentation—contributes to and actualizes its content.

5. After the publication of "The Hollow Men" in 1925, Eliot became a convert to Anglo Catholicism. After his conversion, he published a series of poems focusing on the difficulties and potentialities of faith, entitled "The Four Quartets." Contrast the "Hollow Men" to "The Four Quartets." In particular, pay attention to what is different about the symbolism in these poems. How is faith, for example, represented symbolically in "The Four Quartets" as opposed to "The Hollow Men?"

Howl

by Allen Ginsberg

Content Synopsis

"Howl" is a complex, powerful poem, with themes woven together out of a series of surreal, political, and religious images and symbols. It is best to approach the poem through its three sections, breaking down each into movements of images that let the power and the meaning of the poem slowly build. Like many other poems, the sound of "Howl" must be considered a part of its meaning. Ginsberg stated the lines of "Howl" to be 'breath lines,' crediting Whitman, the Hebrew rhythms of the Old Testament, Christopher Smart, and William Blake as influences in the composition of the poem. (Ginsberg). Specifically, the sound is inherently a part of the form and content of the poem. The long free lines represent a consciousness free from formal and social constraints. As Ginsberg said, "Howl" was his "original blow for freedom" (Tytell 104). Lee notes that critics "often refer to 'Howl' as the most important poem since "The Wasteland," arguing that it helped free American poetry from New Critical hegemony by proclaiming loudly; that free verse, the personal, and the political belonged again in the poetic vernacular"(Lee 360).

The poem's opening line has become one of the most famous in American poetry. It serves as an opening into the experience of madness, drugs, prophecy, and a new vision that compose the field of the first part of the poem: "I saw the best minds of my generation destroyed by madness, starving hysterical, naked" (I.1). Insanity is portrayed not as a clinical state, but as a state of vision and experience, an existential quest for experience and perception outside the normal bounds of society. Madness is invoked through two main means: an excess of experience (in the Blake sense of "the road of excess leads to the palace of wisdom") and drug use.

Drugs are a consistent image in the poem. Throughout the poem drugs are used both as a means to follow Beat ideals by dropping out of mass/conformist society, but they are also a means to achieve a visionary or state. A state of gnosis is an ecstatic one in which a person, either through drugs or other mystic or shamanistic practices breaks through everyday perception and achieves a sense of unity with the divine or eternal. Visions are often granted to the Gnostic in this state. In "Howl," drugs are described as "the ancient heavenly connection to the starry dynamo in the machinery of the night" (I.3). Drugs are one path to the visionary state, a way to connect with the universe and offering perceptions outside of conditioned consciousness. In fact, Ginsberg wrote Part 2 of "Howl" after a psychedelic experience with peyote. In this sense, drug use in the poem can be related to the vision quest of shamanism, except in Ginsberg's version, the artist replaces the medicine man. The religious implications of the drug state are reinforced through the image of angel-headed hipsters and illuminated states. The same figures who "ate fire in paint hotels or drank turpentine in Paradise Alley" also "studied Plotinus Poe St. John of the Cross telepathy and bob Kabbalah" (I.24).

In "Howl," the Beats are repeatedly referred to as "angels," to connect those in search of the new consciousness or new vision ("who drove cross country seventy-two hours to find out if I had a vision or you had a vision or he had a vision to find out Eternity" (I.60)) with the prophetic tradition. The quest for "kicks" was not just an epicurean activity, but also a serious search for freedom and new meaning in an America growing more conformist and authoritarian. The "madman bum and angel beat" (I.76) is also a stance of freedom and individual expression. The bohemian rejection of society is a hermetic and holy act.

As the poem builds through Part One, the imagery of madness morphs into other realms of activity. A series of political images ("burned cigarette holes in their arms protesting the narcotic tobacco haze of Capitalism" (I. 31) gives way to a series of biographical and sexual images. The point, however, would be that these confessional acts of accepting one's sexuality are political. There is a sense of Ginsberg finally accepting his homosexuality in a liberatory confession of the self, but there is also the presence of the Beat concern with not repressing human sexuality; that repressing sexuality, hetero or homosexual was part of the conformist authoritarianism of 1950's America.

Part Two of the poem presents a powerful symbol of what drove the "best minds" of a generation to madness: Moloch. It would be useful to understand the origins of the term before explicating Ginsberg's use of the term. Moloch was originally a Canaanite fire god whose worship centered around child sacrifice. In medieval texts, Moloch became one of the princes of hell, and in Milton's "Paradise Lost," he is the demon of blood, rage and battle who argues for eternal warfare against

heaven. Moloch was also used as a symbol of industrialism's destruction of the human spirit in Fritz Lang's film "Metropolis."

Ginsberg makes use of all of these associations. In "Howl," Moloch represents all that is evil, mechanical, militaristic, and materialistic in American society. Moloch is a "sphinx of cement and aluminum," "the crossbone soulless jailhouse and congress" (II.82), "Moloch whose mind is pure machinery! Moloch whose blood is running money! Moloch whose fingers are ten armies!" (II.83). Corporate, conformist America has aligned itself with the god of war and Moloch demands a sacrifice of children, the young minds destroyed in the first part of the poem. In the face of "Moloch whose love is endless oil and stone," (II.85) the only sane response is insanity, which leads into Part 3 of the poem.

Carl Solomon becomes the anchor symbol of this section, and the repeated line "I'm with you in Rockland" the bond of solidarity and love that represents the only hope of escape. Ginsberg met Carl Solomon while both were patients at a New York mental hospital (see Biographical Context). Ginsberg uses the madhouse as a symbol of repression of the individual, both in an artistic and political manner. The state declares those who do not conform-who are individuals-insane, and locks them away. However, the outsider position of the madman, of the inmate, of the Beat, becomes the position from which to imagine alternatives to American society/Moloch: "I'm with you in Rockland/ where you accuse your doctors of insanity and plot the Hebrew socialist revolution against the fascist national Golgotha" (III.107). Ultimately, however, it is not just the political but the spiritual that will rejuvenate America. It is not Ginsberg or Solomon that needs rehabilitation, it is America. "I'm with you in Rockland / where we hug and kiss the United States under our bed sheets the United States that coughs all night and won't let us sleep" (III.110).

Historical Context

The first major reading of "Howl" occurred on October 7, 1955 at the famous Six at Six Gallery reading. The title referred to the six poets who read at the Six Gallery: Gary Snyder, Philip Whalen, Michael McClure, Kenneth Rexroth, Philip Lamantia, and Allen Ginsberg. Kerouac and other Beat notables attended. As Ginsberg read "Howl," the crowd became spellbound. Kerouac noticed the jazz rhythms of the poem, chanting, "Go, Go" (one of the key words from his novel "On the Road" and the title of John Clellon Holmes' Beat novel "Go") as Ginsberg read. By the end of the reading, Rexroth, the eldest poet of the group, broke out in tears.

While the Great Depression and World War II influenced the Beats, the major historical influences are 1950's America and the Cold War period. Ginsberg and other Beats reacted to what they saw as the extreme conformity of 1950's Eisenhower's America. They saw older American expressions of individuality being replaced by corporatism, strip malls, and tract housing, all of which stressed similarity and conformity instead of difference and individuality.

The Cold War provided another historical context. The presence of the Atom Bomb, first dropped in 1945, and the prospect of atomic war with the Soviet Union permeated Beat consciousness, but was particularly important for Ginsberg, given his leftist tendencies and the politics of his mother, who was a member of the American Communist Party and used to take Ginsberg to hall meetings and the hear leftist political speakers. However, the Cold War was also seen as an excuse for eliminating civil liberties and enforcing a conformist "American Type" on everyone. Loyalty oaths, witch hunts, and the other tactics of McCarthyism were seen as the ultimate opposite to the image of a free and loving America. As Lee has recorded, "social histories of the 1960's often cite 'Howl' as the most famous embodiment of a structure of feeling—youthful, dissatisfied, rebellious—that would coalesce into the New Left" (360).

Lawrence Ferlinghetti's City Lights Publishing first published "Howl and Other Poems" in 1956. In May of 1957 the book was censored, and Ginsberg and his publishers were charged with promoting obscenity. Ginsberg and Ferlinghetti challenged the charges, and their victory in the trial brought Ginsberg and his poem national acclaim and publicity.

Societal Context

The word "beat" first came to the attention of the main writers of the group through Herbert Huncke in 1944. Huncke introduced William Burroughs to the street connotations of the term, specifically in relation to being outside the social order and being able to "score" drugs in any city. Burroughs then passed it on to Ginsberg and Jack Kerouac. Kerouac and John Clellon Holmes further refined the literary and generational meaning of the term The word had a street usage of 'tired' or 'down and out' or those at the very bottom of society, but it also came to have a spiritual meaning as well, as in 'beatific' or 'beatitude, especially in the hands of Kerouac. The term came to represent an entire sub-culture of young people fed up with the conformist careerist path America had taken, and felt no place in such a society. It was generally an anti-authoritarian set seeking new experiences and attempting to break the social and politic taboos of previous generations. This included experimentation with drugs and challenging segregation.

It can be argued that, with the exception of literature, no other artistic context had as much influence on the Beats as Jazz music. Jazz artists were there heroes of the Beats, and jazz music became a lesson in composition and form. The improvisational method of jazz was directly incorporated into Beat theories of writing, and jazz rhythms helped form the styles of the Beat writers. Ginsberg specifically credited jazz musician Lester Young for the tone of "Howl."

Religious Context

Ginsberg wrote, "The appeal in "Howl" is to the hermetic tradition of art" (Ginsberg xi). It is through this lens that the Jewish, Christian, and hermetic imagery should be read. Hermetic tradition would refer to "occult" or hidden meanings in a Gnostic sense, where direct experience creates knowledge and understanding. As Ginsberg noted about the religious imagery in the poem, "overt intention of this mystical name dropping was to connect younger readers, Whitman's children, already familiar with Poe and Bob, to older Gnostic tradition" (Ginsberg 126).

Scientific & Technological Context

Ginsberg's poetry is often portrayed as a reaction or an opposition to what has been called the "military industrial complex." Just as the "Moloch" imagery of Part 2 serves to indict the growing corporatism of American Life, much of Ginsberg's later poems attack specifically the American military machine and the corporate world that feeds it. For Ginsberg, this military/financial hub became a symbol of a culture of death, a culture that prioritizes money, power, and violence over love, peace, and individual rights. Ginsberg's ultimate nemesis remained the atomic bomb.

The presence of psychoanalysis can also be felt in the poem. The Beats in general, and Ginsberg in particular were proponents of Freudian and Reichian analysis. Besides their time in mental institutions, both Ginsberg and Kerouac underwent voluntary Freudian psychoanalysis at the hands of Burroughs, who was not professionally certified as an analyst, but Burroughs had undergone analysis himself, and read all of Freud, so the group felt confident in his ability. The Beats were also early students of Wilhelm Reich, and agreed with his theories of sexual repression and character armor. Beat themes of confession, openness, and expressed sexuality have roots in their study of Reich.

Biographical Context

Ginsberg was born in Newark, New Jersey on June 3rd 1926. His father was Louis Ginsberg, a minor American lyric poet, and his mother Naomi was an active leftist. Both parents influenced Ginsberg artistically and politically, however, his mother's mental breakdown and eventual confinement to an asylum for paranoid schizophrenia left deep impressions on his psyche. At Columbia University and the surrounding environs, Ginsberg met Jack Kerouac and Lucien Carr and began a series of literary experiments with them, creating what they called a "New Vision." While in New York, he also met William Burroughs, Neal Cassidy, and the hipster/petty criminal Herbert Huncke, who introduced Ginsberg to New York's bohemian (Beat) and underground subculture. Ginsberg was arrested with Huncke, and was sentenced to psychoanalytic treatment at the Columbia Psychiatric Institute. While there, he met Carl Solomon, and the two spent their time at the institute engaged in literary discussion.

In 1954, after traveling through America, Mexico, and South America, where he took the psychedelic plant yage, Ginsberg settled in San Francisco. He became a part of the literary and Beat subculture of the Bay Area, meeting poets Kenneth Rexroth and Gary Snyder, painter Robert LaVigne, publisher/owner of City Lights Books Lawrence Ferlinghetti, and Peter Orlovsky. The last two were key in Ginsberg's life. Orlovsky became Ginsberg's lover and partner, and allowed him to accept his homosexuality, and Ferlinghetti became Ginsberg's publisher.

Frank Casale, Ph.D.

Works Cited

Ginsberg, Allen. *Howl: Original Draft Facsimile*. Ed. Barry Miles. New York: Harper Perennial. 1995.

Lee, Ben. "Howl and Other Poems: Is There an Old Left in the New Beats." *American Literature*. 76.2 (2004) 367-389.

Tytell, John. *Naked Angels*. New York: Grove Weidenfeld, 1976.

Discussion Questions

1. Discuss the differences between the three sections of the poem.
2. Discuss how Ginsberg uses political imagery in the poem.
3. Discuss the use of the drug imagery in the poem.
4. The opening line "I saw the best minds of my generation destroyed by madness, starving hysterical, naked" is one of the most famous lines in American poetry. How does this line set the tone for the poem as a whole?
5. Ginsberg wrote the poem out of a sense of desperation at the direction of the American government during the Cold War, when some people wanted to trade civil liberty and freedom for security. Is it possible to relate this attitude to the world today?
6. Sexual expression is a major component of the poem. Discuss Ginsberg's attempt to escape sexual repression through his poem.
7. Discuss the importance of jazz to the poem.
8. "Howl" is an urban, city-centered poem. Discuss this aspect of the poem.
9. One line reads, "Who threw potato salad at CCNY lecturers on Dadaism." Define Dada, and explain why this is a relevant or ironic image.
10. Discuss the formal importance of the repetitive line openings in one of the three sections of the poem. ("Who" in Part 1; "Moloch" in Part 2; "I'm with you in Rockland" in Part 3).

Essay Ideas

1. Explain the Moloch symbol in depth. What does it symbolize? How is it described?
2. From the opening to the closing lines of the poem, insanity or mental illness is invoked and described in "Howl." Write an essay exploring the centrality of this theme to the poem.
3. Write an essay detailing the relationship of the poem to Beat culture in general.
4. Walt Whitman is often described as an influence on Ginsberg's work in general and "Howl" in particular. Write an essay exploring this influence.
5. Write an essay which explores the use of religious themes and images in the poem. How did Ginsberg make these traditional themes serve his purposes?

I, Too, Sing America

by Langston Hughes

Content Synopsis

The poem "I, Too, Sing America" by Langston Hughes is inspired by and in response to Walt Whitman's famous poem, "I Hear America Singing." Whitman's poem, in one unified stanza, celebrates working Americans in all their differences. In five halting stanzas, Hughes' poem addresses the social inequality that is predicated on race in America. The speaker of "I, Too, Sing America" says that he also celebrates America, but since he is the "darker brother," he is forced to eat in the kitchen segregated from everyone else. Even though the speaker is excluded, he laughs and grows strong looking forward to the future when he will "be at the table when company comes." He is confident that someday people will see how "beautiful" he is and be ashamed of their previous prejudice. The single-line final stanza highlights the speakers' refusal to be forgotten through the statement, "I, Too, am America."

Symbols & Motifs

Hughes plays off Whitman's reference to America singing in "I, Too, Sing America." The speaker in Hughes' poem is also singing; although he is forced to do it from the kitchen. The kitchen serves as a metaphor to demonstrate the segregation and exclusion that Blacks were subjected to in the first half of the 20th century. The speaker has hope and faith, however, that tomorrow will be better and, "nobody'll dare say to me, 'eat in the kitchen' then." The poem's sentiment is anticipation for the day when African Americans will be treated as equal to white men, with everyone eating together.

Historical Context

Langston Hughes' success coincided with the beginning of the Harlem Renaissance; a time when African Americans were thriving in the fields of art, music and literature. During the 1920s, black artists were achieving wide spread recognition for the first time. At this time, performers such as Louis Armstrong and Bessie Smith played for black and white audiences alike in Harlem nightclubs. Harlem became a cultural hub where writers such as Zora Neale Hurston, Claude McKay, and Langston Hughes migrated to in efforts to immerse themselves in the thriving community of arts and letters. As more and more Blacks moved north, the art of the Harlem Renaissance evolved, addressed more urban topics, and focused on social injustice.

Societal Context

Langston Hughes was an outspoken advocate for the rights of Blacks. Before Hughes returned to the U.S. from Europe in the early 1920s, he was denied passage on a ship because of his race (Poetryarchive. com). "I, Too, Sing America" was written out of anger and the general frustration at the slow progress from slavery to equality. During the 1920s, the Black population in the North nearly doubled and doors were opening, but segregation was still in full effect. The Ku Klux Klan had a large following and lynchings were still occurring at an alarming rate ("The Rise and Fall of Jim Crow"). While conditions were better for Blacks in the North, they were far from perfect. Racism pervaded overcrowded cities and job prospects were scarce. Many Blacks fought for the lowest paying, least desirable jobs because they were denied better opportunities ("The Rise and Fall of Jim Crow"). The Jim Crow era was still largely in effect across the country. Hughes said, "From a whole race of people freed from slavery with nothing . . . it has not always been . . . but the Negro people believed in the American Dream . . ." (Poetryarchive. com). Hughes acknowledged that society had come a long way since slavery but urged people to realize that there was still a long way to go.

Religious Context

"I, Too, Sing America" does not have a specific religious context.

Scientific & Technological Context

"I, Too, Sing America" does not have a specific scientific or technological context.

Biographical Context

Langston Hughes was born in 1902 in Joplin, Missouri to an abolitionist family (Jackson). He started writing poetry in the eighth grade, but was encouraged by his father to study engineering (Jackson). He attended Columbia University briefly but dropped out to pursue a career as a writer. He was an avid reader and admired poets such as Walt Whitman, Edgar Lee Masters, and Carl Sandburg (Simes and Wahlgreen 760).

His first poem, "The Negro Speaks of Rivers," was published in Brownie's Book (Jackson). Other early poems were published in the magazine "Crisis" which was run by the National Association for the Advancement of Colored People (NAACP) (Poetryarchive.com). He traveled to Africa, Russia, and

Europe on a freighter in 1923, moved to Harlem in 1924, and found inspiration in the clubs where he would listen to jazz and blues music (Jackson). He moved to Washington D.C. for a year in 1925 and met poet Vachel Lindsay at a restaurant where Hughes was bussing tables (Simes and Wahlgreen 760). He left a few of his poems at Lindsay's table and Lindsay liked them so much that he read them at a public reading that night; an event which made Hughes a minor celebrity for a time (Simes and Wahlgreen 760).

In 1926, Hughes' first book of poetry, "The Weary Blues," was published and he moved back to Harlem. His poetry embraced the Black experience and often imitated jazz and blues music. Later in his life, he wrote poems specifically to be accompanied by jazz music (Simes and Wahlgreen 760). Hughes died from cancer in 1967. He had a successful career for over 40 years during which he published poetry, short stories, scripts, plays, and autobiographies (Jackson). He is the first black person known in the United States to support himself solely through his writing.

Jennifer Bouchard, M.Ed.

Works Cited

_____. *African American Poetry*. Englewood Cliffs, New Jersey: Globe Book Company, 1993.

Hughes, Langston. "I, Too, Sing America." *Elements of Literature: Fifth Course, Literature of the United States*. Austin: Holt, Rinehart, and Winston, 2003. 740.

Jackson, Andrew. "Langston Hughes." *Red Hot Jazz*. 26 March 2008. <http://www.redhotjazz.com/hughes.html>.

Sime, Richard and Bill Wahlgreen, eds. *Elements of Literature: Fifth Course, Literature of the United States*. Austin: Holt, Rinehart, and Winston, 2003. 760-763.

_____. The Poetry Archive. *Langston Hughes*. 2005. 14 April 2008. <http://www.poetryarchive.org/poetryarchive/singlePoem.do?poemId=1552>.

Discussion Questions

1. What is the tone of the poem?
2. Who are "they" in the poem?
3. How does Hughes use metaphor to express his hopes and frustrations?
4. How will life be different for the speaker "tomorrow"?
5. How are the first and last lines of the poem different?
6. Why might it be useful to have two people write about the same topic?
7. Do you think that Hughes' poem is more complementary or more oppositional to Whitman's poem?
8. How might a contemporary black poet write about this topic today?

Essay Ideas

1. Read more poetry by Langston Hughes and write an essay in which you analyze his poetic style, themes, and structure.
2. Write an essay in which you compare and contrast the poetry of Langston Hughes to the poetry of Walt Whitman.
3. Explore visual art produced during the Harlem Renaissance such as the paintings of Aaron Douglas or the photographs of James Van Der Zee and compare to the poetry of Langston Hughes.
4. Research the Harlem Renaissance and write an essay analyzing why it ended and generalize how the Harlem Renaissance contributed to the future Civil Rights Movement.
5. Write your own poem in which you express your frustration at being left out or excluded.

Ezra Pound, pictured above, wrote "In a Station of the Metro," featured opposite. Photo: National Portrait Gallery, Smithsonian Institution; gift of Friends of Marcella Comes Winslow

In a Station of the Metro

by Ezra Pound

Content Synopsis

A two-line poem, Ezra Pound's "In a Station of the Metro" represents a great concentration of form and effect. The title states the speaker's location, while the pair of lines that follow juxtaposes two images:

> The apparition of these faces in the crowd
> Petals on a wet, black bough.

First, the speaker registers the faces of the commuters who are waiting for or disembarking from the train. The word "apparition" suggests a sudden and unexpected appearance, as if the speaker was not paying attention to his surroundings and then, all at once, took notice. Following hard on the first, a second image comes to mind, for the faces suggest to the speaker "petals on a wet, black bough." A weaker poet would feel compelled to make the comparison explicit, adding a phrase such as "these faces in the crowd / that are like petalslip." Pound knows this sort of linking phrase is unnecessary. Actually, the poem contains no verb at all. The phrases do not make up a complete sentence, nor are the two lines grammatically linked. Instead, one image follows immediately on the other, and the reader must make the same connection that the speaker in the metro station did. Just as the faces suddenly appeared to the speaker, bringing to mind a second, poetic image, so do these lines suddenly appear to the reader. The poem reenacts the telescopic, associative properties of the mind at work.

Pound's poem is reminiscent of the Japanese haiku, in which three lines of five, seven, and five syllables respectively contrast two or three images. Matsuo Basho's classic poem, "Furu Ike Ya," "The Old Pond," serves as a representative example of the genre. It is worth looking at the poem in Japanese . . . even if one does not speak the language . . . in order to understand the form (note that Pound himself was fascinated by Chinese and Japanese ideographs, and the later poems in his epic work "The Cantos" are studded with these characters). Below is the poem in Japanese, followed by a translation of the Japanese characters into syllables, followed by Robert Hass's English translation. All three versions are taken from Hiroaki Sato's collection "One Hundred Frogs."

古池	furu ike ya	The old pond—
蛙飛び込む	kawazu tobikomu	frog jumps in,
水の音	mizu no oto	sound of water.

While Pound is freer with his syllable count than Basho is or another haiku poet would be, his lines of eight, twelve, and seven syllables nevertheless echo the short-long-short pattern of the haiku. As in a haiku, the images of "In a Station of the Metro" are linked associatively rather than grammatically; the three lines represent not a complete sentence, but a series of phrases each containing a separate image. Yet Pound's poem transposes the haiku, which could be considered a pastoral form, to the modern environs of a Paris subway station. Nature makes its way into the poem only because it is a point of reference in the consciousness of the speaker. "In a Station of the Metro" is therefore a fascinating appropriation of form, a poem that links East and West, the urban and the pastoral, and appearance and reality.

Historical Context

As short as "In a Station of the Metro" may be, it can serve to illustrate the central tenets of Imagism, a literary movement that Ezra Pound helped found. Writing about "In a Station of the Metro" in his 1916 book "Gaudier-Brzeska," Pound explained:

> The 'one image poem' is a form of super-position, that is to say, it is one idea set on top of another; In a poem of this sort one is trying to record the precise instant when a thing outward and objective transforms itself, or darts into a thing inward and subjective (89).

In focusing on the boundaries between the objective and the subjective, Pound was engaging in the great cultural and artistic project of his time. From the visual arts to the hard sciences, the great innovators of the 1910's and 1920's explored the relationship between subjective appearance and objective reality. The Cubist paintings of Picasso, for example, juxtapose and layer multiple perspectives of a single object; the faces and bodies of the women in "Les Mademoiselle des Avignon" (1907) are arresting in part because we see them simultaneously in profile and straight on. Einstein's theories of special and general relativity, which the physicist developed in a series of papers published between 1905 and 1915, posited that time itself is relative to an observer's perspective. In philosophy and psychology, too, the great minds of the time were exploring the relationship between what happens and what is perceived to have happened. In his book "Matter and Memory," Henri Bergson

posits that the images one "remembers" are more a part of the present than they are of the past: ". . . from the moment it becomes image, the past leaves the state of pure memory and coincides with a certain part of my present" (140). By Bergson's lights, the speaker in the Metro station can see both the crowd before him and the image of the rain-soaked branch as part of his present reality; both are available to him here and now, because both are images in his mind. Pound's Imagism . . . ; and this brief poem which seems a crystallization of the movement . . .; is very much part of the zeitgeist of the early twentieth century.

Societal Context

One should not let this poem's title, with its reference to the Paris Metro, distract one from its real subject: it is not the train itself, but rather the people who ride the train, that fascinate Pound. Compare for a moment the two major forms of transportation available to a twentieth or twenty-first century commuter: the automobile and the train or subway. Driving or riding in a car can be insulating experiences, in which each driver is shut off from his fellow commuters. Rail travel, however, is a quasi-communal experience. Crowds of commuters wait on the same platforms, squeeze into the same cars, and follow the same routes. There is a delicate balance between the public and the private in such a crowd: the commuters are at once physically close and psychically apart. For the people-watcher as much as for the poet, riding the metro is an opportunity to observe people without needing to interact with them.

It is worth comparing Pound's treatment of the Paris metro with his friend and sometime-collaborator T.S. Eliot's treatment of the London tube. For Eliot, who took the tube to work for years, the underground constitutes a void of time and space that allows for reflection and introspection. Eliot's prophetic character, the Rock, claims: "The desert is not only around the corner, / the desert is squeezed into the tube-train next to you." In the "Four Quartets," the desert or purgatorial aspects of the underground are made more explicit. The descent into the underground station invites commuter and reader alike to "descend lower" into "internal darkness." Riding the tube forces the rider to confront his own internal life:

Or as, when an underground train, in the tube,
    stops too long between stations
And conversation rises and slowly fades into
    silence
And you see behind every face the mental
    emptiness deepen
Leaving only the growing terror of nothing to
    think about ("East Coker III").

The London Underground for Eliot, like the Paris Metro for Pound, is a place of meditation and transformation. The commute involves not a diffusion of purpose, but a concentration of it. For Eliot and Pound alike, going down into the subterranean station suggests the classical descent into the underworld. In this hidden world, the poet has a chance to see inner and outer realities that may not be available to him in the light of the sun.

Religious Context

In a poem as short as "In a Station of the Metro," every word is important. Pound could have chosen to begin his poem with "The appearance of these faces in the crowd." The phrases would still make sense, for the faces do appear to be like "petals on a wet black bough." Instead, however, Pound uses the less common word "apparition." The words "appearance" and "apparition" share a common root, the Latin participle "apparre," meaning "having come into view." Yet "apparition" carries metaphysical and religious connotations that "appearance" does not. In supernatural terms, an apparition is a ghost or a specter. In the context of Catholicism, it is the physical manifestation of a spiritual being: an angel, a saint, or the

Virgin Mary. The Vatican's Congregation for the Doctrine of Faith has even published a document laying out the criteria for judging the validity of such apparitions: "Norms of the Congregation for Proceeding in Judging Alleged Apparitions and Revelations." Pound's diction therefore lends his poem. …and his speaker's vision of the crowd … a distinctly religious cast. As the words "revelation" and "epiphany," two other terms that originated in theology but have been appropriated for literary purposes, apparition retains its metaphysical connotation. Standing on a Paris Metro platform, the poet's stand-in has a vision that partakes of the transcendent. He sees an everyday image before him, and then sees it anew through the eyes of the poet. The poet's act of seeing is a quasi-religious one, and his metaphor making . . .; his transformation of a crowd of people into petals on a bough is less simile than sacrament.

Scientific & Technological Context

The city itself might be considered humanity's greatest social and technological achievement. In Ian McEwan's novel "Saturday," protagonist Henry Perowne looks out from his window over London at night, and is filled with wonder at this vast system:

Henry thinks the city is a success, a brilliant invention, a biological masterpiece—millions teeming around the accumulated and layered achievements of the centuries, as though around a coral reef, sleeping, working, entertaining themselves, harmonious for the most part, nearly everyone wanting it to work.

The city works not only because of the people who inhabit it, but also because of the layers of infrastructure and subsystems of which these people make use. The underground train, subway, or metro should figure prominently among "the accumulated and layered achievements of the centuries." These public transportation systems were vital to the late nineteenth and early-twentieth growth of metropolises such as London, New York, or Paris.

The first lines of the Paris metro were dug in anticipation of the Paris World Exposition of 1900. London could already boast of its underground and New York of its competing private subway lines and the Parisians felt they needed to have a comparable system to serve and impress the crowds that would flood the city for the fair. From the start, the Paris Metro was an iconic system. Hector Guimard's famous beaux-arts entrance gates, with their sinuous cast iron lines framing the legend "Metropolitain," brought high style to what might have been a purely functional design element. Many of Guimard's original gates are still in use in Paris, while one is on display in the garden of The Museum of Modern Art (Museum of Modern Art Online 2007). When Ezra Pound rode and wrote about the Paris Metro, the system was not even fifteen years old. Yet the metro had already become an integral part of Parisian life and of modernity. Like Guimard's entrance gates, the metro itself was both a functional invention and a thing of beauty. Much the same could be said of Pound's poem.

Biographical Context

William Wordsworth famously defined poetry as "emotion recollected in tranquility." The poet has the experience of feeling an emotion deeply, and later finds the words to recapture that feeling and to share it with his reader. Such a definition certainly seems apropos to Pound's "In a Station of the Metro." Rarely does a poet so precisely identify the experience out of which a poem was born as Pound does here:

Three years ago in Paris I got out of a "metro" train at La Concorde, and saw suddenly a beautiful face, and then another and another, and then a beautiful child's face, and then another beautiful woman, and I tried all that day to find words for what this had meant to me ("Gaudier-Brzeska" 89).

Pound relates not only the crowd of faces that he saw, but the struggle he undertook to find words to describe this scene. He goes on to say, "And that evening, as I went home along the Rue Raynouard, I was still trying, and I found, suddenly, the expression. I do not mean that I found words, but there came an equation" (90). Here Wordsworth's formulation of the poetic act begins to fail us, for Pound does not use his poem to describe the emotion he felt. While his recollection in his memoir is studded with references to himself and his feelings, there is no "I" in the poem itself. Perhaps this is in part what Pound means by finding "an equation" to express the scene on the Metro platform. It is as if the poem is not a subjective recollection, but rather an objective formula.

If Wordsworth's definition of the poetic helps us understand the process, by which Pound reflected on his experience, T. S. Eliot's rebuttal of Wordsworth may help us to understand the product of that reflection. Eliot argued that Wordsworth was wrong in seeing poetry as an act of personal reflection on past experience. In "Tradition and the Individual Talent," Eliot wrote that poetry "is not the expression of personality, but an escape from personality" ("Selected Essays" 21). Ezra Pound, the man, disappears as Ezra Pound, the poet, constructs a poem that functions independently of his own experience. Eliot's concept of the objective correlative likewise helps to explain Pound's comment about finding "an equation." Eliot identified the objective correlative as

A set of objects, a situation, a chain of events which shall be the formula of that particular emotion; such that when the external facts, which must terminate in sensory experience, are given, the emotion is immediately evoked (Selected Essays 145).

Pound has successfully created such an objective "formula" in this short poem. He recaptures not the emotion he felt, but rather "the external facts" that provoked that emotion. When the reader encounters the "equation" or "formula" of "In a Station of the Metro," he or she experiences the emotions that come with seeing one's everyday surroundings transformed by the poetic and transcendent gaze.

Matthew J. Bolton, Ph.D.

Works Cited

Bergson, Henri. *Matter and Memory.* New York: Zone Books, 1991.

Eliot, T. S. *The Complete Poems and Plays.* New York: Harcourt, Brace & World, 1962.

_____. *Selected Essays.* New York: Harcourt, Brace & Company, 1932.

"Hector Guimard." *The Museum of Modern Art: The Collection.* 2007. 8 Dec. 2008 <http://www.moma.org/collection/browse_results.php?criteria=O:AD:E:2407&page_number=1&template_id=6&sort_order=1>Pound, Ezra.

Gaudier-Brzeska. *A Memoir.* New York: New Directions, 1970.

_____. *Selected Poems.* Edited with an introduction by T.S. Eliot. London: Faber and Faber, 1948.

Sato, Hiroaki. *One Hundred Frogs: From Matsuo Basho to Allen Ginsberg.* New York: Weatherhill: 1995.

Discussion Questions

1. What is the mood of the poem? What emotion was it that Pound felt in the Metro station and tried to recapture in his poem?
2. Is being part of this crowd of commuters an alienating experience or a communal one?
3. What is the relationship between the crowd and the petals on a bough? Is it simply that the one looks vaguely like the other, or does the comparison set up a deeper series of parallels?
4. What is the nature of the "apparition" that the speaker sees? Does a poet or artist see the world differently than others do? Is it a different intensity of seeing or a different kind of seeing altogether?
5. Have you yourself ever had the experience of seeing an ordinary scene suddenly transformed or made extraordinary? Discuss the experience and speculate as to why an ordinary image or everyday scene can sometimes capture one's attention and become a source of fascination.
6. How does this poem blur the lines between poetry and painting?
7. In this poem, an American in Paris writes in a Japanese form. How have the traditional boundaries between cultures and languages become blurred in the twentieth and twenty-first centuries? How have they been reinforced?
8. Discuss Pound's poem in light of early twentieth-century movements and developments in art and film, such as late impressionism, post-impressionism, cubism, and the rise of the moving picture.

Essay Ideas

1. Read a collection of haiku and compare Pound's poem to this classical Japanese form. How does he appropriate and redeploy the conventions of this form?
2. Explore the fascinating connections between Japanese and French culture, paying particular attention to the late nineteenth century craze for "Japoinese." Read "In a Station of the Metro" in light of these connections.
3. Relocate Pound's poem in the context of another short form, such as the aphorism, the proverb, or even the joke. How do very short pieces of writing work?
4. Do a close reading of the poem, discussing its diction, rhyme scheme, rhythm, and meter.
5. Classical epics such as "The Odyssey" and "The Aeneid," as well as later works such as Dante's "Divine Comedy" and Milton's "Paradise Lost," feature a descent into the underworld. Read one or more of these accounts of the underworld and draw parallels with Pound's crowd of subterranean commuters.
6. Compare Pound's poem to the work of some of his Modernist contemporaries. Consider as a point of comparison Eliot's treatment of modern urban commuters in "The Waste Land."
7. Read James Joyce's short story cycle "Dubliners," and compare the Joycean epiphany to Pound's "apparition."

Journey of the Magi

by T. S. Eliot

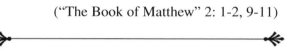

"Now when Jesus was born in Bethlehem of Judeae in the days of Herod the king, behold, there came wise men from the east to Jerusalem, saying 'Where is he that is born King of the Jews? For we have seen his star in the east, and come to worship him.' . . . and, lo, the star, which they saw in the east, went before them, till it came and stood over where the young child was. When they saw the star, they rejoiced with exceeding great joy. And when they were come into the house, they saw the young child with Mary his mother, and fell down, and worshipped him: and when they had opened their treasures, they presented unto him gifts: gold, and frankincense, and myrrh."

("The Book of Matthew" 2: 1-2, 9-11)

Content Synopsis

"Journey of the Magi" is a poem narrated by one of the three magi, the wise men, or kings from the East who, according to Matthew's Gospel, traveled to Bethlehem to worship the infant Jesus. Although Eliot's Magus has had many years to reflect on this experience (for he notes that the journey took place "a long time ago"), he has not yet grasped the significance of what he witnessed in the manger at Bethlehem (32). Indeed, he is unable or unwilling to describe the Epiphany, or presentation of the Christ child, and focuses instead on the arduousness of his journey. Nevertheless, the experience has had a profound impact upon him. "No longer at ease" among his own people, the Magus finds himself musing on questions of life, death, and the afterlife (41). Caught in a time between Christ's birth and his death, the Magus knows the "old dispensation" is no longer valid, but has not yet received the gospels that would tell him of the new dispensation of Christianity (41).

The poem opens with a five-line quotation describing a long and difficult journey through the dead of winter. Eliot has taken this passage from a sermon on the journey to Bethlehem by Lancelot Andrewes, a seventeenth century preacher in whom the poet had taken an intense interest. A year before publishing "Journey of the Magi," Eliot wrote an essay on Andrewes, and a year later, in 1928, he would publish a book of essays entitled "For Lancelot Andrewes." Eliot's own words then build on the winter scene Andrewes describes: "And the camels galled, sore-footed, refractory / Lying down in the melting snow" (6-7). The Magus contrasts the difficulty of the journey with the pleasures he and his companions have left behind in their eastern kingdoms. They "regretted / The summer palaces on slopes, the terraces, / And the silken girls bringing sherbert" (8-10). The primary meaning of "regret" in this context is "to miss or pine for," but the word may also imply that the magi are already beginning to renounce the easy sensuality of their former way of life. In this respect, the journey itself becomes a form of penance or purgation.

Because the cities they enter are "hostile" and because of trouble with "the night-fires going out and the lack of shelters," the magi decide to "travel all night / Sleeping in snatches" (13, 14, 17-18). Note how the Magus's reason for traveling by night subverts the account of the journey in the Gospel of Matthew, in which the magi travel by night because they are following a guiding star. Eliot's wise men have no such guide and therefore are plagued by doubts and fears. The Magus notes that they traveled with "voices singing in our ears, saying / That this was all folly" (19-20). Presumably, these are the remembered voices both of the magi's countrymen in the east, who disparaged their mission, and of skeptical strangers whom they have met on the way.

In the second stanza, the magi arrive at a "temperate valley" at dawn (21). This landscape stands in sharp contrast to the bleak, snowy terrain of the first stanza. The valley is "wet, below the snow line, smelling of vegetation / With a running stream and a water-mill beating the darkness" (22-23). As the Magus continues to describe the locale, the reader begins to realize that the sights and inhabitants of the valley are charged with symbolic resonance that looks ahead to the life, death, and resurrection of Christ. The stream, for example, may symbolize Christ's claim to be "the water of life" (Revelation 21:6). The "three trees on the low sky" are a foreboding of the three crosses on Mount Calvary, on one of which Jesus will be crucified (24). The "old white horse" which "galloped away in the meadow" is something of a crux (25). Perhaps the horse is a symbol of what the Magus will later call "the old dispensation," a set of religious beliefs that must give way to the teachings of Christ (41). Passing a tavern, the Magus sees "Six hands at an

open door dicing for pieces of silver, / And feet kicking at empty wine-skins" (27-28). The first line suggests both the Roman soldiers who would gamble for Christ's clothing at the foot of the cross as well as the thirty pieces of silver for which Judas would betray Christ. The second line looks ahead to Christ's question "will you pour new wine into old skins," which calls for a new religion to express a new faith (Matthew 9:17).

The scenes in the valley have a proleptic quality, in that they encode information about future events. Ironically, their significance is lost on the Magus, who dutifully recalls what he saw but is unable to explain. There is a great gap between what the Magus has seen, without having understood, and what the reader has understood, without having seen. This issue of seeing and understanding is complicated further by the Magus's silence regarding the scene in the manger. His description is compressed and laconic: "we continued / And arrived at evening, not a moment too soon / Finding the place; it was (you may say) satisfactory" (29). Throughout this stanza, the Magus has been reporting what he saw without editorial comment. Now, when he comes to the end of the journey and the heart of his story, he comments on what he saw without reporting it. We hear nothing of the manger, the child, or the presentation of gifts. Instead, we have a one-word summation. Note, too, that the Magus further distances himself from this part of the story by attributing this word to his listener in conditional, parenthetical phrase: "it was (you may say) satisfactory" (31). Thus while the Magus has detailed the sights and sounds of his journey, the Epiphany itself is veiled behind a maddeningly unsatisfactory word.

There has been much critical debate about the word "satisfactory." Some critics have read into this a note of disappointment and embarrassment. The Magus glosses over the particulars of the nativity scene because the manger was not a suitable place for a king to have been born. He may fear that the humbleness of the place would cause his audience to doubt the importance of Jesus' birth. Others argue that the word refers to the prophecy that led the magi to take their journey in the first place, and means simply that the birth of Jesus satisfied the conditions of that prophecy. A third reading might take the word as a deliberate understatement on the part of the Magus, a recognition that words cannot do justice to what he saw in the manger. This reading puts more weight on the parenthetical phrase "(you may say)." You may say it was satisfactory, the Magus implies, but I will say nothing.

In the third stanza, the Magus speaks of his current situation, trying to come to terms with why and how the journey has changed him. He notes that "all this was a long time ago, I remember, / And I would do it again" (32-33). He then says "set down / This set down / This" (33-35). This directive indicates for the first time the occasion on which the Magus is speaking: he is back in his eastern palace, many years after his journey, dictating to a scribe or recorder. Critic Brian Barbour proposes that this recorder is none other than Saint Matthew the Evangelist, who is gathering first-hand reports in order to write his gospel. The Magus's insistence that this figure "set down" his next words establishes both that he has reached a critical point in his story and perhaps that he sees this as his definitive statement. Note how the Magus's directions spill across the line in a disjointed fashion: not "set down this" but "set down / This." This rupturing of the verse may capture the Magus' own consternation as well as the gap between the words he speaks and the words the scribe sets down in the poem. Certainly, these lines draw the reader's attention to issues of oral and written text.

The question that the Magus is so adamant be set down is this: "were we led all that way for / Birth or Death?" (35-36). In the eight lines which close the poem, the Magus uses the word "birth" eight times and "death" nine times. The words begin as a pair of opposites—"Birth or Death?"—

but gradually start to shade into each other. The Magus notes "I had seen birth and death, / But had thought they were different" (37-38). The journey was like a death for the Magus and his companions, and returning to their Eastern kingdoms did not feel like a rebirth. Rather, they find themselves "no longer at ease here, in the old dispensation / With an alien people clutching their gods" (41-42). Alienated from his own people and customs, the Magus says, "I should be glad of another death" (43). In his conflating of death and birth, the Magus is voicing the central creed of Christianity: that by dying one is reborn. The Magus's ninth iteration of the word death calls for a ninth iteration of the word birth. Death and birth are no longer opposites, as they were in the old dispensation, but complements. The Magus longs not for death, but for spiritual rebirth.

Historical Context

London in the 1920's was the seat of literary Modernism. Eliot's circle of friends and colleagues included Ezra Pound, who was instrumental in the publication of "The Love Song of J. Alfred Prufrock" in 1915 and who later edited "The Waste Land;" Virginia and Leonard Woolf, who published several of Eliot's poems at their Hogarth Press; novelist Wyndham Lewis, who edited the Modernist journal "Blast." He rubbed shoulders with W. B. Yeats and, on a visit to France, with James Joyce. Eliot's editorship of the journal "The Criterion" further exposed him to contemporary fiction and poetry, while the book reviews that he wrote incessantly gave him a venue in which to explore his interest in the literature of the past, particularly that of the Elizabethan and Jacobean playwrights.

Modernism might best be defined by Ezra Pound's dictum to "Make it New." Literature must develop new forms to accommodate and express both enduring values and the realities—be they valuable or not—of the modern age. The publication in 1922 of James Joyce's "Ulysses" and

Eliot's "The Waste Land," both of which draw on classical texts, myths, and archetypes to represent the modern condition, brought Modernism into the public eye and signaled just how important this movement would be for novels and poetry alike. After "The Waste Land," Eliot was lionized as the spokesperson for twentieth-century poetry and an authority on the literary tradition.

The 1920's saw dramatic developments in other arts as well, many of which exerted an influence on the literature of the time. It was the decade, for example, in which jazz came into its ascendancy. An aficionado of the music halls, Eliot was greatly taken with this new form of music. Eliot had begun to work with its syncopated rhythms in "The Waste Land," which contains snatches of a ragtime song, "That Shakespearean Rag." However, it was in the middle of the 1920's that he began to experiment with a work in which a mode of phrasing based on jazz rhythms would play a central role. This project, which would eventually become the unfinished play Sweeney Agonistes, was published just prior to "Journey of the Magi" under the title "Wanna Go Home, Baby?" These fragments of a verse play fuse jazz age patter with the conventions of the Greek tragedy. "Journey of the Magi" seems far removed from the world of jazz until one considers that it, like that distinctly American art form, it is built on a layering of voices and a reinterpreting of what has been said before.

Eliot's art was always deeply rooted in Biblical and classical sources, and in this respect "Journey of the Magi" runs counter to the general trend of 1920's secularist culture. Eliot's conversion to the Church of England in 1927, just two months before publishing the poem, baffled friends and critics alike. Those who had read "The Waste Land" and "The Hollow Men" as sounding the death knell of the European Christian tradition could not understand why Eliot would accept the dogma and scriptures of the most orthodox and hierarchical of English denominations. It would not be an overstatement to say that some, including Ezra Pound, saw Eliot's conversion as a betrayal of his youthful ideals.

One is therefore tempted to read the Magus as a stand-in for Eliot himself, one who finds himself living among "an alien people." Such a reading renders English and American culture of the 1920's a time of "summer palaces on slopes, the terraces, / and the silken girls bringing sherbert" (9-10). The mechanized brutality of the World War I trenches lay in the past, while the gathering storm in Germany could not yet be felt abroad. As did their counterparts in the United States, English men and women of means enjoyed something of a giddy time, and England could be said to have enjoyed its own "roaring twenties." Likewise, the country would feel some of the impact of America's stock market crash of 1929, which ended the roaring twenties. Yet throughout the second half of the decade, Eliot was engaged in a spiritual and intellectual struggle that might be at odds with the wider values of the times.

It is worth commenting not only on the time in which Eliot wrote "Journey of the Magi," but on the historical setting of the poem itself Perhaps the most obvious point to be made is that Eliot's setting is deliberately anachronistic. By beginning the poem with a quotation from a seventeenth century preacher, Eliot signals that the words of his poem are not literally the words of the Magus. In this respect, Eliot's monologue is distinctly different from those of Victorian practitioners of the form, such as Robert Browning and Alfred Lord Tennyson, which created and maintained the illusion that one was listening in on a voice from the past. The proleptic sights of the temperate valley likewise frustrate the idea of the Magus's account being a historical one. Time and space seem to work differently in the valley of Bethlehem, with objects and people taking on symbolic or archetypal significance that cannot be explained through science or history. Critic Daniel Harris argues that this deliberate anachronism effectively critiques the notion that linear time represents progress. Recreating the world of the Magus would not bring poet or reader any closer to the reality of the incarnation of Jesus Christ, which must be apprehended outside of the confines of linear, historical thought.

Thus, Eliot's poem does not attempt to recreate a specific point in time or space: the poem readily admits that it is impossible to recapture the historical moment of the magi. Eliot is fascinated by time—indeed, it is the word that appears with the greatest frequency in his collected poems. His later "Four Quartets" would be explicit studies of time past, present, and future. It is perhaps not surprising for a poet whose work revolves around the dialogue between the literature of the classical world and the rhythms and preoccupations of the contemporary one to see the notion of historical time as a chimera.

Societal Context

Eliot began to write about and to practice Christianity at a time when the Church of England's influence, like that of so many other Christian denominations, was waning. In Eliot's unfinished drama "The Rock," written a few years after "Journey of the Magi," the people of London complain "we have too many churches, / and too few chophouses" (21-22). Not only had the church lost its spiritual standing in London, but also London was losing its churches, many of which had been demolished or were scheduled for demolition. Eliot decries this practice in "Lancelot Andrewes" and subtly mocks it in the notes to "The Waste Land." For Eliot, the loss of faith in the church meant a concomitant loss of culture. Seen in this context, Eliot's 1927 baptism into the Church of England and his subsequent writings on explicitly religious themes is a reactionary move.

In the years following his conversion, Eliot would become increasingly interested in social rather than literary criticism. Works like "After

Strange Gods" (1934) and "The Idea of a Christian Society" (1939) address directly what Eliot saw as a loss of religion and culture in modern society, and lay out some of the means by which the traditions of a homogeneous Christian society might be reestablished.

Eliot did not believe that morality and ethics can exist independent of religious faith, and that one can abandon the faith without abandoning morality. A problem arises, however, one or more generations after this loss of faith. Eliot argued that because the various forms of humanism and liberalism drew their strength from the Christian faith, they therefore lose strength with each successive generation. He asks in a 1928 essay on the humanism of Irving Babbitt: "Is it, in the end, a view of life that will work by itself, or is it a derivative of religion which will work only for a short time in history, and only for a few highly cultivated persons?" (128). The loss of England's churches and the decline of England's church would translate into a loss of culture and morality for the English masses.

Religious Context

In equating the birth of Christ with "bitter agony" and death, and in his own readiness for "another death," the Magus has expressed, as many critics have noted, the central tenet of Christian faith (39, 43). Yet what the Magus might welcome almost as much as another death would be a creed and a ritual. The mass of both the Anglican and the Roman Catholic Church, after all, offers believers each week "another death" in the form of the Eucharist, the bread and wine that represent the death of Jesus. The Magus's dissatisfaction largely arises out of his inability to articulate, lacking a church and the New Testament, the divine plan of which he has witnessed a part. The "old dispensation" no longer holds, but the Magus, who was once both wise and happy, lacks the philosophical and theological formulations necessary to live happily in the new one (41). The Magus is trapped in one of what Eliot elsewhere refers to as history's "cunning passages": a time after the Incarnation but before the Crucifixion and Resurrection—or, at least, before news of those events and their significance has spread ("Gerontion" 35). In Eliot's construction of early Christianity, the Magus must wait not only for the death, resurrection, and Jesus, but also for the scriptures and practices that will make clear the implications of those events.

Yet it is not enough to say that "Journey of the Magi," or any other poem for that matter, is a poem about Christianity. Rather, one must determine what kind of Christianity the poem presents. "Journey of the Magi" seems to grow out of the orthodoxies of the Church of England (also called Anglicanism or English Catholicism), to which Eliot had converted a few months before publishing the poem, rather than out of the Unitarianism of his boyhood. The Magus has seen Jesus with his own eyes, but he needs the church, the gospels, and the ritual of the mass to make clear to him what he has seen. In this respect, "Journey of the Magi" may be a refutation both of Unitarianism and of its religious and literary offshoot, Transcendentalism.

A movement, which began in New England as a reaction to the strict Calvinism of the Puritan Churches, Unitarianism, eschews ritual, dogma, and ecclesiastical hierarchies, stressing instead the universality of Christ's message and the oneness of all Christian churches. In placing great emphasis on education, ethics, and the necessity of performing works to the public good, Unitarianism is a product and a producer of nineteenth-century American Humanism. Unitarianism also gave birth to Transcendentalism, a more radically individual form of Unitarianism, which proposed that the individual might apprehend the divine through nature and reflection. Emerson, Thoreau, and Whitman were all Transcendentalists.

The Church of England therefore represented a radically different faith than the one in which Eliot had been raised. Eliot in his middle years chose for himself a faith that stressed orthodoxy, ritual, and rite. In his 1926 essay "Lancelot Andrewes," Eliot wrote, "The Church of England is the creation . . . of the reign on Elizabeth. The via media which is the spirit of Anglicanism was the spirit of Elizabeth in all things" (1932: 341). The Church of England, apparently, was the only denomination that would meet the spiritual and aesthetic needs of a poet and nascent playwright who located his creative inheritance in Elizabethan and Jacobean England.

Scientific & Technological Context

Modernism is bound with the scientific and technological developments of the nineteenth and twentieth centuries. Eliot, too, mused on how the technologies of modern life were influencing not merely the themes, but the forms and rhythms of contemporary literature. He wrote in 1926, "Perhaps the conditions of modern life (think how large a part is now played in our sensory life by the internal combustion engine!) have altered our perception of rhythms" (Smith 51). Eliot believed that poetry would have to accommodate these new rhythms if it were to remain a true and relevant rather than an artificial and precious.

The dehumanizing experience of the World War I trenches, in which soldiers were killed like cattle by machine guns and mortars, further wrenched literature away from the pastoral or contemplative mode. Literature after the war needed, on some level, to acknowledge the barbarism that the modern age had unleashed. "The Waste Land," for example, echoes the destruction of the war through its ruptured, disjointed form and its ironic juxtaposition of texts.

Yet perhaps more central to Eliot's poetry than developments in the hard sciences are those in the social, psychological, and philological ones. The anthropological studies of James Frazer and Jessie Weston were tremendously influences on Eliot at the time that he composed "The Waste Land."

A different social science may help contextualize "Journey of the Magi": nineteenth-century Higher Criticism. This movement, which began in Germany, involved using textual and linguistic analysis to uncover the many hands and many voices that went toward making the Bible. This application of scientific empiricism to a sacred text produced responses among Christian churches and individuals. Responses ran the gamut from the reactionary stance of the Roman Catholic Church, which declared in a papal bull the doctrine of the "inerrancy of the Bible," to the humanistic position of critic Matthew Arnold, who declared that the Bible has the truth of poetry rather than the truth of a historical document. Eliot seems to be commenting on the idea of textual and spiritual authenticity by creating a document that is deliberately ahistorical, yet may be true.

Biographical Context

Born into a prominent St. Louis family in 1888, T.S. Eliot was raised a Unitarian. He attended Harvard and in 1914 moved to England, where he studied philosophy at Oxford University. The next year he married an Englishwoman, Vivienne Haigh-Wood, and began pursuing a rigorous program of writing criticism and book reviews. He worked as a middle school teacher, as an extension lecturer at University College, and as a clerk at Lloyd's Bank before eventually moving in editing and publishing. In 1922, he became editor of "The Criterion," while in 1926 he left the bank to take a position with the publishing House Faber & Gwyer.

Eliot published "The Love Song of J. Alfred Prufrock" in 1915, followed by the collection "Prufrock and Other Observations" in 1917. This was followed by Poems (1920) and his first book of criticism, "The Sacred Wood" (1920), which gathered excerpts from some of the dozens of book reviews and critical pieces Eliot had written over the previous five years. In 1922, he published "The Waste Land." The great acclaim with which "The

Waste Land" was received proved something of a burden to Eliot. He entered a dry spell, unable to find a new direction for his creative energies. He published "The Hollow Men" in 1925, but as this poem drew on some of the same materials and drafts as had "The Waste Land," and elaborates on the desert landscapes of the earlier poem, it reads as a coda rather than a new start. In 1926 and 1927, he published two fragments of the verse drama "Sweeney Agonistes," a work Eliot never completed. Critic John Timmerman sees Eliot in the years after "The Waste Land" as "unable to find a new voice—a theme and a way of expressing it—that would incarnate his own sense of spiritual reality" (17).

In 1927, Geoffrey Faber, for whose publishing house Eliot worked as an editor, asked Eliot to write a poem for his series of "Ariel Poems," illustrated booklets released at Christmas. This commission would prove the means by which Eliot broke his writer's block, freeing him to write in a mode which departed both from the one he had so successfully deployed in "The Waste Land" and "The Hollow Men" and from the dramatic one which so stymied him in "Sweeney Agonistes." Eliot would go on to write three more "Ariel Poems" between 1927 and 1930: "Marina," "Animula," and "A Song for Simeon." One piece that began as an "Ariel Poem" would eventually become "Ash-Wednesday" (1930), Eliot's great six-part poem of conversion.

The year 1927 found Eliot charting a new course for himself not only in his poetry, but also in his spiritual life. In June, Eliot was baptized, in a ceremony veiled in secrecy, into the Church of England. The next day the Bishop of Oxford confirmed him. One must know something of the history of the Eliot family to understand the magnitude of Eliot's decision to renounce the Unitarianism of his boyhood. Eliot's grandfather, William Greenleaf Eliot, had moved from Boston to St. Louis in 1834 to found the city's first Unitarian Church.

He went to St. Louis with the intention of putting down deep roots. "If I come," he said, "I come to remain, and to lay my ashes in the Valley of the Mississippi" (Charlotte Eliot 15). Eliot helped to shape nineteenth century St. Louis by founding or strengthening a number of its religious, educational, and philanthropic institutions. He was one of the founders both of the city's public school system and of Washington University, the first university west of the Mississippi. Although he died the year before Thomas Stearns Eliot was born, William remained a presence in the Eliot household throughout the poet's boyhood.

To reject this Unitarian legacy was therefore a monumental decision for Eliot, one at which he arrived only after much deliberation. He seems to have found in the Church of England a sense of orthodoxy, tradition, and aesthetics, which made the religion of his family, seem hollow by comparison. He also found in his new faith a doctrinal rigor that contrasted with the relativism and humanism of the Unitarians. In 1924, Eliot had scrawled on an envelope: "There are only 2 things—Puritanism and Catholicism. You are one or the other. You either believe in the reality of sin or you don't—that is the important moral decision" (Gordon 213). Believing in sin, Eliot believed in Catholicism. When in November of 1927 Eliot adopted British citizenship, he further distanced himself from his American Unitarian roots.

Appearing in print on August 25, 1927, "Journey of the Magi" is the first work Eliot published after his conversion. It signaled a great redirection of interest and energy for Eliot, and came as a surprise to readers who thought of him only as the poet of "The Waste Land." "Journey of the Magi" sounds the theme of spiritual awakening which will reverberate through all of Eliot's

future compositions, from plays like "Murder in the Cathedral" and "The Family Reunion" to the poetic cycle "The Four Quartets." With the publication of this short poem, Eliot had found a new voice. It is hard therefore not to read the Magus as a refracted version of Eliot, a convert who longs for "another death"—the death of his old life—and for rebirth into a new identity and a new faith.

Matthew J. Bolton, Ph.D.

Works Cited

Barbour, Brian M. "Poetic Form in 'Journey of the Magi'." *Renascence: Essays on Values in Literature* 40 (1988): 189-196.

Burgess, E. F. "T. S. Eliot's 'The Journey of the Magi'." *Explicator* 42 (1984): 36.

Eliot, Charlotte C. *William Greenleaf Eliot: Minister, Educator, Philanthropist*. Boston and New York: Houghton Mifflin, 1904.

Eliot, T. S. *For Lancelot Andrewes*. London: Faber and Faber, 1928.

_____. "Selected Essays." *Selected Essays: 1917-1932*. New York: Harcourt, Brace and Company, 1932.

_____. *The Complete Poems and Plays: 1909-1950*. New York: Harcourt, Brace & World, 1962.

Gordon, Lyndall. *T. S. Eliot: An Imperfect Life*. New York: Norton, 1998.

Harris, Daniel A. "Language, History, and Text in Eliot's 'Journey of the Magi'." *PMLA*. 95 (1980): 838-856.

Smith, Carol H. *T. S. Eliot's Dramatic Theory and Practice: From Sweeney Agonistes to The Elder Statesman*. Princeton: Princeton UP, 1963.

Timmerman, John H. *T. S. Eliot's Ariel Poems: the Poetics of Recovery*. Lewisburg: Bucknell UP, 1994.

Discussion Questions

1. How do the poem's line breaks reflect the emphasis that the Magus puts on different aspects of his story or reflect the emotion with which he recalls his story?

2. Which was more important for the Magus, the journey or the destination? Does his account succeed in communicating the relative importance of each?

3. What would a psychologist or psychiatrist say of the Magus's present state of mind and of how his account of the journey reflects this state of mind? What diagnosis or advice might he or she offer the Magus?

4. The Magus describes his own countrymen as "an alien people clutching their gods." How do you think his people see him?

5. The poem plays with the gap between experience and understanding. Must one experience an event firsthand to understand it? Must one understand an experience to be changed by it? Who is in a better position to understand the Epiphany, the reader or the Magus?

6. What do you believe accounts for the Magus's one-word summation of the scene in the manger?

7. What sort of effect does the birth of Christ seem to have on the "temperate valley" and its inhabitants?

8. In what ways does Eliot seem to be deconstructing or challenging the notion of linear time and historicity through the structure and contents of "Journey of the Magi"? What is the function of anachronism in this poem?

9. The Victorian dramatic monologue, developed by poets such as Robert Browning and Alfred, Lord Tennyson, was structured around a situation in which a speaker addresses himself to a silent auditor. What can you deduce about the Magus's silent auditor?

10. Is the Magus likely to reason and intuit his way toward a full understanding of Christian doctrine, or has he already reached the apex of his understanding? In other words, does he already possess all of the experience and information necessary to apprehend the new dispensation, or is he lacking some vital fact or revelation?

Essay Ideas

1. Eliot wrote three other Ariel poems: "Marina," "Animicula," and "A Song for Simeon." Compare any of these to "Journey of the Magi," drawing thematic and formal connections across the poems. "A Song for Simeon," which like "Journey of the Magi" is narrated by a figure from the New Testament, might be a particularly good choice.

2. In the poem's last stanza, the word "birth" is used eight times and the word "death" nine times. Trace the shifting meanings of the two words and the shifting relationship between them.

3. Read Eliot's essay "For Lancelot Andrewes," which is contained in his volume "Selected Essays." Compare the "conversion" of the Magus to the tenets of the Anglican faith as Eliot expresses them in this essay.

4. Contrast Eliot's poem with the account of the journey in the Gospel of Matthew. How does Eliot deviate from this source? How is his Magus story different in theme from that of the gospel?

5. Read one of Eliot's earliest poems, such as "The Love Song of J. Alfred Prufrock" or "Portrait of a Lady." Compare the alienation of Eliot's earlier protagonists to that of the Magus.

The Love Song of J. Alfred Prufrock

by T. S. Eliot

Content Synopsis

T. S. Eliot's poem is one of the most famous and most influential examples of literary modernism; its publication not only helped launch the career of one of the most important poets of the twentieth century but also helped introduce a completely new way of thinking about and writing poetry. The poem can be (and has been) approached from numerous perspectives (see Blalock 53-83 and McDougal 180-81), and no brief treatment can hope to do it justice. Yet the work's title already suggests the kind of irony that is typical of so much modern verse; the words "love song" suggest a tender, romantic mood that is immediately undercut by the prissy, pompous, slightly ridiculous, and somewhat bourgeois name of "J. Alfred Prufrock." The title is our first indication, then, that Eliot is out to undercut our standard expectations. Another surprise is the Italian epigraph from Dante, the great religious epic poet of the middle ages. Eliot was an immensely learned writer who believed that each individual literary work was necessarily part of a long literary tradition; each work was influenced by tradition and, if successful, in turn helped modify that tradition. "The Love Song," like much modern poetry, greatly depends on allusiveness and implication (see Smith 90-92); rarely is meaning in a modern work explicitly stated or proclaimed. A reader must therefore be able to respond to indirection, connotations, subtle clues, and ambiguous imagery. The quotation from Dante consists of words spoken by

a shameful sinner, trapped in hell, who promises to reveal the details of his life only because he thinks his words will never be repeated on earth and thus ruin his worldly reputation. The epigraph is therefore, like the title, ironic. The serious epic context of the epigraph will seem somewhat grandiloquent in light of the ensuing poem, but the implication that we are entering a kind of private hell and will be addressed by an embarrassed speaker, will be perfectly appropriate. To add to the irony, Prufrock's shame will not stay hidden but will, by the end of the poem, be obvious to every reader (although, to make the irony even tighter, the precise reasons for his shame will never be revealed).

The poem begins abruptly with a simple, clear, first-person invitation, although our impression of simplicity does not last long: "Let us go then, you and I, / When the evening is spread out against the sky / Like a patient etherized upon a table" (1-3). Who, after all, is this "I," and who is the "you" being addressed? Already Eliot is creating a tone of uncertainty and suspense. Perhaps the phrasing alludes to the journey through Hell in the Dante's "Inferno," with Virgil leading Dante on a tour of the underworld. Line 2 introduces a darkening world (through the reference to "evening"), but so far nothing in the poem is especially disturbing. In line 3, however, we first glimpse the kind of startling, unexpected, and even shocking imagery for which the moderns are often known: the evening is now compared to "a patient etherized upon a table." The imagery implies sickness, numbness, dissection—connotations that will later seem perfectly appropriate to the mood and manner of the rest of the work. The irregular line-lengths, the unpredictable rhymes, the deliberately "unromantic" and even depressing urban imagery (as in lines 4-7) all exemplify a "new" kind of poetry intended to do justice to the complexities, uncertainties, and alienation of modern life. The imagery of the opening stanza is anything but glamorous or appealing (for example, "restless nights in one-night cheap hotels" [6]), but it is often vivid, precise, and concrete (for instance, "sawdust restaurants with oyster shells" [7]). Eliot's intention is not so much to state a meaning as to create a mood, and he does this (like many of his modernist successors) not only by relying on memorable images but also through unexpected juxtapositions (as in the reference to an argument that is both "tedious" and "insidious" [8-9]). The narrative structure of the poem is by no means simple or obvious, for just when we are introduced to the idea of an "overwhelming question" (10), our natural curiosity about that question is rebuked and we are implored instead to continue with our mysterious journey. By the end of the opening stanza, it is obvious that in one respect we, as readers, are the "you" of line 1, that the "I" is Prufrock himself, and that we are accompanying him on a tour of the twilight zone of his own disturbed and disturbing psyche.

Because the poem does take us inside of Prufrock's mind, the structure of the work often seems random. The sudden introduction of two lines that at first appear unconnected to anything that has come before—lines that will, however, later be repeated exactly and may thus be more important than they initially appear. "In the room the women come and go / Talking of Michelangelo" (13-14). Here as elsewhere the poem seems to juxtapose the trivial and the profound, implying idle gossip about a great artist but also introducing, for the first time in the work, the topic of women and thus of sexuality—topics that will become increasingly important

as the work proceeds. As Cleanth Brooks notes, Prufrock "is uneasy in the company of women—it may be significant that the original title of the poem was "Prufrock among the Women"—and he is terrified of making a faux pas" (82).

At this point, however, the poem makes another sudden shift: in stanza three the focus turns to "yellow fog" (15), an image presumably implying the air pollution of a large industrial city and thus reinforcing the anti-pastoral tone already established in stanza one. This "yellow smoke" (16) is incongruously (and thus memorably and freshly) described as if it were a relaxed, lazy animal, and although the precise purpose of this passage is by no means clear, it contributes to our sense of moving through a strange, unpredictable world that can be both alluring and disconcerting. Eliot's craft as a poetic musician is especially apparent in this stanza, as he combines, with masterful skill, repeated phrases, alliteration, assonance, simple diction, odd imagery, and heavily emphasized verbs ("Licked," "Lingered," "Let," "Slipped," "Curled" [17-22]). Repetition (which gives the poem an almost hypnotic but also insistent effect) is used with special effectiveness in stanza 4, especially in the obsessively repeated phrase "there will be time" (23, 26, and 28). The irony, of course, is that Prufrock feels he is running out of time; he thinks the time he has already used has been wasted and meaningless, and that the time that lies ahead of him promises only more of the same hypocrisies (27), vacillations (32-33), and middle-class trivialities (34) with which he is so obviously disgusted. The poem is not only a self-indictment of Prufrock's own life but also a condemnation of the superficial life of his whole class, culture, and era. It is, like many another modern poem, an implicit rejection of uninspired, uninspiring modern times.

Prufrock personifies the paralysis, the indecisiveness, the uncertainty, boredom, fragmentation, solipsism, disillusionment, passivity, and isolation that Eliot (and many other modern writers) considered so typical of twentieth-century culture, especially after the shock of the "Great War" (World War I), which destroyed so many lives and so many pre-war illusions about the health of Western civilization. Prufrock is afraid to act ("Do I dare? . . . Do I dare?" [38]), even when the stakes are relatively trivial. He feels old before his time ("With a bald spot in the middle of my hair" [40]). He obsesses about others' opinions ("They will say: 'How his hair is growing thin!'" [41]). He lacks the healthy vigor of a less sophisticated age or class ("They will say: 'But how his arms and legs are thin!'" [44]). He feels trapped in an era in which personal and social times are meaningless, without any larger point or purpose ("I have measured out my life with coffee spoons" [51]). He assumes that other people are mainly indifferent or hostile ("I have known them all already, known them all / The eyes that fix you in a formulated phrase" [55-56]), and he assumes that any independent action on his part will be considered either ill-mannered or presumptuous ("So how should I presume?" [54; see also 61 and 68]). He does seem sexually interested in women ("And I have known the arms already, known them all— / Arms that are braceleted and white and bare / (But in the lamplight, downed with light brown hair!)" [62-64]) but he also seems too timid to act on any sexual impulse. Unable to establish a vital connection with any other person, any higher being, or any larger goal, he wanders through his life as he wanders through the streets of the giant, impersonal metropolis in which he resides. Fearing loneliness but feeling unable to challenge or defeat it (72), he sometimes wishes he could simply disappear or lose his oppressive human self-consciousness (74).

Imagery and themes initially enunciated in the first major portion of the poem are reiterated in the second, where once again a mood of lassitude (77-78) and middle-class comfort (79) is strangely juxtaposed with imagery of odd intensity (80-81) and even Biblical allusiveness (82-83), only to

be undercut with almost bathetic irony (85) and a pathetic confession of fear (86). We are no closer to understanding Prufrock's precise predicament now than we were earlier, and indeed his unwillingness (or inability) to explain himself clearly is part of his reticent, awkward, painfully self-conscious character and reflects his lack of full self-comprehension. He cannot explain himself because he finds it impossible to understand either himself or his circumstances with any clarity or depth. Nevertheless, it increasingly appears that his problem revolves around his relationship with a woman with whom he would like to communicate but from whom he expects no understanding or sympathy (96-98). Some analysts believe that Prufrock wants to propose marriage; others think he instead merely wants to make a sexual proposition. In either case he cannot bring himself to broach the "overwhelming question" (93), fearing that the woman he addresses, after "settling a pillow or throwing off a shawl, / And turning toward the window, should say: / 'That is not it at all, / That is not what I meant, at all'" (107-110). Prufrock's fear of his own inability to explain himself (104) is compounded by his fear of this woman—who seems to know precisely what she thinks, and who is not afraid to say so. By the end of the second major portion of the poem Prufrock seems (and feels) even weaker and more emasculated than before.

Part 3 is the shortest section—as if the poem, like Prufrock himself, is running out of steam and lapsing into quietude. It begins with a strong assertion, but one that is merely negative: "No! I am not Prince Hamlet, nor was meant to be" (111). In the tragicomedy that he thinks his own life has become, Prufrock sees himself as merely a bit player, and an "almost ridiculous" one at that (118). The most daring acts he can imagine himself committing involve wearing his (thinning) hair in a newly fashionable style or running the risk of soiling his clothes by eating a potentially messy fruit (122). The woman who has preoccupied him, on and off, throughout the poem has now dropped out of the picture completely, only to be replaced by mythic, imaginary "mermaids singing, each to each" (124), but Prufrock no sooner mentions these enticing figures than he immediately confesses, "I do not think that they will sing to me" (125). Here as earlier, an appealing or portentous possibility is instantly undercut, and the same pattern is repeated in the poem's final lines, where Prufrock imagines the mermaids "riding seaward on the waves" (126) in a seascape that is both vigorous and energetic (127-28) and appealingly calm (129-30). His dream concludes, however, with ominously abrupt irony: "human voices wake us, and we drown" (131).

Historical Context

Much of the commentary on the historical contexts of Eliot's poem deals with literary history. "Prufrock" has been seen as a rejection of the kind of poetry often favored by the Romantics and Victorians (see Spurr 34-36). The poem is thus self-consciously "new" or "modern"; it represents a deliberate break with the ways of writing and thinking of the immediate past. At the same time, this work (along with Eliot's writings in general) has been seen as being indebted to the "Metaphysical" poets of the seventeenth century, especially Donne—poets whom Eliot admired for their ability to combine profound feeling with complicated thought. Critics have traced echoes or parallels in this poem from such earlier writers as Dante, Dostoevsky, Laforgue, Marvell, and Shakespeare (to mention just a few), and almost everyone who writes about the poem would agree that the more one knows the history of Western literature (including the Bible), the better one can appreciate the subtleties of Eliot's art. However, a knowledge of broader kinds of history can also help us better understand this poem. Although Eliot began writing the poem before the First World War, it was first published during the war and had its greatest impact in the years and decades immediately

following that cataclysm. World War I is usually considered a major turning point in the history of Western civilization. It was the first "modern" war, fought with weapons that represented the very latest in technological advances (such as machine guns, battleships, airplanes, tanks, poison gas, etc.). It was a particularly destructive war, and it was fought for reasons that seemed (especially later) to make no great sense. The war thus came to be viewed as symbolic of the worst aspects of modern civilization, and Eliot's poem can be read as a both a symptom of, and a protest against, the sicknesses of modern life—particularly its moods of alienation, ugliness, and loss of ultimate meanings. Thus, if "Prufrock" is one of the first modern poems, it is also one of the first (and best) indictments of the modern age. It was an age that seemed, to Eliot and many of his contemporaries, a shallow, feckless, materialistic era that lacked any sense of higher purpose or meaning.

Societal Context

Societal Contexts are obviously among the most important aspects of this poem. Although the work takes us inside the mind of Prufrock, it also offers a chilling depiction of the alienating society he inhabits. The poem focuses especially on the kinds of large, impersonal cities that were becoming increasingly common in Eliot's day—cities such as St. Louis (where he grew up), Boston (where he attended college), Paris (where he visited), and London (where he eventually came to reside). Aspects of all these cities are arguably reflected in the poem, and in fact, in an earlier manuscript of the lyric, the emphasis on urban life was even stronger than in the work as it presently stands. The poem offers glimpses of the urban poor (as in the reference to "lonely men in shirt-sleeves, leaning out of windows" [72]), but its main focus is on the upper- or upper-middle class society into which Eliot himself was born and with which he would have been most personally familiar. His depiction of that society is hardly flattering: its way of life revolves around empty chitchat, superficial interactions, self-conscious pretension, surface politeness combined with backstabbing gossip, and, in general, an utter lack of authenticity, compassion, or deep affection. It is a society that emphasizes proper appearance and conventional behavior over real or sincere engagement—a society so over-refined that it has lost touch with any kind of true vitality. The mermaids who enter the poem in its closing lines seem to symbolize the kind of natural beauty and mythic power that are otherwise so lacking in Prufrock's environment, but the mermaids (after all) are mere fictions, mere figments of Prufrock's imagination. Even his brief dream of them cannot last, and in the final line of the work he feels suffocated not by literal death but by a return to the lifeless, meaningless society—the metaphorical hell—in which he feels condemned to spend his days. The mermaids are the enchanting (but illusory) antitheses of the forbidding, distant, unsympathetic women with whom he normally interacts, and one of the clearest indications that Prufrock is not only personally handicapped but is living in a stunted society is the fact that he never seems able to establish a genuine connection with the women around him. To them he is simply an object of pity, amusement, and condescending gossip. If Prufrock is at all typical or symbolic of modern man, then the future of modern society (at least in the diagnosis offered by this poem) seems bleak.

Religious Context

The importance of religious contexts to "Prufrock" is obvious from the opening epigraph from Dante, and that importance is later reinforced by the obvious allusion to the biblical John the Baptist (82-83) and from the even more explicit reference to the biblical "Lazarus" (94, although scholars have debated about which of the two Lazaruses mentioned in the Bible is primarily meant). In later years, Eliot would become more and more prominently identified with a conservative brand of Christianity, but even in this very early poem one senses his dissatisfaction

with the spiritual sterility of modern life. Prufrock is rootless and alienated, cut off from belief in any higher purpose or higher being that might give his life a sense of meaning or direction. He wanders through "narrow streets" (70) that symbolize the narrowness of his own (and his culture's) existence and vision. He speaks mysteriously and repeatedly of an "overwhelming question" (10, 93), but he seems to lack any explicit interest in the largest questions that have preoccupied religious thinkers in all times and places. Rather than seeing Prufrock as a particularly neurotic or peculiarly stunted individual, it seems better to view him as Eliot probably did: as a typical product of a modern era that was fast losing its grounding in the accepted truths of Western Christianity. Prufrock is a symptom of the spiritual decay of his time; like the speaker of the opening epigraph, he is confined to a kind of hell, but to a hell that was now merely metaphorical and no longer accepted as reflecting literal truth.

Scientific & Technological Context

Although science and technology are not strongly emphasized in "Prufrock," they are present by implication. The opening image of a "patient etherized upon a table" (3) is one of the most obvious and most memorable examples of scientific, technological imagery. In addition, the later reference to "yellow smoke" (16) also suggests the air pollution that was one of the most obvious results of modern technology and the Industrial Revolution, which had come to dominate modern culture, especially in the ever-growing cities. The references to "cheap hotels" (6) and "sawdust restaurants" (7) also imply this process of increasing urbanization, as do the references to "chimneys" (19) and "terrace[s]" (20). One of the most startling and unforgettable of all the scientific images in the poem appears when Prufrock imagines himself "sprawling on a pin, / . . . pinned and wriggling on the wall" (57-58), as if he were an insect scrutinized by an entomologist. Later Prufrock refers to a recent technological innovation: a "magic lantern," which he imagines as being capable of throwing his "nerves in patterns on a screen" (105). Here as in the reference to being "etherized" or "pinned," science is not presented in the most attractive terms; it is associated with forces that are deadening, dirtying, and desiccating. Because Eliot associated science and technology with industrialism and with the rise of modern, mass, urban civilization, it is not surprising that the few explicit or implied references to such contexts in this poem are not particularly appealing.

Biographical Context

Eliot (1888-1965) was born into a prominent, wealthy family in St. Louis—a family with strong connections, in turn, to leading families in Boston, where Eliot attended college at Harvard. By personal background and by education, then, the poet was himself quite familiar with the kind of superficially "polite" bourgeois society he mocks in this poem, and indeed some analysts have seen in Prufrock a reflection of Eliot's own insecurities, anxieties, self-disgust, and lack of self-confidence. One prominent critic to the regimented demands in particular, has even related "Prufrock," on Eliot's time that the poet himself faced as a student (Kenner 22). Eliot himself disdained biographical approaches to poetry in general and to his own poetry in particular, arguing that the best poetry is impersonal. However, this attitude on Eliot's part has not discouraged biographical readings of his works, and in fact, his attempts to discourage such readings have often incited them. In any case, poems such as "Prufrock" clearly reflect Eliot's own interest in writing a new kind of poetry—a poetry that would be the antithesis of the softness, sentimentality, and excessive emotionalism he disliked in bad Romantic verse and that would also stand opposed to the oracular, stilted pomposity he associated with too many bad imitators of Milton. Instead, Eliot sought to write a kind of poetry that would be full of irony, ambiguity, wit, and unsentimental precision, especially in the use of imagery

often taken from mundane, unexpected, or "unpoetic" contexts. The life of any great writer is influenced at least as much by what he reads as by what he does, and surely, this is true in the case of T.S. Eliot. "Prufrock" reflects Eliot's reading not only of all the sources to which he obviously alludes in the poem, but also of all the kinds of writers—including the English metaphysicists, the Jacobean dramatists, the French symbolists, the modern imagists—he admired and sought to imitate. The poem also reflects his personal conviction that Western civilization, in the early twentieth century, had reached a point combining crisis and sterility, and that poetry could best help renew its culture (if such renewal were possible at all) by honestly and unflinchingly diagnosing the modern condition rather than ignoring or denying its ills. Prufrock himself proclaims that he is "no prophet" and that his poem deals with "no great matter" (83), but Eliot himself would have seen his own role as partly prophetic, and he would have seen the underlying subject of his poem as "great matter" indeed. Eliot is a prophet in the sense that he seeks to speak unpleasant but important truths to a society that may not want to hear or listen. Eliot did not see the role of the poet as simply to amuse or entertain; instead, he saw the poet as being chiefly obliged to speak honestly, freshly, and compellingly to an audience that had largely lost sight of (and interest in) the serious purposes of life.

Robert C. Evans, Ph.D.

Works Cited

Blalock, Susan E. *Guide to the Secular Poetry of T.S. Eliot*. New York: G.K. Hall, 1996.

Brooks, Cleanth. "Teaching 'The Love Song of J. Alfred Prufrock.'" *Approaches to Teaching Eliot's Poetry and Plays*. Ed. Jewel Spears Brooker. New York: Modern Language Association, 1988. 78-87.

Eliot, T.S. "The Love Song of J. Alfred Prufrock." *The Norton Anthology of English Literature*. Ed. M.H. Abrams and Stephen Greenblatt. 7th ed.

2 vols. New York: W.W. Norton, 2000. 2: 2364-2367.

Kenner, Hugh. *The Mechanic Muse.* New York: Oxford University Press, 1987.

McDougal, Stuart Y. "T.S. Eliot." *Sixteen Modern American Authors. Volume 2: A Survey of Research and Criticism since 1972.* Ed. Jackson R. Breyer. Durham, NC: Duke UP, 1990. 154-209.

Smith, Grover. "'Prufrock' as Key to Eliot's Poetry." *Approaches to Teaching Eliot's Poetry and Plays.* Ed. Jewel Spears Brooker. New York: Modern Language Association, 1988. 88-93.

Spurr, David. "Eliot, Modern Poetry, and the Romantic Tradition." *Approaches to Teaching Eliot's Poetry and Plays.* Ed. Jewel Spears Brooker. New York: Modern Language Association, 1988. 33-38.

Discussion Questions

1. How does the use of such words as "you," "us," and "our" contribute to the poem's effectiveness?
2. How is the lack of a regular, predictable stanzaic pattern appropriate to a poem such as this?
3. What do the various kinds of repetition—especially of images and phrases—suggest about the nature of Prufrock's mind or psychology?
4. What attitude, or combination of attitudes, does the poem encourage us to take toward Prufrock? How sympathetic should our responses to him be?
5. Discuss the attitudes toward women implied by this poem.
6. What are some particular examples of phrasing in this poem that suggest the specific social class of Prufrock and his acquaintances?
7. What are some ways in which the poem creates in its readers some of the same sense of frustration, uncertainty, indecision, and suspense felt by the speaker?
8. The epigraph that opens the poem implies that Prufrock is in a kind of hell. What are some specific ways in which his experience seems hellish?
9. In what ways does Prufrock resemble Shakespeare's Hamlet, and in what ways does he not?
10. Which images in this poem do you find most effective, and why?

Essay Ideas

1. Read a detailed biography of Eliot and discuss this poem in relation to the poet's own life.
2. Read a detailed history of Europe and America in the first two decades of the twentieth century and discuss this poem in relation to the life of that era.
3. Using a basic introduction to literary theory, discuss this poem from at least three different theoretical perspectives (for instance, archetypal, feminist, and Marxist).
4. Compare and contrast this poem with a similar work, such as Philip Larkin's "Aubade."
5. Study the meaning of literary "modernism" and discuss the ways in which this is a "modernist" poem.

Luke Havergal

by Edwin Arlington Robinson

Content Synopsis

Written in iambic pentameter, this four-stanza poem opens with the speaker telling Luke Havergal to "Go to the western gate" (1) where the crimson leaves hang from the vine, and wait and for "what will come" (3). The speaker tells Luke Havergal that if he listens there, "she," presumably Havergal's deceased lover, "will call" (6). Lines 1 and 7 repeat "Go to the western gate, Luke Havergal."

In stanza 2, the speaker tells the speaker that there is "no dawn in eastern skies to rift the fiery night that's in your eyes" (9). However, at the western gate, the "dark will end the dark." Even God "slays himself" and "hell is more than half of paradise" at the western gate.

The speaker reveals in stanza three that he has come "out of the grave" to talk to Luke Havergal (17). The speaker tells him that there is only "one way to where she is" and if he has faith, he cannot miss (21-22).

The final stanza revisits the first and the speaker tells Luke Havergal to "Go to the western gate" (25). He tells him to go before the crimson leaves are blown away and if he listens, "she will call" (30).

Symbols & Motifs

The western gate clearly represents the barrier between life and death. The speaker tells Luke Havergal that if he goes to the gate, he will hear his love call, however, he does not tell Luke Havergal to go through the gate to the other side. It is unclear whether the speaker is beckoning Luke Havergal to commit suicide or simply to confront his lover's death and find closure (Adams).

The crimson leaves that hang from the vine have a symbolic significance as red is a potent color symbol. The color may represent sin or sacrifice, as it is the color of blood, or it may represent love. Further, because leaves turn red they fall and die, the fact that the speaker tells Luke Havergal to go to the western gate before the leaves blow away suggests that the opportunity to connect with his dead love is likewise ephemeral.

Historical Context

"Luke Havergal" does not have a specific historical context.

Societal Context

Although he lived during the rise of modernism, Edwin Arlington Robinson used to more traditional forms and styles and is considered a Romantic poet. Romantics believed in the power of intuition and emotion over rational thought, and this belief is reflected in "Luke Havergal" as its speaker is a voice from another world who advises the title character to go to the western gate to hear his dead lover's call. Robinson's poetry delivered an atmosphere of mysticism and gloom, a reflection of what appeared to be his rather joyless life (Ellman and O'Clair 211). In a short span of time, from 1893 to 1899, Robinson lost his parents and his siblings and was twice refused by the woman he loved.

Religious Context

"Luke Havergal" does not have a specific religious context except that it acknowledges a belief in life after death. The speaker comes "out of the grave" to tell Luke that his love will "call" if he goes to the western gate, assuming that her spirit can communicate with the living. Robinson was not a Christian, and he insisted that there was no "philosophy" in his work (Ellman and O'Clair 211).

Scientific & Technological Context

"Luke Havergal" does not have a specific scientific or technological context.

Biographical Context

Edwin Arlington Robinson was born in 1869 in Head Tide, Maine and lived in the town of Gardiner until age 27 (Beers and Probst 644). Robinson based the town of Tilbury, which frequently appeared in his poems, on Gardiner (644). His father, Edward, was a successful lumber merchant and politician. A shy and quiet child, Robinson was fascinated with words and spent much time trying to find and learn new and difficult ones (Smith). At a young age, he realized that he wanted to be a poet and was tutored by a neighbor, Dr. Alanson Schumann (Smith). In 1890, Robinson's brother Herman married Emma Shepherd, the woman whom Robinson himself had hoped to marry. This love triangle is believed to have influenced his poetry for years to come (Smith). After high school, Robinson attended Harvard University, but he was forced to drop out and return to Gardiner as his family's finances began to decline (Smith).

His father died in 1893, and he lost his mother in 1896, just before the publication of his first book, "The Torrent and the Night Before" (Smith). In 1899, his brother Dean died of an overdose. Herman became an alcoholic after his business failed, and he, too, died a short time later. Robinson's most famous poem "Richard Cory" is suspected to be based on Herman's life (Smith).

At age 27, he moved to New York City to pursue his career as a writer. There, he revised "The Torrent and the Night Before" into the book, "The Children of the Night," which became his first commercial publication (Smith). He worked odd jobs for a year, then President Theodore Roosevelt, a fan of his poetry, offered him a job as a clerk in the New York Custom House (Beers and Probst 644). Robinson worked there for five years, until the end of Roosevelt's term. His next volume of poetry, "The Town Down the River" was published in 1910, and he dedicated it to Roosevelt (644).

In 1911, Robinson was invited to join the MacDowell Colony, artists' colony in Peterborough, New Hampshire, for working writers, artists, and composers. He continued to spend his summers at the MacDowell Colony until his death in 1935 (Beers and Probst 644). Robinson's traditional poetry became quite popular despite the growth of Modernism during his lifetime (644). He won the Pulitzer Prize three times.

Jennifer Bouchard

Works Cited

Adams, Richard P. "The Failure of Edwin Arlington Robinson." *TSE: Tulane Studies in English*. Vol. 11 (1961): 97-51.

Beers, Kylene and Robert Probst, eds. *Elements of Literature: Fifth Course, Literature of the United States*. Austin: Holt, Rinehart and Winston, 2003. 409-417.

Ellman, Richard and Robert O'Clair, Ed. *The Norton Anthology of Modern Poetry*. 2nd Ed. New York: W.W. Norton and Company, 1988. 210-213.

Robinson, Edwin Arlington. "Luke Havergal." *The Norton Anthology of Modern Poetry*. 2nd Ed. New York: W.W. Norton and Company, 1988. 210-213.

Smith, Danny D. "Biography of Edwin Arlington Robinson." Gardiner Public Library. 29 April 2009. <http://www.earobinson.com/pages/HisLife.html>.

Discussion Questions

1. How would you describe tone of the poem?
2. Who is the speaker of the poem?
3. What is the effect of the repetition in the poem? What purpose does it serve?
4. Do you find irony in the poem?
5. What are the main themes of the poem?
6. What images are used in the poem? And why do you think Robinson chose them?
7. Why do you think the speaker wants Luke Havergal to go to the western gate?

Essay Ideas

1. Read a few of Robinson's other poems, and write an essay in which you describe and analyze Robinson's poetic style.
2. Compare this poem to others that deal with the death of a loved one. Compare and contrast the poems in terms of style, tone, symbolism, and theme.
3. Write a poem in which you approach the subject of death from the perspective of the living.
4. Write a poem in which you approach the subject of death from the perspective of the dead.

Metaphors

by Sylvia Plath

Content Synopsis

"Metaphors," an early poem by Sylvia Plath, dates back to 1959, one year before "Colossus," the collection that established her as a serious new poet, was published. Like other early poems such as "Lorelei," "Full Fathom Five," or "Suicide off Egg Rock," "Metaphors" impresses readers with its clever formal technique and precise use of language.

Take Plath's choice of genre, for instance. "Metaphors" belongs to a type of poetry known as Riddle poems. Riddle poems, found in almost all cultures, are built on the fundamental referential power of language, or the power of a word, or groups of words to call into the listener's mind, other related words, or concepts. Riddle poems achieve this transference of meaning through the creative use of rhetorical tropes such as metaphor, metonymy, simile, synecdoche, and precise, pithy, concrete imagery. Like Haiku and other short poetic forms, riddle poems aim to say more with less, ranging between 9 and 15 lines, each line usually no more than nine syllables, with an internal beat that functions as a rhyme when rhyme is absent, and plenty of assonance and alliteration. Here is an example from the "Red Book of Exeter," an Anglo-Saxon anthology of riddles, over a thousand years old: "A wonder on the wave / Water became bone." The answer to this riddle is, of course, "Ice on a lake or seashore." Riddle poets build their riddles around a unique, arresting, central image. They often extend or embellish this image by ascribing more elaborate and surprising attributes and associations to the subject of the riddle. The rule of a good riddle poem, however, requires that all images collectively should point only towards one correct answer, which is the subject of the riddle. The listener of the riddle, in turn, decodes these images and discovers the answer. The subject of riddle poems can be what we traditionally consider an abstract entity: an emotion such as "love" or "fear," or a concrete object, such as a fruit, vegetable or animal.

"Metaphors" begins with Plath providing a metaphoric clue to the riddle's answer: "I am a riddle in nine syllables" (1). This refers both to the syllabic form of this riddle poem as well as the first item in a list of clues that will help solve the riddle. "Nine" here refers to both the nine syllables that make up the first line, as well as the nine months of pregnancy. Right at the outset of the poem, Plath focuses on the physical changes brought about by pregnancy. By following Plath as she builds the riddle of pregnancy, we arrive at an understanding of Plath's complex attitude towards the subject of pregnancy itself.

The speaker in the poem begins her discussion of being pregnant by describing herself as "an elephant," and "a ponderous house" (2). While the image of an "elephant" refers to an obvious weight gain as a condition of pregnancy, it also brings with it unflattering associations of slow and difficult gait, and an overall sense of a largeness that is somewhat distressing to the speaker, a normal experience for most pregnant women. An elephant is also a large object that you cannot ignore; it cannot be hidden or concealed, just as pregnancy cannot be hidden or concealed. The next image, however, is rather unique, and shows the tension between traditional wisdom and a rebellious psyche that animates much of Plath's poetry. The speaker who describes herself as an "elephant," also equates herself to a "ponderous house." Like "elephant," "ponderous" has unseemly connotations of corpulence, boredom and fatigue; like an elephant, a house cannot be concealed either. However, the noun it modifies is "house," a word that suddenly and surprisingly introduces a note of concern for the welfare of the child. The speaker sees herself as a shelter for the child growing inside her.

The speaker uses the image of "A melon strolling on two tendrils" (3), a comical, even ridiculous image, to describe the pregnancy that has deformed her body. Here again, we can see how this seemingly self-deprecating image of a woman reduced to her protruding stomach supported by fragile tendril-like legs contains within it a natural metaphor of fruition. The melon fruit is the most valuable part of the plant and a plant with no fruit is a useless, failed plant. The size and weight attributes introduced with "elephant" and "house," and here expanded in the contrasting image of a melon strolling on tendrils also draw our attention to the incongruous picture of a small woman trying to support a pregnant stomach that is too big for her slight frame.

The fourth line "O red fruit, ivory, fine timbers!" (4) consolidates in a simple list form the metaphoric fruits of labor described in the first three lines. Metaphors of pregnancy use the word "labor" to describe the final stage of pregnancy where the mother pushes the child out of her body.

Just as a child is the "fruit" of its mother's "labor," the "red fruit" in this line is the fruit of the melon, its most valuable part, and the "ivory" is the most valuable part of the elephant, and "fine timbers" stands for the "house" (2) that sheltered the child for nine months. By listing the most valuable part of a melon, an elephant, and a house, Plath moves away from metaphor to metonymy: naming a thing by describing with what it is most commonly associated. The speaker moves away from listing her personal experience of pregnancy-the swelling, the largeness, the deformity-to persuade us of the fruits of such a labor. With all the distresses named, pregnancy produces something valuable. Pregnancy confirms value to the mother.

In "This loaf is big with its yeasty rising" (5), the speaker once again takes up the motif of the process of confirming value to an object by transforming it, by helping it become its most useful self. A pregnant woman is a loaf of bread that is rising; unleavened bread is not a source of pleasure or value. The next line "Money's new-minted in this fat purse" (6) is the most concrete image of pregnancy as an economic role and destiny for women. The various images up to this point all suggested the body of the mother as a raw material that has the potential to produce something of great value: the child. In this metaphor of the mother and child, newly minted money in a fat purse, we find this economic relation in its most eloquent and surprising incarnation.

If the image of the "ponderous house" (2) suggests shelter it also reminds readers of the inevitable event of children leaving their parents' house. The birth of a child, its expulsion from the mother's body prefigures a greater leaving, that of children transitioning into adulthood and autonomy of their own. Thus the idea that the mother's body is a shelter for the child, a "house" (2), also introduces the idea of the lack of permanence associated with a house. Such a transitory experience is coded into the line "I am a means, a stage, a cow in calf" (7), when the speaker presents herself as a threshold, a temporary stage, a liminal space for the child on its way to becoming a discrete self. The mother is a "means," a path, a tool, a "stage" in the life cycle of the child, or a "stage" where the great drama of creation in being enacted. The metaphor of motherhood unites these two images with the concrete image of a "cow in calf."

The metaphoric clues share in the folklore of pregnancy in the line "I've eaten a bag of green apples" (8). Here, the speaker refers to the strange cravings of pregnancy. "Apples" of course, have a poetic resonance all of their own, which might fit this poem as well. The human drama of birth and death in western theology starts with the fall of Adam and Eve after Eve eats the forbidden apple from the Tree of Knowledge. Certain theological traditions believe that God expelled Adam and Eve from the Garden of Eden for fear that they might eat of the Tree of Life, the fruit of which confers immortality to those who partake of it. In blending associations of the forbidden fruit with procreation, Plath seems to be hinting at pregnancy and birth as the human way to achieve immortality.

If we sensed ambivalence in the speaker about the experience of her pregnancy thus far, the concluding line of the poem makes this tension powerfully audible. In "Boarded the train there's no getting off" (9) the speaker concludes her discussion of pregnancy as a journey that once commenced could not be stopped. The tension between pleasure and pride in being a proud worker producing a valuable product, the child, and the complementary feeling of being trapped by the child growing within her is most palpable in this line.

Formal Qualities

Plath was gifted in the craft of poetry and even in an early poem like "Metaphors," there is evidence of great formal control. The poem is a controlled exercise in number 9, which is the number of months in the duration of a human pregnancy, and the unifying theme of the poem. "Metaphors" is a riddle poem written in nine lines of nine syllables each. The first word of the poem "I" is the ninth letter of the alphabet, and the word "pregnancy" has nine letters. Each line is a metaphor for pregnancy, with pregnancy being the riddle, and its clues drawn from domains as different as nature, biology, architecture, economics, travel, and cooking. Plath's early poems show her experimenting with irregular and esoteric rhyme schemes, but "Metaphors" has an internal rhythm rising out of assonance, an example of which is the repetition of the leisurely, long /i/ sound. Perhaps the most obvious clue to the riddle is "I've eaten a bag of green apples" (8), the word "green" conjuring up images of an unnatural gustatory preference, often associated with the strange food cravings of pregnancy.

"Metaphors" is an early example of what was to become Plath's major achievement in her later, mature poems: finding her authentic voice, and to write, "What I really feel" (Kendall 9). In her journals, Plath admitted to feeling constrained and inhibited by the strict verse forms that she used for her compositions, and observed that "my main thing now is to start with real things: real emotions [. . .] and get into me, Ted, friends, mother and brother and father and family" (Kendall 9). As a contemporary reviewer remarked "I am struck, in reading a lot of her poems together, by her posture vis-à-vis her material which is one of considerable objectivity, even when the material is her childhood, her Muses, her pregnancy" (Wagner-Martin 31). "Metaphors," with its artful control of the metaphoric structure, successfully combines technique with emotional complexity, private thoughts with public concerns, theme with form.

Interpretations

In "Metaphors," we see a poet trying to resolve conflicting emotions towards pregnancy and motherhood. Each metaphor evokes images that are self-deprecating, judgmental, and rebellious all at the same time. The confusion within the speaker as to whether pregnancy is the natural fulfillment of her destiny as a woman is ultimately due to the received wisdom of the Fifties, which predicated a woman's success on how well she fit the conventional roles of a wife and mother. The most compelling oppositions in the poem are between what the speaker describes as her destiny to be "a means," "a stage" (7) for her child to come into being. The poem leaves us with a sense of helplessness on behalf of the speaker, who seems to perceive and articulate an authentic dissatisfaction with her ascribed role as a procreator, and yet, does not see any way out of it. When perceived in this light, the riddle and the answer to the riddle are more complicated than what the metaphors suggest; for the speaker, and perhaps for the poet as well, the riddle has no clear-cut answer.

Historical Context

When asked if she addressed historical concerns in her poetry, Plath observed that "the issues of our time which preoccupy me at the moment are the incalculable genetic effects of fallout and a documentary on the terrifying, mad, omnipotent marriage of the big business and Military in America [. . .]. Does this influence the kind of poetry I write? Yes, but in a sidelong fashion" (Kendall 170). Plath has been linked with the confessional school of poetry of the late 50's. She has also been linked with such names as Robert Lowell and Anne Sexton, who wrote largely autobiographical poems, revealing personal details and building private symbols with a candidness that was in direct opposition to the "impersonality" theory of poetry that characterized much of the poetic output of the first half of the twentieth century. Images of the holocaust, of the Nazi death camps, the Napoleonic wars, the Pilgrim fathers and Ku Klux Klan figure in Plath's poems, but mainstream Plath criticism tends to agree that Plath used historical events

and details in a confessional manner for emotional effect, and not to engage with the issues of such events themselves. Plath herself commented that her "poems do not turn out to be about Hiroshima, but about a child forming itself finger by finger in the dark" (Kendall 170).

It is possible, however, to see that Plath dealt with history with a small "h," women's history, to be exact, in a manner that was shockingly unique for a "tranquil fifties" poet. "Metaphors," is a good example of such an engagement. Pregnancy was not a celebrated theme for poetry, specifically, the gross, unflattering portrayal of the woman's body, or the suggestion that pregnancy and motherhood deformed the female body. Perhaps equally shocking was the unspoken question in the poem: are pregnancy and motherhood a woman's destiny? Plath died before the very public social and cultural revolutions of the Sixties, but asking or hinting at such questions places Plath, a largely private poet, at the cusp of an era of noninvolvement ending and the birth of a new social order. The sense of being trapped in a destiny that is ineluctable, pregnancy and motherhood, the metaphor of being on a train of which there is no getting off (9) is the anguish of a poet, who sees an era ending, but does not see a new one beginning.

Societal Context

Following on the heels of World War II, the Fifties saw the official inauguration of the Cold War between the Western bloc and the Soviet bloc with the invasion of South Korea by North Korea and the partition of Vietnam into two countries based on political ideology. In the U.S, the fifties was a decade of optimism and cheerful self-confidence, at least for mainstream America. After the Great Depression and World War II, Americans were largely in favor of settling down and stability, and this decade saw the "nuclear family" firmly entrenched in popular imagination as an economic and ideological unit.

In particular, American women, who were largely liberated from their domestic roles during the War years, found themselves pushed back to the traditional role of being a wife and mother, a subservient partner to the man, who was the head of the nuclear family. This was the "baby boom" generation. "Metaphors" highlights the thinly veiled dissatisfaction of a woman who cannot decide whether motherhood fulfills her destiny or merely entraps her. The metaphors in the poem capture a woman at a transitional moment in her life; she is on her way to becoming a mother. However, the images mix pleasure with anguish; a sense of doom reverberates in the last line: "Boarded the train there is no getting off" (9).

As with Emily Dickinson, another poet who was born ahead of her times, Plath too achieved critical and popular acclaim posthumously. Although she wrote serene and playful poems about her children and Nature, a large part of her woman-centered poems deals primarily with candid and largely pessimistic details of her personal life. Moreover, they deal with her relationship with a tyrannical and emotionally unavailable father, a placid bond with a traditional mother, her whirlwind courtship and marriage to the English poet Ted Hughes, her expatriate life in England, her bouts of depression and institutionalization, her anxieties over her creative power, the dissolution of her marriage, her husband's adultery, and her suicide attempts. What Plath shares with her contemporaries in the confessional school of poetry of the fifties is her choice of this material for her poetry; but in her poems, she manages her autobiography with passion and detachment at the same time. In a decade that sought to restore "normalcy" in social and familial structures, with patriarchy and segregation taking their last gasps before the civil rights activism of the Sixties, Plath's poems proved to be difficult fare for ordinary readers.

Thus, "Metaphors" engages with the social issues of the day in a "sidelong fashion" as Plath herself remarked (Kendall 170). A riddle poem about pregnancy becomes a vehicle to raise questions about the identity of women itself.

Religious Context

Sylvia Plath was born and brought up in the Unitarian faith, but she became interested in both Anglicanism as well as Judaism towards the end of her life. In her largely autobiographical novel "The Bell Jar," Plath's heroine Esther Greenwood speaks for Plath's own religious beliefs when she expresses her disbelief in "life after death or the virgin birth or the Inquisition or the infallibility of that little monkey-faced Pope" (Kendall 115). If there is one recurring religious motif throughout Plath's poem, it is the pitting of a specific theology against maternal love. In such poems as "Nick and the Candlestick," we see a mother's anguished concern for a child who is defenseless against the world with its numerous dangers, including "piranha/Religion" (Kendall 124).

"Metaphors" with its insistence on procreation and birth invests woman, mother, with the creative power of a God. By aligning herself to the natural cycle of creation, through such metaphors as "red fruit," (4) and devoting a poem to the "riddle" of conception and birth, "Metaphors" appears to pose a challenge to organized theology. "Metaphors" does not provide us with a complete religious picture the way a later poem such as "Mary's Song" does; the vision of creation it paints is fraught with anguish expressed in the metaphor of pregnancy as a journey, or "Boarded the train there's no getting off" (9).

Scientific & Technological Context

References to science and technology in Plath's poetry are largely unflattering; in "Lady Lazarus," for instance, the speaker offers her body to Nazi doctors/torturers as their "opus." Plath also spoke out against nuclear fallout, and what she saw as the militarization of American culture in the 50s with its nuclear deterrence program (see Historical Context above). "Metaphors" does not show much evidence of science or technology issues, though, as in all her poems, the precision of Plath's metaphors point towards her keen powers of observation, and an empirical bend of mind. The "fine timbers" of the house (4), the melon supported by the fragile tendrils (3), and the loaf big with yeasty rising (5) are examples of domestic science, appropriate for the able housewife, perhaps the persona in the poem.

Biographical Context

Sylvia Plath was born in Boston in 1932, the oldest child of Otto Plath, a German immigrant, who taught zoology and German at Boston University, and Aurelia Plath, an educated Austrian immigrant, who was content to be a homemaker. Plath's father, who figures prominently in many of Plath's poems, was a brilliant scholar and an unavailable father, while Plath's bond with her mother seems to have been an unremarkable one, at least in her early years. When Plath was eight years old, Otto Plath died of an untreated gangrene of diabetic origin. Her mother undertook secretarial work to support the family while encouraging Sylvia to be an exceptional student.

Plath excelled in her studies and won a scholarship to the prestigious Smith College after graduating from Wellesley High School. She earned her master's degree in English Literature from Cambridge University in England, which she attended on a Fulbright scholarship. Plath met the English poet Ted Hughes (who later became the poet laureate of England) at Cambridge and after a whirlwind romance married him.

After a brief stay in the U.S., the couple moved permanently back to Devon, England, in 1959, when "Metaphors" was written. Plath's literary career had an early start with a prize-winning story, "Sunday at the Mintons" (1952) in the "Mademoiselle" fiction contest. While acting as a secretary to her husband's poetic work, Plath was determined to establish herself in a career of writing. "Metaphors" written in England in 1959 was probably composed at the outset of Plath's first pregnancy; her daughter, Freida, was born in 1960, also the year that saw the publication of her first book of collected poems "The Colossus." Many of the poems in "The Colossus" revolve around Plath's characteristic concerns as a poet; a thematic preference for the inner lives of women, fear and paranoia of the external world, the horrifying lessons of history, men who control and manipulate women, doubts about self-worth, and above it all, the creative assertion of the self and the poet's ego. Plath was an ambitious poet obsessed with perfecting her poetic voice.

"Metaphors" is a woman-centered poem that embodies Plath's characteristic self-doubt. Questions about identity loom at the forefront of this poem where through a series of surprising metaphors, Plath persuades us to question the uses of pregnancy and motherhood for women, in their journey to define themselves. It is an unapologetic list of distresses and doubts commonly "felt" by most pregnant women, but rarely articulated, for fear of disturbing the sacred image of motherhood. A woman who complains about her pregnancy could not possibly be a reliable mother. That is what Plath's speaker sets out to do in an almost playful fashion in this poem: casting herself in a comical light, calling herself an "elephant," (2) "a melon," (3) which hides her dissatisfaction at the distress caused to her body by the pregnancy.

Plath left her marriage with Ted Hughes in 1962, after discovering his affair with another woman. She wrote the most disturbing and brilliant poems in the last year of her life, often writing at night after her children were in bed. On February 11, 1963, in her thirtieth year, after making sure that her children would not be harmed, she turned on the gas in the kitchen oven, stuck her head inside, and killed herself.

It is a truism to say that writers plumb their lives for creative material. Plath did not conceal her private grief from her readers; however, she managed this grief without sentimentality and solipsism, but with an ear to the latent music of all scenes of melancholy. The formal control that animates "Metaphor" from its first word "I" to the last shocking image of a train-trap governs the best and most mature of Plath's poems. We read them to learn how to ask questions of this monster, grief.

Gayatri Devi, Ph.D.

Works Cited

Bassnett, Susan. *Sylvia Plath*. Towata, NJ: Barnes & Noble, 1987.

Kendall, Tom. *Sylvia Plath: A Critical Study*. London: Faber & Faber, 2001.

Meyering, Sheryl L. *Sylvia Plath: A Reference Guide*. Boston: G. K. Hall, 1990.

Newman, Charles. H., Ed. *The Art of Sylvia Plath: A Symposium*. Bloomington: Illinois UP, 1970.

Wagner, Linda W. Critical Essays on Sylvia Plath. Boston: G. K. Hall & Co., 1984.

Discussion Questions

1. Identify the tenor and vehicle for all the metaphors in the poem. Map the exact attribute for each metaphor used by Plath in this poem.
2. What is the speaker's attitude towards her body in "Metaphors"?
3. What is the theme of "Metaphors"? Where in the poem did the theme become apparent to you?
4. Why do you think Plath titled this poem "Metaphors"?
5. What is the speaker's attitude towards pregnancy in this poem?
6. What is the tone of this poem? To whom do you think the poem is addressed?
7. Write five new metaphors for pregnancy in the manner of metaphors used by Plath.
8. Would you consider pregnancy and childbirth riddles? Why or why not? Why does Plath consider her pregnancy to be a riddle?
9. Compare "Metaphors" with "Barren." What inferences can you make about Plath's attitude towards motherhood as evidenced in these two poems?
10. What does "Boarded a train there's no getting off" mean in this poem?

Essay Ideas

1. Would you consider "Metaphors" to be a woman-centered poem? Why? If not, why? Support your position with close reading and interpretation of the poem.
2. Identify the source and target domains used by Plath to create her metaphors for pregnancy. Now using the same domains, try creating your own metaphors for motherhood. Write these metaphors of motherhood out as complete statements and explain their meaning to us. Summarize the tonal quality of these metaphors and show us what your list of metaphors tells us about your attitude towards motherhood.
3. According to "Metaphors," is pregnancy and motherhood a choice for women? Are women free to choose or are they not free to choose? What does the poem seem to suggest on this issue? Support your answer with close reading and interpretation of the poem.
4. What does the poem "Metaphors" tell you about poetry as a form and its capabilities? Is "Metaphors" a good and able representative of the genre of poetry? If yes, why? If no, why? Support your position with well-argued reasons.
5. Rewrite "Metaphors' into a simile poem by changing each metaphor into a simile. Compare and contrast the metaphor version with the simile version. Which one is more poetic? Why?

The Mother

by Gwendolyn Brooks

Content Synopsis

Gwendolyn Brooks' "The Mother," was first published in 1945 in a set of poems called "A Street in Bronzeville" within a book of the same title. Like many of the other poems in the set, "The Mother" is presented through first-person narration from the perspective of a resident in a public housing project. The title itself introduces the ironic conflict: the speaker is not literally a mother, for her pregnancies have ended in abortion, yet she addresses the children who were never born as if they were present to hear her meditation. Through this monologue, the speaker reveals her powerful feelings regarding her choices.

The first ten-line stanza sounds less personal than the rest of the poem because the speaker uses the second-person "you" to generalize, starting with the straightforward: "Abortions will not let you forget" (1), and continuing with a series of conflicting images that reflect a sense of loss and hint at the reasons for having the abortions. These are "the children you got that you did not get" (2). At the time of the abortion, they were "damp small pulps with a little or with no hair" (3), but had they been allowed to "[handle] the air," they could have become "singers and workers" (4). Not all the missed opportunities are positive: "You will never neglect or beat / Them" (5-6). However, most of the motherly activities suggest affection, such as "wind[ing] up the sucking-thumb" (7) or

"scuttl[ing] off ghosts that come" (8). Lines nine and ten use positive connotation and metaphor to suggest the mother's powerful desire to have had what she did not have: "You will never leave them, controlling your luscious sigh/ Return for a snack of them, with gobbling mother-eye."

Starting with line eleven, the tone turns more personal as the speaker shifts from "you" to "I," and the conflicts become even stronger than before: "I have heard in the voices of the wind the voices of my dim killed children." The word "killed" indicates the powerful sense of guilt the speaker feels. In her imagination she has given birth ("contracted") and she has breast-fed the "dim dears" (12-13). Her confused feelings are then illustrated through a series of "if" clauses that leads to a paradox. First, the speaker reveals that she has previously said, "Sweets, if I sinned, if I seized/ Your luck/ And your lives" (14-16), and "If" she has deprived them of the good and bad experiences of life, including their "births" and "names" (17) their "baby tears" and "games" (18), their "stilted or lovely loves," "tumults," "marriages, aches," and "deaths" (19), and "if" she has "poisoned the beginnings of [their] breaths" (20), then "Believe that even in my deliberateness I was not deliberate" (21). In other words, she deliberately chose to end the pregnancies, and with those decisions, she ended the potential for life with all its turbulence and pleasures, but she did not intend to do harm. Nonetheless, her sense of guilt is there, and she accepts responsibility: "Though why should I whine, / Whine that the crime was other than mine?" (22-23). Whoever is responsible, the children, if they are to be seen as children, are "dead" (24), or they "were never made" (25). However, even her attempt to make that distinction torments the speaker:

> But that, too, I am afraid,
> Is faulty: oh, what shall I say, how is the truth
> to be said?
> You were born, you had body, you died.
> It is just that you never giggled or planned
> or cried. (26-29)

The poem concludes with a final message to the children who never became children:

> Believe me, I loved you all.
> Believe me, I knew you, though faintly, and I
> loved, I loved you All. (30-32)

The repetition show the power and sincerity of the voice, and setting "all" onto the last line by itself suggests not only that the speaker has had multiple abortions but also that each had an identity for her, and an impact on her life.

Formal Qualities
The first ten lines are in couplets, after which the rhyme scheme becomes irregular. Despite the irregular pattern, all but four lines rhyme with a line next or near to it. Brooks asserts her freedom to vary line length and rhythm for effect.

Interpretation
While this poem has been criticized for its ambivalence toward the subject of abortion, some commentators argue that women who have had abortions know that Brooks' sympathies lie with the mother and the difficult choices she has had to make because she knows she could not have properly provided for the children (Guy-Sheftall 157).

More important than whether the poem is for or against abortion rights is the depth of the conflicts faced by the speaker as expressed by the ironies, paradoxes, and repetitions in the poem.

Historical Context
In most states, abortion in the early stages of pregnancy was legal until the period of 1860 to 1880, when prohibitions were enacted forbidding all abortions except for "therapeutic" reasons, usually defined as a threat to the mother's life. However, abortions remained common. They were performed by midwives, by physicians in their offices, or in hospitals. Family physicians who did not perform abortions themselves often referred patients to colleagues who did. In many cases, the women seeking abortions already had several children, and could not see how they could afford to raise another (Reagan 158-159).

With the Great Depression of the 1930s, abortion rates increased as many men and women lost their jobs, family incomes decreased, and more and more women who could find work had to help support their families. Women would frequently be fired if they were pregnant. "Since black women lost their jobs in disproportionate numbers," Reagan adds, "their need may have been greater than that of white women" (135).

Because it was illegal, midwives and physicians performing abortions when the mother's health was not clearly endangered could be arrested, but most arrests and trials occurred only when the patient had died after a procedure. Around 1940, police began raiding doctors' offices or taking in women for questioning as they left from having abortions. One effect of this was "the destruction of a system that had worked well for both women seeking abortions and for physicians. This system had created a space in which thousands of women obtained safe abortions from skilled physicians" (Reagan 161). Police and prosecutors frequently compelled the patients to testify in open court, which resulted in public embarrassment. Reagan speculates that this "new repression of abortion was a reaction against the apparent changes in gender and growing female independence. During the Depression, women had cut their fertility and appeared to be leaving the home and motherhood for the workplace. World War II accentuated these trends" (162) as women often took jobs in the war industry while men fought overseas. It was near the end of the war that Brooks wrote her poem.

Another change in the early 1940s was the establishment of hospital committees that evaluated whether an abortion met the definition of "therapeutic." These committees would sometimes require a second opinion before allowing the procedure, thereby adding to the cost to the woman as well as the time required. Consequently, abortions became more and more difficult for poor women to obtain (Reagan 172-178).

Societal Context

As Leslie J. Reagan explains in her study, "When Abortion Was a Crime," "Most doctors encountered women patients seeking abortions who told similar stories of poverty, excessive childbearing, and illegitimacy. Numerous individual physicians violated the official medical norms that condemned abortion because they could not ignore the dilemmas described by their patients" (158). As is noted in the Historical Contexts section, the Depression of the 1930s added to the economic and social pressures already faced by many women. Poverty, unemployment, the threat of losing a job due to pregnancy, the financial strains of having too many children, and the shame of being an unmarried mother in a society that stigmatized out of-wedlock births, fueled these pressures.

Religious Context

The speaker in this poem explores moral issues from a personal standpoint without reference to religion. At the time the poem was written,

abortion was generally seen as a social problem rather than a religious one. Of the major organized religions in the United States, only the Catholic Church took a stand against all abortion, condemning the general practice in 1869 and specifically opposing therapeutic abortions in 1895. Protestant churches tended to accept the law of the time, permitting abortion when the mother's life was threatened. Jewish tradition had long held the life of the mother to take precedence over that of the unborn child (Reagan 7).

It was not until the 1950s and 1960s that organized protestant denominations became major voices against abortion.

Scientific & Technological Context

Abortion had always involved certain health risks, but until the twentieth century, so did childbirth. Common abortion procedures often involved injecting chemicals into the womb in order to induce a miscarriage. In the early 1900s, doctors increasingly used curettes, spoon-shaped scraping devices, as part of the process, which increased chance of perforating the uterus and causing infections.

By the 1930s and 1940s, abortions had been made safer, and when infections did occur, they could be better treated with new sulfa drugs and antibiotics. The increased use of blood transfusions in case of hemorrhage further reduced the rate of mortality following abortions.

Biographical Context

"The Mother" is not autobiographical. Like many of Brooks's poems, it employs a first-person speaker to give voice to an underclass that is traditionally rarely heard in poetry.

Gwendolyn Brooks was born in Topeka, Kansas, on June 7, 1917. Within months, her family moved to Chicago, which remained Brooks's home for the rest of her life. She was the oldest child of three in a loving but strict family.

She was a shy child, and at a young age showed an interest in poetry, which her mother encouraged. She was writing poems at seven, and published her first poem in 1930. In her youth, she had the opportunity to meet Langston Hughes and James Weldon Johnson. Through her reading, she was influenced by modern poets, such as Ezra Pound, T.S. Eliot, and E.E. Cummings. By the age of seventeen, she was writing a weekly poetry column for a newspaper. She also became involved in the civil rights movement, serving as publicity director for the Chicago NAACP.

In 1938, she married Henry Blakely, and had her first child, Henry Jr., in 1940. Her daughter, Nora, was born in 1951. While living in a kitchenette apartment on the south side of Chicago, she continued writing poetry, and in 1945, she published her first collection, "A Street in Bronzeville," which included "The Mother." The book was well received, and Brooks was awarded a Guggenheim Fellowship to help fund her as she continued her work. Among her other honors was a fellowship to the American Academy of Arts and Sciences.

Brooks's next collection of poems, "Annie Allen" (1949), earned her even more praise and honors, including a Pulitzer Prize (the first awarded to an African American woman) in 1950. Her work continued to win her awards and honors through the rest of her life. She taught at a number of colleges, including Columbia College in Chicago, Columbia University, University of Wisconsin, and Chicago State University. In 1968 she was named Poet Laureate of Illinois, and in 1985 the Poetry Consultant to the Library of Congress. She died at the age of 83 on Dec. 3, 2000.

Michael L. Schroeder, Ph.D.

Works Cited

Brooks, Gwendolyn. "The Mother." *Selected Poems*. New York: HarperCollins, 1963.

Guy-Sheftall, Beverly. "The Women of Bronzeville." *A Life Distilled: Gwendolyn Brooks, Her Poetry and Fiction*. Ed. Maria K. Mootry and Gary Smith. Urbana: U of Illinois P, 1989. 153-161.

Reagan, Leslie J. *When Abortion Was a Crime: Women, Medicine, and Law in the United States, 1867-1973*. Berkeley: U of California P, 1997.

Discussion Questions

1. Consider the many different ways in which the "children that you did not get" are referred to in the first stanza. What is the effect of listing such a range of activities and experiences?

2. Identify paradoxes in the poem and discuss how such apparently contradictory statements can convey powerful meaning.

3. Examine the metaphor in lines 9-10 and discuss what it implies about the speaker's feelings.

4. Note the shift from second-person in the first stanza to first-person in the second. Discuss the ways in which this shift affects meaning.

5. The poem includes a number of examples of alliteration and assonance. Discuss whether such repetition of sounds adds to the meaning and effectiveness of the poem or not.

6. Discuss the environment and time period in which this poem is set. How did factors like the Depression, the Women's Rights Movement, and scientific advancements influence the instance of abortion?

7. Discuss how this poem makes you feel. How do you think Brooks feels about abortion? Has the poem changed your view on it?

8. Abortion remains a hot topic in our culture today; discuss the aspects of the poem that you feel are still relevant today, as well as those that were time-specific.

Essay Ideas

1. Some critics have complained that the poem does not take a clear stand on the abortion issue. Write an essay in which you use details from the poem itself to argue that the poem does suggest that safe and legal abortions serve a social need, that abortions are wrong, or that the ambiguity itself poses a powerful statement about the issue.

2. Write an essay exploring the ironies of the poem, starting with the title and considering the implications of other examples of situational irony.

3. Write an essay that describes how the poem transcends a solely personal experience. How does it reflect on society as a whole and go beyond the voice of the narrator? Cite examples from the poem, keeping in mind the social and historical background of the time.

4. Write an essay that discusses the possible reasons and motivations behind this poem. Why would Brooks write on such a sensitive topic? Keep in mind how the poem made you feel, as well as how critics and audiences have received the poem in the past.

5. Compare "The Mother" with Lucille Clifton's "Lost Baby Poem." Discuss how the poems convey similar or different sentiments regarding abortion. Also, focus on the tone, scope, and settings of the poems.

My House

by Nikki Giovanni

Content Synopsis

"My House" is typical of Giovanni's work in many ways. It emphasizes individuality—a common theme in her writings—but it also stresses mutuality and affection (similarly important motifs in her works). Love, especially physical love, is strongly stressed in this poem (as it is in other works by Giovanni), and the speaker of the poem is the assertive, self-confident woman who often appears in her writings. The voice of the speaker here is direct, plain, colloquial, unpretentious, and even whimsical. The poem itself is written in free verse, without rhyme, without any conventional stanza structure, and without any fixed or standard meter. In all these ways, "My House" is a perfectly recognizable work by Giovanni.

The title of the poem already implies that the emphasis of this work will be upon developing the speaker's individuality and independence. This is a woman who apparently owns her own home and who therefore has a significant measure of autonomy. She is an adult but, as will soon become clear, she is a young adult who has not lost her sense of playfulness. Her house reflects her uniqueness as well as her strong sense of self-possession and self-confidence. At the same time, the speaker of this poem seems modest and unpretentious—traits already implied by the absence of capitalization throughout the poem, particularly when she refers to herself in the very first word of the poem as "i" (1).

"i" is a highly appropriate opening word in a poem that so strongly emphasizes the speaker's autonomy. The first line of the poem stresses the speaker's desires, but that emphasis is immediately balanced in the second line by on the mention of some other, unnamed person, the unspecified "you." The pronoun "you" is given the last position in the second line, just as the word "i" had been given the first position in the opening line, achieving symmetry, highlighted by the fact that both lines contain five syllables. The speaker's desire to "kiss" the addressee of the poem immediately gives the work a sensual tone, but the sensuality is muted at first. The speaker may have said that she wanted to "be there to love you," phrasing which would have been more abstract; or she could have used stronger, perhaps more vulgar verb than "kiss." Instead, she introduces a sensual tone in the second line while also keeping that tone somewhat restrained.

The sensuality becomes more explicit in the next three lines (each of which contains six syllables, making them a roughly defined unit), in which the verb "kiss" is emphasized repeatedly, and the language becomes highly rhythmic using such repetition (3-5). Now the focus of the poem shifts to the physical, and the speaker stresses the desires of the "you," who possesses not only physical desires but also physical needs. However, in line five, the focus moves once more to the speaker's desires. Yet in the sixth and final line of the opening stanza—which is also the longest line in the stanza, receiving special emphasis—the stress is emphatically on the speaker, her house, her plans, and her life. The opening stanza, then, exhibits a balance between the self and other, between self-respect and mutual desire, and between autonomy and affection. It is straightforward and unadorned: it lacks the devices of complex imagery, metaphor, and simile (not to mention meter and rhyme) that many of Giovanni's readers might expect. The speaker declares her independence not only by emphasizing her house and her own life but also by avoiding all standard, conventional norms that most people might expect and even desire in a poem.

In the second stanza, the emphasis is once again placed on physical contact and on sensual desire, but again, the desire and contact seem muted. The poem focuses on the physical act of hugging, but nothing more explicit or daring. Line 8 emphasizes the speaker's yearning to hug (so that self-assertion is balanced by a confession of "need"). Line 9 emphasizes the speaker's more autonomous desire (she "want[s]" to hug; she no longer "need[s]" to hug). Line ten then shifts to the pleasure and desires of the addressee. The repetition of the word "hug" in these lines highlights the poem's sensuality, but the tone here is almost childlike and playful, as the speaker herself acknowledges when she asks whether her words "sound like a silly poem" (11). Here again, as throughout the first two stanzas, the speaker directly addresses "you," thus adding to the poem's sense of intimacy. At the same time this poem may refer to a specific person, it might just as easily be read to be addressing the reader of the work. The poet is conscious of herself as a poet; she is engaged in a direct relationship with another person, but she is also aware that she is crafting a work of art from that relationship, and she is aware that her work of art is being read—and judged—by others.

Stanza 3 begins with the same language and same concerns highlighted in stanza one. However, after the first line, it offers a significant departure. Suddenly, the poem becomes sensual in a new way by emphasizing food rather than physical affection. Suddenly, too, the poem is full of striking, memorable imagery, with its references to "pork chops," "sweet potatoes," and "yams" (13-15). The speaker effectively uses repetition to give her work a highly rhythmical quality ("and 133 and 133; and" [12-14]), but she also knows how to break those rhythms and head off in an new and unexpected direction, as she does in lines 16-17 ("cause i run the kitchen / and i can stand the heat"). If most of stanza three emphasizes the speaker's willingness to work, the last two lines reiterate her autonomy, her resilience, and her self-respect.

Having ended stanza three by emphasizing the "heat" (17), in the opening of stanza four, the speaker shifts to the external cold of "winter" (18)—a shift that is typical of the frequent unpredictability of this poem, its spontaneity and vitality. This third stanza implicitly describes a different kind of creativity than that stressed in the second stanza. The second stanza implied the speaker's talents as a cook; the third stanza implied her talent as a seamstress. Both roles are conventionally feminine roles, but the speaker of this poem seems anything but a stereotypical woman. Her ability to make a "quilt" out of different types of unwanted fabric is relevant to her ability to make a poem out of the miscellaneous items of common phrases and images. Her poem has a preplanned design, but it is simple, just like her quilt. Then, she once again calls attention to the fact that she is aware of herself as a poet (22-23). Here and throughout the work, she invites us to judge the poem even before we have finished reading it. She seems highly self-confident, but at the same time, she seems highly conscious of the kind of impact she is having on her readers. By raising the possibility that her poem may be "silly" (23), she reveals a vulnerability and modesty and playfulness that balance her general sense of confidence and self-assertiveness.

Stanza 5—the shortest of the poem—exhibits Giovanni's spontaneity. The speaker clarifies her thoughts to herself as much as she clarifies her desires for her lover or the reader; the poem thus becomes an act of self-exploration and self-discovery. The striking emphasis in this stanza on the single word "warm" (25) returns us, once again, to the sensuality that has been stressed before, but here, the emphasis is more on sensual comfort than on sensual pleasure. The speaker here seems as much a caregiver as a lover—just another of the many ways in which she emerges from this poem as a highly balanced figure. Such balance is stressed, for instance, in stanza six, in which the speaker confesses that although the windows of her house may be "dirty" (25), this only means that "if i can't see out sometimes / they can't see in either" (28-29). The speaker seems self-content in her self-containment, but not in a condescending or anti-social way. She is happy with herself, but she also seems to possess a good sense of self-mocking humor, as she shows once more when she raises the possibility again that perhaps her work really is "a silly poem" (36).

In stanza eight, the poem returns to sensual imagery, this time combining the affectionate language of the first two stanzas with the emphasis on the preparation of food. In this stanza, the poem uses highly memorable language involving "fudge" (38), which is vividly described as "chocolate warmth" (40). The imagery of touching one's "lips" to the fudge (39-40) looks back to the earlier imagery of kissing (2-5), just as the reference to "warmth" (40) looks back to the similar imagery in line twenty-five. The poem is more carefully unified than it might first appear, and indeed such unity is especially apparent in the final stanza. In the last section, the poet nicely balances the phrases "my house" and "your poem" (48-50), and the nouns in each of these phrases echo key

words from the rest of the work. The poem began by stressing the speaker; it ends by stressing the unnamed lover she has been addressing throughout the work. The poem, however silly it may seem to her, to the lover, or to others, is finally offered as a kind of gift, and the concluding stanza emphasizes balance not only in its phrasing but also in the kind of loving relationship it ultimately implies.

Historical Context

The most important aspect of the historical context of this poem is the text's place in the history of American poetry. Giovanni was writing in the aftermath of literary modernism, a movement that often produced—especially in the works of such writers as T. S. Eliot and Ezra Pound—poetry that was deliberately difficult, allusive, and arcane. "My House," like Giovanni's poetry in general, does not fall within the modernist tradition, and in some ways, the poem can be seen as a declaration of independence not only from literary modernism but also from other traditions of verse in the English language, especially traditions that emphasized conventional stanza patterns, metrical patterns, or need for rhyme schemes. The poem is written in free verse, and this is one of the ways it is a deliberate rebuke to what might be considered the artful artificiality of much of the poetry that preceded it. Giovanni is writing in the tradition of such other free spirits as Walt Whitman, Langston Hughes, and William Carlos Williams. Her poem reflects the heavy emphasis on freedom and self-assertion that were typical of American culture in the decades including (and following) the 1960s.

Societal Context

The fact that the speaker of the poem is a young, independent, self-confident, and playful woman reflects, in part, the resurgence of feminism in the 1960s. The speaker of the poem desires the company of the addressee, but not in any subservient way. She addresses "you" as an equal, and although she is willing to cook, provide warmth, affection, and sensual pleasure, she does all of these things on her own terms, in her own way, and in her own house. The fact that the author of the poem was, at the time of its composition, a young black woman is significant as well in the context of the African-American Civil Rights Movement (1955-1968). The poem thus reflects the rise of a new generation of self-confident, self-assertive black writers, both male and female. Nevertheless, Giovanni does not emphasize matters of race nearly as much as she focuses on social class. The young female speaker of the poem is not obviously black, but she seems not of an upper economic class: she has to gather patches for a quilt, she does her own cooking, the food she cooks is common and inexpensive, and the windows of her house need cleaning. The social circumstances of the speaker are modest, but the speaker herself exudes vitality and self-confidence.

Religious Context

Religion plays no great or obvious role in this poem — a fact that is itself significant. This is a poem about secular, sensual love, not about the love generally associated with religious faith. The speaker's focus is on the here-and-now—on the pleasures of this life rather than on the potential rewards or punishments in a life hereafter.

Scientific & Technological Context

Science and technology are not especially important in this poem. The speaker is a modern, free-spirited woman, but she is also a woman who does her own cooking, makes her own quilts, cleans (or does not clean) her own windows, and bakes her own fudge. She is, in other words, associated with many of the traditional domestic tasks that have often been assigned to (or taken on by) women and she seems to do these tasks as they have been done for centuries. Nothing about her lifestyle suggests that she is living a scientifically or technologically

advanced existence. Her life is simple in almost every way.

Biographical Context

Nikki Giovanni (1943—) won early attention as an outspoken poet of black revolution and black pride. Many critics have admired her early fiery poetry. Others, however, find much of her early work simplistic and propagandistic, although it is undeniably an accurate reflection of the spirit of the times. Seen against the background of the highly political and race-conscious poetry of the 1960s, a work such as "My House" appears universal in its concerns, tone, topics, and themes. The race of the speaker is never made explicit, and indeed even the speaker's gender is never explicitly mentioned. "My House" is an important transitional poem in Giovanni's career, foreshadowing her movement away from a strict and narrow concern with politics and race. Its tone and focus also indicate a broadening of her writing that becomes increasingly clear as her career continued to develop.

Robert C. Evans, Ph.D.

Works Cited

Carson, Warren J. "My House." "Magill's Survey of American Literature". Revised Edition. Pasadena, CA: Salem Press, 2007. EBSCO *Literary Reference Center Plus*. Web. 22 Aug, 2010. <http://search.ebscohost.com/login.aspx?direct=true&db=lkh&AN=MOL9830000806&site=lrc-plus>.

Cook, Martha. "Nikki Giovanni: Place and Sense of Place in Her Poetry." *Southern Women Writers: The New Generation*. Ed. Tonette Bond Inge. Tuscaloosa: U of Alabama P, 1990. 279-300. Print.

Fowler, Virginia C. *Nikki Giovanni*. New York: Twayne, 1992. Print.

Giovanni, Nikki. "My House." *My House: Poems*. New York: William Morrow, 1972. 67-69. Print.

Harris, William J. "Sweet Soft Essence of Possibility: The Poetry of Nikki Giovanni." *Black Women Writers (1950-1980): A Critical Evaluation*. Ed. Mari Evans. New York: Doubleday, 1984. 218-28. Print.

Juhasz, Suzanne. *Naked and Fiery Forms: Modern American Poetry by Women, A New Tradition*. New York: Harper and Row, 1976. Print.

McDowell, Margaret B. *Groundwork for a More Comprehensive Criticism of Nikki Giovanni." I Belief vs. Theory in Black American Literary Criticism*. Ed. Joe Weixlmann and Chester Fontenot. Vol. 2. Greenwood, FL: Penkeville Publishing Company, 1986. 135-60. Print.

Discussion Questions

1. How do the final words of the first two lines create a false expectation about the structure of the poem? How might the final two words of lines 3 and 4 seem, at first, to confirm that expectation? How might the number of syllables and the rhythms of the first two lines also create certain expectations about the structure of the poem (expectations that are later undermined)?

2. Discuss the effects — and effectiveness — of line seven. How does it offer a marked shift from the preceding lines? Count the number of syllables in lines 1-6 and then count the number of syllables in lines 6 and 7. How do the preceding lines disrupted by lines 6 and 7 establish the pattern, and why might the poet want to disrupt that pattern?

3. Why does the speaker use the word "cause" (6) rather than the more "correct" word "Because"? How does her use of the word "cause" already help to characterize her and imply something about her personality and values?

4. How does the relationship between lines 8-10 resemble a kind of hugging? How, in other words, do the lines almost "hug" one another?

5. Discuss the foods mentioned in lines 13-15. How do those references contribute to the tone and atmosphere of the poem? What other kinds of food might the speaker have mentioned if she had wanted to create a significantly different effect?

6. Look up the etymology (word history) of the word "yams" (15) and discuss some possible reasons that the speaker may wish to use that word instead of "sweet potatoes" (14). What may this preference suggest about the speaker's background and heritage?

7. Is there anything possibly confusing about the idea of gathering patches for a quilt in carpet stores (19-21)? Can you explain this language?

Essay Ideas

1. How would you categorize this poem and why? What kind of poem is it? Support your answer with detailed evidence from the poem itself.

2. Discuss this poem within the context of other poems published in the same volume of Giovanni's poems (a volume also titled "My House"). How is this poem typical of that volume? How is it distinctive?

3. Giovanni is often thought of as a distinctively "black" writer with strong "revolutionary" political views. How and why might this particular poem appeal to a wide variety of readers who may not share Giovanni's ethnic heritage or political opinions?

4. How and why might feminist critics react to this poem? Is there anything about the poem that might disturb them? Is there anything about the poem they might especially enjoy?

5. Discuss all the ways in which this poem carefully balances a focus on the speaker with concern for others.

My Mother's Body

by Marge Piercy

Content Synopsis

Piercy's poem on the death of her mother opens with imagery that sounds almost primitive and primeval, as if the speaker of the poem is in touch with ancient myths about the rhythms of life and death, and especially with fears about the latter. References to "the dark socket of the year," "the pit" and to "the cave where the sun lies down / and threatens never to rise" (1-3) recall ancient fears associated with winter, a season when all light and life could seem to be on the verge of extinction. Thus, the speaker already begins to associate the potential death of the world with the actual death of her own mother, the source of her own life, the light of the speaker's own world. The opening stanza also makes effective use of such devices of sound as alliteration (as in line one and especially in line four) and assonance (particularly at the end of line five).

Primeval language continues in the second stanza, as the speaker vividly describes how "hawkfaced pain seized" her mother is (6). Pain is compared to a deadly bird of prey, while the speaker's mother is implicitly compared to a creature too weak to defend herself against attack. The speaker's mother is thrown by pain, so that she falls with a "sharp / cry" (7-8)—the line—break giving strong emphasis both to the adjective and to the noun. The imagery then jumps to a more modern, more human context: the mother's cry is compared to "a knife tearing a bolt of silk" (8). This phrasing juxtaposes strength (the knife) and weakness (the silk), as it juxtaposes something common (the knife) with something precious (the silk). The speaker's "father heard the crash" (a nicely onomatopoeic word) "but paid / no mind, napping after lunch" (9-10). This is the first and only explicit reference to the father in the poem. In his one appearance, he seems guilty of indifference or neglect. The rest of the poem will be concerned not with the family as a whole but (as the poem's title had already implied) with relations between mother and daughter.

Based on the evidence provided by stanza three, the bond between these two persons seems almost mystical or supernatural: although the daughter is "fifteen hundred miles north" (11) when her mother is assaulted by pain, that pain sank "talons" into the daughter's skull "and crouched there cawing" (13-14). This language echoes the earlier language of line six, so that the pain experienced by the mother is somehow felt simultaneously by the daughter, implying (if perhaps somewhat improbably) the depth of the almost supernatural bond they share. The extrasensory nature of the connection between mother and daughter continues in lines 17-18, and it is in the latter line that the specific ethnic and religious background of the family becomes clear. Apparently, they are of Jewish ancestry in the mention of "Chanukah" (18). In four stanzas, the poem moves from seeming to be rooted in ancient general human myths about winter and the loss of sunlight to being rooted in the specific legends of a particular religious subculture. Stanza 4, though, is linked with stanza one by their shared emphasis on the loss of light. Both stanzas also implicitly emphasize one of the main themes of the whole poem: the passage of time.

Stanzas 5 and 6 develop the emphasis on Jewish traditions and Jewish beliefs even more explicitly than stanza four. Piercy deals with a universal human fact (the fact of death, especially the death of one's mother), but she now places that fact in a highly particular, highly personal context. The specific domestic details of stanza five help root the poem in the speaker's own background and experiences, but the imagery of "tops turn[ing] like little planets" (26) also helps provide a kind of cosmic perspective that mixes with, and complicates, the speaker's intimate personal memories. Finally, in a line typical of the way this poem blends different kinds of connotations, the speaker says in line thirty that "the room stopped spinning"—an image that unites the earlier allusions to Jewish traditions and the motion of the planets with a common, colloquial image of disorientation and perplexity. Here, as so often in this poem, Piercy mixes imagery (taken from widely different aspects of experience), and blends all those aspects together so that they implicitly comment on and enrich one another.

Stanza 7 emphasizes a pattern of imagery that now begins to run throughout the poem, thereby adding both to its unity and to its variety. The body of the speaker's mother is compared to a "thin, "empty dress," just as her "clothes" are compared to "curtains / hanging on the window of what had / been your flesh" (32-35). These kinds of comparisons had already been anticipated in the reference to "veils of wax" (20), but now such language will be used far more often and emphatically. In stanza 8, the sense of cultural complexity becomes even

stronger. The poem had already moved from a kind of broadly human emphasis in stanzas 1 and 2 to a more specifically Jewish focus in stanzas 4 through 7. However, we are reminded, in stanza 8, that this Jewish culture is situated inside a broader culture that is a crude mixture of the Christian and the secular. Finally, stanza nine—the concluding stanza of part one—sums up what has come before. The somewhat playfully alliterative reference to "Pelicans with pregnant pouches" (41) echoes the reference to "beaches" (40). The reference to "pterodactyls" recalls the references to birds of prey in line six and lines 13-14. Line 43 echoes lines 17-19, and line 45 echoes line 18 in particular. In short, the final stanza of part one implicitly summarizes much that had come before it, and the final words of the stanza—"went out"—seem especially appropriate to a poem about the loss of life and light.

Large portions of part 2 echo imagery from part 1. Thus, the image of memories "shrouded in dropcloths" (47) echoes lines 32-35, while the reference to light, in line 49, echoes all the light imagery used earlier in the poem. The reference to a "scrim" (51) recalls the earlier references to "veils" (20) and to "curtains" (33), while the description of "fingers tearing at the flimsy curtain" (52) echoes lines 8, 13, and 33 in particular. Here, as so often throughout her poem, Piercy achieves a subtle kind of unity by using understated echoes. The poem may seem random and spontaneous in its structure, but it actually achieves far more coherence than may be immediately obvious. The poem thus seems credible as a series of haphazard thoughts, even as it also achieves a kind of underlying artistic unity.

Typical of the kind of coherence the poem displays is the sort of extra-sensory perception (and connection) described in line 55. Clearly, this line echoes such earlier lines as 11, 12, and line 43. Similarly, line 55 also reiterates the heavy emphasis on the passage (and the fluidity) of time, that is a major theme of this poem. Section two of the poem takes us into the past of the mother's life, presenting her as a young woman, her life filled with dreams and aspirations but already filled, too, with its share of disappointments. In this section of the poem, Piercy further develops the idea of a deep, almost spiritual connection between mother and daughter—an idea already implied in the opening section, especially in lines 11-15 and 17-19. Now the poem begins to imply that the identities of mother and daughter are almost permeable or interchangeable: the daughter acts as a kind of mother to her mother in the last four stanzas of part two. Part 2 ends with a particularly effective word, as the daughter imagines herself giving to her mother what her mother's "youth had wanted" (72). The word "wanted" here does double duty, since it can refer both to what her mother's youth had desired but since it can also refer to what her mother's youth had lacked.

Part three of the poem continues to elaborate on earlier imagery and themes, even as it also broadens its focus to include, at least initially, the poem's readers in its concerns. By opening, asking "What is this mask of skin we wear, / what is this dress of flesh" (73-74), the speaker implicitly speaks for all humanity, thereby reminding us that we are all as impermanent and mortal as her mother has proven to be. Line 74, in a fashion typical of the way this poem is structured, echoes line 32, while line 74 is also typical in its effective use of both assonance and alliteration ("dress of flesh"). Meanwhile, line 75 offers a subtle but clear allusion to the "coat of many colors" worn by Joseph in the Bible. In this instance as so often elsewhere, Piercy manages to keep her poem sounding plainspoken, colloquial, and conversational while also keeping it from being more than merely simple or boringly drab.

By the time part three reaches lines 79-81, the speaker has once again begun to narrow her focus to herself, her mother, and her own family line. Indeed, she mentions the names of Piercy's own grandmother and mother specifically (83-84), so

that the poem deals with issues that are at once broadly human and highly autobiographical. Crucial to the entire work is the statement: "My mother is my mirror and I am hers" (88). This line builds on the idea (already strongly emphasized) of the close connection between this mother and this daughter, whose identities have come to seem, by this point, almost inseparable. Once again, "dress" imagery helps unify the poem (94), and once again, passages from later in the poem echo earlier passages, as lines 97-98 echo lines 70-71, but here the echo is ironic. As part three concludes, the speaker implies not only the love she and her mother have shared but also the tensions and hostilities that have divided them. The mother is no longer presented simply as a victim or a saint but as herself a victimizer (98-100). Lines 101-02 echo lines eight and thirteen, but now the mother is the one who inflicts pain, not merely the one who suffers from it. Even in a poem clearly meant to extol her mother, Piercy cannot deny the complicated truth of her mother's complex moral nature.

Having implicitly criticized her mother in part three, Piercy now implicitly criticizes herself in part 4. The first stanza describe the speaker's exaggerated, unfounded fear of her mother's power (ironically, she feared the very kind of union with her mother that she now yearns for and praises), while the second stanza describe the mother's efforts to dominate the once-young but now mature daughter. In this final section of the poem, the speaker recalls, relives, explains, and thus transcends her earlier tensions with her mother. It is a measure of the poem's honesty that it is more than hagiography, more than the celebration of a saint; it is a forthright and thus credible account both of her mother's attractiveness and of her failings.

In the poem's final lines, the speaker is able to see herself as the daughter of her mother's "dream," language that typically looks back to the daughter's dream earlier in the poem (55). As the poem concludes, the speaker imagines her newly dead mother revitalized and reborn, "alive in my eyes, my breasts / my throat, my thighs" (135-36). The mother is dead physically, but she is also alive physically in her daughter's flesh. Most important, she lives on in her daughter's soul and personality—a personality more daring than her mother's and also more free, and thus able to give life to her mother's own deepest aspirations: "What you / did not dare in your life you dare in mine" (138-39).

Historical Context

Although this poem focuses clearly on the speaker and on the speaker's mother, the work is also set firmly within a variety of historical contexts—contexts that include prehistory, as in the reference to the "pterodactyls" (42), ancient history (2-3), and Biblical history, as in the allusion to the story of Joseph (75). The poem also suggests life in early twentieth—century America (59-60 and 113), as well as life in the latter half of the twentieth century in Florida, a place where many elderly people took up residence in search of a warmer climate. In order to understand the poem, it helps to know that Wanamaker's (60) was a major department store company headquartered in Philadelphia and that a "flapper" (113) was a fashionable young woman of the 1920s. Historical allusions are significant in the poem, but the poem is never so heavy with them that it becomes incomprehensible without extensive notes.

Societal Context

Although this poem is obviously highly personal, it also reflects significant social changes that occurred during the lifetimes of the speaker and her mother. Perhaps the most important of these changes resulted from the rise of feminism, which became an especially powerful social force during and following the 1960s. The speaker clearly believes that she benefited from the greater personal freedom that became increasingly common during this period. She also sees her mother's life as having been handicapped, in many ways, by the society in which she grew up—a society that placed clear restraints on the lives of women. In the penultimate stanza of part three, the poem seems to reflect the tensions that existed between women of the speaker's generation and women of her mother's generation. The same tensions are also reflected in stanzas 3 through 5 of part 4. Ironically, in a poem that celebrates and commemorates her mother, the speaker also spends much space describing the conflicts between them—generational conflicts that were typical of the society of the late twentieth century.

Religious Context

Religion plays a very significant role in this poem, especially because of all the allusions to the Jewish religion, particularly in part one of the work. The speaker seems to have grown up in a Jewish household and seems familiar with, and respectful of Jewish customs. At the same time, the speaker does not call upon God for any kind of consolation as she tries to deal with her mother's death. Her tone and attitude in the poem seem to reflect the increasing secularism of the late twentieth century, when many Jews were primarily Jewish in culture rather than in any deeply, profoundly spiritual sense. Religion provides a valuable context for understanding this poem.

Scientific & Technological Context

Science and technology are not especially important in this work. The poem is primarily about personal relationships, not about material progress. The major emphases of the poem are psychological and even moral rather than scientific or technological.

Biographical Context

Piercy was born in 1936 to a father of Christian heritage who married a woman of Jewish ancestry—a fact that seems relevant to the various religious references in this poem, especially since Piercy herself was raised within the belief system of Judaism. Although Piercy came from a strongly working class background, she quickly developed an interest in literature, but not the sort of highly intellectual, difficult, modernist literature that was fashionable at the time. "My Mother's Body" clearly reflects a more colloquial, plainspoken attitude toward poetic style; Piercy's work is more obviously in the tradition of Walt Whitman and William Carlos Williams than in the tradition of such frequently opaque modernists as T. S. Eliot or Ezra Pound. The poem also reflects Piercy's especially close relationship with her mother, even though that relationship was often troubled at times, particularly when Piercy herself became a somewhat rebellious young woman. In addition, the poem clearly shows the strong influence of feminism on Piercy's life and on her perceptions of the lives of other women, particularly her mother.

Robert C. Evans, Ph.D.

Works Cited

Gilbert, Sandra. Review of "My Mother's Body" by Marge Piercy. *Poetry* 147.3 (December 1985): 159-61. Print.

Lancaster, Ian. "Commentary on Marge Piercy's 'My Mother's Body.' *Representative Poetry Online*. University of Toronto, 2003. Web. 28 Aug. 2010. <https://tspace.library.utoronto.ca/html/1807/4350/poem1613.html>.

McManus, Terry. "Marge Piercy—Biography." *Marge Piercy*. margepiercy.com, 2009. Web. 28 Aug. 2010. <http://www.margepiercy.com/main-pages/biography.htm>.

Moramarco, Fred, and William Sullivan. "'A Whole New Poetry Beginning Here': The Assertion of Gender." *Containing Multitudes: Poetry in the United States since 1950*. Boston: Twayne, 1998. 163-94. Print.

Piercy, Marge. "My Mother's Body." *The Art of Blessing the Day: Poems with a Jewish Theme*. New York: Knopf, 1999. 19-25. Print.

Walker, Sue. "Marge Piercy: An Overview." "Ways of Knowing: Essays on Marge Piercy". Mobile, AL: Negative Capability, 1991. 132-47. Print.

Discussion Questions

1. Why do you think the poem pays so little attention to the role of the father in this family? Why (and how) is he mentioned merely in lines 9-10?

2. What is the potential double meaning of the reference to a "great vessel" in line 15? How does the word "vessel" seem to have one meaning when it is imagined as being "filled with water" but another meaning when it is imagined being filled with "oil or blood" (16)?

3. Explore the symbolic meanings of Chanukah (18) and discuss their relevance (sometimes ironic) to this poem.

4. In what various ways do lines 36-40 contain language that seems crude or unnatural?

5. How is the language of lines 53-54 paradoxical, and how is such language typical of the poem as a whole? How does the somewhat abstract language of these lines compare and contrast to language elsewhere in the poem?

6. Why does the speaker include the precise details mentioned in lines 56—57? What do these details suggest about her mother's life, and what does their inclusion suggest about the speaker's own motives as a poet?

7. Discuss the rhythm of lines 58-60, and discuss the rhythm of lines elsewhere in the poem. Why might rhythm seem especially important in a poem that lacks a standard meter? Why "does" the poem lack a standard meter, and why does it lack rhyme? Why do you think that the poet chose to avoid these common features of poetry?

8. What common device of sound is used in line 64, and where else is that device used throughout the poem? What other devices of sound does Piercy use in this poem? Where does she use them, and why are such devices especially important in a poem that lacks rhyme and a regular metrical pattern?

9. What is anaphora, and how and why is it used in lines 79-81? Is it used anywhere else in the poem?

10. Is there anything unusual about the rhythm of line 100? Is there anything especially appropriate and/or ironic about the rhythm of that line?

Essay Ideas

1. Trace a major pattern of imagery—such as the pattern of references to clothing—throughout the poem and discuss the significance of that pattern. How does the pattern contribute to the meaning, structure, and effectiveness of the poem?

2. Write an essay in which you discuss some particularly effective examples of phrasing in this poem, including uses of irony, juxtaposition, ambiguity, and paradox. How and why, for instance, is the phrase "bark of wrinkles" (92) effective?

3. Make a list of the number of people mentioned or implied in this poem, then make a list of their characteristics and discuss the ways in which they are characterized. Who emerges from the poem as the most attractive character? Explain why.

4. Discuss the various ways in which the word "you" is employed in this poem. Who is referred to by "you," and how and why are such references used? How are they effective in various ways?

5. Discuss the relations between the various parts of the poem. For example, how does part 1 prepare for and/or differ from part 2? How does part 4 related to part 1? What do the various parts have in common? How are they distinct?

Claude McKay, pictured above, wrote "America," featured on page 21 of this volume. Photo: Library of Congress

My Papa's Waltz

by Theodore Roethke

Content Synopsis

The poem is written in iambic trimeter, a meter that imitates the rhythm of both ordinary English speech and of the waltz (a three-beat dance). However, the iambs fight with the trimeter, slowing the poem down and making it jolt along awkwardly, just like the waltz itself. This stop-and-start rhythm is reinforced by punctuation at the end of every second and fourth line, which divides each stanza into two nearly freestanding sentences. When the poem is read aloud, its elements fail to concur with one another, reinforcing the poem's central irony: a dance, which metaphorically suggests two people joyfully moving in harmony with one another, reveals painful disharmonies.

The poem's narrator, a young boy, describes an impromptu dance that takes place in the family kitchen on evening as the narrator's father "waltzes" him around the room. The poem, written in iambic trimeter to match the traditional three-beat tempo of a waltz, describes the complicated emotions the young boy feels as his father waltzes him "off to bed."

Many children and parents have playful bedtime rituals that express their affections for one another. The narrator of this poem describes his "Papa's Waltz" differently. From the first stanza, where the narrator describes how "the whiskey on your breath/Could make a small boy dizzy" and characterizes himself as hanging on "like death," the reader becomes increasingly aware that this waltz communicates both love and fear, and physical as well as emotional pain.

The personal pronouns "my," "you," "we," and "I" suggest that the poem is addressed to the family circle—father, mother, and child. The setting, the family's kitchen, is unsettled by the father-and-child waltz, which is more like roughhousing than a genteel dance. The mother remains on the sidelines, frowning, as the dance's rough rhythm makes the pans slide from the kitchen shelf.

While the first two stanzas describe the smell of the father's whiskey breath and the sound and feel of the pans bouncing, the third stanza is located firmly in the boy narrator's sight and feeling. His head is at the level of his father's belt-buckle, which scrapes the boy's right ear, and the hand that holds his is battered; its palm "caked hard by dirt." The alternating end-stopped lines reinforce the awkwardness of the dance as the poem itself refuses to "flow" regularly along the three-beat time of a waltz.

The last stanza juxtaposes all of the poem's conflicted themes and emotions: the father "beats" time on the child's head with his dirty hand, and dances the child off to bed with the child "still clinging" to his father's shirt. The poem's ironies emphasize the complexity of the child/parent relationship. On the one hand, the dance seems to suggest abuse: the child holds on "like grim death" and finds his Papa's version of waltzing both physically and emotionally painful. This pattern seems psychologically accurate inasmuch as psychoanalysts concur that abused children are often willing to collude with their abusers in exchange for love and attention. The child perseveres in the dance, possibly because he relishes his father's ritual of playfulness and affection in the midst of a life where hard labor and obligation are the norm. While the poem can be read as a thinly veiled story about an abusive relationship between father and son, it also captures some of the fundamental joy a child experiences when playing with a parent and receiving that parent's undivided attention.

Symbols & Motifs

The waltz is a well-known romantic pair dance that became popular in the nineteenth century. Most readers associate waltzing with genteel balls accompanied by orchestras. The poem's many ironies originate in the contrast between our stereotype of the waltz as a graceful, romantic dance and the strange and awkward "dance" that the "Papa" of the title creates with his son (the "small boy" first-person narrator identified in line 2). Though the waltz is usually considered a heterosexual courtship ritual, in this poem, Roethke imagines something quite different. Instead of the father romantically dancing in the kitchen with the mother, he dances with the son while the mother looks on angrily; possibly, because of the mess they are creating in the kitchen, and possibly, because she feels left out of the ritual. The waltz should be genteel and graceful, as the partners barely touch one another and whirl predictably and gracefully across the floor, in time with the music and with the movements of other dancers. This "waltz" is jolting and awkward.It is painful for the child well as his father who exudes whiskey breath, "beat(s) time on my head/ With a palm caked hard by dirt."The child's ear is scraped by his belt-buckle when the father misses a step.

Dance itself is often compared to conflicts, especially when a pair of dancers uses the dance to express hostility and conflict as well as love and attraction. The dance of death, a familiar trope in western literature since the Middle Ages, conceptualizes death as a bridegroom who courts and dances with his potential victim. Roethke's dance may describe death or simply the kind of conflict that develops as fathers begin to challenge their sons.

When the dancers' stomping feet make the pans "slide from the shelves," the father and son seem to be enjoying the triumph of pleasure over orderliness. The mother frowns because she is unable to abandon her world of hard-won labor (emblematized by the kitchen) for the carelessness of play. Instead of the father romantically dancing in the kitchen with the mother, he dances with the son, and the mother looks on angrily; possibly, because of the mess they are creating in the kitchen, and possibly because she feels left out of the ritual.

Historical Context

"My Papa's Waltz" is part of a larger body of work Theodore Roethke produced that interrogates the complex relationship he had with his father, Otto Roethke, whom he remembered as a stern and unforgiving man, but to whom he was intensely devoted nonetheless. This relationship may be understood in generational terms. Otto Roethke and his brothers had emigrated to the United States from Prussia in 1870 in search of a better life. Part of a generation of immigrants that came in huge numbers in the nineteenth century, they exchanged the political turmoil of Eastern Europe for the hard labor of immigrants "starting over" in a new and unfamiliar culture. Though Otto Roethke loved his work in the greenhouses he owned with his brothers; he worked hard with his hands all his life and had little understanding of the son who excelled at academics and sought to join the world of writers rather than of laborers. Like all fathers, Otto

Roethke wanted his son to enjoy an easier life than his own. Had he survived to witness his son's academic success, he would probably have been puzzled by the new world emerging in the twentieth century and embodied by his poet son, who shared his interest in plants but lacked his workaday stamina and focus on material survival. The world Otto Roethke's son inherited, which would feature two major world wars, a great depression, and massive social changes, further unsettled the stability of the heritage that the Roethke family had provided.

Societal Context

The waltz is a nineteenth-century dance that was considered scandalous when first introduced, because it involved two partners constantly touching and fast, whirling movement around the dance floor. By the beginning of the twentieth century, this dance had become accepted and commonplace, and had made inroads into the folk world, as we see here, as the uneducated father and his son "romp" together in a kind of parody folk version of the original high-society dance. As father and son waltz together in the kitchen, the larger figure of the father grotesquely overpowers that of the young son, who hangs on with grim determination. The frowning mother looks on from the sidelines. In this poem, the waltz—supposedly a light, flirtatious dance in high society - becomes a metaphor for family relationships.

As critics have noted, Roethke made some important changes in revising the poem for publication. He changed the narrator's gender from a "small girl" to a "small boy," possibly to avoid implications of sexuality in his portrayal of the parent/child dance. Roethke also altered several words in the poem to intensify the impression of brutality, changing the phrase "kept time" to "beat time," for example. Roethke's revisions suggest that he was seeking a balance of pleasure and pain in his depiction of the ambiguous ritual between father and son (McKenna 34-9). These changes

reflect a growing willingness, in twentieth-century America, to confront and elucidate conflicts between parents and children, a topic that many writers had been unwilling to approach openly in previous eras.

Religious Context

The poem does not have a specific religious context; as a lyric poem, it focuses squarely on a brief, shared family experience that is secular.

Scientific & Technological Context

Nature, for Theodore Roethke, was an overmastering symbol of life. He was particularly absorbed by a fascination with the life cycle of plants, especially those who undergo dormancy, transformation, and change. His family had long been involved in cultivating plants - in Germany, his grandfather had been Bismarck's chief forester—and when Roethke's father and brothers emigrated to the United States in 1870, they established themselves in the trade they had begun in Germany: horticulture. Though Roethke did not follow their example, the traces of the family love for the cultivation of plants are everywhere in his poetry and prose. His fascination with the cycles of nature—the life cycle of plants, for example—is matched, as in "My Papa's Waltz," with a fascination with the growing-up of a young boy who must wrestle with a human father who is every bit as challenging as the natural world.

Biographical Context

Theodore Huebner Roethke (1908-1963) was born and raised in Saginaw, Michigan, the son of German immigrants. His father owned a greenhouse and many of Roethke's poems focus on images of plants and growth. His father died in 1923, when Roethke was still a teenager, and this event apparently affected the young poet deeply. Roethke fulfilled the "American Dream" by distinguishing himself as a student, graduating with highest honors from the University of Michigan in 1929.

Though his family wanted him to become a lawyer, he dropped out of law school after a single semester, decided to become an English professor, and received his master's degree in 1936 from Harvard. He spent the remaining years of the Great Depression and World War II teaching at several universities, including Lafayette University. He was expelled from this position in 1940, a year when he became emotionally involved with fellow poet Louise Bogan, who was to become one of his most important supporters. After an itinerant career in several academic positions, Roethke landed a full-time teaching position at the University of Washington in 1947. In 1953, he married Beatrice O'Connell, a former student of his at Bennington College. She was an understanding and supportive wife and made possible the posthumous publication of his last volume of poetry, "The Far Fields," which went on to win the National Book Award.

Roethke was sensitive and emotionally intense, and craved fame throughout his life. Roethke suffered from mental illness, probably bipolar disorder, which was exacerbated by alcoholism. He was plagued by frequent nervous breakdowns, but because of his dedication to his work as a teacher and poet, managed to keep his position at the University of Washington. Intensely introspective and demanding of himself, Roethke was renowned as a great teacher, though sometimes incapacitated by an ongoing bipolar condition. He was also highly self-critical and produced less and less as he grew older, though he continued to spend the same amount of time and energy working on his poems. His collection, "The Waking: Poems 1933-1953," won the Pulitzer Prize for poetry in 1954. Other awards include Guggenheim Fellowships in 1945 and 1950, and a National Book Award and the Bollingen Prize in 1959 for "Words for the Wind" (1958). He died of a heart attack while swimming at a friend's house in 1963 at the age of 55.

Lisa Jadwin, Ph.D.

Works Cited

Balakian, Peter. *Theodore Roethke's Far Fields.* Baton Rouge: Louisiana State UP, 1989.

Fong, Bobby. "Roethke's 'My Papa's Waltz.'*College Literature.* 17.1 (1990): 79-82.

Galvin, Brendan. "Kenneth Burke and Theodore Roethke's 'Lost Son' Poems." In *Theodore Roethke.* Ed. Harold Bloom. New York: Chelsea House, 1988. 85-112.

Janssen, Ronald R. "Roethke's 'My Papa's Waltz.'*Explicator* 44.2 (Winter 1986): 43-44.

La Belle, Jenijoy. *The Echoing Wood of Theodore Roethke.* Princeton, New Jersey: Princeton UP, 1976.

Malkoff, Karl. *Theodore Roethke.* New York: Columbia UP, 1966.

McKenna, John J. "Roethke's Revisions, and the Tone of "My Papa's Waltz." *ANQ* 11.2 (Spring 1998): 34-9.

Parini, Jay. *Theodore Roethke, an American Romantic.* Amherst: U of Massachusetts P, 1979.

Seager, Allan. *The Glass House: The Life of Theodore Roethke.* New York: McGraw-Hill, 1968.

Walker, Ursula Genung. *Notes on Theodore Roethke.* Charlottesville, Virginia: Bibliographical Society of the University of Virginia, 1968.

Roethke, Theodore. "My Papa's Waltz."*The Norton Anthology of Modern Poetry.* Eds. Richard Ellmann and Robert O'Clair. 1st Ed. New York: W. W. Norton & Company, 1973: 755.

Discussion Questions

1. How is this bedtime ritual like or unlike those that you experienced as a child?
2. What is the father trying to communicate to the child?
3. How does the mother respond to the dance, and why?
4. Is there anything abusive suggested in the relationship between the father and son?
5. What is the poem's rhyme scheme, and why did Roethke choose it?
6. To what extent is the father aware of how the child is perceiving the dance?
7. What other kinds of life experiences might the "waltz" symbolize?
8. Why does the narrator choose to focus on this particular experience with his father?
9. The father's dirty hands and large size can seem brutal, but what other, more positive associations, can those characteristics evoke?
10. Compare this poem to other poems that are recollections about childhood (see "Complementary Texts"), and explain what it shares with those poems, and how it is different from them.

Essay Ideas

1. Describe the way in which Roethke invokes the child's sense perceptions to describe the dance.

2. Roethke's diction contrasts violent-sounding words like "death," "battered," "beat," and "hard," with more playful words like "dizzy," "romped," "clinging," and "waltzed." How does this word-choice reflect the poem's themes?

3. What, in your view, is the significance of the fact that the "waltz" takes place as the father is putting the boy to bed?

4. How does the disparity between the partners reflect the traditional disparity between the male dancer and female dancer in the waltz?

5. How does this poem challenge your perception of relationships between parents and children?

Old Possum's Book of Practical Cats

by T. S. Eliot

Content Synopsis

A collection of poems on the subject of raffish, anthropomorphized cats, "Old Possum's Book of Practical Cats" is Eliot's attempt to write children's literature and nonsense verse in the tradition of Edward Lear or W. S. Gilbert. It is a light-hearted departure for a poet better known for high-modernist works such as "The Waste Land" and "Four Quartets," and for religious-themed plays such as "Murder in the Cathedral." "Practical Cats" is perhaps most familiar to readers as the libretto for the Andrew Lloyd Webber musical "Cats."

"Practical Cats" is a loosely grouped series of portraits, connected by a shared theme and meter rather than by an overarching plot or a developing storyline. Yet Eliot does make a few gestures toward narrative wholeness. The collection is bookended by "The Naming of Cats" and "The Ad-dressing of Cats," two poems which speak of cats and their relationships to people rather than presenting a portrait of a specific cat. "The Pekes and the Pollicles," which comes in the middle of the collection, is primarily a narrative rather than a monologue or portrait, and might serve as a sort of climax to the work. Finally, some of the criminally minded cats who feature in their own poems, such as Mungojerrie and Griddlebone, will subsequently be mentioned as subordinates of Macavity, the "Mystery Cat" who is behind any number of feline malfeasances in and around London.

The first poem in the collection, "The Naming of Cats," suggests that cats have three names: one for public use around the household, one for their more mischievous, out-of-doors prowling, and a third "effanineffable" name which, in moments of leisure, a cat sits silently contemplating (*Complete Poems and Plays* 149). The poem gives Eliot scope to list strange and unique names of cats. Much of the fun of this piece comes from the rhyming of real words with nonsense ones: "Of names of this kind I can give you a quorum / Such as Munkustrap, Quaxo, or Coricopat, / Such as Bombalurina, or else Jellyorum— / Names that never belong to more than one cat" (149). Eliot gave his own cats equally silly names, such as Pettipaws or George Pushdragon (Ackroyd 251). Owning, naming, and writing about cats therefore seem to have offered the poet one more venue in which to exercise his love of words.

The next few poems are portraits of individual cats, each one given a distinct and anthropomorphized identity. "The Old Gumbie Cat" keeps the house in order by putting the mice and cockroaches to useful tasks. "The Rum Tum Tugger," on the other hand, is obstinate and contrary: "If you offer him pheasant he would rather have grouse. / If you put him in a house he would much prefer a flat / If you put him in a flat then he'd rather have a house" (153). Here Eliot uses very long lines of fourteen syllables. By burying a rhyming word in the middle of each line (for example, the first line above ends with "grouse," and midway through the next line the rhyme "house" appear), he renders such long lines silly. The poem's refrain, moreover, contains two very short lines: "For he will do / As he do do / And there's no doing anything about it!" (153). This counterpointing of very long with very short lines and these jangling rhymes and repetitions give the poem a rollicking tone.

"Growltiger's Last Stand" tells of a fierce, piratical cat who lives on a boat with his lover, Griddlebone. Jealous Siamese cats board Growltiger's ship and force him to walk the plank. It may come as a shock, to a twenty-first century reader, to come across a reference to the Siamese cats as "Chinks:" "With a frightful burst of fireworks the Chinks they swarmed aboard" (152). In the context of a nonsense poem meant for children, the epithet seems particularly offense and gratuitous, important neither to the story nor to the rhyme scheme. There has been much debate in recent years about anti-Semitism in poems such as "Gerontion" and a handful of other Eliot poems. Perhaps this line in "Practical Cats" is also worth some debate.

"The Song of the Jellicles" talks of a group of cats rather than a single one, describing the Jellicle cats and the preparations they make for the "Jellicle Moon and the Jellicle Ball" (156). Relentlessly rhythmic, exactly rhymed, with more than half its lines beginning with the words "Jellicle Cats," the poem is hypnotic, managing to be both whimsical and haunting.

Eliot's next pair of cats are thieves and saboteurs: "Mungojerrie and Rumpleteazer had a very unusual gift of the gab, / They were highly efficient cat-burglars as well, and remarkably smart at a smash-and-grab" (156). Much of the fun of this poem is found in the reactions of a hapless family—presumably the cats' owners—to Mungojerrie and Rumpleteazer's crimes: "Or after supper one of the girls / Suddenly missed her Woolworth pearls: / Then the family would say: "It's that horrible cat!" Like Growltiger and several of the cats to come, Mungojerrie and Rumpleteazer are anthropomorphized

into colorful criminals who have "really a little more reputation than a couple of cats can very well bare" (156). Old Deuteronomy has a different sort of reputation: his claim to fame is his tremendous old age. When Deuteronomy suns himself, villagers close roads and shut down pubs so as not to disturb his sleep. As in many of the poems, the comic situation of "Old Deuteronomy" revolves around making a cat the center of human activity.

The full title of Eliot's next poem, phrased in the language of an Elizabethan broadsheet, summarizes its action neatly: "Of the Awefull Battle of the Pekes and the Pollicles: Together with some Account of the Participation of the Pug and Poms, and the Intervention of the Great Rumpuscat" (159). Two packs of dogs, the Pekes and the Pollicles, aided by their allies the Pugs and the Poms, ready for a great fight. Just as the dogs have squared off, they are interrupted by the appearance of "the GREAT RUMPUSCAT" (160). He is fearsome to behold: "His eyes were like fireballs fearfully blazing, / He gave a great yawn, and his jaws were amazing" (160). The Rumpuscat chases the dogs away, bringing peace to the park and street once more. As happens at several other points in the collection, notably in "On Ad-dressing a Cat," cats establish themselves as superior to dogs.

More of Eliot's individual portraits follow "The Pekes and the Pollicles." Mr. Mistofelees is a conjurer: "At prestidigitation / And at legerdemain / He'll defy imagination / And deceive you again" (161). "Macavity: The Mystery Cat" is the cat presented on the grandest scale. "The bafflement of Scotland Yard," Macavity is responsible for crimes committed by a criminal syndicate of cats he holds under his sway (163). Eliot, a lifelong fan of Arthur Conan Doyle's Sherlock Holmes stories, must have had Holmes's nemesis Dr. Moriarity in mind when he created Macavity. Like Moriarity, Macavity is a gentleman turned criminal mastermind.

"Gus: The Theater Cat" is the poem that most clearly approaches the dramatic monologue, in that the bulk of the poem is narrated by Gus himself. In keeping with the conventions of the traditional Victorian dramatic monologue, there is a gap between how Gus thinks of himself and how the reader thinks of him. Though he brags of his great acting career, the reader suspects that Gus is not so much a has-been as a never-was. "Gus" is perhaps the most purely witty of the cat poems, an incisive little satire: "He loves to regale them, if someone else pays, / With anecdotes drawn from his palmiest days" (164). The poem is also full of cat puns: an appreciative audience, for example, gives not a standing ovation but "seven cat-calls" (164). Two more portraits round out the collection. "Bustopher Jones: The Cat about Town" is a bon-vivant, while "Skimbleshanks: The Railway Cat," keeps order on the Night Mail train. Later editions include a final portrait, "Cat Morgan Introduces Himself," in which a cat that inhabited the offices of Eliot's London publishing house talks of himself in an East End Cockney accent.

The collection ends with "The Ad-dressing of Cats," which both serves as a summation of what has come before, and tries to answer the question, "How would you ad-dress a Cat?" (169). The first and last poems of the collection therefore treat not individual cats, but relationships between cats and humans. This movement into and then back out of a fantastical world is familiar to readers of Lewis Carroll. The two "Alice" books begin and end with Alice safely at home rather than wandering the topsy-turvy world of Wonderland. Similarly, Eliot, in this collection's first poem, moves us into the "effanineffable" world of the cat, and in the last draws us back out into a more familiar world in which the proper relationship between cats and humans is restored.

Historical Context

Childhood is both a biological reality and a social construct. It can be difficult, living in the twenty-first century, to distinguish between the two. Yet if one goes back to medieval art and literature, for example, one finds a representation of childhood that stands in sharp contrast to our own. In early modern Europe, children were generally depicted as little adults: smaller, weaker, but not fundamentally different from the fully-grown men and women around them. In paintings, they bear the proportions of the adult figure; in literature, they talk with the language of an adult. Childhood as we know it today is a Romantic creation. It was Wordsworth who argued that children come into the world "trailing clouds of glory" and that "the Child is Father of the man" ("Ode: Intimations of Immortality," 64; "My Heart Leaps Up," 7). The Victorians took their cue from the Romantic poets of the early nineteenth century, creating a decidedly sentimental culture of childhood. Not only did children begin to figure prominently in literature (think of Dickens' Tiny Tim, for one) but literature was written specifically for children. If the Romantics created childhood, the Victorians created children's literature. In previous centuries, children might have been given "The Pilgrim's Progress" to read. In the nineteenth century, they were given Carroll's "Alice in Wonderland" and Edward Lear's "The Owl and the Pussycat." This new literature recognized fundamental differences between children and adults, playing with nonsense words and, indeed, non-logical thought in a way that both mimics and encourages the developmental processes of children. It is the Victorians who begin to write works for children that are not explicitly didactic. Similarly, there is a double-awareness to the best of Victorian children's literature: it can be enjoyed both by children and by adults. "Peter Pan," for example, was made a great success not only by children, but also by adults who loved the play.

Eliot therefore owes a debt to Carroll, Lear, J. M. Barrie, and other Victorian poets and writers of children's verse. Eliot's invented nonsense words, such as "jellicle" and "pollicle," are reminiscent of the nonsense words in Carroll's poem "Jabber-wocky:" "'Twas brillig, and the slithy toves / Did gyre and gimble in the wabe" (1-2). In "Through the Looking Glass," incidentally, Alice follows her cat, Dinah, through the mirror and into Wonderland. In terms of both the rhythm and the theme of his cat poems, however, it is Lear to whom Eliot is most indebted. Eliot had previously mimicked Lear in his poem "How Unpleasant to Meet Mr. Eliot," a burlesque of Lear's "How Pleasant to Meet Mr. Lear." Lear's poems, such as "The Owl and the Pussycat," use the galloping rhythms of the limerick or nursery rhyme to recount the adventures of anthropomorphized animals. Indeed, Eliot's own nom-de-plume for "Practical Cats," Old Possum, reverses the anthropomorphic process by identifying the author with an animal. Eliot turns a nickname that Pound had given him (because of his ability to "play dead" by not revealing what he is thinking) into a full-fledged persona.

Societal Context

The English have long regarded the lower classes and the criminal element (which at many points in English history have been thought synonymous) with an uneasy admixture of horror and fascination. This anxiety manifests itself in an impulse to romanticize the criminal. For, indeed, English literature offers a host of cutpurses with hearts of gold, from Robin Hood to the Artful Dodger. As an Anglophile and as an American born to an elite family (Eliot's grandfather founded the Unitarian church in St. Louis as well as Washington University), Eliot shares this preoccupation with a streetwise, criminal milieu to which he himself had little direct access. In Part II of "The Waste Land," in experimental works such as "Sweeney Agonistes," and in some of his unpublished verse, he explored the patterns of speech and behavior of the lower classes and of criminals. "Practical Cats" gives him license both to celebrate and to contain criminal and anti-social behavior by attributing

it to brigand cats that steal, fight, and commit all sorts of sabotage.

Notice, therefore, how many of Eliot's cats are anthropomorphized into charming criminals. Growltiger is a gallant pirate, Mungojerrie and Rumpelteazer are suave burglars, Macavity is a criminal mastermind wanted by Scotland Yard. The cat poems quite literally "domesticate" criminality by equating it to the sly or mischievous activities of housecats. Those cats that are not explicitly criminals, such as Gus, the Theater Cat, nevertheless live a hardscrabble life. Gus is down on his luck, willing to trade his stories for "a toothful of gin" (165). Like Charlie Chaplin's Little Tramp, he is a sentimentalized version of the urban poor. "Practical Cats" is therefore one more entry in the canon of the sentimentalized English rogue or ne'er-do-well.

Scientific & Technological Context

"Skimbleshanks: The Railway Cat" is a great paean to train travel. Although Eliot traveled, by train, plane, and automobile, it is only the train—railroad and underground alike—that his poetry valorizes. In "Skimbleshanks," he captures the rhythms and sights of traveling on a night train. God is in the details, and this poem works precisely because Eliot has so keenly observed the details of railroad travel. It begins, for example, with that awareness of minutes rather than hours that the train's timetable demands: "There's a whisper down the line at 11.39 / When the Night Mail's ready to depart" (167). One would be hard-pressed to find a better description of traveling in a sleeping car than that of the third stanza, beginning "Oh it's very pleasant when you have found your little den / With your name written up on the door. / And the berth is very neat with a newly folded sheet / and there's not a speck of dust on the floor" (168). The passage evokes not merely the physical space of the sleeping car berth, but the sense of comfort and security it provides its inhabitant.

Skimbleshanks is "in charge of the Sleeping Car Express," smoothing the way for the train and its passengers (167). Confident that Skimbleshanks is on duty, passengers can sleep soundly. The poem conjures that sense of drifting asleep on a moving train and waking to find it has already passed through several stops. The narrator treats the reader as a fellow passenger, informing him of what Skimbleshanks has been doing while he has been asleep. "You were fast asleep at Crewe and so you never knew / That he was walking up and down the station; / You were sleeping all the while he was busy at Carlisle, / Where he greets the station master with elation" (169). The reader is ensconced in his sleeping car berth, whereas Skimbleshanks is integrally involved with the business of running the train. Skimbleshanks emerges as a sort of ghost in the locomotive machine, a presence that gives train travel a human—or rather, a feline—touch.

Religious Context

Andrew Lloyd Webber's musical "Cats" (1981), based on "Practical Cats," is explicitly Christian in some of its symbolism and staging, most notably in a final scene of apotheosis in which Grizabella seems to ascend into Heaven. "Practical Cats," on the other hand, is only implicitly religious. Nevertheless, one can identify strains of Christianity and Buddhism running through Eliot's cycle of poems.

Eliot wrote "Practical Cats" subsequent to his 1927 conversion to Anglicanism, and this fact alone might prompt one to read the work as engaging, on some level, with Christian themes and symbols. The first poem in the collection, "The Naming of Cats," may evoke the doctrine of the trinity by declaring that cats have "three different names" (149). Certainly the cat's third name partakes of the religious: the cat sits in "rapt contemplation," thinking of "his ineffable effable / Effanineffable / Deep and inscrutable singular Name" (149). Is it God, or perhaps the nature of the soul, that both is and is not "effable" (able to be described

in words)? Eliot's coinage of the word "effanineffable" may be an attempt to capture the seemingly opposite qualities that religious faith unites: effable revelation and ineffable mystery.

The image of one sitting in "rapt contemplation" may call to mind Buddhist meditation rather than Christian prayer. The Buddha, after all, achieved enlightenment by sitting in contemplation under a fig tree. Eliot had an abiding interest in Buddhism, which he had studied at Harvard and to which he briefly considered converting. Buddhism and other eastern religions figure into several of his poems and plays, including "The Waste Land." In "The Naming of Cats," as in "The Waste Land," Eliot seems to be fusing elements of Eastern and Western religious practices and beliefs to create a composite faith.

Read in light of "The Naming of Cats," some of the protagonists of the subsequent poems might take on religious dimensions. The "GREAT RUMPUSCAT," for example, comes down upon the feuding Pekes and Pollicles with the power and rage of an Old Testament prophet or a Jove, his eyes "like great fireballs fearfully blazing" (160). Webber, in his musical, recast some of the characters into Biblical archetypes, transforming the sleepy Old Deuteronomy into a quasi-divine patriarch. Yet one must be careful not to read too much into these poems. "Practical Cats" is by no means an allegory, and neither Christianity, Buddhism, nor any other religion will serve as a skeleton key to unlock a pattern of encoded meaning across the poems. Nevertheless, in a handful of passages—particularly at the conclusion of "The Naming of Cats"—Eliot subtly shifts from writing about the feline to writing about the divine.

Biographical Context

St. Louis-born and Harvard-educated, Thomas Stearns Eliot lived most of his adult life in England, where he came in 1913 to study at Oxford. Although Eliot finished his doctoral dissertation, the First World War prevented him from returning to Harvard to defend it and receive his degree. In 1915, he abandoned academia for the life of a poet and writer. He married an Englishwoman, Vivienne Haigh Wood, and took up residence in London. He spent the next decade working at a furious pace: teaching, reviewing books, and eventually working at Lloyd's bank. He published "Prufrock and other Observations" in 1917, which was followed by two more books of poetry and a collection of essays drawn from his book reviews, "The Sacred Wood." In 1922, he published "The Waste Land," to great critical acclaim.

The 1920's were a time of great personal and professional change for Eliot. His marriage grew ever more fractious, while the new fame that "The Waste Land" had brought him proved burdensome. He struggled to break a poetic writer's block and to find a new theme and mode of verse that would be substantively different from "The Waste Land." In 1926, he left Lloyd's to take a job as editor at the publishing house Faber & Gwyer. The next year, in 1927, he converted to the Church of England and adopted British citizenship. His poems after the conversion, such as "Journey of the Magi" and "Ash Wednesday," took on explicitly religious themes and forms. He took steps to transform his home-life, as well: by the end of the decade, he had separated from Vivienne, who within a few years would be committed to an institution.

At the time, he began composing the poems that would become "Old Possum's Book of Practical Cats," Eliot was living what Gordon Lydall calls, in the title of one of her biographies of the poet, his "new life." A de-facto bachelor for the first time in fifteen years, Eliot spent a good deal of time with the families of his friends Frank Morley and Geoffrey Faber, for whose publishing house Eliot worked as an editor. "Practical Cats" grew out of doggerel rhymes that he composed to entertain the Morley and Faber children. Eliot

himself was childless, and he may have seen these young people as surrogates. One of his poems of the late 1920's, "Marina," seems a cry to a vanished child, twice bearing the refrain, "O my daughter" (6, 36).

Yet it is not enough to say that a practical occasion—an interest in entertaining a few children—led Eliot to write "Practical Cats." How do we place these nonsense poems in the larger context of Eliot's life and career? Certainly, they look back, with their bouncing rhythms, made-up words, and larger-than-life characters, to the obscene "Bolo" and "Columbo" poems that Eliot included in letters to a handful of male friends, including Conrad Aiken, Ezra Pound, and James Joyce (Ricks 320). These bawdy doggerel verses are decidedly not for children, treating the sexual grotesqueries of a sailor named Colombo and a new world King named Bolo. Eliot excised them from his journal, and it was not until the 1990s that they were publicly printed. As Eliot's celebrity grew during the first half of the twenties, and as he became more religious during the second half of the decade, he took increasing pains to shape his public image. Obscene verses did not fit with the persona he created for himself. "Practical Cats," on the other hand, is a socially acceptable, desexualized way to be silly. The impulse behind the two sets of poems may therefore be much the same: the desire of a reserved, self-conscious man to act or speak absurdly.

"Practical Cats" therefore presents Eliot in a different light than do his weightier poems. Here is the Eliot who, as a young man, frequented music halls and boxing matches and who, in middle age, formed a Sherlock Holmes fan club and enjoyed watching Marx Brothers movies. "Practical Cats" was more than a diversion for Eliot: it reflects, no less than does a poem like "Ash Wednesday," his abiding interests.

Matthew J. Bolton, Ph.D.

Works Cited

Ackroyd, Peter. *T. S. Eliot: A Life*. New York: Simon & Schuster, 1984.

Eliot, T. S. *Old Possum's Book of Practical Cats*. New York: Harcourt, Brace, & Jovanovich, 1939, 1972, 1982.

_____. *The Complete Poems and Plays: 1909-1950*. New York: Harcourt, Brace &World, 1962.

_____. *The Waste Land: A Facsimile and Transcript of the Original Drafts including the Annotations of Ezra Pound*. Ed. Valerie Eliot. New York: Harcourt Brace Jovanovich, 1971.

_____. *Inventions of the March Hare*. Ed. Christopher Ricks. New York: Harcourt Brace, 1996.

Gordon, Lyndall. "Eliot's New Life." New York: Farrar Straus Giroux, 1988.

Wullschlager, Jackie. *Inventing Wonderland: The Lives and Fantasies of Lewis Carroll, Edward Lear, J. M. Barrie, Kenneth Grahame, and A. A. Milne*. New York: Free Press, 1995.

Discussion Questions

1. How do you see these poems as being linked? Is there a master plot or narrative that seems to bind them together?
2. To what extent is this collection a children's book? Are there passages that seem more geared toward a child and others that seem more geared toward an adult?
3. Does the same character narrate these poems all? Does the Old Possum of the title have any real identity that emerges across the poems? Pay particular attention to the first and last poems in the collection.
4. Eliot converted to the Church of England about a decade before publishing "Practical Cats," and much of his criticism and poetry after the conversion explicitly addressed religious issues. Do you see any religious, Christian, or spiritual overtones or symbols in "Practical Cats?"
5. Does "Practical Cats" function as social criticism? How do individual portraits of cats comment on issues of poverty, crime, race, class, or gender?
6. While the title of the work refers only to cats, dogs also appear in the collection several times. Contrast Eliot's dogs with his cats. How do the dogs serve as a foil for the cats? How is their relationship with humans and with each other fundamentally different from those of the cats?
7. At what points does "Practical Cats" seem to reach beyond the boundaries of comedy toward some more profound statement? Are there points in the collection where comedy gives way to tragedy or pathos?

Essay Ideas

1. Explicate the rhyme scheme and metrical pattern of any one of these poems. What is the relationship between meter and meaning, sound and sense? How do rhyme, rhythm, and meter help to produce or reinforce the meaning of the poem? Are some rhyme schemes or meters inherently silly?
2. We recognize a distinctly Shakespearean quality to Shakespeare's work, whether we are reading one of his tragedies or one of his comedies. Contrast one or several of the cat poems with one or more of Eliot's "serious" poems. What emerges as distinctly "Eliotic" in such a comparison? Some poems to consider might include "The Love Song of J. Alfred Prufrock," "Portrait of a Lady," "The Waste Land," "The Hollow Men," and "Marina."
3. Compare "Practical Cats" to the book for Andrew Lloyd Webber's musical "Cats." How did Webber change or revise Eliot's collection in creating the script for the musical? What was imposed on Eliot's work and what was lost?

One Art

by Elizabeth Bishop

Content Synopsis

One of the finest examples of the form, Elizabeth Bishop's villanelle "One Art" is a tightly structured poem that actively works against its own structure. It resists the stringent demands of its form, erecting a kind of psychological dam, where the calm surface belies the enormous strain of welled-up grief. Though Bishop wrote during the rise of "Confessional" poetry—a term usually applied to a poet, like Sylvia Plath, whose power is in unconcealed emotion—Bishop's poem is nothing if not an exercise in restraint, working both with and against a challenging form. The way she works with, and against, this formalist aesthetic creates a poem that is ambiguous, layered with meanings and possibility.

The first line of the poem begins with a statement that is itself full of ambiguity: "The art of losing isn't hard to master" (1). On one hand, the poet seems to be announcing something important, something decisive. Yet what is the art of losing? Are we meant to recognize it as something else, or literally, as in losing our keys? The second stanza, with its playful "lose something every day" (5), does not sound serious at all. After all, nothing lost so far is irreplaceable. However, as the refrain returns, the poem seems straining to keep its playfulness. The voice proclaiming, "The art of losing isn't hard to master," sounds less and less sure of itself as the poem goes on, and the losses are

added up. First, there are some pedestrian things like keys or an "hour badly spent" (6). However, the losses grow like weeds: "places" and "names" (8) in the third stanza, then "my mother's watch" (11) and "three loved houses" (12) in the fourth. By the time the poet has lost "two cities," (13) "rivers, a continent" (14) the refrain feels as hollow as a supermarket condolence card. At the end, when the final loss—"you"—is incurred, the poet has clearly "lied," or at least, denied the pain of these disastrous losses.

When we reach the last refrain, a parenthetical directive— "(Write it!)" (22)—provides the necessary crack in the formal armor of the poem. The poet is revealed as someone urging herself to be happy, as someone might repeat a mantra in order to calm herself. In this case, however, the mantra is the refrain of "no disaster," which in the end turns out to have been a lie: they are disasters, every one. The voice that takes over for two words in the last line has been the poet's true voice, masked (mastered, you might say) by the form and the tone of the poem.

Historical Context

The villanelle as a form traces its roots to 15th Italian pastoral poetry—the word itself means "rural" or "rustic" and is derived from villano, Italian for "peasant." However, the 16th century poet Jean Passerat probably codified its modern form requirements. The form consists of five tercets and a final quatrain, with the first and last lines of the first tercet reoccurring as a refrain, and then, in the final quatrain, as the final couplet. An old pastoral poem might begin its first tercet thus:

The fields are flowering, the roses bloom
Where Alessa my fair-haired beauty walks
Toward the blue ocean in the afternoon.

The built-in strength of the villanelle is its repetition. As the reader hears, and comes to expect the refrain, the refrain itself often changes its mood. Here, for instance, the scene is happy: we take the image of the sea and the roses to mirror the beauty of Alessa. In the middle tercets of the poem, however, she might drown, and the refrain "Down to the bright blue sea" becomes ominous instead. At the ending quatrain, the refrain "Down to the bright blue sea" might be elegiac:

Now the rains have come and the autumn
    moon,
The crops have been cut to the stalks.
No fields are flowering, no red roses bloom,
Just the cold blue ocean in the afternoon.

The refrain, as it progresses, relatively unchanged syntactically, undergoes a full change in emotion. In addition, because we hear the refrain—this would have been sung, not read—repeatedly throughout the poem, we not only expect it, but we become particularly attuned to any slight change. This is the power of form at its most basic: it provides a structure where the reader thinks he knows what is coming. It is then up to the author to either fulfill that expectation or—as Bishop does here—subvert it.

"One Art" appears in the collection "Geography III," published in 1976. Although she had won numerous awards, including the Pulitzer Prize for "Poems: North & South—A Cold Spring" twenty years before, Bishop remained insecure about her poetry. Additionally, the poetry zeitgeist of the 70's

was the Confessional style, an intimate, sometimes claustrophobic approach to poetry that relied on secrets and events of the poet's life to create shock, sympathy, or anger in the reader. Many of the Confessional poets wrote in free verse in an attempt to liberate themselves from the constraints of form, a gesture that symbolically liberated them from the canon. Formal perfection was out; raw energy and unsettling honesty, such as one found in Robert Lowell and Sylvia Plath's poems, was in. In this context, the formality of Bishop's verse must be appreciated for what it says as well as what it refrains from saying. Where Lowell and Plath were comfortable with including biographical information no matter how personal and detailed (Lowell went so far as to include letters from his wife, verbatim, in "The Dolphin"), Bishop's poetics were far more armored; she censured Lowell after this in a letter, reminding him "art isn't worth that much" (Goldensohn 227). Although free, confessional-sounding verse has ultimately triumphed in poetry journals and classrooms, "One Art" survives as one of the great formal successes of this period of American poetry.

Societal Context
"Elizabeth Bishop is spectacular in being unspectacular," wrote the poet Marianne Moore in a review of "North and South" ("Complete Prose" 406). Indeed, Bishop's poems often are not spectacular, nor do they overwhelm with virtuosic cascades of language. However, today Bishop stands as perhaps the most celebrated mid-century American female poet.

Moreover, she stands as the most relevant figure from that era, having survived the Modern, Formalist, Confessional, and Post-Modern eras with her reputation and admirers intact. During her lifetime, in comparison, esteem for her work was limited to a small number of admirers, her close friend and widely acclaimed poet Robert Lowell among them. Today, Lowell, as well as other then-popular poets like Theodore Roethke, Weldon Kees, and John Berryman lags behind Bishop in anthologies and academic studies; her poems are more widely read than any female author save Emily Dickinson.

In 1976, when "Geography III" was published, Bishop was teaching at Harvard. She was well regarded but by no means the major presence in the canon that she is today. Dana Gioia, who was a student at the time, sent in an appreciative remembrance after her death in 1979 to "The New Yorker" because, as he later writes in the "New Criterion," "I was worried that she would be forgotten" (2). The 10 poems of "Geography III," which are some of her best—"One Art" and "In the Waiting Room" among them—were well-received, but when she died three years later her relatively slim collection of work was not seen as the major contribution it is today. In a prophetic moment, Lowell, who himself was America's premier poet at the time, wrote in a letter that Bishop's language and images seemed to "belong to a later century." This description has proved correct, as the 20th and 21st centuries have seen an incredible increase in the volume of study on her life and work.

In an article in "The New Criterion" Gioia speculates that Bishop's later ascendancy can partially be attributed to the academy's increased interest in marginalized and displaced voices. Bishop occupied an almost constant status as outsider, since she was often a stranger to her surroundings, living a peripatetic life from such a young age. Additionally, Bishop's status as a lesbian has encouraged study of her poems using ideas from gender studies and Queer theory.

However, Gioia concludes, these factors are secondary to the poems themselves in making Bishop so popular. Comparing her to Keats, Gioia writes that Bishop possessed what Keats described as "negative capability," a term describing the poet's state of ambiguity and mystery. "She had a native genius for reflecting the rich complexity of experience without reducing it into abstraction or predetermined moral judgment," writes Gioia, echoing Moore's description, "She is inclusive by being artfully inconclusive" (8). "One Art," ending as it does with an inconclusive, mysterious conclusion, is emblematic of this quality.

Religious Context

Although not immediately apparent, Bishop counted the devotional poetry of George Herbert as a major influence on her work. In their modesty and relentless pursuit of accuracy, Elizabeth Bishop's poems do resemble Herbert; both of them seeking to put into words what Herbert calls in his poem "Prayer(I)," "A kind of tune, which all things hear and fear." Like Herbert, Bishop's "One Art" possesses a kind of humility in the face of loss, never defiant or boastful. What might be called the reverent aspect of Bishop's work is never explicitly religious—her awe is reserved for the natural and unnatural world—and though the poem may not be about God, it is certainly about belief. Herbert's quality of doubtful belief and resolution, so central to the tension of his poems, is shown here in the last lines of "The Affliction": "Ah my dear God! though I am clean forgot, / Let me not love thee, if I love thee not" (65-6). The ambition of the poem is simply to be as true to the poet's emotion, a task that requires enormous courage. It is quite similar to "One Art," where Bishop dramatizes the tension between what we would like to feel—what we say we feel—and what we do feel.

Scientific & Technological Context

Though her writing is not directly interested in science, Bishop has always been noted for an obsession with accuracy and classification. As a tourist and perpetual visitor in Brazil and on her other journeys, she often made studies of birdlife, plants and people. Her interest, however, is not in finding the correct scientific names of things, but in determining the most effective and honest way to describe them. Technologically speaking, the advent of air travel shows up as an influence on some of her poems—it certainly facilitated some of her globetrotting as well. There are not enough poems, however, that explicitly deal with technology to rightly call it a concern of hers. A rare example is "Night City," where her description of the city from the plane is both surreal and dangerous: "Broken glass, broken bottles, / heaps of them burn" (3-4). The plane's vantage point, far from a convenience, reveals the destruction on the ground.

Biographical Context

Although she maintained that one need not know the biography of a poet in order to appreciate the poem, Bishop's life certainly informs and enlarges the scope of her own poetry, which often alludes to real experiences of her life. "One Art," for example, is a kind of biography of loss, and each item lost does have a corresponding biographical loss. When she was five years old, her mother was committed to a sanitarium in Dartmouth, Nova Scotia after a prolonged period of mental illness. Her father died when she was eight months old and Bishop was left in the care of her mother's parents, who took her to the Nova Scotia town of Great Village. Bishop was to move from Nova Scotia in 1917 to Worcester, Mass, to live with her father's parents, and then to her aunt's house a year later. At the age of eight, she had lived in four households with four different families; the themes of travel and loss became intertwined at a young age.

In 1930, Bishop enrolled at Vassar, where she majored in English Literature and co-founded the school's literary magazine, *Con Spirito* and served as the editor of the college yearbook. The most important event of her college life occurred in 1934, however, when she first met the poet Marianne Moore. The friendship between them lasted until Moore's death, and was instrumental in bringing Bishop to New York, where she moved after graduation. Moore wrote an introduction for the first publication Bishop received, a group of poems

in the anthology "Trial Balances." Moreover, the two women discussed and criticized each other's work; Bishop was heavily influenced by the interplay between formal structure, rhyme, and rhythm that is a hallmark of Moore's work.

Bishop traveled extensively throughout her life. In the three years following her graduation she lived mostly in Paris, and took multiple trips throughout Europe, Morocco, and Florida, where she lived briefly in Key West. In 1942, on a trip through Mexico, Cuba, and Haiti, she met Lota de Macedo Soares, a Brazilian woman from a prominent family in Rio de Janeiro; in 1951 the two would begin living together in Brazil. By this time, Bishop was an acclaimed, if not wildly popular poet, having been offered a Guggenheim Fellowship in 1947, an appointment as Consultant in Poetry at the Library of Congress in 1949 (similar to the current position of Poet Laureate), and an award from the American Academy of Arts and Letters in 1950. However, she continued to have trouble with depression and alcoholism, problems that had not been helped by her lifestyle in New York. Her trip to Brazil was part of an around-the-world tour she hoped might be a welcome break from the pace and anxieties of the city—she later wrote to Lowell "I was miserably lonely there most of the time" (Goldensohn 9). However, upon arrival, Bishop had a violently allergic reaction to a cashew she ate, and was hospitalized for five days. Soares, who Bishop had planned to visit, invited her to extend her stay and recuperate her home, which was a meeting place for many Brazilian architects and writers. Bishop accepted and ended up staying for over a decade.

Bishop and Soares lived together intermittently in Rio, in Petropolis, and in a 17th century house in Ouro Preto, Brazil. At the beginning, Bishop's life in Brazil had a cathartic effect on her health and poetry; she began to confront her longstanding addiction to alcohol and her depression. As her career flourished, though, their relationship began to deteriorate. The publication of "Poems:

North & South—A Cold Spring," which combined her first book with new poems, won the Pulitzer Prize in 1955. "Questions of Travel," her third collection, was also well received, and dealt with familiar themes of travel, displacement, and tourism: "Should we have stayed home and thought of here?" she asks in the title poem (14). However, there were significant strains in her relationship with Soares at this time, who was afflicted by her own problems with depression and anxiety. Bishop spent less and less time in Brazil, teaching instead at universities in the U.S. and coming back to Brazil intermittently. In September of 1967, while visiting Bishop in New York, Soares overdosed on sleeping pills in an apparent suicide.

After her partner's death, Bishop lived primarily in Boston, teaching at Harvard and writing the poems that would be published in "Geography III." She continued to travel extensively (a partial list of places includes Yugoslavia, Ecuador, Norway, Sweden, and the Galapagos Islands), and in 1976 received the prestigious Books Abroad/Neustadt Award, the first American and first female recipient. On October 6, 1979 she died at home in Boston.

Andrew Allport

Works Cited

Bishop, Elizabeth. *The Complete Poems*. New York: Farrar, Straus and Giroux, 1993.

———. *One Art: Letters*. Ed. Robert Giroux. New York: Farrar, Straus, and Giroux, 1994.

Gioia, Dana. *From Coterie to Canon*. The New Criterion. Vol. 22, No. 8. April 2004.

Goldensohn, Lorrie. *Elizabeth Bishop: The Biography of a Poetry*. New York: Columbia UP, 1992.

Moore, Marianne. *Complete Prose*. New York: Viking, 1986. 406-7.

Discussion Questions

1. The difficulty, and pleasure, of "One Art," is the masterful tone of the poem, which manages to incorporate many emotional registers. Where specifically do these changing tones—happy, melancholy, sardonic—surface in the poem? How are they created?

2. Read "One Art" aloud. How do its rhymes and rhythms affect a recitation? What differences do you so between the poem on the page and aloud?

3. The final command to "Write it!" is direct and urgent. But who, exactly, is being told what? Who is speaking to whom, and why is the command so striking?

4. For all the repetition, the first lines of the poem remain ambiguous. What, exactly, is "The art of losing"? Why is it an art? What other clues in the poem lead the reader to consider other meanings of "losing" and "art"?

5. "One Art" began as a piece of prose. Imagining what it might have looked like, compare its first versions to the final villanelle form. What does the poem gain by its present form? More generally, how do poems in form—sonnets, sestinas, rhymed verse—differ from free verse?

6. How much about Bishop's life do you think we need to know in order to make the poem effective? Does the biographical "truth" matter in a poem?

7. Bishop's language is emphatically plain: Marianne Moore said she was "spectacular in being unspectacular." How does her style here prove this paradox? What is "unspectacular" about the poem?

8. What role does travel play in "One Art"? How many kinds of travel are represented here? How does travel appear to relate to "losing"?

9. "One Art" can be read as a kind of lesson: "Practice losing," she tells the reader. Why would Bishop choose to frame the poem in this context? Who is giving the lesson, and who is learning it?

Essay Ideas

1. Write a villanelle. The poem must be 6 stanzas, with 5 tercets and 1 quatrain. You may change the refrain only slightly. After you have finished, write a short paper describing the difficulties you faced in the composition—what are the factors for success in this form? What makes it challenging or interesting?

2. Bishop's "Armadillo" is a poem in conversation with Robert Lowell's "Skunk Hour." The poems are addressed to the other poet, and the vision of the natural world, as it comes into contact with humans, is central to both. What fundamental differences are there in the poets' styles? How do the poems speak to these differences?

3. How would you describe the tone of "One Art"? Do its rhymes and asides seem playful or old-fashioned; formulaic or technically deft? How and why does the tone change in the poem?

4. "You'd just wish they'd keep some of these things to themselves," Bishop told "Time" in 1967 for their cover story on Robert Lowell, whose Confessional style included brutal truths about his own troubled life, even excerpts from his wife's anguished letters. In the ensuing 30 years, poetry, at least in the popular imagination, seems to mean something closer to the free verse confessions of Lowell and Sylvia Plath than Bishop's formal poem, "One Art." In what ways does Bishop keep things to herself in this poem? What clues—or even confessions—does she make to the reader?

5. Compare Bishop's "The Fish" with Marianne Moore's poem of the same name. Bishop sent Moore the poem, writing that she is "afraid it is very bad, if not like Robert Frost, perhaps like Ernest Hemingway!" ("Letters" 87). How do these two poems reflect the differences and similarities of the two? How do they illustrate Moore's influence and Bishop's resistance to it?

Pictured above is Edgar Allen Poe's New York cottage. Poe's "The Raven" is featured on page 159 of this volume.
Photo: Library of Congress

The Possessive

by Sharon Olds

Content Synopsis

"The Possessive" appears in the third sequence of poems entitled "The Mother" in Sharon Olds' first collection of poetry, "Satan Says" (1980). This poem is representative of one dominant strand in Olds' work that draws on her experiences as a mother. While Olds is noted for her use of autobiographical material, this poem is distinct from her other work in that it does not portray a bodily experience such as sex or childbirth. Instead, it takes note of a small but significant moment in a mother-daughter relationship and makes it universal.

In this poem, the speaker gazes at her daughter, who has just returned from the barber, "that knife grinder" (4). While the daughter's age is not mentioned, the speaker expresses a feeling of coming detachment and battle, indicating that she is a pre-adolescent. The theme of battle is underscored throughout the poem by the repetition of violent language and imagery. The "edge" of the daughter's hair has been "sharpened" as if it were a sword (5). The image of the daughter, with a "blade of new bangs" (7) hanging over her eyes like "paper-cuts" (12) evokes the image of a soldier in a "bright helmet" (15) with eyes "like carbon steel" (9). The detachment between the speaker and the daughter is repeated using the words "distance" and "Distant" next to each other in the same line (17). The daughter's eyes have now become

full of "the watch fires of an enemy," as if containing troops lying in wait (19).

The title refers to the use of the word "my" in the poem where the speaker refers to "my daughter" in an attempt to make sense of the gradual separation of daughter from mother (1, 14). While the daughter "started from next to nothing" (13) in the speaker's body, she is a separate being who looks at her mother "as if across a/great distance" (16-17). Before going to get her hair cut, the daughter's hair was "wispy as a frayed bellpull." A bellpull is a cord or handle used to pull a bell, usually connected with a bell to call a servant. This image evokes a little girl who might be 'pulled' into acquiescence but now she has become a little soldier, someone separate and distinct from the mother (3). The choice of title indicates that the speaker is questioning the use of the grammatical possessive form "my" to describe her daughter, an attitude announced at the beginning of the poem with the line "as if I/owned her" (1-2). The speaker calls attention to the possessive pronoun in order to highlight the inevitable loss that occurs between child and parent as the child grows up and becomes her own person. That the child is coming into "possession" of herself might be read in the line where she has "had the edge of her hair sharpened." This puts emphasis on the daughter's control in her haircut; by the end, however, she has not fully entered the battle yet, as the passive tense suggests in the line "Distant fires can be/glimpsed in the resin lights of her eyes" (17-18).

While this free-verse poem does not follow any regular rhyme or rhythm, the repetition of sounds in some of the lines draws attention to the poem's theme and imagery. "Daughter" and "her" in the first and second lines create an internal rhyme, which could delineate the underlying significance in pronoun usage, from "my" to "her." The use of two similar-sounding but different-meaning words, "spliced" and "sliced," emphasizes the change in the relationship between mother and daughter from being connected to being separated (11). Two words in perfect rhyme, "bangs" and "hangs," are separated by a line break and appear within a stanza that is almost completely taken up by monosyllabic words (7-8). The effect of this is that the stress falls on each world almost equally and that they themselves sound like they are being "banged" out in a steady, spondee rhythm, which stresses every syllable, as if a drum beat preceding a battle.

The first three sections of "Satan Says" are organized into the stages of a woman's life: daughter, woman (which includes wife/lover), and mother. The last section, entitled "Journey," might be read as corresponding to the last phase, that of old age or what might be called the time of the "crone," a time when a woman looks back on her life and prepares for death. The connotation of "journey" also might be that of a time when she is freed from the identities of daughter, lover, and mother in order to discover her own identity. In "The Possessive," the speaker repeats and reinforces the underlying motifs and themes of the collection as a whole as one of both connection and separation, as the daughter begins to repeat the same cycle as the mother.

Historical Context

In assigning a whole section of poems under the title, "Mother," Olds places herself in a tradition of mother-poets. In America, this begins with one of our oldest poets, Anne Bradstreet, who lived and wrote during the colonial period. Critic Susan MacCallum-Whitcomb explains that prior to industrialization, the home was the basic economic unit, with husband and wife working together (41-42). The rise of industrialization in the nineteenth century, among other phenomena, gave way to a social system that separated women and men into more distinct roles, with men entering the public sphere for work and women dominating the private sphere of the home. Writing, while an activity that can be done in the spaces of time between meals, diaper changes, and other duties, came to be seen as more a separate vocation. Still many women did write, and enjoyed popularity as a result. Yet their success remained only popular, as "[s]erious critical consideration was only reserved for men speaking to men about topics that were assumed to be of significance to the world at large," and in that day and age, the concerns of a mother, restricted to the private sphere, did not fit into that assumption (MacCallum-Whitcomb 43). By the middle of the twentieth century, a few women poets, such as Anne Sexton and Sylvia Plath, emerged who not only had families, but also wrote about them. Still, it was not until the Women's Movement of the 1970s that "women's" topics became acceptable subjects for serious poetry.

"Confessional" was a tag assigned to poets in the 1950s and 60s by literary critics to denote a new strand in poetry that addressed intimate, personal topics. These poets included Sylvia Plath, Anne Sexton, John Berryman, and Robert Lowell. Lowell has been condemned, in particular, for using actual letters from his ex-wife in his poetry. Sexton wrote about such previously taboo topics as menstruation and abortion; both she and Plath wrote poems about their own suicide attempts and their battles with mental illness. More recently, Sharon Olds has been placed into the category of "confessional" poet, while she prefers to call herself a poet who writes "apparently personal" poems (Interview with Laurel Blossom). Perhaps an even better moniker is one taken on by the editors in their subtitle of "After Confession: Poetry as Autobiography." While "confessional" has an overtone of confessing sin or shame, "autobiographical" is more wide-ranging and flexible. It is more accurate at describing Olds' poetry, which draws on both positive and negative moments in a particular woman's life. While the moment described in "The Possessive" is charged with conflict, it is not one that would be unfamiliar, or shameful, for most readers. Read alongside such explicit poems as "The Language of the Brag," which describes the physicality of childbirth, "The Possessive" represents a broader range of Olds' work as containing a multiplicity of a woman's experience. While Olds acknowledges that Sexton and Plath did important work in opening up the family as an appropriate subject for poems, she looks to other poets as her teachers-Muriel Rukeyser, with whom she took a class, Ruth Stone, Philip Levine, Adrienne Rich, and Galway Kinnell are some she names (*Interview with Laurel Blossom*). A later collection, "The Father," which chronicles Olds' relationship with her dying father, has been criticized by another poet, Louise Gluck, for lacking "ambivalence toward the self," a quality she identifies as necessary for "emotional authority" (245). "The Possessive," however, reads as one of ambivalence on the part of the mother looking at her daughter, so in this instance might be read as containing what Gluck perceives lacking in "The Father." However, a close reading of "The Possessive" shows that Olds does write about ambivalence. In this case, she explores a mother's ambivalence towards her growing daughter.

Societal Context

Psychoanalytic critique can provide a useful lens to examine more deeply the depiction of the relationship between mother and daughter in "The Possessive." In 1978, Nancy Chodorow explored the social configurations of mothers and children from the viewpoint of psychoanalysis in her landmark text, "The Reproduction of Mothering: Psychoanalysis and the Sociology of Gender." Here she describes the psychoanalytical interpretation that, with both sons and daughters, "a mother is likely to experience a sense of oneness and continuity with her infant. However, this sense is stronger, and lasts longer, vis-à-vis daughters" (109). Mothers often experience daughters as "an extension or double of herself." Other accounts also suggest that mothers normally identify more with daughters and experience them as less separate" (109). Because of this, "separation and individuation remain particularly female developmental issues" (110). As observed in the synopsis of the poem, "The Possessive" is principally about a mother's recognition of her daughter becoming a separate individual, and psychoanalysis presents a variety of issues that arise in this process.

"In the classical account of the feminine Oedipus complex, a girl totally rejects her mother when she discovers that her mother cannot give her a penis," Chodorow notes (114). While nothing in the poem explicitly points to a reading of the daughter's rejection on these terms, another poem in "Satan Says" suggests that this analysis might provide one possible explanation for the battle imagery in "The Possessive." In "The Sisters of Sexual Treasure," a poem that appears within the second sequence, "Woman," the speaker and her sister are triumphant that they are "out of our/mother's house" (1-2) to pursue sex with men, whose bodies "were like our father's body!" (6) Their sexual activities "proved our theory of the lost culture:/that if Mother said it wasn't there, / it was there" (17-19). Certainly, the speaker in this poem exudes a tone of the rebellious daughter, here specifically manifested in the form of an alliance with men and a rejection of women, at least of the mother figure. "The Possessive" brings the speaker full circle to her own position as mother confronted with a daughter's rebellion.

If we are to take the daughter as pre-adolescent, we might read her as entering a critical phase in her development, as well as in her relationship with her mother. According to Peter Blos, in the classic psychoanalytic construct, adolescence marks a period where "a child of either gender must give up its incestuous love objects (parents, siblings, parent substitutes) in favor of other primary objects in order to be able to go out into the non-familial relational world" (Chodorow 134). While a son struggles as a young child to separate himself from the mother, a daughter's struggle is more acute in adolescence because, as mentioned before, she has not had to separate herself from the mother to the extent that a boy often does. Chodorow further explains:

> Before she can fully develop extra familial commitments, therefore, a girl must confront her entanglement in familial relationships themselves. It is not surprising, then, that as Blos and other analysts point out, the pubertal/adolescent transition is more difficult and conflictual for girls than for boys, and that issues during this period concern a girl's relationship to her mother. (135).

In "The Possessive," the daughter's trip to the barber seems to be a trip she takes without the mother, and while there she has her hair cut into a style that her mother finds startling. In itself, this rebellious act marks individuation of the daughter from the mother. Furthermore, the barber might be construed as a male lover. Just as a first sexual experience changes the body, penetrates the female body, 'slicing' it perhaps, the barber 'slices' the daughter's previously 'spliced' hair. Hair is often seen as a source of power as well as an attribute of beauty for a woman. This observation enriches the reading of the poem as a metaphor for the coming transformation of the girl from the daughter—'owned' by

the speaker as indicated by the possessive "my"— to a woman separate and distinct from the speaker.

The response of the speaker is one of ambivalence, as she questions the use of the possessive. She recalls when her daughter was "next to nothing" (13) in her body and she struggles to "find/ another word" for the girl she observes (14-15). The ambivalence is also a classic marker of this phase in the mother-daughter relationship:

> "Mothers feel ambivalent toward their daughters, and react to their daughters' ambivalence toward them. They desire both to keep daughters close and to push them into adulthood. This ambivalence in turn creates more anxiety in their daughters and provokes attempts by these daughters to break away" (Chodorow 135).

This break, for many mothers and daughters, signals a coming "disaster." In the poem, this is made abundantly clear in the imagery of the fires of a coming war. Despite the war imagery, however, psychoanalysts view the later outcome after this phase as largely positive. This is due to "the retention of preoedipal (sic) attachments to their mother, growing girls come to define and experience themselves as continuous with others. The basic feminine sense of self is connected to the world" (Chodorow 169). This connection is manifested throughout the poems in "Satan Says." In particular, "The Possessive" gives depth to the ways in which the poet grapples with a girl becoming a woman, completing the circle begun with the image of the little abused girl locked in a box in the first poem, "Satan Says."

Religious Context

While the title of the book in which "The Possessive" appears is "Satan Says," many of the poems do not address religious themes in any perceivable way. However, if analyzed as a part of a larger whole, the poem points to readings of the mother as a Christian figure capable of both punishment and redemption. In Christian theology, motherhood occupies a sacred role in its connection to the Virgin Mary, the mother of Jesus. While previously a subject treated with dismissal, at best, by literary critics in the nineteenth century, motherhood has been recovered as a legitimate basis for experiences described and explored in the poems. This tradition of mother-poets, described in Historical Context, draws on the Christian elevation of the family in Puritan society during the colonial period. Susan MacCallum-Whitcomb points out that during the colonial period, women poets actually had some advantages over their nineteenth-century counterparts because of the elevated status of the family in society due in large part to Puritan beliefs; "[t]herefore, everything related to the creation of the family was considered significant" (40). Thus, Christian doctrine gave legitimacy to a tradition of poetry about motherhood. As Calvinists raised Olds, and perhaps she is drawing upon her own religious roots in claiming motherhood as a rightful subject for poetry. Certainly, the imagery in "The Possessive" suggests a pivotal moment in the life of both mother and daughter, one that she compares to a time of war. With such imagery, she places the struggle between mother and child within the frame of the larger issues of life and death, issues that very much fall within the domain of the religious and spiritual.

Scientific & Technological Context

The connection between biology and psychology is subtly explored in "The Possessive." While the poem describes a girl's haircut, the haircut stands for something much more significant: the coming onset of puberty, which the speaker can see in her daughter's eyes like "the watch fires of an enemy" (19). According to developmental psychologist Sheila Greene, puberty is a significant period in a girl's life in that it "marks a transition from childhood to adulthood. As a girl's body turns into that of a woman she confronts the meaning of what it is to be an adult woman in her culture" (85). For many theorists, "this realization constitutes a crisis for many young women" (85). Such a crisis might manifest in various ways, but certainly one common feature is rebellion against the mother. Greene, however, resists making biological change a central feature of the study of women's development, though she acknowledges it as "an intrinsic part of women's life" (96). The work of Nancy Chodorow, addressed more fully in the Societal Contexts section, explains a way of seeing this process from a psychoanalytic/sociological point of view.

Biographical Context

Born in 1942 in San Francisco, Sharon Olds has described herself as the daughter of "hellfire Calvinists." She received a bachelor's from Stanford University and then went to Columbia University in New York City to pursue a doctorate. She completed the PhD with a dissertation on Emerson but decided to trade in an academic career for the pursuit of her own poetry. Her first collection was "Satan Says," perhaps titled so because, as she describes it, Olds decision to become a poet was a deal with the Devil:

> I had finished my graduate work, I suddenly felt free. I was leaving graduate school with an actual degree, the piece of paper in my backpack and it came to me to call up Satan, which really meant myself, a certain part of my own mind. But I didn't know psychology then. So I said to Satan, I will give up all I've learned at graduate school, not really letting on how much that was, if I can just write my own poems even if they're bad. And so that was my pact. ("Question and Answer").

Jacque Kahn observes that this vow "freed her to develop her own voice," resulting in a first collection of poetry which startles readers with its "candid language and explicit imagery." He argues, "'Satan

Says' transgresses socially imposed silences. The poems explore intensely personal themes with unflinching physicality" ("About Sharon Olds").

"Satan Says" was published in 1980 by the University of Pittsburgh Press and received the inaugural San Francisco Poetry Center Award. Recognition continued with her subsequent books. "The Dead and the Living" won the 1983 Lamont Poetry Prize and the National Book Critics Circle Award. "The Father," published in 1992, was a finalist for the National Book Critics Circle Award. Her other books are "The Gold Cell" (1987), "The Wellspring" (1996), "Blood, Tin, Straw" (1999), and "The Unswept Room" (2002). She has also published two collections of her selected work, "The Matter of This World" (1987) and "Strike Sparks" (2004). Sharon Olds' poems are widely anthologized and have been translated into seven languages. With a Lila Wallace-Readers' Digest grant, she founded a program for teaching writing to the disabled in New York in 1993. From 1998 to 2000, Olds was the New York State Poet Laureate. She is currently on the faculty of the creative writing program at New York University.

Olds' work has variously been described as exhibiting "relentless courage" (Kahn) and of being "self-indulgent" (Dillingham). Despite what a reader might think, there is no question that her work has taken on subjects rarely before written of in poetry, especially by a woman. Its representations of sexual and bodily experiences validates that she is a writer that has "no use for poetic politesse" ("Merriam-Webster's Encyclopedia of Literature" 831).

Alyssa Colton, Ph.D.

Works Cited

Chodorow, Nancy. *The Reproduction of Mothering: Psychoanalysis and the Sociology of Gender. Berkeley.* Los Angeles, and London: U of California P, 1978.

Dillingham, Thomas F. "About Sharon Olds." *The Continuum Encyclopedia of American Literature.* London, New York and Harrisburg: Continuum Publishing, 1999. Rpt.in Nelson. 23 March 2006. <http://www.english.uiuc.edu/maps/poets/m_r/olds/about.htm>.

Feaver, Vicki. "Body and Soul: The Power of Sharon Olds." *Contemporary Women's Poetry: Reading/Writing/Practice.* Eds. Alison Mark and Deryn Rees-Jones. New York: St. Martins, 2000. 140-156.

Gluumlck, Louise. "The Forbidden." *Proofs and Theories: Essays on Poetry.* New York: HarperCollins, 1994. Rpt. in Sontag and Graham. 244-253.

"Graduate Program Faculty." *Creative Writing Program, New York University.* 27 March 2006. <http://cwp.fas.nyu.edu/page/faculty>.

Greene, Sheila. *The Psychological Development of Girls and Women: Rethinking Change in Time.* London and New York: Routledge, 2003.

Kahn, Jacque. "About Sharon Olds." In *Nelson.* 23 March 2006. http://www.english.uiuc.edu/maps/poets/m_r/olds/about.htm.

MacCallum-Whitcomb, Susan. "Claiming Our Birth-Write: The Poetry of American Mothers." *This Giving Birth: Pregnancy and Childbirth in American Women's Writing.* Eds. Julie Tharp and Susan MacCallum-Whitcomb. Bowling Green, OH: Bowling Green State U Popular P, 2000. 39-54.

Nelson, Cary, ed. *Modern American Poetry: An Online Journal and Multimedia Companion to the Anthology of Modern American Poetry.* Ed. Cary Nelson. 1999. Department of English, University of Illinois at Urbana-Champaign.

_____. "Olds, Sharon." *Merriam-Webster's Encyclopedia of Literature.* Ed. Kathleen Kuiper. Springfield, Mass: Merriam-Webster, 1995. 831.

_____. "Question and Answer following Reading, January 29, 1998." *Writers Online 2, no. 3* (summer 1998). New York State Writers' Institute, University at Albany, State University of New York. 27 March 2006. <http://www. albany.edu/writers-inst/olv2n3.html#olds>.

____. *Satan Says*. Pittsburgh: U of Pittsburgh P, 1980.

____. "Sharon Olds." Interview with Laurel Blossom. *Poets & Writers Magazine* (September/ October 1993): 30-32. Rpt. in *Nelson*. 23 March 2006. <http://www.english.uiuc.edu/maps/ poets/m_r/olds/excerpt.htm>.

Sontag, Kate and David Graham, Eds. *After Confession: Poetry as Autobiography*. St. Paul, MN: Graywolf Press, 2001.

Discussion Questions

1. How much does the use of sound contribute to the meaning of the poem?
2. Do you find the image of the "bellpull" and the soldier image she uses contradictory?
3. What is the significance of the title? How is it reinforced in the poem?
4. What is the "story" in this poem? Who is speaking?
5. Which images or phrases do you find most intriguing or appealing? Are there any that do not ring true?
6. Does this poem prompt any particular memories for you of moments between child and parent?
7. What is the significance of the haircut?
8. If another poem were to be written from the daughter's point of view, what do you think it might say? What images might it include?
9. How does this poem compare and speak to other poems in the collection?
10. Imagine a poem where a mother looks at a son after a haircut. How might it read differently, if at all?
11. Rewrite the poem in prose and share with a partner or group. Discuss your writings.

Essay Ideas

1. Examine the use of imagery and sound to develop the theme of the poem.
2. Write a line-by-line explication of the poem, drawing on your own interpretations for the images.
3. How does the poem complement other poems in the collection?
4. Drawing on background research on the development of girls, explain how the poem brings the concerns of the mother to the foreground.
5. Compare "The Possessive" to other poems about puberty and/or mothers and daughters.

The Raven

by Edgar Allan Poe

Content Synopsis

The publication of "The Raven" in February 1845 brought Poe unprecedented renown both at home and abroad. It is a captivating poem, one that has lived up to its creator's conception of what a poem should be. According to Poe, a poem's province is to be beautiful and to have a universal appeal, and this has been the enduring legacy of "The Raven." Its haunting narrative, its excellent workmanship, and its truthfulness to the human heart and mind have made it one of the best loved poems in the English language. When one year later Poe wrote "The Philosophy of Composition," he drew heavily on "The Raven" to exemplify the process of literary creation. Critics have hailed the poem as a superb reflection of the inner realities of a tortured mind, of the loneliness and alienation that lie in the deepest recesses of the human psyche. Coming long before Freud's theories of the unconscious mind made their debut, the poem looked ahead of its time, heralding the modernist approach to art.

As Poe himself explains, the situation depicted in the poem is rather unusual, but it is still within the realm of reality. It focuses on an encounter between a man and a raven, the man expecting an obliging interlocutor in the bird but finding instead a creature who confirms his worst fears. The poem starts with the narrator reflecting on events that take place on a stormy, dreary December night, which he, being an avid reader, begins by poring over a book on "ancient lore." He has almost fallen asleep when a gentle tapping on his door suddenly startles him. Not expecting visitors at this hour of the night, he still tells himself that the rapper is no other than a fellow human being coming to pay a social visit. However, more than the "quaint" book he is reading or the stormy night outside has stirred the man's emotional state on that night. He has spent the whole evening being tortured by his memories of Lenore, his dead beloved, and has waited for the morning to rescue him from his gloomy thoughts. With a mood favoring superstition, he is on edge, terrified by the slightest movement around him, down to the rustling of the purple curtains lining the windows of his room.

Pulling himself together, the man walks to his door, reciting an apology for his delayed response. He finds no one near his door, nothing other than the tempestuous darkness of the night. However, he still lingers by the door "peering" into the gloom, feeling fearful and hopeful at the thought of encountering Lenore. He whispers her name only to hear the night's echo of his own voice. Back into his chamber, he hears the self-same tapping, only louder this time, at his window. He tries to calm his racing heart by rationalizing the tapping as the work of the wind; but to his utmost puzzlement, the window admits a "stately raven," who, rather unceremoniously, makes himself at home by perching on a bust of Pallas Athena, the Greek goddess of wisdom and the arts. It is the perfect perch for a proud bird, which now looks more distinctly black for the whiteness of the bust's marble.

At this stage, the man could not help being amused by the raven's grave, hence comic, behavior. Not expecting an answer, he asks him about the "lordly" name he happened to have on "the Night's Plutonian shore"—the underworld in Greek mythology. The raven says "Nevermore." Although fascinated by the raven's ability to vocalize, the man is reluctant at first to give much weight to his "sad" word; it seems to bear "no relevancy" to him at this stage. The raven, he mutters, will fly away in the morning, just as "other friends" had done before, just like his own hopes. To this, the bird responds by "nevermore." Trying again to rationalize the uncommon occurrences of the night, the man dismisses the gloomy word as the raven's "stock and store," gathered from an "unhappy master," whose unyielding circumstances made him repeat "nevermore." The explanation, however, fails to abate the rising tension in the speaker's mind, and he follows by wheeling his seat closer to the bird to ponder further his humorless word. This physical proximity soon begins to signal the presence of psychological affinities between man and bird marked initially by the man's gradual abandoning of rational analysis of the bird's behavior.

The "grim, ungainly, ghastly, gaunt, and ominous bird of yore" assumes even darker hues as the poem progresses. He is now a creature whose "fiery eyes" have penetrated the speaker's heart, sending him to feel afresh the loss of Lenore—she will "nevermore" press the velvet lining of the seat he now occupies. This remembrance of Lenore brings with it a waft of incense to the speaker's being, sending him to say that this may be the work of angels bringing him, wretched as he is, a respite from his anguish over his beloved's death. Once again, his wish is denied by the raven's answer "nevermore." At this stage, the man's agitated nerves take the poem to higher levels of tension.

Since he expects the response "nevermore," he asks the bird all the questions that have so far unhinged his being, deriving a kind of perverse pleasure from thus tormenting himself. He implores this ominous "prophet," this "thing of evil," who may have been sent by the devil to his "horror-haunted" house, to tell him whether there will ever be a "balm in Gilead" for him. Here he echoes the Bible's Jeremiah, who too in torment poses this rhetorical question. (Gilead, a mountainous area east of Jordan, is well known for the medicinal quality of its plants.) The bird's retort of "nevermore" brings the narrative to its climactic moment in which a frenzied speaker asks the bird if he will ever in the "distant Aidenn" (paradise), embrace his angelic Lenore. The raven says "nevermore."

Satiated with self-torture, the man orders the bird to leave his place, viewing him as the incarnation of his pain. "Take thy beak from out my heart," he bids the bird, and demands that he leave no trace of his black plumage in his chamber. The bird's ready answer to this dismissal is yet again "Nevermore." He remains forever perched on Pallas Athena's bust. By now, however, the narrative's symbolic bent, which links the black bird to the man's sordid mood, has been firmly established. The raven clearly comes across as the speaker's double or alter ego, a projection of the horror-laden contents of his psyche. The two creatures converge in the final lines of the poem as the man's soul takes a permanent abode in the shadow of the bird cast by the lamp on the floor. The bird's sad and lonely word, uttered now by the man himself, concludes the poem and seals the man's unhappy fate.

It is rather ironic that a poem which has widely appealed to children and youths should also embody so much despair. One of the poem's overriding themes is loneliness, felt in the finest fibers of the speaker's soul. The narrative begins with the bereaved lover seeking companionship in an ancient book, alienated as though from both the present and the future. Not having anyone to speak to, he has developed the habit of speaking to himself and now to the irrational bird. The vents he has to the outside world, his door and window, open to darkness and storm. And instead of a guest, or even the ghost of his lover, he has a raven whose sole word confirms the dreary monotony of his life. He is damned to loneliness in this world and the hereafter; not even death would bring him "nepenthe" or relief. His sense of doom is archetypal, finding, therefore, a subtle echo in the reader's being, regardless of age or education.

Historical Context

"The Raven" is simply timeless, not just because it has survived the test of time, but also because of the absence in it of any dates or references to historical events. Set in the antebellum South, the poem makes no allusion to either slaves or masters. Although the speaker seems to lead the leisurely life of aristocrats and lives in a house with lavish furnishings, his situation hardly makes a political statement: the "richly furnished" room where the man is placed has more to do with Poe's intention to "designate Beauty as the province of the poem" ("Philosophy of Composition"). Besides, it is more pertinent to Poe's purposes to free the poem from the complications of slavery (which is certainly not beautiful). With no one to wait on him or solicit his comfort, the speaker stands as the archetypal lonely man, removed from all references to time.

Societal Context

Like history, society has no place in the poem, which practically exists in a social vacuum. With a raven for a guest who outstays his welcome and who links the past with the present, the speaker seems to have no hope of being with fellow human beings. The best he can do is to fill his world with memories of Lenore when he is not struggling with his mental demons. Needless to say, the absence of society, which is artistically deliberate, goes to buttress the theme of alienation in the poem. The man

gradually descends into full-flown psychosis obviously for being alone with his gloomy thoughts, which populate his world with dark creatures like the raven.

With alienation as its focal point, the poem, however, does not fail to reflect the society which produced the writer himself. It voices the melancholia and the fatalism which characterize the literature and culture of the Old South. In an attempt to evaluate Poe, the Southern writer Allan Tate asserts that the "forlorn demon" is "with us like a dejected cousin . . . This is the recognition of a relationship, almost of the blood, which we must in honor acknowledge: what destroyed him is potentially destructive of us (40). Needless to say, the raven himself is a part and parcel of Southern superstition, which associates the black bird with death.

Religious Context

The speaker is obviously a man who has been brought up on Biblical stories and on Christianity's orthodox doctrines of heaven and hell. Furthermore, his readings in classical mythology have acquainted with ancient beliefs, to which he repeatedly alludes in the poem. But with all his religious schooling, the speaker is hardly at peace with either himself or with the larger forces of his universe. He is hopeless right from the beginning, unable to deal with his anguish over the loss of Lenore. Even when he momentarily thinks that God may still extend his mercy to him in a draft of "nepenthe," the bird's rejoinder "nevermore" puts an end to all his wishful dreams. Images of hell rather heaven dominate his thinking and radiate throughout his tale. For instance, he is ready to view the raven as a native of the "Night's Plutonian shore," the underworld in Classical mythology, as soon as he lays his eyes on him, even before the bird has uttered his lonely word. This vision of the bird can only be confirmed in the rest of the poem, and the speaker can only lose all prospects of redemption, grace, and salvation. As in the case of the Biblical Jeremiah, there is no "balm in Gilead" for him. He is damned in this world and the one to come, and certainly has no hope of being with the "saintly" Lenore. For now, however, his "horror haunted' home can host only demonic creatures like the raven.

Instead of faith, the poem resonates with superstitions and primitive fears. The speaker is driven to "fantastic terrors" by the tapping on his door and the rustling of his curtains. It is his jagged nerves that give form to the "ominous" black bird, who continues to croak "nevermore."

Scientific & Technological Context

Composed during times when science was forging ahead with new discoveries and when life is rapidly yielding to the mechanization of labor, "The Raven" notably shuns all reminders of either science or technology. The poem's gothic atmosphere, its use of archaic words ("quoth," "hath," "thy," "thou," "betook, etc."), its sentimental personae (poring over a volume of "forgotten lore"), its distinct aura of superstition, and its uncanny world of death and demons take it back to an earlier, slow-paced, and antiquated existence. Although Poe was quite modernistic in his theories about literature and in his secular approach to art, he was wary of science and tended to side with the Romantic poets, such as Wordsworth and Keats, in viewing science as destroying life's beauty. This is the theme of his "Sonnet—To Science," in which he speaks of the age's scientific spirit as antagonistic to poetic imagination and life's magical qualities: "Why prey'st thou thus upon the poet's heart, / Vulture! whose wings are dull realities!"

In *The Philosophy of Composition*, Poe speaks of the mathematical precision of "The Raven" and the "mechanical approach" he followed while writing it. However, apart from its flawless metrical design, the poem is spawned by deeply felt, tumultuous feelings. It is charged with a forceful current of primeval fears, especially of death and annihilation.

Biographical Context

Those who are familiar with Poe's life rarely fail to see the link between his personal experience and his literary work. Indeed, it has been a commonplace among Poe's critics and biographers to stress the effect of the author's childhood and upbringing on his fiction and poems. In one of his poems, "Alone," Poe himself credits the sorrow, which overwhelmed his adult life to childhood incidents. The writer's unlucky childhood, which starts with the poverty of his biological parents, the absconding of his alcoholic father when he was an infant, and the death of his mother when he was barely two years old, were quite likely to leave some indelible scars on his psyche. The story that Poe remained with his mother's corpse for a whole night in December 1811 has often been cited as a childhood trauma which may have contributed to the emotional collapse and suffocating melancholia which he was to suffer from later in life. It is on a stormy December night that the raven, a symbol of death, enters the speaker's life, never to leave it again.

Poe's disturbed adulthood, his alcohol abuse and manic depression, could also have been fed by his relationship with his foster parents, a prosperous Richmond couple who took him in after the death of his mother. Biographical records stress that although the couple took good care of Poe's financial needs and provided him with excellent schooling, they somehow failed to understand or minister to his emotional needs. His foster mother, Fanny Allan, was a hypochondriac who found it difficult to satisfy the young Poe's starvation for love; his foster father, John Allan, was unable to bond with the teenage Poe, who had been steadily growing up into a solitary and unapproachable youth. He found him sullen and ungrateful, especially during his short career at the University of Virginia, where Poe, who suffered from low self-esteem, was apparently spending beyond his means and ended up in debt. Their relationship never really recovered after an intense argument the two of them had, which led to Poe's disownment and disinheritance by his father.

Poverty and debt remained Poe's constant companions until his death, embittering his life, and making him feel guilty about his responsibilities towards his own family. Poe sold "The Raven" for only $15, and his other manuscripts did not fare much better in comparison. His work as an editor, reviewer, and critic was never adequately paid despite his competence and successful efforts to increase the readership of the journals he edited and contributed to. Naturally, Poe's drinking and gambling habits aggravated his financial situation and often threatened his work stability. However, the luxury and social status, which Poe had coveted all his adult life, were transferred to his protagonists, aristocratic men like the poetic persona in "The Raven." And yet the loneliness, the psychotic disorders, and the self-torment which Poe suffered from until his death were also handed down in sizeable portions to these protagonists. Beyond the exterior details of his lifestyle, the man in "The Raven" is a projection of Poe himself: his fears, his sense of alienation, and his despair. The "demon" in the speaker's mind is found elsewhere in Poe's writings; in "Alone," for instance, another Poe-like speaker portrays his depressed spirits as "a demon in my view."

The sorrow, which the man in "The Raven" undergoes following the death of his beloved Lenore, also has its parallel in Poe's personal life, namely his grief over the loss of his young wife, Virginia, who, like his mother, died of consumption, or what is now known as tuberculosis. Indeed, Virginia was going through the terminal stages of her illness when Poe was writing "The Raven." On the other hand, the speaker's hopelessness regarding a union with Lenore in another world could be related to a sense of guilt Poe himself felt regarding his marriage at the age of twenty-six to his first cousin, Virginia Clemm, who was barely thirteen. Incest, in fact, is a theme that runs through many of Poe's fictional works (notably "The Fall of the House of Usher"), but this poem's conception of the "pure" and "saintly" Lenore may have to do with Poe's desire to free his marriage from notions of sin and defilement.

Sanna Dhahir, Ph.D.

Works Cited

Poe, Edgar Allan. "Alone." *Eris Etext Project*. 1 February 2007. http://www.informations.com/etexts/literature/american/1800-1899/poe-alone-426.htm.

_____. "The Philosophy of Composition." *The Norton Anthology of American Literature*. Shorter 6th ed. Ed. Nina Baym. New York: Norton, 2003 (748-56).

"The Raven." *The Norton Anthology of American Literature*. Shorter 6th ed. Ed. Nina Baym. New York: Norton, 2003 (697-700).

_____. "Sonnet—To Science." *The Norton Anthology of American Literature*. Shorter 6th ed. Ed. Nina Baym. New York: Norton, 2003 (748-56).

Tate, Allen. "Our Cousin, Mr. Poe." *Poe: A Collection of Critical Essays*. Ed. Robert Regan. New Jersey: Prentice Hall, 1967.

Discussion Questions

1. In the "Philosophy of Composition," Poe explains that the raven can be seen as a projection of the speaker's psyche. In what way(s) is this depicted?

2. Does the poem's speaker reflect his creator? If you agree, focus on three points in which distance is almost non-existent between the two.

3. In structuring "The Raven," Poe claims to have started it at its climactic moment. Which part of the poem is this? If not sure about your answer, you can go to Poe's illustration of this issue in "The Philosophy of Composition."

4. As a poet and artist, Poe found in the scientific bent of his age a spoiler of life's magical qualities. However, the poet's religious sentiments, including his conception of heaven and hell, could be described as being somewhat in line with 19th century skepticism, which was directly influenced by scientific discoveries. Do you agree? Why? Why not?

5. While he greatly cherishes the memory of Lenore, the speaker also finds it a source of extreme anguish. Can you identify this duality in his view of Lenore? Which of the two voices predominates, love or anger?

6. Poe's tendency to use archaic expressions has to do with his intention to augment the gothic atmosphere of "The Raven." Identify Poe's archaism and discuss its function in the poem.

7. Poe frequently alludes to Greek and Roman mythology in the poem. What function(s) do these serve? Explain with references to the poem.

8. The poem also alludes to the Bible. Discuss Poe's use of biblical allusions.

9. According to Poe, the events in the poem are mostly within the realm of reality. Do you agree? Why? Why not?

10. When do events turn to be purely symbolic? Can these parts be explained as manifestations of subconscious reality?

11. Despite its somber tones, "The Raven" has some comic moments. Which situations make us smile? Why?

Essay Ideas

1. According to Poe, the poem must aim to be beautiful. Write an essay discussing the aesthetic qualities of "The Raven."

2. The raven can be seen as a cluster of symbols. Discuss the symbolism invested in the poem's black bird.

3. Write a character sketch of Poe's persona in "The Raven."

4. Themes of alienation, depression, and death predominate in this poem. Discuss one or more of these themes, focusing the various elements that make them prominent

5. Write an essay discussing the gothic elements employed in "The Raven."

The Road Not Taken

by Robert Frost

Content Synopsis

"The Road Not Taken" is a four-stanza poem written in tetrameter with the following rhyme scheme: abaab dedde fgffg hihhi. The effect is a rhythmic, yet conversational, voice that mimics the effects of both walking and talking. The speaker of the poem narrates a time in his life when he was walking in the woods and he came across a fork in the road, "two roads diverged in a yellow wood." In the first stanza, the speaker notes that he is only one person and cannot travel both roads, so he tried to look as far down each as path as he can to see where they go.

In the second stanza, both paths look "fair" and the last one he looks at seems better because it was "grassy and wanted wear." However, the following lines contradict this statement when the speaker notes that both paths look equal.

The speaker reveals in stanza three that on that particular morning, neither path had been "trodden." He decides to go with the second path and "keep the first for another day" but he recognizes that one path often leads to another and doubts if he will ever return to this spot.

In stanza four the speaker foreshadows the future and predicts he will say "with a sigh" that years ago he took the road "less traveled by and that has made all the difference." He predicts that the path he will chose will affect his life greatly, in fact make "all the difference," but the fact that he tells this with a sigh indicates that he will have some questions about where the other path may have brought him.

Symbols & Motifs

The two roads clearly represent the choices people have to make in life. Sometimes people come to a crossroads in life and need to decide where to turn. Just like walking in the woods, the tricky part with choosing a path in life is that one decision leads to another and "way leads on to way" and it is impossible for a person to return to the place he started if he determines that he made the wrong choice. The well-worn path seems to indicate the safer choice, although Frost's contradiction in the second stanza hints at the fact that both paths really are the same. What may seem like the better choice is not always so. The road less traveled is the unknown, possibly riskier route. The woods symbolize the obstructions that prevent a person from seeing where his choice will lead.

The fact that the poem is titled "The Road Not Taken" rather than "The Road Taken" emphasizes the mystery that surrounds the choices that people make—specifically, the path not chosen. Because one cannot go down two roads at once, there is no way to be certain where different choices would have led.

Historical Context

In 1912, Robert Frost wrote a letter to his literary editor, Susan Hayes Ward, in which he shared with her a time when he was walking in the woods one evening (Frost 603). During his walk, he encountered another man coming down an intersecting path. As the two men got closer to one another, Frost imagined that the man was his own image (Frost 603). As he got even closer to meeting, Frost imagined absorbing "this other self" but instead he pauses and lets the man pass by. Three years after this incident, Frost wrote "The Road Not Taken." In 1915, Robert Frost and his family moved to New Hampshire after three years in England. His return may have sparked reflection and a revived appreciation for walking in the woods of New England.

Frost also explained another inspiration for this poem at the 1953 Bread Loaf Writer's Conference. He said that he was thinking about a friend of his who had gone off to war and always regretted not choosing the other road. The real internal conflict for his friend, though, was that he knew if he did choose the other road, he would have been sorry he did not go off to help in World War I (Classic Poetry Pages). Frost was moved by the man's awareness that people cannot be in two places at once, nor can they see into the future to determine which choice is the better one.

Societal Context

The outbreak of World War I in 1914 would have made this poem easy for Frost's contemporaries to relate. "The Road Not Taken" is a timeless poem because it addresses a universal conflict in life. People must make decisions that shape their life. The risk and struggle with making these decisions is that nobody knows how they will turn out or where the road will end.

Religious Context

Frost did not ascribe to any particular religion although he read the Bible quite frequently. He is quoted as saying, "I don't go to church, but I look in the window" (Thompson). "The Road Not Taken" explores the author's belief in free will

and the power of human beings to shape their own lives.

Scientific & Technological Context

"The Road Not Taken" does not have a specific scientific or technological context.

Biographical Context

Robert Frost was born in San Francisco, California on March 26, 1874. His father was from Lawrence, MA but moved out to California seeking success as a journalist (Thompson). Both his father and his mother were well-educated and qualified teachers (Thompson). His father died when Robert was eleven and his mother moved him and his younger sister back to Lawrence where she worked as a schoolteacher to get by. He attended Lawrence High School where he discovered his love of poetry and met his future wife, Elinor White (Thompson).

White and Frost married in 1895 and both worked as teachers until 1900 when, after his mother's and their first child's death, they became farmers in Derry, NH (Thompson). They had five children and Frost wrote poetry at night (Thompson). In order to support his growing family, Frost returned to teaching until 1912 when he sold the farm and moved the family to England (Thompson). While in England, Frost published two collections of poetry, "A Boy's Will" and "North of Boston" (Poets.org). They returned in 1915 to avoid the heightening dangers of the war (Thompson).

Frost and his family returned to America to discover that his poetry was critically acclaimed. They settled in Franconia, NH and Frost began to work on his third poetry collection. In 1920, the Frosts moved to Shaftsbury, VT where they remained for the next twenty years (Thompson).

After his wife and son died, Frost moved to Boston and Amherst where he taught and lectured at colleges (Thompson). He died in 1963 at the age of 88. In his lifetime, he published 14 collections of poetry and won four Pulitzer Prizes (poets.org). Although often referred to as a poet of New England, Frost presented ideas and emotions that went much deeper and had universal appeal (Poets.org). President John F. Kennedy remembered the poet by saying, "He has bequeathed his nation a body of imperishable verse from which Americans will forever gain joy and understanding" (Poets.org).

Jennifer Bouchard, M.Ed.

Works Cited

Classic Poetry Pages. 2003. *Lemon8 Design & Development.* 29 January 2008. http://poetrypages.lemon8.nl/life/roadnottaken/roadnottaken.htm.

Frost, Robert. "Crossing Paths." *Elements of Literature: Third Course.* Austin: Holt, Rinehart and Winston, 2000, p. 603.

Frost, Robert. "The Road Not Taken." *Elements of Literature: Third Course.* Austin: Holt, Rinehart and Winston, 2000, p. 602.

Poets.org. 1997. *The American Academy of Poets.* 29 January 2008. http://www.poets.org/poet.php/prmPID/192.

Thompson, Carole. "Places and Poetry." *The Friends of Robert Frost.* 29 January 2008. http://www.frostfriends.org.

Discussion Questions

1. Why do you think Frost writes about roads that go through the woods versus a meadow or a town?
2. What does the speaker mean when he says he kept the other road for another day? How do you know he realizes his choice of path is final?
3. What path did the speaker choose?
4. What do you think the speaker means when he says his choice "has made all the difference?"
5. What is the tone of the poem?
6. Identify the contradictions in the poem. Why did Frost include them in the poem?
7. Why did Frost entitle the poem "The Road Not Taken" instead of "The Road Taken"?
8. Do you think people ever go back and try another road in life? Give examples.
9. If we cannot ever go back and redo our choices, what is the point of reflection and regret?
10. This poem was written in 1915. Do you think it is more or less relevant today?

Essay Ideas

1. Write your own road poem. Think about another traveler, setting, and attitude toward all of the roads that life offers.
2. Write about an important turning point in your life. Discuss how it changed your life and imagine how your life would have been different if you had made a different choice.
3. Describe and analyze Frost's literary style. Focus on his descriptions, the structure of the poem, the rhyme, and meter. Compare this poem to some of Frost's other works.
4. Write an essay in which you analyze the poem from the point of view of another character in literature (e.g. Holden Caulfield, Atticus Finch, Romeo Montague, and Macbeth).
5. Compile a collection of poems and songs that deal with a similar theme regarding life's choices. Write an introduction to your collection identifying unifying ideas and evaluating the overall message of the collected works.

Sestina

by Elizabeth Bishop

Content Synopsis

The poem's setting is the inside of a simple, rural house. An "old grandmother" (2) sits in the kitchen with a small girl, her granddaughter, reading jokes from an "almanac" (5), a compendious book full of astrological and meteorological data that could also include general information and humor. However, there is some pain behind the laughter; the grandmother is "talking to hide her tears" (6). As they engage in the placid domestic activities of a rainy afternoon—having tea, reading, drawing pictures—the house itself, and the objects within it, comes alive. The voices of household objects speak to the child as she sits engaged in the creative act of drawing "another inscrutable house" (29). We hear these voices as they call out to the child: "It was to be, says the Marvel Stove. / I know what I know, says the almanac" (25-6). The short scene that the poem captures is both plainly realistic and charged with the fantastic. Each ordinary object in the small room becomes alive, filling the domestic setting with strange actions and associations. The poem's ending phrase—" another inscrutable house" (37)—refers to both the picture the child is drawing in crayon, and the house she is drawing it in.

Elizabeth Bishop, more than any other mid-20th century poet except perhaps Richard Wilbur, is known for her use of forms and formal structure. However, a mark of Bishop's mastery of

form is how lightly the poem wears it. Though it announces a formal enterprise in its title, "Sestina" is not a difficult or convoluted poem. In fact, it is deliberately simple, perhaps in an effort to reflect the language of the child, using only the present tense and creating a narrative of visual, rather than cerebral, events. The form itself demands the reoccurrence of images, most notably the "tears" that are initial hidden by the grandmother. These hidden tears turn up in the following stanzas in the grandmother's cup of tea, the child's picture, and the almanac's "little moons" (33); they permeate the house, and can be seen everywhere. This vision is present only to the child, however, who is continually "watching" (14). As the poem unfolds, "watching" becomes a kind of imagining, and then a kind of creating. The child sees "the teakettle's small hard tears" (14) and the "clever almanac" (18) which is also seen as a bird that "hovers half open above the child" (20). The first line of the envoi, the last three-line stanza, is a bittersweet combination of the productive process of planting and the stasis of grief: "Time to plant tears, says the almanac" (37).

A central question of "Sestina" is the position of the speaker. Although the poem is predominately in the point-of-view of the child, there are moments, such as the second stanza's "She thinks" when its shifts to the perspective of the grandmother (7). Also, some of the vocabulary—"equinoctial tears"

(7) and "inscrutable house" (39), for example—is decidedly adult. This shifting perspective, which moves between the child, the grandmother, and a narrating voice, gives Bishop a tonal freedom in the poem to speak in many different registers, and to employ both realism and fantasy in the poem.

Historical Context

"Elizabeth Bishop is spectacular in being unspectacular," wrote the poet Marianne Moore in a review of "North and South," Bishop's first book (*Complete Prose* 406). Indeed, Bishop's poems often are not spectacular, nor do they overwhelm with virtuosic cascades of language. However, today Bishop stands as perhaps the most celebrated mid-century American female poet. Moreover, she stands as the perhaps most relevant figure from that era, having survived the Modern, Formalist, Confessional, and Post-Modern eras with her reputation and admirers intact. During her lifetime, in comparison, esteem for her work was limited to a small number of admirers, her close friend and widely acclaimed poet Robert Lowell among them. Today, Lowell, as well as other then-popular poets like Theodore Roethke, Weldon Kees, and John Berryman lags behind Bishop in anthologies and academic studies; her poems are more widely read than any female author save Emily Dickinson. In a prophetic moment, Lowell, who himself was America's premier poet at the time, wrote in a letter that Bishop's language and images seemed to "belong to a later century." This description has proved correct, as the 20th and 21st centuries have seen an incredible increase in the volume of study on her life and work. "Sestina" appeared in "Questions of Travel," Bishop's third collection, published in 1965, a decade after her last book, "Poems: North & South—A Cold Spring," won the Pulitzer Prize. Its critical success added to her already-established reputation among many prominent poets in America such as Robert Lowell and John Ashbery. However, Bishop never was a tremendously confident

poet, nor a prolific one (her "Complete Poems" run fewer than 300 pages; Lowell's over 1,000; Ashbery will probably triple that). Her practice of composition, focused as it was on the visual and on landscapes, was influenced less by autobiographical events than by changes in scenery, of which she had many.

Two of Bishop's most famous poems, "One Art" and "Sestina," are examples of two of poetry's most difficult forms, the villanelle, and the sestina, both of which demand a strict adherence to formal set rules. Unlike the villanelle, which relies on enchained rhymes as well as the repetition of a refrain, the sestina, whose form was codified by French balladeers in the 13th century, relies primarily on repetition of the six end words of the first stanza. Each of these words—in this case, "house," "grandmother," "almanac," "stove," and "tears" in order of their first appearance—must be used to start a following stanza. Moreover, the last end word becomes the first end word in the following stanza, creating a link, as we see here in the last line of stanzas two and the first line of stanza three: "She cuts some bread and says to the child, // It's time for tea now; but the child" (12-13). A sestina with six initial lines must have six six-line stanzas, with the end words alternating so that each stanza begins with a different word and no two have the same order. The final three-line stanza, also called an envoi, must contain the six end words in the reverse order of their first appearance, so that the last word of the poem is always the last word of the first line. Like the strange, cozy house that is the setting of the poem, the sestina offers an uncanny, almost claustrophobic space to the reader. When read aloud, the sestina has the power to alert the listener to the subtle connections of repetition, rather than the more familiar connections of rhyme.

Societal Context

Bishop wrote many of the poems in "Questions of Travel" while living in Brazil with Lota Soares, to whom she dedicated the book. Unlike many of her contemporaries in America, who were actively opposing U.S. foreign policy and the escalating war in Vietnam in their poetry and actions, Bishop separated herself from the tumultuous events in the U.S. (although Brazil had its own political and societal unrest, including an overthrow of the government during her time there). The settings of "Questions of Travel" range in geography, and are arranged in two sections, "Brazil," and "Elsewhere." The poem "Sestina" appears, as do a few others set in Nova Scotia, in "Elsewhere," along with poems set in Maine, Washington, D.C., and Massachusetts. However, the bulk of the collection is clearly situated in the culture and geography of Brazil, where she had established a real home for the first time in her life. There, she kept in regular correspondence with her American friends, especially Robert Lowell and Marianne Moore, but the people and the landscape of her adopted country shaped her writing. As the Brazilian landscape provided her with inspiration, she was also able to write about earlier, biographical landscapes in "Questions of Travel." As Elizabeth Goldensohn points out in *Elizabeth Bishop: Biography of a Poetry*, the poems of Questions of Travel "reaffirm a spatial orientation over temporal focus" (193).

In an article in "The New Criterion" Gioia speculates that Bishop's later ascendancy to her current reputation can partially be attributed to the academy's increased interest in marginalized and displaced voices. Bishop occupied an almost constant status as an outsider, since she was often a stranger to her surroundings, living a peripatetic life from such a young age. Additionally, Bishop's sexual orientation—she was a lesbian, in a time and place when homosexuality was neither condoned nor understood by the mainstream—has encouraged study of her poems using ideas from gender studies and Queer theory. However, Gioia concludes, these factors are secondary to the poems themselves in making Bishop so popular. Comparing her to Keats, Gioia writes that Bishop possessed what Keats described as "negative capability," a term describing the poet's state of ambiguity and mystery. "She had a native genius for reflecting the rich complexity of experience without reducing it into abstraction or predetermined moral judgment," writes Gioia, echoing Moore's description, "She is inclusive by being artfully inconclusive" (8). The form of "Sestina" echoes this feeling of inconclusiveness by allowing only a only certain number of end-words; by limiting what she can say, Bishop is able to speak freely.

Religious Context

Although not an immediately religious poem, "Sestina" does touch on the mystical and magical presences of what might be called spirits. The almanac, in particular, with its omniscience, can be seen as a divine presence: it "hovers" (20), both "birdlike" (19) and perhaps angelic above the two women. As in another Bishop sestina, "A Miracle for Breakfast," the ordinary, and in both cases domestic objects, are infused with spiritual meaning. The stove, which is a "Little Marvel," echoes the description of a child but also describes the miraculous, ordinary inventions and rituals within these poems.

Scientific & Technological Context

Bishop was a poet interested in the folk sciences, rather than cutting-edge technological or scientific advances, of her day. She prefers in her poems to dwell on anachronistic versions of science: "Geography III" begins with the misstatement that the earth is "Round, like a ball" (6) instead of elliptical. Furthermore, her preferred engagement with science is one of childhood scholarship, and she returns repeatedly to the young age when we learn the fundamental (and sometimes wrong) facts about our world. The "clever almanac" (18), whose pages include calendars of the moon's phases, tide tables, and times of dawn and dusk, emblematic of this knowledge, is a kind of rural schoolbook. The farmer's almanac would also have advice on crops, rainfall patterns, and any number of articles, jokes, and stories to while away long winter nights (or rainy fall days, as in "Sestina"). The almanac's information infuses the scene: it has predicted the "equinoctial tears" (7) of the grandmother; later "the little moons" (33) which illustrate the lunar cycle, fall into the child's drawing.

Biographical Context

Although she maintained that one need not know the biography of a poet in order to appreciate the poem, Bishop's life certainly informs and enlarges the scope of her own poetry, which alludes obliquely, when it does at all, to biographical experiences.

From an early age, Bishop had to deal with loss and displacement. When she was five years old, her mother was committed to a sanitarium in Dartmouth, Nova Scotia, after a prolonged period of mental illness. Her father was already gone, having died when she was eight months old, so Bishop was left in the care of her mother's parents, who took her to the Nova Scotia town of Great Village. This age and landscape are described in "Sestina," and in the prose stories "Primer Class" and "In the Village" (*Collected Prose*). Her grandmother had a glass eye, which, Bishop wrote, "made her especially vulnerable and precious to me" (Goldensohn 138). However, Bishop moved from Nova Scotia in 1917 to Worchester, Mass, to live with her father's parents, and then to her aunt's house a year later. At the age of eight, she had lived in four households with four different families; the themes of travel and loss became intertwined at a young age. As author Bonnie Costello notes, Bishop's poetry, despite domestic settings as in "Sestina," illustrates that "a house is no shelter from pain and loss" (199).

In 1930, Bishop enrolled at Vassar, where she majored in English Literature and co-founded the school's literary magazine, "Con Spirito" and served as the editor of the college yearbook. The most important event of her college life occurred in 1934, however, when she first met the poet Marianne Moore. The friendship between them lasted until Moore's death, and was instrumental in bringing Bishop to New York, where she moved after graduation. Moore wrote an introduction for the first publication Bishop received, a group of poems in the anthology "Trial Balances." Moreover, the two women discussed and criticized each other's work; Bishop was heavily influenced by the interplay between formal structure, rhyme, and rhythm that is a hallmark of Moore's work.

Bishop traveled extensively throughout her life. In the three years following her graduation, she lived mostly in Paris, and took multiple trips throughout Europe, Morocco, and Florida, where she lived briefly in Key West. In 1942, on a trip through Mexico, Cuba, and Haiti, she met Lota de Macedo Soares, a Brazilian woman from a prominent family in Rio de Janeiro. In 1951, the two would begin living together in Brazil. By this time, Bishop was an acclaimed, if not wildly popular poet, having been offered a Guggenheim Fellowship in 1947, an appointment as Consultant in Poetry at the Library of Congress in 1949 (similar to the current position of Poet Laureate), and an award from the American Academy of Arts and Letters in 1950. However, she continued to have trouble with depression and alcoholism, problems that had not been helped by her lifestyle in New York. Her trip to Brazil was part of an around-the-world tour she hoped might be a welcome break from the pace and anxieties of the city—she later wrote to Lowell "I was miserably lonely there most of the time" (Goldensohn 9). However, upon arrival, Bishop had a violently allergic reaction to a cashew she ate, and was hospitalized for five days. Soares, who Bishop had planned to visit, invited her to extend her stay and recuperate her home, which was a meeting place for many Brazilian architects and writers. Bishop accepted and ended up staying for over a decade.

Bishop and Soares lived together intermittently in Rio, in Petropolis, and in a 17th century house in Ouro Preto, Brazil. At the beginning, Bishop's life in Brazil had a cathartic effect on her health and poetry; she began to confront her longstanding addiction to alcohol and her depression. As her career flourished, though, their relationship began to deteriorate. The publication of "Poems: North & South—A Cold Spring," which combined her first book with new poems, won the Pulitzer Prize in 1955. "Questions of Travel," her third collection, was also well received, and dealt with familiar themes of travel, displacement, and tourism: "Should we have stayed home and thought of here?" she asks in the title poem (14). However, there were significant strains in her relationship with Soares at this time, who was afflicted by her own problems with depression and anxiety relating to her job as a city planner. Bishop spent less and less time in Brazil, teaching instead at universities in the U.S. and coming back to Brazil intermittently. In September of 1967, while visiting Bishop in New York, Soares overdosed on sleeping pills in an apparent suicide.

After her partner's death, Bishop lived primarily in Boston, teaching at Harvard and writing the poems that would be published in *Geography III*. She continued to travel extensively (a partial list of places includes Yugoslavia, Ecuador, Norway, Sweden, and the Galapagos Islands), and in 1976 received the prestigious Books Abroad/Neustadt Award, the first American and first female recipient. On October 6, 1979, she died at home in Boston.

Andrew Allport

Works Cited

Bishop, Elizabeth. *The Complete Poems*. New York: Farrar, Straus, and Giroux, 1993.

____. *One Art: Letters*. Ed. Robert Giroux. New York: Farrar, Straus & Giroux, 1994.

Costello, Bonnie. *Questions of Mastery*. Cambridge: Harvard UP, 1991.

Gioia, Dana. "From Coterie to Canon." *The New Criterion*. Vol. 22, No. 8. April 2004.

Goldensohn, Lorrie. *Elizabeth Bishop: The Biography of a Poetry*. New York: Columbia UP, 1992.

Moore, Marianne. Complete Prose. New York: Viking, 1986. 406-7.

Discussion Questions

1. The sestina, like many poetic forms, began as an oral form, and it repetitions were intended to keep a listener attentive to the poem. On the page, the end-words may appear more obvious than aloud. Listen to Bishop's "Sestina" and try to keep track of the six end-words. How does the poem emphasize, or de-emphasize them?

2. What are the differences between how the words appear in each stanza? Do they take on additional and/or alternate meanings?

3. How does Bishop manipulate the tone or mood of the poem? What would you describe as the central feeling(s) in "Sestina?"

4. In the poem, Bishop uses only simple, present tense and short, declarative statements. Bishop's language is emphatically plain: Marianne Moore said she was "spectacular in being unspectacular." How does her style here prove this paradox? What is "unspectacular" about the poem?

5. Who is speaking in "Sestina"? What different points of view is the reader given?

6. Why does Bishop choose to animate the "Marvel Stove" and the almanac with speech? What are the stove and book saying, and what purpose does their speech serve?

7. At the beginning of the poem, we learn that the grandmother is "laughing and talking to hide her tears" (6). Is it important that we know why she is crying? How does the poem avoid, or perhaps answer obliquely, this question?

8. Why is the title of the poem simply "Sestina"? Why do you think Bishop chose to call it this, instead of, say, "Fall in Nova Scotia," or "Drawing Lesson"? What sorts of information does the title give us, and what does it leave out?

9. How does the form of the poem affect its content? That is, how do the requirements of the sestina—the six-line stanzas, the repeated end-words—affect the scene and action of the poem?

Essay Ideas

1. "You'd just wish they'd keep some of these things to themselves," Bishop told *Time* in 1967 for their cover story on Robert Lowell, whose Confessional style included brutal truths about his own troubled life, even excerpts from his wife's anguished letters. In the ensuing 30 years, poetry, at least in the popular imagination, seems to mean something closer to the free verse confessions of Lowell and Sylvia Plath than Bishop's formal poem, "One Art." In what ways does Bishop keep things to herself in this poem? What clues—or even confessions—does she make to the reader?

2. Bishop's "Armadillo" is a poem in conversation with Robert Lowell's "Skunk Hour." The poems are addressed to the other poet, and the vision of the natural world, as it is exposed to humans, is central to both. What fundamental differences are there in the poets' styles? How do the poems speak to these differences?

3. The end-words of a sestina are enormously important, since they are repeated so often. What is the connection between the six words here: "house," "grandmother," "almanac," "stove," and "tears"? Do the words change throughout the poem? What kinds of changes do they undergo?

4. In many poems, including "The Man-Moth," "Questions of Travel," and "Sestina," tears play a crucial role in Bishop's imagery. Using these examples or others of your choosing, analyze the appearance and meaning of these tears, which not always emotional.

5. Write a sestina. Try to be creative in the way you use the end-words, varying your syntax without sacrificing clarity. The end words must be used in reverse order in the final three-line stanza, the envoi.

6. Compare the scene in "Sestina" to that of "Manners" and "First Death in Nova Scotia," the preceding and following poems, respectively, in "Questions of Travel." How do the poems describe a similar place, and what differences/similarities in style do you see between them?

The poster above advertises a performance of Edgar Allen Poe's poem, "The Raven," which is featured on page 159 of this volume. Photo: Library of Congress

Still I Rise

by Maya Angelou

Content Synopsis

Written in 1978, "Still I Rise" is a poem of pride and protest in which the speaker says that despite the history of oppression for Blacks, she will rise. The poem begins with the speaker saying, "You may write me down in history with your bitter, twisted lies . . ." to acknowledge the prejudice that has pervaded American history. She continues that no matter what she is subjected to, she will always overcome.

The poem is nine stanzas long and is filled with accusations and rhetorical questions directed at the oppressor. Questions such as "Do you want to see me broken?" and "Does my haughtiness offend you?" challenge the oppressor. Meanwhile, the speaker asserts her confidence and strength in spite of, or perhaps because of, the challenges in her life and the life of her people with statements like, "I walk like I've got oil wells pumping in my living room."

The first seven stanzas are each four lines long and the second and third lines rhyme with one another. This gives the poem a rhythm and consistency that reflects the speaker's unyielding determination to succeed. The last two stanzas, however, break from this pattern. The eighth stanza is six lines long and ends in a couplet, while the final stanza is nine stanzas long with five of the lines repeating the words, "I rise." The break from routine and the growing length of the stanzas achieves the effect of the speaker rising out of the

poem and give her final words more weight and greater impact on the reader.

Angelou also incorporates anaphora, similes, and metaphors throughout the poem to illustrate the resilience of the speaker regardless of what befalls her. She says, "You may shoot me with your words, You may cut me with your eyes . . ." but she laughs in the face of this hate because she knows that like dust, like hope, like air, she will rise. She compares herself to a "black ocean, leaping and wide," an indication of the infinite power of her resilience. She closes the poem claiming that she is the "dream and the hope of the slave" followed by the thrice repeated phrase, "I rise." Angelou captures the both the repression and the progress of the African American people over the course of history.

Symbols & Motifs

Much of Angelou's poetry possesses a lyrical, jazzy quality and "Still I Rise" is no exception (Cecil). This quality is no surprise as Angelou admits to being heavily influenced by the works of poets such as William Shakespeare and Langston Hughes as well as Negro spirituals and Bible hymns (Bartow). Likewise, Angelou often centers her work on themes of Black discrimination and oppression (Cecil).

Throughout the poem, Angelou refers to earth, air, and water. She compares herself to dust, air, and the ocean. She says that "with the certainty of tides" she will rise. Angelou makes a connection with nature and its ability to persevere throughout eternity.

Historical Context

In writing this poem, Maya Angelou is able to honor the hard work and strength of her ancestors who suffered through slavery. She is also able to acknowledge the many years of discrimination and subjugation that followed. From slavery to the present, African Americans have told stories out of the need to express their feeling and be heard (Moss). Topics often revolve around sadness, anger, hard work, and discrimination, but also about unity and persistence (Moss). Angelou incorporates all of these emotions into her poem. Stories were often told through song so Angelou's use of rhythm in "Still I Rise" pays respect to that tradition.

Societal Context

"Still I Rise" is a poem that addresses the plight of American Blacks, but has a message that can traverse racial and cultural boundaries because it is about overcoming adversity. Although written in the 1970's, the poem has a timeless quality because of the universality of its conflict and the optimistic, determined nature of its message. In one interview, Maya Angelou explained that even though she writes from personal experience, she does not necessarily write about her own life. She is instead, "thinking about a particular time in which I lived and the influences of that time on a number of people . . . I used . . . myself—as a focus to show how one person can make it through those times" (Cecil).

Religious Context

"Still I Rise" does not have a specific religious context.

Scientific & Technological Context

"Still I Rise" does not have a specific scientific or technological context.

Biographical Context

Maya Angelou was born as Marguerite Johnson in St. Louis, Missouri in 1928. When she was three years old, her parents divorced and from that point forward, she spent much of her childhood in Stamps, Arkansas living with her grandmother whom everyone called "Momma." In Stamps, she learned what it was like to live as a black person in a white dominated society (Cecil). She returned to live with her mother in St. Louis for a short time and returned to Stamps after her mother's boyfriend (Cecil) raped her. At age fifteen Angelou moved to San Francisco and became pregnant at age sixteen with her only child, a son named Clyde. Her experiences were later captured in her first autobiography, "I Know Why the Caged Bird Sings." She continues to tell her story in three subsequent autobiographies.

Angelou has published multiple collections of poetry including "Just Give Me a Cool Drink of Water 'fore I Diiie" in 1971, "Oh Pray My Wings Are Gonna Fit Me Well" in 1975, "Wouldn't Take Nothing for My Journey Now" in 1993 and "A Brave and Startling Truth" in 1995 (poets.org).

In addition to writing, Maya Angelou is also an actor, singer, dancer, director, and civil rights activist (poets.org). In 1959, she was asked by Martin Luther King Jr. to become the northern coordinator for the Southern Christian Leadership Conference (poets.org). Two years later, she spent one year in Egypt with a South African activist to whom she was briefly married (Encyclopedia Britannica). She worked as an associate editor for the only English news weekly in the Middle East. From 1964 to 1966, she edited the *African Review* in Ghana (poets.org). Maya Angelou broke new ground in 1971 as the first black female director in Hollywood. She was nominated for a Tony award in 1977 for her performance in the renowned epic "Roots" (poets.org). In 1993, President Bill Clinton asked her to write and deliver a poem that became "On the Pulse of the Morning" at his inauguration.

Jennifer Bouchard

Works Cited

Angelou, Maya. "Still I Rise." Poets.org. *The Academy of American Poets*. 4 April 2008. http://www.poets.org.

Bartow, Anna. *Autobiography: Maya Angelou*. 2008. Yale New Haven Teachers Institute. 5 April 2008. http://www.yale.edu/ynhti/curriculum/units.

Cecile, Kelly Holland. *Maya Angelou*. 1998. University of North Carolina. Edited by Mark Canada. 5 April 2008. http://www.uncp.edu/home/canada/work/canam/angelou.htm.

"Maya Angelou." *Encyclopedia Britannica*. 2002. PBS.org. 5 April 20008. http://www.pbs.org/wnet/aaworld/reference/articles/maya_angelou.html.

"Maya Angelou." Poets.org. 4 April 2008. *The Academy of American Poets*. 4 April 2008. http://www.poets.org.

Moss, Barbara. *How the African American Storyteller Impacts the Black Family and Society*." 2008. Yale New Haven Teachers Institute. 5 April 2008. http://www.yale.edu/ynhti/curriculum/units.

Discussion Questions

1. What is the tone of the poem?
2. Who is the "you" in the poem?
3. Who is the "I" in the poem?
4. How does the reader distinguish between the private "I," and the collective "I," the representation of all Afro-American women?
5. Identify the sensory details that Angelou uses to help strengthen her message.
6. What are some of the things that Angelou compares the speaker's hope to? Why?
7. What is the effect of Angelou's use of parallelism and juxtaposition of the words "you" and "I"?
8. What is the effect of the repetition of the last three lines of the poem?
9. What is the message of the poem?

Essay Ideas

1. Write an essay in which you analyze how Angelou's use of tone, personification, metaphor, and allusion help the reader to understand and enjoy the poem's message better.
2. Evaluate Angelou's use of sexuality in the poem and an element of power and confidence. Discuss the effect of this on the overall message and tone of the poem.
3. Write your own poem using the same title. What obstacles are you overcoming and how will you rise above them?

Stopping by Woods on a Snowy Evening

by Robert Frost

Content Synopsis

"Stopping by Woods on a Snowy Evening" is one of the most widely read and widely loved of all American poems. Its title already sets an appealing mood, implying rest, relaxation, contemplation, and calm. The title suggests a voluntary action undertaken in an appealing environment during peaceful conditions. (The effect would be entirely different, for instance, if the poem were entitled "Stranded in the Forest during a Nighttime Blizzard.") The poem itself, however, will ultimately prove more complicated-and even disturbing-than its title may suggest. Nevertheless, the beginning of the work could not seem simpler or less complex. Every word of the opening line (like most of the rest of the words in this poem) is monosyllabic: "Whose woods these are I think I know" (1). The line makes a simple statement; it constitutes a single, simple sentence; and even its rhythm is not complex, since its meter is a perfect example of four iambic feet. (In other words, in each pair of syllables, the first is unaccented and the second is accented, so that this line, like almost all the other lines in the poem, has the following basic rhythm: da-dum, da-dum, da-dum, da-dum [see also Monte 280]). Although the meter of the poem is mostly regular and predictable, however, the poem never seems monotonous or trite; Frost manages to make its rhythm sound perfectly colloquial and conversational, as if we are genuinely hearing a real person speaking in the natural accents of everyday talk.

Even in the first line, however, subtle complications emerge. The very first word, for instance, implies an owner of the woods. Although we often think of nature-and especially of forested areas-as wild, free, and untamed, these woods actually belong to someone; they are someone's property. Already, then, the poem begins to suggest distinctions between self and other, between freedom and restraint, and between the personal and the social-distinctions that will become increasingly important as the work proceeds. Although the poem centers on the perceptions and experiences of the unnamed, unknown speaker, his very first perception is less of the woods themselves than of the fact that the woods are not his. They belong to someone else. The speaker never enjoys a pure, unmediated relationship with (or contemplation of) the woods themselves; his experience of them is already colored by his awareness that they are someone else's property, and his experience of them is also colored by his own acute self-consciousness, particularly his concern with being observed himself while he observes the woods. Already, then (in the very first line), Frost has introduced one of the major tensions implicit in this entire work-a tension between the private self and the social self, between the independent observer and the observer who must be conscious of himself in relation to others.

Lines 2 and 3 introduce more emphasis on the unnamed owner of the woods; he lives in "the village," a place symbolically associated with society, with other people, and thus with the social obligations that will later prove so important in this poem. The entire first stanza, in fact, is overshadowed by the speaker's awareness of this anonymous owner; the woods are "his woods" (4), and the speaker can only enjoy contemplating them if he can assure himself that the owner "will not see me stopping here" (3). Paradoxically, this emphasis on the owner of the woods suggests a great deal about the speaker himself; he seems a private man and a respecter of others' property; perhaps he is somewhat shy, and certainly, he is concerned with what others may think or say about him. His language seems plain, direct, and uncomplicated, yet his concern to remain unobserved arouses our curiosity about his precise thoughts and motives. He wants his experience of the woods to be as private as possible, and yet his experience of them is enshrined in one of the best-known poems in the English language. By the time we have reached line 4, therefore, our attention is focused not only on the peaceful landscape implied by the title but also on the personality of the unnamed speaker and on his complex attitudes toward other people.

Another means by which Frost introduces subtle complexity into a seemingly simple poem involves the poem's rhyme scheme. Normally a poem with stanzas comprised of four lines would consist of simple couplets (aa / bb) or (even more commonly) of alternating rhymes (ab / ab). Frost, however, chooses a highly unusual rhyme scheme for his opening stanza and for the following two: he rhymes the first, second, and fourth lines, introducing a non-rhyming word into the third line of each of the first three quatrains. Then, to complicate matters even further, he makes the last word of each third line anticipate the rhyme-words of the first, second, and fourth lines in the following stanza. The rhyme scheme of the first three stanzas thus consists of the following pattern: aaba / bbcb / ccdc. Finally, to make the structure of the poem even more complex, and to lend the last stanza a strong sense of finality, Frost closes the poem with the following emphatic rhymes: dddd. This is one of the most unusual rhyme schemes in all of English poetry. Yet the poem never seems self-consciously clever or overtly witty. Instead, the complex rhyme scheme, with its heavy emphasis in the final stanza on similar-sounding words (all of them monosyllabic), ironically contributes to the poem's impression of plain, blunt, laconic speech, as if the speaker is so focused on the woods and on his own thoughts that he cannot be bothered to search out highly varied rhymes. Both in technique and in theme, therefore, the poem is a fascinating combination of apparent simplicity and deeper complexity.

Stanza 3 introduces a third "character" into the poem: in addition to the speaker and the owner of the woods, we now meet the speaker's "little horse" (5). Here as before, whatever the speaker says about someone else (whether it be the owner of the woods or even the horse) tells us much about himself. Since the man who owns the woods is not present to observe (and judge) the speaker, the speaker now assumes that his horse "must think it queer / To stop without a farmhouse near" (5-6). Once again, then, the speaker seems highly self-conscious about his act of stopping to observe the woods, but his tone at this point seems less truly uncomfortable than in stanza one. To be observed, even potentially, by the human owner of the woods (an owner, moreover, who is male, as is presumably true of the speaker himself) is an unappealing prospect; to be observed by the "little horse" is another (and far less unsettling) experience. The adjective "little" implies the speaker's affection toward the horse and makes the horse seem unthreatening, while the mere fact of ascribing thoughts to the horse makes the animal seem a companion rather than an indifferent, uncomprehending beast.

Even the adjective "queer" implies merely amused befuddlement rather than some harsher judgment (as such alternative adjectives as "mad," "crazed," or "absurd" would imply). Alone with his horse, with not even "a farmhouse near" (6), surrounded on one side by "the woods" and on the other by a "frozen lake" (7), the speaker can begin to relax and can even presumably smile at himself as he imagines what his horse must think of this pause in their journey. Yet in this stanza, as in the first, we as readers are invited to contemplate not so much the woods themselves as the speaker contemplating the woods. We are invited to wonder what he is thinking and how he is feeling, though his exact thoughts and feelings remain a mystery. Frost creates an atmosphere of uncertainty and suspense; he leads us to wonder why indeed the speaker has stopped, what precisely the speaker is thinking, why the speaker is so concerned to remain unobserved, and why exactly the speaker feels so uncomfortable for having paused. Never, though, does Frost answer these questions, and the fact that they are left hanging is just one more way in which the poem is more complex than it initially seems. The woods provoke the speaker's thought; the speaker provokes ours.

In stanza 3, the horse "gives his harness bells a shake / To ask if there is some mistake" (9-10). Paradoxically, it is the horse who seems more concerned with keeping on schedule, with sticking to a routine, than the man. Perhaps Frost is implying that animals, unlike humans, are not made for contemplation or reflection; perhaps he is suggesting that animals are not likely to pause to notice beauty, consider nature, or ponder their relations with the world around them. On the other hand, perhaps he is simply implying that the horse is cold and wants to keep moving to generate warmth. In any case, the stanza further deepens our sense of the speaker's isolation. Earlier he assumed that the owner of the woods would not understand why he had paused to stop and now he assumes that his horse is impatient with his pausing. In each of the first three stanzas, then, the emphasis has been as much on the reaction of others to the speaker (and on the speaker's reactions to them) as on the speaker's response to the woods or the other natural surroundings. In stanza three, however, his characterization of the wind as "easy" and of the flakes as "downy" (12) implies his ability to appreciate the peace and softness of a gentle snowfall on a calm night. Such details, though, gain their real impact when we recall that the speaker had earlier referred to the present night as the "darkest evening of the year" (8) and that he had earlier referred to the lake as "frozen" (7). These facts give a literally dark, cold edge to the picture that balances, and complicates, the more appealing details of the scene. The speaker's perception of the environment is neither simple nor simplistic; the scene may be beautiful in one respect, but in another respect (as the horse's "shake" perhaps implies) it can also seem forbidding. Once more Frost implies a kind of complexity-both in the landscape and in the speaker's perceptions of it-that prevents the poem from seeming naive or sentimental. The last line of stanza two thus balances (and is balanced by) the last line of stanza three.

Balance and complexity are again the hallmarks of the masterful fourth (and final) stanza. Now, for the very first time, the speaker explicitly characterizes the woods in openly emotional language. Earlier he had merely reported, in a simply factual tone, that the woods were "fill[ing] up with snow" (4); now, however, he calls them "lovely, dark and deep" (13). "[L]ovely" is the key word; it implies as much about the speaker as it says about the woods. It suggests his ability to perceive and appreciate beauty; like the reference earlier to the "little horse," it therefore suggests a "lovely" (and loving) aspect to his own character. It is a word conventionally associated with softness and femininity, and it thus reveals a side of his personality that the speaker might normally be reluctant to share, especially with another male (as lines 3-4 suggest). The adjectives "dark and deep" can also be read as implying the speaker's emotional response to the woods, or they can be read as more neutrally descriptive. In either case, they balance "lovely," for they imply that the woods are not only attractive but also potentially threatening, or at least ominous and disturbing. The darkness and depth of the woods-whether literal, metaphorical, or both-make them beyond human control, perhaps even beyond human understanding. Seen from one perspective, the woods are "lovely," seen from another perspective, they can appear somewhat menacing or unsettling. Perhaps, from yet another perspective, even the darkness and depth of the woods can seem appealing, especially if these traits are associated with a kind of "death-wish" on the speaker's part (Ciardi 15; see also McLaughlin 313). This could mean a desire to cease participating in the daily struggles of life, to take refuge in a kind of rest that might seem attractively "dark and deep" (see Thompson 26; Unger and O'Connor 599-600). Whether these adjectives, then, are interpreted as neutral, ominous, or seductive, they help contribute to the complex tone of the poem as a whole.

The poem ends, however, not by emphasizing the woods themselves but by stressing instead the speaker's obligations elsewhere-the "promises" he feels committed "to keep" (14). The fact that they are "promises to keep" (rather than "duties to fulfill" or "burdens to discharge") implies the speaker's sense of ethical responsibility, his moral commitment to other people. He feels the weight of his "promises" (the only word in the poem with more than two syllables [see also Monte 280]). Once more, an awareness of others enters the speaker's consciousness (and ours). However attractive or fascinating the woods may seem, the speaker feels impelled to move on: he has "miles to go before" he can "sleep" (15)-a statement that at first seems simply literal but whose meaning is deepened, and made metaphorical, when the speaker repeats it, making it the very last line of the work. The "sleep" mentioned in line 16 is often interpreted as the symbolic sleep of death, an interpretation that makes the speaker's journey not simply a movement through space from one point to another but also the larger journey of life, from the womb to the grave. The tone of the last line can be interpreted as one of weariness, resignation, or determined commitment, or perhaps as all at once. Certainly, the repeated phrasing of the last two lines gives the poem one last complex twist, yet the effect of the line is typical of the poem as a whole: it is quiet, it is understated, and it relies on subtle implication rather than overt statement. Like the woods themselves, this line (and the poem as a whole) invites our contemplation and reflection. The poem functions for us as the woods function for the speaker: it gives us a chance to pause, to ponder, to admire. Inevitably, however, we-like the speaker-must finally move on.

Historical Context

Frost's lyric can profitably be examined not only within the contexts of literary history but also within the broader historical context of the era in which it was first written (as well as the time that has elapsed since then). The most striking aspect of the poem from a literary-historical point of view is its extreme accessibility. Frost, after all, was writing during the hey-day of modernism, an international movement that affected not only literature but also all the other arts. For instance, by the time Frost's poem was first published in 1923, it had been ten years since Stravinsky had unleashed his stridently avant-garde ballet "The Rite of Spring" on a shocked music world. Braque and Picasso had similarly unsettled the world of painting with their unconventional cubism. Most relevantly, T. S. Eliot had charted new (and, to some readers, unattractive and incomprehensible) directions in poetry with the publication of such works as "The Love Song of J. Alfred Prufrock" (first printed in

1917), while the even more unconventional Ezra Pound had been publishing practically a book a year of deliberately innovative verse since 1908. James Joyce's path-breaking and puzzling novel "Ulysses" had been appearing in serial form from 1918 to 1920 and was first printed entirely in 1922. Similarly, Eliot's lengthy poem "The Waste Land" (the instantly acknowledged masterpiece of modernism) appeared in print just a few months before Frost's lyric. Eliot's poem thus probably had no impact on the composition of Frost's "Stopping" (although see Hamilton 125), but "The Waste Land"-at least in technique, structure, manner, and form-symbolizes almost everything that Frost's lyric is not. "The Waste Land," for example, comes equipped with a Greek and Latin epigraph, unpredictable meter, an unconventional rhyme-scheme, quotations from French and German literature (in French and German), puzzling historical allusions, and footnotes provided by the poet himself. And, all of that happens just in the first eighty lines! By contrast, Frost's poem seems immediately clear and accessible: its debts to earlier (and more conservative) traditions of poetry are signaled by its use of quatrains, its simple meter, its plain speech, and its straightforward themes. Part of the historical importance of Frost's poem, therefore (and of Frost's writings in general), is its importance as a symbolic alternative to the stylistic modernism that dominated so much of twentieth-century art. Frost's poem is unforbidden, and the general ease and openness of his style, in this work and others, helps explain his enormous popularity.

Frost's poem can also be related to non-literary historical developments. The poem was first published, after all, during a period of rapid industrialization and urbanization, when the kind of rural landscape and rural lifestyle implied by this lyric were increasingly becoming outdated (and thus subjects for nostalgia). World War I had recently devastated Europe and had shaken Western civilization to its core, but Frost's poem implies an admiration for such traditional values as an appreciation of beauty as well as an appreciation of personal responsibility. In a world that was becoming increasingly unpredictable and uncertain, Frost's poem speaks to (and for) ancient patterns of thought, feeling, and life.

Societal Context

The society implied in "Stopping by Woods" is a rural society of the sort that was fast disappearing during the time when Frost wrote. It is a society in which property rights are important and in which most property is still owned by males (1-4). It is a society that values the work ethic and ethical obligations of all types, especially "promises" made to others (14). It is a society in which males are the ones who tend to go off to work and in which males are the primary breadwinners. Thus, it is a society in which men value themselves (and are valued by others) for the work they do, the income they earn, and the social obligations they fulfill. There is precious little time for philosophizing or aesthetic contemplation (let alone artistic creativity) in this society. Most people resembling Frost's speaker were relatively poor (or were certainly lower middle class); they had to be concerned with the opinions of others, and they had to be concerned with making a living rather than reflecting, too often or too long, on life's meanings or complexities. The audience for whom Frost wrote-and who embraced Frost as they embraced no other modern poet-was an audience that appreciated plain speech, traditional forms, and the kind of thoughts and feelings a "common man" could share and comprehend. In the plain-speaking, clear-thinking, sensitive but unsentimental speaker of Frost's poem, many of Frost's first and subsequent readers saw reflections of their own better selves, and in the realistic society Frost evokes (with its beauties as well as its obligations) many of Frost's readers saw reflections of the society they themselves inhabited and the kind of life they themselves lived.

Religious Context

The relevance of religion is even less obvious to this poem than the relevance of science and technology. God is never mentioned or clearly implied; even the precise thoughts of the speaker as he contemplates the woods are unclear: the most explicit thing he says about them is that they are "lovely, dark and deep" (13). Frost's own religious beliefs are a matter of uncertainty and even controversy (see Cook and McWilliams 386-90), and the poem itself certainly stakes out no obvious religious position. Perhaps that fact, however, is significant, especially if we read the final lines as implying something about the nature of life (and death). Many readers believe that the last line does allude to the final and most permanent kind of "sleep," and some readers have even argued that the speaker is tempted by a desire to die (Ciardi 15). The poem can be read as implying, however, that life's obligations must be accepted, not refused, and that death will come when it comes and may even be a kind of rest. The philosophy the poem implies seems more Stoic than overtly Christian; certainly, a different kind of poet could easily have turned the poem into a sermon. Frost, however, does not; in this sense, as in most others, he lets readers draw their own conclusions.

Scientific & Technological Context

At first glance, Frost's poem seems to have almost nothing to do with science and technology. However, that, of course, is precisely why these topics are relevant to this lyric. The poem was written, after all, during a period of intense scientific and technological innovation. Automobiles had been mass-produced beginning in the first decade of the twentieth century; airplanes had already proven useful as weapons in World War I; more and more of the U.S. was powered by electricity; radio broadcasts became common beginning in 1922; factory jobs were increasingly typical; and the list

could easily be extended. Yet Frost's poem reflects none of these developments. The speaker still travels with a horse and sleigh; the nearest community is not a huge city but a small "village" (2); the nearest residence is not an urban tenement but a rural "farmhouse" (6). Frost's poem evokes simpler times and a simpler life, and in the decades since the poem was first published it has taken on an even greater air of quaintness and nostalgia. It would be difficult to write such a poem (with such a setting and such a speaker) today, when the pace of scientific and technological change has accelerated even more than was true when Frost first composed the work. Frost wrote the poem at exactly the moment when the kind of relatively uncomplicated rural life the poem depicts and celebrates had begun to slip irretrievably into the past.

Biographical Context

Frost himself admired this poem, once remarking that the work contained "all [he] ever knew," yet he often expressed annoyance with the elaborate interpretations the work provoked (see Greenburg and Hepburn 12). He particularly rejected claims that the poem implied any kind of "death-wish" (Henry 69), and when "a friendly critic asked if the last two lines in 'Stopping by Woods' referred to going to Heaven, and, by implication, death, the poet replied, 'No, all that means is to get the hell out of there'" (see Greenburg and Hepburn 13). According to David Hamilton (relating a story reported by N. Arthur Bleau):

> "'Stopping by Woods' was [Frost's] favorite poem because it arose from a particularly bleak Christmas and the 'darkest evening of the year' just before it. Having no money, Frost loaded a wagon with farm produce and went to town, but he found no buyers and returned empty-handed, without even small gifts for the children. He felt he had failed his family, and rounding a bend in the road, by

woods, and quite near his house, the horse, who seemed to understand his mood, and who had already been given the reins, slowed and stopped, letting Frost have a good cry. 'I just sat there and bawled like a baby,' Bleau reports Frost as having said." (127)

Frost also claimed that he had written the poem in a burst of inspiration after working long and hard on a different piece, although Hamilton thinks that the idea that "Frost finished it at one sitting seems a bit of a stretch since drafts exist that indicate his revisions" (128-29). Critics have even debated how Frost intended the poem to be punctuated (Monteiro 38-40). The one aspect of the poem few readers disagree about, however, is its fine artistic success.

Robert C. Evans, Ph.D.

Works Cited

Ciardi, John. "Robert Frost: The Way to the Poem." *Saturday Review 40.* (April 12, 1958).13-15, 65.

Cook, Reginald L., and John McWilliams. "Robert Frost." *Sixteen Modern American Authors. Volume 2: A Survey of Research and Criticism since 1972.* Ed. Jackson R. Breyer. Durham, NC: Duke UP, 1990. 360-403.

Greenberg, Robert A., and James G. Hepburn, eds. *Robert Frost: An Introduction.* New York: Holt, Rinehart, and Winston, 1961.

Hamilton, David. *The Echo of Frost's Woods. Roads Not Taken: Rereading Robert Frost.* Ed. Earl J. Wilcox and Jonathan N. Barron. Columbia: U of Missouri P, 2000. 123-31.

Henry, Nat. "Frost's 'Stopping by Woods on a Snowy Evening.'" *The Explicator* 32.5 (1974): 69.

McLaughlin, Charles A. *Two Views of Poetic Unity.* The University of Kansas City Review 22.3 (1956): 312-15.

Monte, Steven. "Stopping by Woods on a Snowy Evening." *Poetry for Students.* Detroit: Gale, 1998. 1: 279-281.

Monteiro, George. "To point or not to point: Frost's 'Stopping by Woods.'" *American Notes and Queries 16* (2003): 38-40.

Thompson, Lawrence. *Fire and Ice.* New York: H. Holt, 1942.

Unger, Leonard, and William Van O'Connor. *Poems for Study: A Critical and Historical Introduction.* New York: Rinehart, 1953.

Discussion Questions

1. Frost himself strongly objected to the idea that the last two lines of the poem imply anything about death, and yet many readers have interpreted the lines that way. Should a writer's personal interpretation of his or work have any special authority, or should interpretations be authorized simply by the words on the page?

2. Is the poem more (or less) effective because Frost refuses to spell out a "lesson" or "moral"?

3. How might the tone and the effect of the poem be different if the speaker were stopping by the woods on a spring or summer evening?

4. What can we infer about the personality, character, and lifestyle of the speaker, and what evidence supports those inferences?

5. Are there any details of this poem that might be accused of being sentimental?

6. How does the speaker of the poem try to behave according to conventionally "masculine" ideals? How does he also violate some common "masculine" stereotypes?

7. Should we even assume that the speaker of this poem is a male? What is the evidence for or against this assumption?

8. How would you explain the enormous popularity of this poem? What are some possible reasons that it appeals so strongly to so many readers?

9. In some editions of the poem, line 13 reads as follows: "The woods are lovely, dark and deep." In some other editions, the line is printed as follows: "The woods are lovely, dark, and deep." Does the presence or absence of the extra comma make any real difference?

10. How does the rural setting contribute to the impact of the poem? Could a poem on a similar theme take place within a large city? How might you write such a poem?

Essay Ideas

1. Read a detailed scholarly biography of Frost. What was happening in his life (and in the life of his era) in the years and months preceding his composition of this poem? How might those events have affected the writing of this lyric?

2. Study Frost's own comments about the writing of poetry, including his views of its purpose and value, and then discuss the ways this poem exemplifies his ideals.

3. Using a detailed bibliography of Frost criticism, study a variety of interpretations of this poem. Discuss the strengths and weaknesses of each approach, and explain which analysis you find most convincing.

4. Using a basic introduction to literary theories, discuss the comments different kinds of theorists might make about this poem. How (for instance) might a feminist read this work? How might an archetypal critic respond? What might a Marxist have to say about this lyric?

5. Study the ways nature is often described, not only in Frost's poems but also in American literature in general. How is the depiction of nature in this lyric typical of (or different from) its depiction by Frost or by other American writers?

Wallace Steven has two works featured in this volume:
"Thirteen Ways of Looking at a Blackbird," on page 211, and
"Sunday Morning," opposite. Photo: Library of Congress

Sunday Morning

by Wallace Stevens

Content Synopsis

In this famous work—considered by many critics to be one of the masterpieces of twentieth-century American poetry—the speaker focuses on a financially comfortable female character who spends her Sunday morning relaxing at home rather than attending church services. Her absence from church does not prevent her from meditating about the Christian religion, especially the sacrifice of Jesus on the cross and his supposed resurrection from death; however, she wonders why she should commemorate such historically distant and supernatural events when earth itself has the power to evoke complex emotions and spiritual satisfactions. She implicitly compares Christianity to other supernatural religions, such as those of the Greeks and Romans—religions that, by imagining some supernatural paradise, failed to appreciate all the complex beauty of this tangible earth. Supernatural religions offer, of course, the prospect of an eternal, unchanging happiness, but the speaker concludes that it is precisely the fact and awareness of death, loss, and change that make the beauties of the earth seem so beautiful. Ultimately, the poem concludes that even Jesus himself was simply a person like all other persons: he lived and he died, and the value of his existence lay both in his life and in the death that gave his life its significance. In the final lines of the poem, the speaker asserts that the inevitability of death is precisely what makes life beautiful and valuable.

The socially elevated tone of the poem is established in the first line when Stevens uses a combination of Latinate and French-derived phrasing to describe the woman's "Complacencies of the peignoir"—phrasing that is entirely different in effect than "Laziness in a bathrobe" would have been. The woman featured in this poem is presumably wealthy or at least financially comfortable, and the fact that no male companion is mentioned suggests that she may be an independent, self-reliant figure. This connotation is significant, since independence and self-reliance will turn out to be two of the key themes of this poem. As she lounges at home on a Sunday morning, she indulges in the colors and sounds of nature (including a free-roaming bird that foreshadows the birds that will appear at the very end of the poem), allowing these comfortable sensations to "mingle" and help "dissipate"—if only briefly—her thoughts of Christ's crucifixion ("the holy hush of ancient sacrifice"; [1-5]).

Thoughts of Christ, however, soon intrude once more, and indeed the first stanza of the poem establishes the basic dialogical rhythm that will characterize the entire work. The woman will conduct, within her own mind, a kind of silent debate, as she meditates first on the pleasures of nature and then on the appeal of supernatural consolations. Thus, if the first five lines of stanza one emphasize natural pleasures, the next ten lines emphasize, by contrast, the haunting presence of "silent Palestine, / Dominion of the blood and sepulcher" (14-15). Much as the woman might like to enjoy the sensual pleasures of the moment, she cannot put out of her mind—at least not at this point—the power of the Christian myth. Meanwhile, Stevens has already begun to employ the striking imagery and the lush sound effects that help make this poem so unforgettable, as in the ways "green wings" is echoed by "seem things" in lines 9-10, or in the heavy use of alliteration and other forms of repetition in lines 11-12. Each stanza of the poem consists of fifteen lines, and each line of the poem consists of ten syllables, yet the absence of rhyme and the frequent use of enjambment help the poem flow freely and smoothly, so that the total effect of the work is a combination of order and freedom, of structure and liberty. Just as one of the basic themes of the work is a kind of dialogue between constraint and flexibility, so the same kind of dialectic is reflected in the very structure and phrasing of the poem.

As the second stanza makes clear, this poem is designed not only to reflect thought but also to provoke it. The series of questions asked in this stanza give voice to the meditations of the poems central figure, yet inevitably, those same questions are posed to the reader, too. Why, the speaker wonders, should she pay homage—and make offerings—to the dead (16), including supposedly divine figures (such as Christ) who are as dead as anyone else from the distant past? What is the point of religion if it can only be insubstantial and illusory (17-18), lacking a real physical presence? Are not the real, tangible, visible beauties of the physical world at least as valuable as abstract, disembodied "thoughts of heaven" (19-22)? Part of the power of Stevens' poem is that in discussing earthly beauty, he also recreates it in the sheer richness of his phrasing. This is especially depicted in its striking images (as in the reference to "pungent fruit and bright, green wings") and in its lush sound effects, particularly alliteration (as in the reference

to "any balm or beauty of the earth"). Contemplating a kind of pantheistic thought that foreshadows "new-age" thinking by many decades, the woman of the poem contemplates the idea that "Divinity must live within herself" (23)—that if there is to be anything sacred in her life, she herself (like any human being) must be its source, its focus, and its manifestation.

However, just when the poem may seem on the verge of becoming almost naively romantic (since it emphasizes only the beauty of earthly existence), the speaker acknowledges the darker aspects of life as well, including "grievings in loneliness" (25). The phrasing of the second half of the second stanza emphasizes the sheer complexity of earthly life. It emphasizes both the obvious beauties of spring and summer and the less obvious, more complicated, ones of autumn and winter. Life, the speaker admits, consists of "All pleasures and all pains"; it consists both of the heavy, leafy "bough of summer" as well as the barren, stripped-bare "winter branch" (28-29). The woman's willingness to see and admit both the appealing and the less appealing aspects of natural life makes her vision seem far more mature and sophisticated, by the second half of this stanza, than it might have seemed in the first half. If she is still a romantic, she no longer seems entirely naive, and indeed the language of Stevens' poem manages to combine lush, evocative imagery with plain, straightforward syntax. The poem itself never seems saccharine or sentimental. There are no unqualified, ecstatic exclamations or overwrought, artificial-sounding phrases (at least none that are not obviously intended to be humorous). This is not the sort of romantic poem that might have been written by a late-nineteenth-century imitator of Wordsworth, Keats, or Shelley. This is a romantic poem that anticipates and responds to all the possible objections that might be leveled against it. It is a "thoughtful" romantic poem, not merely an outpouring of sentimental emotion.

Indeed, part of the appeal of "Sunday Morning" is the way it manages to blend lofty romantic ideals with a real sense of humor. Such humor becomes especially obvious in stanza III, which in its first half uses alliteration in a way that is obviously overdone and therefore almost amounts to parody. There Stevens describes the Roman god Jove, whose "mythy mind" lacked any "Large-mannered motions" and who, lacking also a human mother and an earthly place of birth (unlike Jesus), therefore regarded human beings with an almost comical condescension: "He moved among us, as a muttering king, magnificent, would move among his hinds" (32-34). Jove, then, represents a kind of divinity that is about as far removed from real contact or sympathy with humanity as can be imagined: he regarded humans as far beneath him in dignity and power—as mere peasants, laborers, or servants ("hinds"). Stevens has trouble taking such a god seriously, just as few people today take any such gods seriously or regard them as anything more than obvious figments of the human imagination.

In the next few lines, however, Stevens suggests that it was our very dissatisfactions with gods like Jove that led us to desire and imagine a very different kind of god—a god (in the form of Jesus) who was simultaneously human and divine. This was the god whose presence was so accessible that "the very hinds discerned" his birth, signaled by the presence of the "star" of Bethlehem (36-38). In describing the nativity of Jesus, Stevens manages to move from the comic language of a few lines earlier to a lofty, sublime kind of phrasing, yet no sooner is that new tone established than the focus of the stanza suddenly shifts again, as Stevens plainly asks, "Shall our blood fail?" (39). Here as so often elsewhere, this is a poem that is full of surprises; we can never quite anticipate what Stevens will say or do next—a fact that gives the poem much of its suspense and interest. Relying once again on a series of questions that help the poem continue

to seem literally thought-provoking (and non-dogmatic), the next few lines quickly move away from any focus on Jesus and ask whether the earth itself may come to seem "all of paradise that we shall know" (41). In the space of a few lines, then, Stevens has traced the evolution of human religious thought from ancient polytheism (in which the gods seemed remote from humans) to Christianity (in which God became a man) and finally to modern atheism (in which there is no need for gods because we can no longer take any gods seriously). By the end of this stanza, the poem seems (but only momentarily "seems") to be celebrating this naturalistic, atheistic vision, in which nature itself will appear to be enough for us. In this new dispensation, there will no longer need to be any supernatural yearnings, and thus "The sky will be much friendlier then than now" (42). The earth will seem our own (and our only) home, not a mere way station in the progress toward some imagined, fictitious, supernatural heaven. Once we have been able to dispense with longings for the supernatural, we will seek contentment in the beauties of nature and in the moral and emotional beauty of "enduring love" (44).

Just when the poem seems to have reached a kind of emotional and logical climax, however, the woman poses new questions. She admits that she is happy with the beauties of nature (such as the loveliness of birdsong), but she concedes that such beauties can always and only be temporary, and she wonders how she can feel contentment when such beauties inevitably pass away (46-50). Now, in response to such concerns, the voice of the poem becomes even more emphatic and affirmative—indeed, almost prophetic. The poem ticks off an impressive, evocative list of magical, mythical, but imaginary beliefs and places, but the very words with which the list begins ("There is not any") denies the reality of these things even as the things are named. Stevens manages to evoke the beauty of these myths even while acknowledging that myths are precisely what they are and have always been (51-56). None of them, the poem asserts, "has endured / As Aprils green endures" (56-57). None of these myths, in other words, is or can ever be as enduring as the beauties of nature. In addition, none of these myths can ever be as enduring as the memories of (and desires for) beauty itself (57-60). It is such memories and such desires that call all myths into being.

The woman of the poem, however, still is not satisfied, and so the back-and-forth motion of the poem continues once more. The woman is quoted as saying, "But in contentment I still feel / The need of some imperishable bliss" (61-62). In other words, the beauties of nature and the satisfactions of love are indeed beautiful and satisfying, but they are not permanent in the way that supernatural happiness seems to be. In response, the voice of the poem replies with one of the most famous and suggestive phrases Stevens ever composed: "Death is the mother of beauty" (63). Only our awareness of mortality, in other words, leads us to truly appreciate—and want to create—beauty and beautiful things. Our awareness that we ourselves are impermanent (as Ernest Becker suggests in his profound book "The Denial of Death") is at the root of all human creativity, including the creativity that leads to human reproduction itself. As the stanza develops, Stevens makes it clear that the consciousness of death leads, ultimately, to the kind of sexual love that produces new humans who in turn become conscious of death and who in turn love and reproduce (63-75). It is the inevitable consciousness of death that causes "boys" to court "maidens," wooing them with gifts as if they were goddesses until the maidens "stray impassioned in the littering leaves" (75)—a wonderful image that implies life-affirming lovemaking amidst the fallen leaves that symbolize death.

In Stanza VI, more questions arise, but now the questions raise further doubts about the alleged attractions of supernatural myths and realms,

making those attractions seem static and artificially perfect. At this point, too, a new and crucial word begins to enter the poem incessantly: "our." The voice of the poem now begins to speak for all humans. This word is reiterated so often that it becomes almost a chant (79-87), until Stevens (in a poem in which repetition is one of the key devices) concludes the stanza by returning to and reasserting his earlier claim: "Death is the mother of beauty, mystical, / Within whose burning bosom we devise / Our earthly mothers waiting, sleeplessly" (88-90). Awareness of death, in other words, is the ultimate source of our instinct to reproduce—the instinct that leads flesh-and-blood mothers (such as the former "maidens" mentioned earlier) to create ever-more flesh-and-blood mothers who give birth to all human life that ever exists and has ever existed. It is the awareness of change that leads us to create imagined places (such as heaven) in which no change ever really occurs, but it is also the awareness of change that causes all creativity. The awareness of death is ultimately the source of all life and of all love and loveliness.

In Stanza VII, Stevens shifts from celebrating female reproduction to celebrating male vitality and creativity, imagining a rite of sun worship that sounds almost pagan (like something out of Stravinsky's "The Rite of Spring"). Stevens foresees a time when men "Shall chant in orgy on a summer morn / Their boisterous devotion to the sun," but he is careful to stress that they will celebrate the sun "Not as a god, but as a god might be" (92-94). They will not make the mistake, in other words, of confusing symbol with reality; they will not worship the sun as a supernatural god but will honor the sun as a symbol of all the power and beauty and life-giving qualities of nature. They will create a kind of masculine music that fills the sky and links them with that sky (not an imagined heaven) and with all the features of the earth (96-101). "They shall know well the heavenly fellowship / Of men that perish and of summer morn"

(102-03). A bond born of their awareness of their own mutual mortality will unite them. Their "fellowship" (a word with strong religious overtones) will seem "heavenly" but will not rely on literal belief in the myth of heaven. Instead, their fellowship will be rooted in the fact of their awareness that they are as ephemeral as the "dew" itself (105).

In the eighth and final stanza, Stevens returns once more to the meditating woman with whom the poem began, and indeed, in this stanzas language and imagery the poem comes full circle, echoing significant phrasing from Stanza I. Now, however, the poem reaches a kind of resolution—or rather, a series of resolutions. In the first place, a disembodied voice announces that "The tomb in Palestine / Is not the porch of spirits lingering. / It is the grave of Jesus, where he lay" (107-09). The tone here is understated but emphatic: there are no longer any questions (although the uncertain source of the voice raises some potential ambiguities). Jesus (according to this voice) was simply a man—like everyone else—who lived and died. However, the fact that he died (and, it is implied, remained dead) does not diminish the value of his life in the least. It is his bond with the rest of humanity that made his life at least as valuable as anyone else's did. Next, after having dealt with the issue of the possible divinity of Jesus (by dismissing that possibility), the poem becomes even more assertive and resolute. The ensuing lines state that human life is "unsponsored, free" (112). In other words, there are no gods who create us or who superintend our existences. We are existentially independent, and in fact this poem anticipates many of the tenets of philosophical "existentialism" before that term had even become a buzzword (as it did in the 1940s and 50s). Finally, in the closing lines of the poem, Stevens again emphasizes (especially by using such words as "we" and "our") the fellowship that unites all humans, and he emphasizes again the beauties of the natural world—the only world that is our only real home. At the same time, in the very

last and very powerful image with which the poem closes, he implies once more the common mortality that unites us not only with each other but also with all other living creatures. There is, in this final suggestion of shared death, a kind of strange and haunting beauty, as the poem describes how, "At evening, casual flocks of pigeons make / Ambiguous undulations as they sink / Downward to darkness, on extended wings" (118-20).

Historical Context

"Sunday Morning," which was first published in 1915, appeared during a time of growing skepticism about traditional religion. Darwinian thought, which became increasingly influential in the latter decades of the nineteenth century, had begun to undermine intellectual confidence in Christian explanations of the universe, but those explanations had already been under serious challenge since at least the rise of the Enlightenment in the eighteenth century and before. In literature, the rise of Romanticism in the nineteenth century both reflected and helped celebrate a growing emphasis on the beauties of the natural world and thus helped contribute to a decreasing interest in the supernatural. Atheism and agnosticism seemed on the ascent (or at least traditional religion seemed in some danger of decline) in the early decades of the twentieth century, especially among educated persons, and so Stevens poem reflects thinking that would have seemed highly relevant to people of many different persuasions at this time.

Societal Context

The woman who is the central figure of this poem seems to be living a comfortable material existence—a fact that may help explain her growing skepticism about religion. She seems to be neither in great need nor in great pain, and so the traditional consolations that religion can provide may seem less urgently attractive to her than they often seem to persons who are hurting or desperate.

The woman is obviously thoughtful and articulate and therefore presumably well-educated or at least well read. She is a meditative, contemplative figure, and she has both the instinct and the leisure to engage in serious thought. She symbolizes the growth of an educated group of religious skeptics during this period, and the fact that she is a woman is itself significant, representing the growth of free thought among a segment of society that had tended to be more pious than most and less capable of independence in many aspects of life. The fact that there seems to be no significant male figure in this woman's life (no husband or beau or father) subtly implies, once more, her basic autonomy, in thought as in various other ways.

Religious Context

Religion is obviously a crucial issue in this poem, and indeed this is certainly one of the greatest poetic statements of atheism or agnosticism in the English language. Unlike other famous poems that deal with the decline of faith (such Matthew Arnolds "Dover Beach" and "Stanzas from the Grand Chartreuse" or Philip Larkin's "Church Going"), the tone of Stevens poem is ultimately not melancholy or sad. Stevens poem does not, finally, regard the loss of faith in conventional religion as something to mourn but, indeed, as something to celebrate or at least to accept and affirm. The poem suggests that gods and heavenly utopias are human inventions, and it suggests that a hard philosophical realism can coexist with (and may indeed be a precondition for) a truly romantic appreciation of life and nature as they really are.

Scientific & Technological Context

Science and technology are not the subjects of much (if any) explicit attention in "Sunday Morning," but the poem can nevertheless be seen as partly a response to the scientific and technological revolutions that had been transforming life in the modern era, especially in the nineteenth and early twentieth centuries. Scientific progress in such fields as geology and biology, to name just two, had begun to erode traditional confidence in religious explanations of the universe. Atheism and agnosticism would probably not have become such powerful forces among intellectuals in the early twentieth century if science had not seemed increasingly capable of explaining the way things really worked. Stevens' poem, in some ways, can be seen as an attempt to retain a kind of mystical appreciation for the beauties and wonders of nature even in the face of scientific and technological progress. His poem manages to be both non-religious and deeply spiritual at the same time. Its spirituality, however, does not rely on supernatural assumptions. It is a spirituality that is fully compatible with modern science.

Biographical Context

"Sunday Morning" is one of the most romantic, ecstatic, mystical, and lyrical works in modern American poetry—qualities which make the fact that its author (1879-1955) was a buttoned-down, reclusive insurance executive seem all the more remarkable. Stevens, like the female persona of his poem, was familiar with reasonably comfortable economic circumstances: his father had been a lawyer, and Stevens himself had been able to attend Harvard University. He studied and practiced law himself, but his romantic impulses were apparent not only in his creative writing but also in his determination to marry an attractive young woman (Elsie Moll)—even though his parents considered her unworthy of their upper-crust son's attentions. By the time Stevens published "Sunday Morning," however, both of his parents were dead, and Stevens himself had long since grown away from the kind of conventional Christianity that his mother had tried to instill in him when he was a boy.

Robert C. Evans, Ph.D.

Works Cited

Becker, Ernest. *The Denial of Death*. New York: Free Press, 1973. Print.

Serio, John N. *Wallace Stevens: An Annotated Secondary Bibliography*." Pittsburgh: U of Pittsburgh P, 1994. Print.

Stevens, Wallace. "Sunday Morning." *Collected Poetry and Prose*. Ed. Frank Kermode and Joan Richardson. 53-56. Print.

Vendler, Helen. *On Extended Wings: Wallace Stevens Longer Poems*. Cambridge, MA: Harvard UP, 1969. Print.

Discussion Questions

1. Compare and contrast the first and last stanzas of the poem. In particular, discuss the change in bird imagery: why does Stevens shift from emphasizing a single cockatoo to emphasizing a flock of pigeons? How does the notion of "freedom" become more complicated in the final stanza?

2. This poem does not use rhymed lines, but rhyme is not altogether absent from the work. Discuss some instances in which rhyming appears, and discuss the particular effectiveness of such rhymes or near rhymes.

3. Discuss the various ways in which Stevens uses alliteration in this poem. Where does the intended effect seem almost comic? Where does it add to the lyrical beauty of the work?

4. Discuss the use of repetition in this work. Where does Stevens repeat words, and what are some of the effects (and effectiveness) produced by such repetition?

5. Discuss some instances in which the language of the poem sounds almost archaic or deliberately old-fashioned. Discuss the effectiveness of some particular instances of such diction, and discuss the reasons why Stevens, in general, may have wished to use such language.

6. Certain phrases in this poem almost function as aphorisms. In other words, they are short phrases that seem to state general truths. Identify and discuss some of these kinds of statements; what are their functions in the poem?

7. This poem is widely considered one of the most lyrical or musical in the English language. How does the poem achieve its musical effects? For example, what is anaphora, and where, how, and why is it used in this poem?

8. Discuss the references to "maidens" and "boys" in Stanza V. How are these two words typical of much of the language of the rest of the poem, especially in their differences from one another? Which of the two words seems more archaic? Why does Stevens emphasize "youthful" sexuality? What do these two words imply about the nature of that sexuality?

9. Discuss the use of balance in the phrasing of this poem. Discuss, for instance, the reference to the "heavenly fellowship / Of men that perish and of summer morn" (102-03). How and why is that phrase balanced, and how is such balance typical of the poem as a whole?

10. Why do you think that Stevens attributes the final comment about Jesus to a "voice" (106-09)? Why is this comment not stated impersonally, as the rest of the assertions in the final stanza are stated?

Essay Ideas

1. Compare and contrast this poem with Edward Arlington Robinsons poem titled "Credo." Compare and contrast it with Matthew Arnolds "Dover Beach." How are the three poems similar and/or different in tones, conclusions, and fundamental assumptions?

2. Compare and contrast this poem with Stevens' poem titled "Of Modern Poetry." How are the two works similar in their fundamental assumptions and in some of the techniques they employ? How do they differ in focus?

3. Read the poem by William Carlos Williams titled "Spring and All." How is that poem similar to "Sunday Morning" in some of its fundamental assumptions and in some of its imagery, but in what ways does that poem seem even more naturalistic and materialistic than Stevens' does? What role does the idea of the divine play in the two poems? In what ways is Stevens's poem more "romantic" than Williams'?

4. What are some reasons that a deeply devout Christian might nevertheless find this poem worth reading?

5. How does the presentation of beauty in this text compare and contrast with its treatment in Stevens' poem titled "Peter Quince at the Clavier," especially in the fourth section of that work?

Allen Ginsberg, pictured above, wrote "A Supermarket in California," featured opposite. "Howl," also by Ginsberg, is featured on page 63. Photo: National Portrait Gallery, Smithsonian Institution; gift of Abe Frajndlich in memory of Regina and Ruven Sapir @Abe Frajndlich 1986/1998

A Supermarket in California

by Allen Ginsberg

Content Synopsis

The poet, in the middle of the twentieth century, alone, his head aching, walks at night, under a full moon, through the streets in Berkeley, California. He thinks of Walt Whitman, the pioneering American poet of democracy and of everyday experience. He is in the middle of the mental act of writing a poem. That act involves a conversation with a precursor, a past poet, whose work he sees himself building upon and extending, finding the motor of his art in his spiritual connection with Whitman.

Searching for democratic imagery like Whitman's, he goes into a supermarket, thinking of Whitman's long lines of poetry, characterized by enumerations of things seen, thought, and felt. He begins by cataloging the shoppers and sees them as the goods they are shopping for, blurring the line between people and their desires. Then he shifts his focus and imagines Garcia-Lorca, the Spanish poet killed by the fascists in Spain in 1936, another of his precursors, lingering by the watermelons, compressing images of poetry and produce.

The poet then addresses Whitman directly, describing Whitman as he sees himself, not idealized but as a lonely man poking among the everyday things and looking for beauty and love, and as a moralist. The poet sees himself in the company of Whitman, surveying the store, enjoying its goods in his imagination and not bound to pay for his pleasures, being within the world of the market, yet free of its constraints.

In his reverie of creation the poet asks Whitman where they are going, noting the supermarket will close in an hour. Then his consciousness shifts. The man whose beard he touched in fantasy becomes what is really left of the man, now, his book. The poet feels the absurdity of his poetic vision, turning the word into the shadow of the flesh. The poet wonders if he and his Whitman will walk together through the night lonely together, past the America of materialism, inside a reality that signifies another America, a Whitmanian idea of a spiritual democracy based on goodwill that has been lost.

The poet concludes by saluting Whitman as a poet who teaches him courage in the face of lost dreams as he wonders what America Whitman could have seen from the world of death as America receded from him.

Symbols & Motifs

The elaborate symbolism of the poem relies on the poet's transformation of words and things into symbols. The supermarket is a supermarket, but it is also the landscape of the poet's consciousness as well as an image of America. The produce and the canned goods he surveys are produce and canned goods, but they are also luminous objects, objects of desire and repositories of emotions that correlate to half-hidden things inside the poet that he needs to release, a force that needs to be produced and reproduced. His headache signifies a tension resulting from something contained within him that oppresses if it cannot burst out. Even the side streets signify something other than themselves because they are "side" streets, not main streets. The poet is a subversive man who sees secret things inside ordinary things.

These symbolic presences in the poem point to the theme of the poet as the bardic seer, the mystically penetrating intelligence who finds the meaning of the world that lies hidden from the ordinary eye. This motif explains the presence of such visionary poets as Whitman and Garcia-Lorca.

Historical Context

The poet places himself within a poetic tradition by introducing the figures of Whitman and Lorca, historical precursors, poets who practiced the kind of poetry he wishes to practice, a poetry of revolutionary consciousness and mystic illumination, a poetry that reveals the transformation of the world latent in the present actualities of the world.

Ginsberg created, and society confirmed, a picture of the young poet walking through the streets and around the supermarkets of Berkeley. This was at the time when his presence was about to burst out as an astonishing phenomenon, and has historical significance for readers more than a half century later. That that picture is ostensibly greater for today's readers is also significant. That said, one of the contingent experiences of reading Ginsberg, even at his moment, was that he and his contemporaries constituted a historical phenomenon for poetry, freeing it from academicism and pretentious intellectualism and giving it the improvisatory swing and subversive hipness of jazz.

Societal Context

The social commentary is implicit in the subversion of the supermarket by its use as a place to shop for imagery rather than for food. Into the realm of antiseptic consumerism, Ginsberg introduces the groping aesthetics of consciousness. He introduces the realm of mystic contemplation into the dominant realm of commerce.

From the second line of the poem the sexual subversion implicit in the poem is revealed. It is a "fruit" supermarket, with the suggestion of homosexuality implicit in the word "fruit" actualized not just by the poet's own homosexuality but also by the homosexuality of his two precursor poets, Whitman and Lorca. Whitman, surveying the grocery boys, was proudly homosexual. Lorca was tormented by his homosexuality. Ginsberg, torn between the two poles, in the poem, is trying to ground himself in an identity acceptable to himself, despite societal constraints.

Religious Context

In the poem, the supermarket becomes a sanctuary—a holy place where the vision of older poets is enshrined and where the young poet can come and seek communion with them. Ginsberg invests the profane—the objects of everyday consumption, with an aura of the sacred by his transforming them into consubstantial elements in his quest for enlightenment and for a place for himself in the realm of the visionary poets, who are not only poets but priests of consciousness.

Scientific & Technological Context

The poem is an artifact of the 1950s. The technologies of advertising, suburban living, and mass production are culturally dominant. The lost America is obliterated by "blue automobiles in driveways."

The poet transforms the technology of the supermarket. Ginsberg transforms a sanitized, but jazzed-up, environment of neon signs and gaudy displays dedicated to the technology of consumption. This transformation only secondarily nurtures the body, but primarily is intended to fuel the machinery of capitalism into a technology of enlightenment where objects become symbols and consciousness expands through its visionary power to see through the objects and find communion with a power of poetic, visionary creation.

Biographical Context

Allen Ginsberg was a cultural phenomenon, a public poet, not only because his themes involved social issues and causes but also because he performed his poems publicly and because his own life, down to its every intimate detail, was the subject of his poetry. Ginsberg was born on June 3, 1926 in Newark, New Jersey, to Louis and Naomi Ginsberg. Louis was a poet and a lifelong high school English teacher. Naomi, early in Allen's childhood, suffered a number of breakdowns and spent much of her life battling paranoid delusions and incarceration in psychiatric hospitals.

From boyhood, Ginsberg kept notebooks in which he wrote about the life around him and of his own feelings, thoughts, fantasies, and ambitions. Ginsberg was a student at Columbia, where he thought he was going to study labor law and carry on in the tradition of his socialist father and communist mother. However, when he discovered literature and began seriously writing poetry, he met people like Lucien Carr, who introduced him to William S. Burroughs and Jack Kerouac. Kerouac was the future author of the culture transforming novel "On the Road, "who in turn introduced him to a host of his bohemian and petty-criminal acquaintances."

Ginsberg's academic career was interrupted by his bohemian pursuits, by his own mystical visions—Blake, for example, came to him as an auditory hallucination and bestowed his prophetic/poetic mantle on him—and by his naive and innocent involvement in getting rid of hot merchandise that others who were imposing on his hospitality had stolen. To avoid imprisonment after they were caught, Ginsberg pleaded insanity. In the psychiatric hospital, he met Carl Solomon, to whom his breakout poem, "Howl," was dedicated.

After his release from the psychiatric hospital, Ginsberg held a number of conventional jobs but also continued to frequent the circles of bohemians, artists, and people in revolt against conventional morality and society. He wrote poetry and began experimenting with changing prose into verse. He veered back and forth between heterosexual and homosexual relationships. It was on October 13, 1955, at a poetry reading at the Six Gallery in San Francisco that Ginsberg first read "Howl" to an audience of poets and bohemians. The poem was immediately a sensation. The poet and owner of City Lights Books, Laurence Ferlinghetti, published "Howl," which then brought worldwide popular recognition both to Ginsberg and to what came to be called the Beat Generation. It was at that time in Berkeley that Ginsberg wrote "A Supermarket in California."

Ginsberg traveled the world, wrote poetry, and campaigned for an end to war and government repression, for the repeal of laws criminalizing homosexuality and the use of marijuana. He was a practicing Buddhist.

Allen Ginsberg died at home, of cancer of the liver, on April 5, 1997. Bob Dylan, Lou Reed, Patty Smith, and John Lennon are among those artists who were influenced by his work.

Neil Heims, Ph.D.

Works Cited

Ginsberg, Allen. "A Supermarket in California." *Howl and Other Poems*. San Francisco: City Lights Books, 1956. Print.

Heims, Neil. *Allen Ginsberg Philadelphia*: Chelsea House, 2005. Print.

Discussion Questions

1. Is there a critique of society implicit in "A Supermarket in California?" What is it? Is it legitimate? If so, in what ways? Is it still applicable?

2. Does "A Supermarket in California" look like a poem? When you read it aloud, does it sound like one? Is it a poem? If not, why not? If you think it is a poem, what makes it a poem?

3. What sense of the role of the poet in society do you derive from reading "A Supermarket in California?"

4. What role do Walt Whitman and Federico Garcia Lorca play in the poem?

5. What does the poem suggest about the youthful search for identity? What things are necessary for a youth to achieve his identity? How are they represented in the poem?

6. Share the experiences you have had that are similar to the one Ginsberg presents in "A Supermarket in California."

7. What is the picture of American society conveyed by the poet in "A Supermarket in California?" Is there more than one America presented by the poem?

8. How does the homosexual subtext affect the poem? Does it diminish its effect or enhance its meaning? Explain your answers.

9. How do you think your vision of reality affects reality itself? Is reality stable and absolute or various and shifting?

10. What is the function of poetry and what is the role of the poet in society according to the poem?

Essay Ideas

1. Explain the importance of long verse lines in "A Supermarket in California."

2. Examine the theme of vision in "A Supermarket in California."

3. Analyze the importance and the role of precursor poets in "A Supermarket in California."

4. Discuss the tension between the commercial culture of consumer goods and the mystic revelations of consciousness in "A Supermarket in California."

5. How does the poet conceive of America in the poem and how does he differentiate the idea of America from the actuality of America?

Take the I Out

by Sharon Olds

Content Synopsis

The title of the poem is a common phrase—a phrase intended to discourage egotism and emphasize the importance of teamwork. The opening half of the poem's first line, however, suggests that the speaker will defiantly disagree with this commonly accepted concept. The first five words of the poem seem to engage in a kind of dialogue with, or offer a kind of rebuttal to, the poem's title, seeming to imply that the poem will paradoxically defend egotism. Those opening five words even manage to mention the crucial word "I" twice. The attitude of the speaker seems informal, and the poem, by beginning with the word "But," seems to plunge right into the midst of an on-going exchange, using a technique known as "in medias res."

By the second half of the opening line, however, the focus shifts from the literal meaning of the word "I" (i.e., the self, the ego) to the figurative meaning of the kind of I-shaped steel beam which the speaker's "father sold." The poem begins to evolve away from an emphasis on the speaker and begins to encompass others, especially the speaker's father and the unnamed persons ("They") with whom he worked with (2). In the space of two lines, the speaker has already established the motifs of family and class as important to the poem. The speaker's father was apparently a salesman who marketed products made by industrial workers. Helping to establish the conversational tone of the entire poem,

the opening lines differ in length (the first line has eight syllables; the second has ten). Line 3 has ten syllables, suggesting the start of some kind of pattern, but then any sense of a strict or rigid order is disrupted by the appearance of line 4, which has twelve syllables. The lines of the poem, so far, are as free flowing as the molten metal they describe, and the absence of rhyme adds to the sense that the poem will be structurally similar to prose rather than to any predictable, formal poem.

To say this, however, is not to say that the poem is lacking in subtle formal features. The opening line, for instance, tends to accentuate each of the odd syllables, as does the second line (at least until the reader reaches the final two words—"pig iron"—which seem equally accented). The first line features heavy assonance by placing the emphasis on the letters "i" and "e," while the second line strongly stresses alliteration thanks to the repeated emphasis on "th" and "p." There is a subtle echo between "sold" (in line 2) and "mold" (in line 3), while there is also an effective slowing of the pronunciation at the end of line 3—a slowing of sound that matches the slowing of movement that the line describes. Line 4 offers a vivid image and more alliteration, while line 5 offers a flood of precise nouns in which the first syllable of each noun is heavily accented, thus giving the line a potent rhythm. Through effective enjambment, the end of the line heavily accents the crucial word "he," so that by this point it becomes quite clear that the poem is emphasizing the speaker's father rather than the speaker herself.

In line 6, the verb "marketed" helps separate the father even more strongly from the workers who actually made the steel beams: he is presented more as a member of the middle class than as a member of the proletariat, an identity reflected by his taste for "bourbon" (line 6). Yet the father's interest in alcohol is immediately balanced by his provision of "Cream of Wheat" (6) cereal for his children, so that the steel he sells is associated with his strength as a father and as a provider for his offspring. The cereal in this case is literally warm, and it is also an iconic American brand, thus helping to give these lines an appealing air of domesticity: the father is presented as a hard worker who cares about his children ("he paid for our dresses" [7]). Even though he does not, help manufacture the steel, he is around it enough that his "metal sweat" seems "sweet in the morning" (9) but "sour in the evening" (10). He is associated with hard work, and his daughter's fond memories of him are vivid, sensual, and detailed. Thus, a poem that seemed to emphasize the speaker herself has evolved, by line 10, into a clear and extended celebration of the speaker's father.

It is in line 10 that the speaker begins to refer to the actual letter "I" itself, a shift signaled by the fact that the "I" here is italicized. She describes the vertical part of the letter as "frail between its flitches," thus using alliteration once more in an ear-catching way. She uses paradoxical wording, pairing an expected phrase ("hard ground") with one that is strikingly unexpected ("hard sky"), and then making what had earlier seemed "frail" now seem strong by using the verb "soars" (12)—a verb that is quickly reinforced by the equally strong verb "rushes" in the next line (13). Now the focus shifts away from the literal letter "I" to its possible symbolism as a token of the connection between the speaker's father "and" mother (14). No sooner is this connection mentioned, however, than it is immediately qualified and complicated when the speaker asks, "What if they had loved each other" [?] (14)—thereby implying that they had not. In lines that speak vividly of the possibility of joinings and connections, the speaker suggests that somehow, a perfect union failed to exist between her own parents. The father, who seems to have been a dependable worker, successful salesman, and reliable parent, seems not to have enjoyed a completely loving relationship with his wife, although the reasons for any flaws in the parents' marriage are not made clear.

Line 17 briefly shifts back to the speaker talking about herself. She recounts how she once saw, recorded on the white cardboard with which shirts are often packed, "the penciled / slope of her [mother's] temperature rising, and on / the peak of the hill, the first soldier to reach / the crest, the Roman numeral I" (18-21). Apparently, her mother kept accurate records of her temperature in order to chart her fertility so that she would know when she was most likely to become pregnant. This careful preparation suggests that the speaker's parents truly wanted to have children, thus also implying that the speaker herself was genuinely loved, even if the love between her parents was somehow imperfect or damaged. The speaker literally embodied the physical bond between her parents; she is the link between the two ends of their figurative letter "I," just as the roman numeral "I," described as "the first soldier to reach / the crest," resembles the first sperm to reach the egg and result in fertilization. Likewise, the repeated, italicized "*I, I, I, I*" of line 22 seem almost to suggest the energy of the sexual act and of sexual climax, while there also seem to be (perhaps) sexual, erotic overtones in the imagery of "identity, head on, / embedded in the poem" (23-24). By the time the poem repeats, in line 24, its opening phrase ("I love the I"), the connotations associated with the crucial letter have become rich and complicated as the poem begins to come full circle.

The circularity of the poem is suggested not only by the way line 24 clearly echoes line 1 but also by the way the imagery of lines 26-27 echoes the imagery of line 4. Earlier in the poem the speaker had referred to the "bending jelly" of steel cooling and hardening in a "bath" of water (4); now the speaker describes how "when I was / born, part gelid, I lay with you / on the cooling table" (26-27). Who, exactly, is the "you" here? Presumably, the "you" refers to the speaker's mother, so that the language balances all the earlier emphasis on the speaker's father. One cannot be as sure of the meaning of this line as of the meanings of earlier lines in the poem, and indeed, as the poem draws to its conclusion, the content becomes far more ambiguous, metaphorical, and suggestive. Thus, in the final lines the speaker asserts that "The I" is a pine / resinous, flammable root to crown / which throws its cones as far as it can in a fire" (28-30). In what senses is the "I" a "pine"? The imagery of "root" and "crown" refers back to all the earlier language suggesting the various ends of various kinds of "I's." However, for the most part the phrasing of the last three lines of the poem seems deliberately mysterious and intentionally ambiguous. The final three lines suggest the continuation of life amidst death—the ways pine trees scatter their seeds when they are engulfed in flames, so that new pines can be born. Clearly, such imagery is relevant to the birth imagery emphasized in lines 25-27, so that while the poem began by stressing imagery associated with mechanical manufacturing, it ends by emphasizing imagery associated with arguably the most meaningful processes of natural birth and reproduction. The first ten lines of the poem were fairly simple and straightforward whereas the final lines are fundamentally more mysterious and suggestive.

Historical Context

Perhaps the most important element in the "historical context" of this poem is its place in the history of American poetry. In its structure as well as in its language, Olds' poem is part of a large-scale rejection of the traditional conventions of English and American poetry. Olds disregards standard features of traditional verse such as distinct stanzas, predictable line-lengths, predictable metrical patterns, and predictable patterns of rhyme. In this sense, Olds' poem is part of a counter-tradition in American poetry most famously associated with the work of the nineteenth-century poet Walt Whitman and continued in the twentieth century with the work of other writers such as William Carlos Williams. The line lengths in Olds' poem range from as few as four syllables to as many as sixteen; most of the lines consist of even numbers of syllables, but some of the lines (in no predictable pattern) consist of odd numbers of syllables. Most of the lines end without punctuation, while some of the line endings are punctuated. Again, however, there is no discernible pattern. In its diction as well as in its structure, the poem is generally colloquial and relaxed. Like many modern poems influenced by the work of such writers as Whitman and Williams, Olds' poem looks and sounds more like prose than poetry. Olds is clearly setting her work apart from what had once been the standard conventions of English poetry.

Societal Context

Olds' writing is often praised for being accessible to a wide range of readers, and this poem certainly conforms to that mold. "Take the I Out" is likely to be of interest to anyone (which is to say, to almost everyone) who has ever been part of a family, to anyone who has ever had vivid memories of his or her father and mother, and to anyone who has ever had memories of childhood and of growing up. Family matters are frequent themes in most of Olds' poetry, and certainly the family depicted here is one to which many readers will be able to relate. The father seems to be a member of the middle class, but he is closely associated with persons of the working class as well. In this poem, Olds offers a picture of a family that has its appealing aspects while also being far from perfect—the kind of family that most of her readers will be able to relate. While some readers find the depictions of family life in other poems by Olds distasteful and repellent, few readers are likely to object to the way the family is presented in this poem. This work, is accessible (and widely socially "acceptable") not only in its style but also in its subject matter.

Scientific & Technological Context

Science and technology play noticeable roles in this work. The first five lines of the poem emphasize steel-making, one of the most important of all modern industries. The steel industry provided economic power to the nations that invested in it and provided economic rewards to the workers and salesmen it employed. By emphasizing the steel industry, Olds helps situate her poem in the modern era, particularly in the early to late twentieth century. The same is true of her apparent references to scientific family planning in lines 18-21, which also help to make the poem seem both a reflection "of" and reflection "on" an era in which science and technology had begun to play increasingly prominent parts.

Biographical Context

Sharon Olds (1942-) is known for writing poems that invite autobiographical interpretations, partly because they frequently present female speakers and partly because they often deal with common, everyday matters such as family life, relations between parents and children, and childhood memories. Sometimes the families depicted in Olds' poems seem dysfunctional; the males, in particular,

can often seem unappealing. Sexuality—often depicted in graphic terms—is a frequent subject in Olds' verse, as are anger and violence that appear frequently in her poetry. Many of the less pleasant aspects of life depicted in Olds' poetry seem rooted in her own personal experiences, especially her unhappy childhood. "Take the I Out," however, offers a generally positive depiction of the life and family relations of its female speaker.

Robert C. Evans, Ph.D.

Works Cited

Bedient, Calvin. "Sentencing Eros." *Salmagundi* 97. Winter, 1993. 169-181. Print.

Burt, Stephen. "Trauma units: Sharon Olds's poems wrestle with the legacy of childhood abuse." *The New York Times Book Review*: *Literature Resource Center* (2002): 22." Web. "19 Sept. 2010."

Campbell, Katie. "Sharon Olds: Overview." *Contemporary Poets*. Ed. Thomas Riggs. 6th ed. New York: St. James Press, 1995. *Literature Resource Center*. Web. 19 Sept. 2010.

Dillon, Brian. "'Never having had you, I cannot let you go': Sharon Olds's Poems on a Father-Daughter Relationship." *The Literary Review* 37.1 (1993): 108-118. Print.

Hoagland, Tony. "The Unarrestable Development of Sharon Olds." *American Poetry Review*. 38.1 (2009): 7-9. Print.

Olds, Sharon. "Take the I Out." *Blood, Tin, Straw: Poems*. New York: Knopf, 1999. 43. Print.

Stone, Carole. "Sharon Olds." *American Poets since World War II": Third Series*. Ed. R. S. Gwynn. Detroit: Gale Research, 1992. *Dictionary of Literary Biography Vol. 120*. *Literature Resource Center*. Web. 19 Sept. 2010.

Discussion Questions

1. How does the third word of the poem already help to characterize the speaker? How does that word help foreshadow much that comes later in the poem?

2. How does the precise language the speaker uses (such as the final two words of line 2 and much of the phrasing in line 5) help to characterize the speaker, and how does such language contribute to the over-all tone of the poem?

3. Discuss the effectiveness of the first and final words of line 3. In particular, discuss the rhythms of both words and the use of vowel sounds in both words.

4. How does the use of enjambment at the end of line 5 help emphasize the verb at the beginning of line 6? Discuss the various verbs associated with the speaker's father in the first ten lines of the poem. How do those verbs help to reinforce one another and create a total picture of the man? Are verbs used as often in describing the speaker's mother? If not, why not?

5. How do lines 6-7 help foreshadow line 9? How does Olds play with sound effects in line 7 and again in line 9? How do lines 8-9 help characterize not only the speaker's father but also the speaker herself?

6. What are "flitches" (11)? How and why is the use of that word effective? How does the use of such a word help characterize the speaker of the poem?

7. How does the kind of language used in lines 13-14 differ from the kind of language used in the first ten lines of the poem? How does the kind of language used in lines 13-14 foreshadow the kind of language used later in the poem?

8. How is the phrasing in lines 14-16 different from the phrasing used in all the earlier lines, particularly in their sentence structure?

9. How and why is the phrase "our I" (25) particularly important? How does that phrase implicitly involve the reader in the broader story the poem implies?

10. What are some possible meanings of the word "you" and "we" in lines 26 and 27?

Essay Ideas

1. Read several essays dealing with Olds' poetry and discuss the various ways in which this poem is typical and/or atypical of her writing, both in style and in themes.

2. Read a number of Olds' poems about parents and discuss the similarities and/or differences between this poem and other poems you examined.

3. Write an essay in which you explain, in detail, why you find this poem either effective, ineffective, or some combination of both.

4. Write an essay in which you place this poem within a larger historical context. For example, examine the references to the steel industry. Examine the references to Cream of Wheat. Examine the references to family planning. Do some basic historical research and discuss the ways in which these references help locate the poem within a particular historical era.

5. Imagine a variety of specific kinds of readers of this poem, and then discuss the various ways in which (and reasons for which) the poem might be expected to those kinds of reasons. For example, why might this poem appeal to anyone who has ever been a father? Why might it appeal to anyone who has ever been a child?

Thirteen Ways of Looking at a Blackbird

by Wallace Stevens

Content Synopsis

Published in 1917, "Thirteen Ways of Looking at a Blackbird" consists of thirteen brief stanzas, separate images, or contemplations that stem from the speaker observing a blackbird.

Each stanza consists of visual images and philosophical meditations. Stevens pares down his ordinary subjects to bare bones images until they become almost foreign (Clark). In doing so, Stevens is able to tread the line between reality and imagination.

The first stanza presents a visual contrast of color and movement. Stevens states, "Among twenty snowy mountains, the only moving thing was the eye of the blackbird." The "eye of the blackbird" transports the reader from a natural world to an imaginary one, as a bird's eye cannot actually move (Maeder). The movement is important as a contrast to the still mountains but also metaphorically as the poem focuses on looking or seeing. The movement of the blackbird's dark eye also sets the mood, as its contrast to the white of the mountains is unsettling.

The second stanza compares the speaker's state of mind, "I was of three minds," to a tree "in which there are three blackbirds." Man is usually referred to as being of two minds, the conscious, and unconscious. Stevens' speaker introduces another level of thought in this stanza, possibly the imagination.

The third stanza brings forth the idea of interconnectedness in nature as the speaker describes the blackbird "whirling in the autumn wind." Stanza 4 also presents images of unity as the speaker suggests that not only are man and woman "one" but also, "a man and a woman and a blackbird are one."

In stanza five, the speaker uses a natural image of the blackbird whistling to reflect on the nature of poetry itself. He states, "I do not know which to prefer / The beauty of inflections / Or the beauty of innuendoes / The blackbird whistling / Or just after." The metaphor illustrates the difficulty in choosing between the act of reading poetry and the way it lingers in the mind afterwards, being in the moment versus the memory of the moment (Maeder).

The speaker studies the blackbird, through an icicle-covered window, walking back and forth in stanza six. In stanza seven, the speaker scolds the men of Haddam for ignoring the blackbird and imagining "golden birds," implying that the men ignore the women "about" them for the imagined perfect ones (Clark).

In stanza 8, the speaker states that, "the blackbird is involved in what I know" again suggesting a unity between man and nature. Stanza 9 reiterates this idea exclaiming, "When the blackbird flew out of sight, / It marked the edge / Of one of many circles," which is a way of saying that the world contains many realms of existence (Leggett).

Stanzas 10 and 11 comment on the arresting quality of the sight of a blackbird. Ten comments on the blackbird flying in a contrasting "green light" which would cause even "the bawds of euphony" to "cry out sharply." In stanza 11, fun is poked at the ignorance of the aristocrat who rides around in a glass coach and mistakes the shadow of his coach for blackbirds (Clark).

Stevens closes his poem with a short stanza of movement, "The river is moving/The blackbird must be flying" followed by a moment of still observation in stanza thirteen. It is snowing in the scene but the speaker focuses on the still image of the blackbird sitting "in the cedar-limbs." The final moment of the poem resembles the opening section of the poem where the focus is on the blackbird in its natural landscape (Maeder). By observing a scene and then zeroing in on a specific image, Stevens conveys the importance of paying close attention to the natural world because of all it can reveal to us (Clark).

Symbols & Motifs

The blackbird is the dominant motif in "Thirteen Ways of Looking at a Blackbird" as it appears in every stanza. It represents an element in nature, a bleak but striking focal point in a vast and multi-faceted world.

Historical Context

Wallace Stevens' poetry was influenced by the modernist movement of the early 20th century. The term modernism refers to the paradigm shift away from 19th century optimism because of World War 1 (*Understanding the Context of Modern Poetry*). Published in 1917, "Thirteen Ways of Looking at a Blackbird" was written at the height of the war. Since the world was no longer considered stable, an aura of futility, loss, and confusion prevailed (*Understanding the Context of Modern Poetry*). This shift is evident in the art and literature of the time which, like Stevens, rejected traditional forms

and themes and set out to create a new art that reflected the times.

Stevens also borrows from the ideas of the Imagist movement, led by Ezra Pound, which was taking place at the same time. Imagism sought to achieve clarity through the expression of crisp visual images, much influenced by the style of traditional Japanese haiku. Stevens experiments with his own unique brand of imagism by exploring the same subject in thirteen different ways.

Societal Context

In accordance with its Modernist sensibilities, the speaker of the poem is detached and only partially present in the poem. The "I" presents itself in only some of the stanzas suggesting that the speaker feels lost in this new, unsettled world. Likewise, the landscape is depicted as desolate, and while the speaker stresses the importance of observing nature, he lacks a true connection.

Religious Context

"Thirteen Ways of Looking at a Blackbird" does not have a specific religious context but does suggest the existence of a world beyond our own as even when the blackbird flew out of sight, "it marked the edge of one of many circles." This implies that beyond our sight are many other worlds or realities.

Scientific & Technological Context

"Thirteen Ways of Looking at a Blackbird" rejects even the small technological advances in society, such as the "barbaric glass" window and "the glass coach," and stresses the importance of observing the natural landscape.

Biographical Context

Wallace Stevens was born on October 29, 1879 in Reading, Pennsylvania. He attended Harvard University from 1897-1900 where he became interested in writing poetry, but he did not graduate (Modern American Poetry). He graduated from

New York law school in 1903 and married Elsie Kachel in 1909 (Modern American Poetry).

In 1915, at the age of 36, his first poem was published (Modern American Poetry). By 1923, Stevens' first book of verse, "Harmonium" was published. Stevens was disappointed with the reviews and ceased writing for the remainder of the decade (Modern American Poetry).

In the meantime, Stevens advanced in his business career, working as a lawyer in New York City from 1908 until 1916 when he moved to Hartford, CT to work at Hartford Accident and Indemnity (Modern American Poetry). In 1924, his only child Holly Bight was born. He became Vice President of his company in 1936 and lived in Hartford for the rest of his life (Modern American Poetry). Stevens traveled regularly to Florida and weekly to New York City (Modern American Poetry).

By the 1930s, Stevens resumed writing and began publishing poems in limited editions. His books published at the time included "Ideas of Order" in 1935, "Owl's Clover" in 1937, "The Man With the Blue Guitar" in 1937 and "Parts of a World" in 1942 (Modern American Poetry). As Stevens grew older, his work became more philosophical and his poetry began to comment on old age and even poetry itself (Modern American Poetry). In 1951, he published a collection of essays, "The Necessary Angel" which included his thoughts on the art form (Modern American Poetry).

Stevens died on August 2, 1955 at the age of seventy-six.

Jennifer Bouchard, M.Ed.

Works Cited

Clark, James A. "Wallace Stevens: A Portrait of the Artist as a Phenomenologist." *Philosophy in the Contemporary World 4.3* (Fall 1997): 1-5.

Leggett, B.J. *Early Stevens: The Nietzschean Intertext.* Durham: Duke UP, 1992. 12 September 2008. http://www.english.uiuc.edu/maps/poets/s_z/stevens.

Maeder, Beverly. *Wallace Stevens' Experimental Language: The Lion in the Lute.* New York: St. Martin's Press, 1999. 12 September 2008.

Modern American Poetry. http://www.english.upenn.edu/~afilreis/88/stevens-13ways.html.

Modern American Poetry. "Wallace Stevens." 12 September 2008. http://www.english.uiuc.edu/maps/poets/s_z/stevens.

Stevens, Wallace. "Thirteen Ways of Looking at a Blackbird." *Modern American Poetry.* 8 August 2008. University of Pennsylvania. 12 September 2008. http://www.english.upenn.edu/~afilreis/88/stevens-13ways.html.

"Understanding the Context of Modern Poetry." *Edsitement: National Endowment for the Humanties.* 16 September 2008. http://edsitement.neh.gov/view_lesson_plan.asp?id=615.

Vendler, Helen. "On Extended Wings: Wallace Stevens; Longer Poems." Cambridge: Harvard U P, 1969, 75-77. 15 September 2008. http://www.english.uiuc.edu/maps/poets/s_z/stevens/blackbird.htm.

Discussion Questions

1. What is the tone of the poem?
2. Identify the sensory details in each stanza.
3. What is the poet's relationship to nature? How does he feel about the natural world?
4. What is the significance of the blackbird? What does it represent?
5. What does Stevens mean when he says that, "A man, a woman, and a blackbird are one"?
6. Why did Stevens decide to make his poem thirteen stanzas?
7. How does each stanza change from the beginning of the poem to the end?
8. Can you describe the speaker of the poem?
9. What do you think is the message of the poem?

Essay Ideas

1. Write an essay in which you analyze how Stevens' use of tone, imagery, metaphor, and symbolism help the reader to understand and enjoy the poem's message and/or effect.
2. Compare and contrast this poem, one of Stevens' earliest, to one or more of his later poems. Evaluate style, tone, subject matter, and aesthetics in your essay.
3. Write a poem "Thirteen Ways of Looking at _____," in which you model Stevens' style in your observations of the object of your choice.
4. Write an essay in which you discuss the theme of alienation in "Thirteen Ways of Looking at a Blackbird."
5. Read Robert Frost's poem, "Stopping by Woods on a Snowy Evening." Imagine Frost and Stevens walking through these same snowy woods together and write a dialogue between the two discussing their ideas about nature.

The Waste Land

by T. S. Eliot

Content Synopsis

"The Waste Land" is perhaps the most important poem of the 20th century, one that has been read as the definitive statement of literary Modernism and as an epitaph for Western culture. Eliot's poetics of allusion calls on the reader to draw connections between his poem and the Western European literary canon. As such, "The Waste Land" reshapes one's understanding of any number of works of literature that came before it. Eliot himself, perhaps best describes the impact of "The Waste Land" in an essay written a few years before the poem was published, claims: "What happens when a new work of art is created is something that happens simultaneously to all the works of art which preceded it" (Selected Essays 15). Eliot's poem is just such a "happening," a new work of literature that changes how one reads literature as a whole.

The epigraph to "The Waste Land," a quotation from Petronius' "Satyricon," announces the themes and methods that Eliot will employ in the poem itself. A braggart traveler claims to have seen the Cumaean Sibyl, a woman to whom the gods gave immortal life, but not immortal youth, such that time wore her to a wasted shell. The Sibyl hangs in a cage, and the local boys taunt her, asking "Sibyl, what do you want?" She replies, "I want to die." The Sibyl might be read as a symbol for Western civilization, which has wasted away to a shrunken, caged version of its former glory.

The epigraph contains two languages, Latin and Greek, and several voices: those of the narrator, the boys, the sibyl, and, somewhere behind these three, Petronius himself. "The Waste Land," like its epigraph, is structured around the juxtaposition of languages and voices.

The first of "The Waste Land's" five parts, "The Burial of the Dead," begins "April is the cruelest month, breeding / Lilacs out of the dead land, mixing / Memory and desire, stirring / Dull roots with spring rain" (lines 1-4). The lines are a perversion of the beginning of Chaucer's "The Canterbury Tales:" "Whan that Aprill with his shoures soote, / The droghte of March hath perced to the roote" (1-2). For Chaucer, April brought a literal and spiritual rebirth, delivering life-giving rain and inspiring "folk to goon on pilgrimages" (12). In Eliot's poem, April with its "spring rain" is instead cruel, in that it recalls a former life (memory) and an unattainable one (desire). Winter, on the other hand, "kept us warm, covering / Earth in forgetful snow" (5-6). Non-existence and forgetfulness are less cruel than rebirth and memory.

Eliot's narrator becomes more distinctly individualized in the next few lines as he recounts a summer trip across Germany. He recalls drinking coffee in the Hofgarten, and suddenly a snatch of conversation, perhaps overheard from the next table, makes its way into the poem: "Bin gar kein Russin, stamm' aus Litauen, echt deutsch" [I am not Russian, I'm from Lithuania-a true German] (12). Eliot is, however opaquely, teaching his reader how to read the poem. One must recognize this voice and language as belonging to a different speaker than the man in the Hofgarten. As with the epigraph, the lines reward the reader who bothers to translate them: they speak of a blurring of cultures and languages that is a recurring theme of the poem. A second narrator, a woman named Marie, then recalls a childhood visit to the house of her cousin, the archduke, where she and the young man went sledding.

A dramatically different voice begins the next stanza, that of an Old Testament prophet such as Ezekial: "What are the roots that clutch, what branches grow / out of this stony rubbish?" (19-20). Here, for the first time, is a vision of the literal wasteland or desert that the poem posits as an analogue for the sterility of modern life. The prophetic voice promises: "I will show you fear in a handful of dust" (30). Lines from Wagner signal another shift of speaker. Then a girl speaks, recalling a moment in a garden of hyacinths. Two more incidents close "The Burial of the Dead." Madame Sosostris, "famous clairvoyante" (43) reads a deck of Tarot cards. Sosostris comes across as a shyster, a greatly devolved version of the Sibyl or the ancient oracle. Nevertheless, there is still a power to the cards, for their faces prefigure the central images of the poem. Sostostris's injunction to "fear death by water," for example, will become the title of the fourth part of the poem (55). Sosostris, like so many denizens of "The Waste Land," is unaware of the power she has inherited. Finally, in lines that echo those of Dante's Inferno, a nameless speaker has an infernal vision of London as an "unreal city" (60). Crossing the square mile of London known as The City, he sees a familiar face in the crowd, Stetson, a veteran of an unspecified war. The speaker challenges Stetson and, in a line borrowed from Baudelaire, the "hypocrite" reader:

"You! Hypocrite lecteur!-mon semblable,-mon freacutere!" (76).

The poem's second part, "A Game of Chess," contrasts two conversations and two marriages. First, a cultured and well-off husband and wife fail to communicate. The woman has a nervous disposition, which, toward the end of her speech, borders on hysteria: "What shall I do now? What shall I do? / I shall rush out as I am, and walk the street / With my hair down so" (131-3). The man is silent and withdrawn, responding to her querulous pleas only with darkly ironic thoughts. Her lines are placed in quotation marks, indicating that they are spoken aloud; his are not. She asks "What are you thinking of? What thinking? What? / I never know what you are thinking. Think" (113-114). To which he silently replies, "I think we are in rats' alley / Where the dead men lost their bones" (116). The second half of "A Game of Chess" focuses on a marriage from a very different socio-economic set. The reader overhears a woman in a pub telling a story about her friend Lil. Lil's husband is coming home from the service, and Lil has used the money he gave her for new teeth to get an abortion instead. The narrator reports her advice to Lil: get some new teeth before Albert gets home, for "he wants a good time, / And if you don't give it him, there's others will" (148-9).

"The Fire Sermon" begins by constructing a vision of modern London out of fragments of sixteenth and seventeenth century English verse. Lines by Spenser, Shakespeare, and Marvell are corrupted and subverted when voiced in the context of the modern city. Eliot quotes, for example, Andrew Marvell's great meditation on mortality, "To His Coy Mistress": "But at my back I always hear / Time's winged chariot hurrying near" (21-22). In "The Waste Land," however, one hears not reminders of mortality, but the distractions of modern life: "But at my back, from time to time I hear / the sound of horns and motors which shall bring / Sweeney to Mrs. Porter in the spring" (196-8). This third part also introduces the character Tiresias, whom Eliot in his notes terms "the most important personage in the poem" (52). In Greek and Roman mythology and literature, Tiresias figures in several stories. Ovid retells the two most famous ones in "The Metamorphoses." Walking through the woods, Tiresias comes upon two snakes copulating. He strikes the snakes with his stick, and as a punishment for disturbing this sacred act, he is transformed into a woman. For seven years, he wanders the earth, looking to find the snakes again. When he finds them, he strikes them again and regains his manhood. A second story builds on the first. Zeus and Juno (Hera, to the Greeks) are arguing about who derives greater pleasure from the sex act, men or women. They turn to Tiresias, who having been both man and woman may draw a comparison. Honest to a fault, Tiresias admits that women take more pleasure. Hera, angry that he has given away her secret, strikes Tiresias blind. Zeus takes pity on Tiresias, and while he cannot counteract Hera's punishment, he grants Tiresias foresight. As the blind seer who knows both past and future, Tiresias figures in a number of works of Greek literature, including "The Odyssey," where he gives Odysseus advice on how to return home, and "Oedipus Rex," in which he knows that Oedipus has unwittingly killed his father and married his mother. In "The Waste Land," too, Tiresias is a witness to a "crime": the loveless liaison between the city clerk and the typist. Eliot's Tiresias retains some of his androgyny, describing himself as "throbbing between two lives, / Old man with wrinkled female breasts" (218-9). He is therefore a particularly expert witness of a loveless, cold-blooded sex act.

"The Fire Sermon" is also notable for its metrical innovation. The stanza beginning "The river sweats / Oil and tar" (266-7) introduces a new rhythm to the poem, one of short, compressed lines of one to eight syllables. This rhythmical variation will return in the last part of the poem. "The Fire

Sermon" ends by juxtaposing the words of representatives of Western and Eastern religion, St. Augustine and the Buddha. Somehow, this juxtaposition produces an independent meaning which fuses some of the tenets of Christianity and Buddhism: "To Carthage then I came / Burning burning burning burning / O Lord Thou pluckest me out" (307-9). Eastern and Western spirituality alike evince a mistrust of the material world and a need to be purged by fires of resignation and redemption.

"Death by Water" is both the shortest and one of the earliest-composed parts of the poem. This brief lyric describes a drowned sailor who undergoes a sort of apotheosis or transformation. Earlier in the poem, the narrator alluded to Shakespeare's The Tempest: "Those are pearls that were his eyes" (48). Part IV builds on this allusion. In Shakespeare's play, the sprite Ariel describes the process by which the sea transforms the body of a drowned king: "Those are pearls that were his eyes / Nothing of him that doth fade, / But doth suffer a seachange / Into something rich and strange" (I.ii.399-402). Here, too, Phlebas the Phoenician suffers a seachange in the depths. This transformation is often read as a symbol of the subconscious processes by which the stuff of life becomes the stuff of art. It speaks of an image that is central to Eliot's earlier poem "The Love Song of J. Alfred Prufrock": "We have lingered in the chambers of the sea / By sea-girls wreathed with seaweed red and brown" (129-30). Note that Part IV also fulfills Madam Sosostris's injunction to "Fear death by water" (55).

The fifth and final part of the poem, "What the Thunder Said," begins with passages evoking Jesus's agony in the garden of Gethsemane the night before he was crucified, the apostles' journey to Emmaus, where they found Jesus's empty tomb and Shackleton's expedition across the Antarctic. It then introduces a landscape that has only been hinted at in Part I: the desert of the red rock. This waterless landscape stands in sharp contrast to the undersea imagery of "Death by Water," and this dialectic of desert and sea remains one of the most elaborately developed sources of tension in the poem. Midway through "What the Thunder Said," the narrator introduces a third geography: the wilderness in which sits an empty chapel. In his notes, Eliot refers readers to Jessie Weston's book "From Ritual to Romance," a study of the ways in which the vestiges of pre-Christian fertility cults manifest themselves in the Christian tradition. Eliot seems to imply that "The Waste Land" is a modern grail legend, and that the overarching narrative of the poem is one of the journey to the empty chapel.

Yet Eliot's notes warrant further scrutiny. Eliot first published the poem in two journals, "The Dial" and "The Criterion," and in neither publication was the work accompanied by notes. When the poem was published as a small book, the editors asked Eliot to flesh out the volume by appending notes to it. Eliot therefore wrote the notes after the poem had been completed. In a 1956 lecture, Eliot termed his notes to the poem "a remarkable exposition of bogus scholarship" saying, "I regret having sent so many enquirers off on a wild goose chase after Tarot cards and the Holy Grail" ("On Poetry" 110).

The poem ends with a crescendo of allusions and references, culminating in the ritualistic closing of the "Brihadaranyaka Upanishad": "Datta. Dayadhvam. Damyata. / Shantih shantih shantih" (433-4). The three Sanskrit words beginning with the syllable "da" mean, respectively, "give," "sympathize," and "control." In a traditional Buddhist story, these are the words that the rumbling thunder speaks. In his notes, Eliot translates "shantih" as "The peace which passeth understanding" (55). Thunder and rain thus bring peace to the wasted land and closure to a poem that has dwelt on sterility and aridity.

Historical Context

"The Waste Land" reflects the senseless destruction of the First World War. Eliot's contemporaries read it as an indictment of that war. Although never explicitly mentioned, the war is present in the veteran Stetson (69), the "falling towers" of the centers of civilization (373), and, more globally, in the sense of desolation and loss which pervades the poem.

Eliot, like most men and women of his generation, was personally affected by the war. He dedicated his first book of poetry, "Prufrock and Other Observations" (1917), to Jean Verdenal, a friend from his time in Paris who was killed in battle. Classmates from Harvard and Oxford likewise met their death in the trenches. Eliot's brother-in-law, Maurice Haigh-Wood, served on the frontlines throughout the war. Although Eliot tried to enlist upon the United States' entry into the war in 1917, he was rejected because of his health. Eliot therefore spent the war years in a London that had been emptied of its young men. He would have walked this ghostly city with a double awareness, thinking both of the grey streets around him and of the brutalities taking place in the European trenches. The narrators of "The Waste Land" are similarly aware of an infernal landscape that underlies their modern city.

Postwar London was the center of literary modernism, and Eliot's circle of friends and associates included Ezra Pound, who was instrumental in the publication of "The Love Song of J. Alfred Prufrock" in 1915 and who later edited "The Waste Land." Virginia and Leonard Woolf, who published several of Eliot's poems at their Hogarth Press, and novelist Wyndham Lewis, who edited the Modernist journal "Blast," were also instrumental in the publication. He rubbed shoulders with W. B. Yeats and, on a visit to France, with James Joyce. Modernism might best be defined by Ezra's Pound's dictum to "Make it New." Literature must develop new forms to accommodate and express both enduring values and the realities-be they valuable or not-of the modern age. Yet these new forms must be rooted in the great art and literature of the past, and indeed must reinterpret the perennial truths of such art for a new age. The publication in 1922 of James Joyce's "Ulysses" and Eliot's "The Waste Land," both of which draw on classical texts, myths, and archetypes to represent the modern condition, brought Modernism into the public eye and signaled just how important this movement would be for novels and poetry alike.

There is yet another historical context in which to read the poem: that of the history of English literature. Eliot argued in his influential essay, "Tradition and the Individual Talent" that "What happens when a new work of art is created is something that happens simultaneously to all the works of art which preceded it" (15). In other words, existing and new works of literature alike must be read in the context of all works of literature, because each work has its place in a historical order. Eliot's poem draws on a tremendous number of sources, and takes much of its strength and meaning through allusion. Yet "The Waste Land" also changes the way in which one reads the literature to which it alludes. When a reader familiar with "The Waste Land" reads "The Tempest," Ariel's song ("Full fathom five thy father lies") has been transformed by its Eliotic context. For the "Waste Land" reader, this passage becomes a new center of the play.

Societal Context

Later in life, Eliot averred that while critics have deemed "The Waste Land," "an important bit of social criticism," he himself considered the poem "only the relief of a personal and wholly insignificant grouse against life" ("The Waste Land" 1). In truth, the poem can be both, for Eliot's personal grouses tended toward social criticism, and he took society's shortcomings very personally.

The product of a classical education and the scion of an old and prominent family, Eliot was both appalled and fascinated by the lower classes. "The Waste Land" is full of characters who speak to a disintegration of the old order. Some of this

disintegration is financial: the upstart city clerk, "one of the low on whom assurance sits / As a silk hat on a Bradford millionaire," is a portrait of uppity petty bourgeois (233-34). The woman in the Hofgarten, who might be German, Russian, or Lithuanian, speaks to a blurring of ethnic, linguistic, and national identity. Eliot longed for a more fixed social order and a homogenous culture. This is what he believed to have existed under the reign of Queen Elizabeth and which he credits as helping to account for the richness and unity of Elizabethan and Jacobean literature ("Selected Essays" 341).

Eliot's interest in shared belief systems and in the cultural and social identities such systems foster helps to explain the appeal that anthropology held for the poet. At the time he was composing "The Waste Land," Eliot was greatly taken with Jessie Weston's "From Ritual to Romance," an anthropology text which argued that any number of religious and cultural institutions have their origins in primitive nature worship and ritual sacrifices. The ritual that most appealed to Eliot was that of the sacrifice of the Fisher King, in which a primitive king or his effigy is drowned or buried in order to appease the gods and hence produce a harvest. It matters little that Weston's work has largely been debunked: she provided Eliot with a framework on which to hang some of his ideas about religion and culture. While Eliot's notes may overstate the centrality to his poem of the Fisher-King ritual, this concept nevertheless goes a long way toward explaining the connections between the poem's broken land, fallen kings, and lost faiths. Eliot also credits in his notes Frazier's "The Golden Bough," a seminal work of anthropology, which he says has "influenced our generation profoundly" (50).

Eliot's interest in anthropology and culture would eventually become a more directed form of social criticism. In "The Waste Land," the people of the unreal city have lost touch with the rituals necessary to bring rain, spring, and rebirth to the land. With this loss of ritual comes a loss of culture and morality. In the years following his conversion to Anglicanism, Eliot would become increasingly interested in social rather than literary criticism. Works like "After Strange Gods" (1934) and "The Idea of a Christian Society" (1940) explicitly address what Eliot saw as a loss of religion and culture in modern society, and lay out some of the means by which the traditions of a homogeneous Christian society might be reestablished.

Scientific & Technological Context

"The Waste Land" is a product of the modern, post-industrial city. To put it another way, the modern, post-industrial city is a wasteland for Eliot. Its citizens have become automatons who function according to the dictates of their workaday schedules:

> A crowd flowed over London Bridge, so many,
> I had not thought death had undone so many.
> Sighs, short and infrequent, were exhaled,
> And each man fixed his eyes before his feet.
> (62-5)

This unreal city is full of reminders of the time, from the bells of averred, which ring "with a dead sound on the final stroke of nine" (the start of the workday), to the publican's recurring cry of "HURRY UP PLEASE ITS TIME" (141). Frank Budgen, an early critic of James Joyce, argues that industrialism has produced the modernist preoccupation with time: "James Watt invented the steam engine and the steam engine begat the locomotive, and the locomotive begat the time-table, forcing men to think in minutes where their grandfathers thought in hours" (129). Men no longer live their lives in accordance with the progress of the sun or seasons, but of the abstract hands of a clock.

Modern technology tends, in "The Waste Land," to cheapen nature and the sublime. Man makes his mark on the river Thames, for example, with "empty bottles, sandwich papers, / Silk handkerchiefs, cardboard boxes, cigarette ends" and, on a larger scale, with the "oil and tar" that the river "sweats" (177-8; 267; 266). Likewise, the introduction of a modern element frequently subverts the narrator's attempt to allude to a line of poetry or a sentiment from a pre-industrial age. The sound of motorcar horns distracts Mrs. Sweeney from what she should be listening for-the sounds of "time's winged chariot" (Marvell 22). Nor is it insignificant that the woman who goes through the motions of a sexual liaison in "The Fire Sermon" is a typist. After her lover departs, "She smoothes her hair with automatic hand, / And puts a record on the gramophone" (255-6).

Yet in other places, modern technology becomes the stuff of lyric poetry: "At the violet hour, when the eyes and back / Turn upward from the desk, when the human engine waits / Like a taxi throbbing waiting" (215-7). Eliot was quite concerned about the implications that technological innovations would have for poetry. He wrote in 1926, "Perhaps the conditions of modern life (think how large a part is now played in our sensory life by the internal combustion engine!) have altered our perception of rhythms" (Smith 51). It would be reductive to read this alteration as wholly negative. In Eliot's later work "Four Quartets," the tube-train becomes a place of contemplation, while in the play "The Cocktail Party" a character declares of an elevator "I like to manage the machine myself—In a lift I can meditate" (311). Eliot seems to measure the value of a particular technological innovation according to whether it leads to distraction or encourages contemplation.

On another level, too, "The Waste Land's" juxtaposition of narrators and of fragments of verse or conversation may owe a debt to the telephone, radio, the gramophone, and other technologies which allowed, for the first time, voice to exist entirely independent of speaker. A poem of disembodied voices, "The Waste Land" could not have been written in any century but the twentieth.

Religious Context

Although raised in a Unitarian family, Eliot was not a practicing Christian at the time he composed "The Waste Land." Yet throughout the teens and twenties, Eliot evinced a wary fascination not only with various denominations of Christianity, but with Buddhism, as well. In 1914 and 1915, he wrote a series of poems that treat martyrdom. "The Love Song of J. Alfred Prufrock" likewise draws on images of Christian martyrs; Prufrock says he, like John the Baptist, has "seen my head (grown slightly bald) brought in upon a platter" (82). However, Prufrock ultimately concludes that he is "no prophet." Both Dante, whom he first discovered at Harvard, and St. John of the Cross, also enthralled Eliot. Nor were his religion interests limited to Christianity. He studied Buddhism at Harvard, attended a few sessions of a Buddhist society at Oxford, and briefly contemplated converting to the Eastern religion. A decade later, Eliot did convert, but not to Buddhism. In 1928, he was baptized and confirmed in the Church of England. The orthodox and ritualized faith of The Church of England, or Anglicanism, stood in sharp contrast to the liberal-humanistic Unitarianism of Eliot's boyhood. One of the challenges for Eliot's biographers, then, is to determine the nature of his religious sentiment and convictions at the time that he was composing "The Waste Land."

"The Waste Land" is shot through with Christian imagery and loci, and the poems' churches, like the rock of Eliot's desert, seem to offer shelter. Amid the "clatter and chatter" (262) of Lower Thames Street, the interior of the church of Magnus Martyr holds "inexplicable splendor of Ionian white and gold" (265). The chapel of "What the Thunder Said" represents a quest's end. While the chapel may be empty, the quester's arrival there seems to invoke presence: a cock on the roof crows, lightning flashes, and life-giving rain finally falls on the broken ground. At the end of both "The Fire Sermon" and of the poem itself, Eliot fuses

Christianity and Buddhism. If anything, the conclusion of the poem falls more heavily in the camp of the latter faith, with the "Datta. Dayadhvam. Damyata" of the Vedic Upanishad providing a sense of structure and peace (432).

Eliot moved ever closer to an Orthodox Christianity in an era in which more and more people were drifting away from the faith. "The Waste Land" offers a bleak vision of modern life, but religion and literature remain the means by which one may transcend this bleakness.

Biographical Context

Thomas Stearns Eliot was born into a prominent St. Louis Unitarian family in 1888. He attended Harvard, where he earned a bachelor's degree in philosophy and a master's degree in English Literature. He began writing poetry and spent a semester in Paris. It was as a Harvard doctoral student that Eliot first came to England in 1914. Having won a traveling fellowship, he studied first in Germany and then, with the outbreak of World War I, in England. He studied philosophy at Merton College, Oxford, and wrote a dissertation on philosopher F. H. Bradley.

In 1915, Eliot abandoned this orderly, academic life by impulsively marrying Vivienne Haigh-Wood, an Englishwoman. Haigh-Wood suffered from a nervous condition and other vaguely diagnosed medical conditions, and their marriage would be a fraught one. It was also in 1915 that Eliot met Ezra Pound, who immediately took Eliot under his wing. Pound, a few years Eliot's senior and already a published poet was instrumental in getting "The Love Song of J. Alfred Prufrock" printed in 1914.

Both his marriage and his new role as a published poet prompted Eliot to remain in England and make his living as a writer. After a brief stint teaching middle school, Eliot adopted a rigorous schedule of writing book reviews and teaching extension college classes. In 1917, he took a job at

Lloyd's Bank in the square mile of London known as the City, where he would work until 1926. Eliot published his first collection of poetry, "Prufrock and Other Observations," in 1917. This was followed by "Poems" (1920), his first book of criticism, "The Sacred Wood" (1920), which gathered excerpts from some of the dozens of book reviews, and critical pieces he had written over the previous five years.

The Eliots' marriage was a trial for both husband and wife, and effectively ended with their separation and with Vivienne's subsequent commitment to a mental hospital in the 1930's. Vivienne's role in the marriage and her impact on Eliot's work has been the subject of gossip, scholarly debate, and even a popular play, "Tom and Viv." It is tempting to read the marriage of "A Game of Chess" as a roman-a-clef, with the woman with the bad nerves standing in for Vivienne and the silent, morbid husband for Eliot. One must note, however, that Vivienne read this episode in Eliot's draft and wrote "brilliant!" in the margin. Certainly, Eliot drew on personal experience in his poetry. The conversation about Lil and her husband, for example, was suggested to Eliot by a conversation he overheard his housekeeper having in the back parlor. However, Vivienne seems not to have read the marriage of the first half of the poem as a betrayal. In print, at least, she was nothing but enthusiastic about the poem. She suggested several other changes to "The Waste Land," and composed the line "What'd you get married for if you don't want children?" ("The Waste Land" 21).

Vivienne contributed to "The Waste Land," but the poem's real editor was Pound. Eliot sent Pound the manuscripts for a long poem called "He Do the Police in Different Voices" (the title is drawn from Dickens) which drew together poems and fragments that Eliot had composed separately and was struggling to hammer into a coherent shape. Here Eliot was following a process he describes in a 1959 interview with Donald Hall of the "Paris Review," as "Doing things separately and seeing the possi-

bility of fusing them together, altering them, and making a kind of whole of them" (Gardner 14). "He Do the Police in Different Voices," contained almost all of the passages, which would become the text of "The Waste Land." Pound's contribution was ruthlessly to excise the text, cutting away many of Eliot's narratives and transitions. Pound summed up his role in the genesis of "The Waste Land" in a poem he appended to Eliot's manuscript: "Know diligent Reader / That on each Occasion / Ezra performed the caesarian Operation" (Letters 498).

The last part of "The Waste Land" was written under very different circumstances than the preceding ones. Eliot suffered some form of nervous breakdown or anxiety attack in 1921, immediately following his mother's first visit to England. Three months leave from the bank allowed him both to recuperate and to finish his poem. At Margate in October, he finished Part III. At a sanitarium in Lausanne during November and December, he wrote parts IV (which was a recasting of an earlier poem) and V. He gave the work to Pound upon returning to London in January 1922, who again edited with a heavy pen. The poem was published later that year.

"The Waste Land" cast a long shadow both on English and American literature and on Eliot's life. In the wake of its success, Eliot was lionized as the most prominent voice of Modernism. Indeed, the great popularity of the poem proved something of a double-edged sword to Eliot, who struggled for the next several years to find a new theme and voice.

Matthew J. Bolton, Ph.D.

Works Cited

Budgen, Frank. *James Joyce and the Making of Ulysses*. Bloomington: Indiana UP, 1960.

Chaucer, Geoffrey. *The Complete Poetry and Prose*. Edited by John H. Fisher. London: Harcourt Brace, 1989.

Eliot, T. S. *Selected Essays: 1917-1932*. New York: Harcourt, Brace and Company, 1932.

_____. *On Poetry and Poets*. London: Faber & Faber, 1957.

_____. *The Complete Poems and Plays*: 1909-1950. New York: Harcourt, Brace & World, 1962.

_____. "The Waste Land": *A Facsimile and Transcript of the Original Drafts including the Annotations of Ezra Pound*. Ed. Valerie Eliot. New York: Harcourt Brace Jovanovich, 1971.

Gardner, Helen. *The Composition of Four Quartets*. London: Faber, 1978. Shakespeare, William. The Riverside Shakespeare. Boston: Houghton Mifflin Company, 1974.

Discussion Questions

1. What might the red rock of "The Burial of the Dead" symbolize? Why does the handful of dust inspire fear? Is there a relationship between the red rock, the desert, and the handful of dust?

2. What seems to be the relationship between reading and writing, or between the study of literature and the creation of it, as manifested in Eliot's use of allusions and quotations?

3. Contrast the two marriages in "A Game of Chess." Do the upper class and the lower class couple suffer from any of the same problems? How do the two conversations serve to illuminate each other?

4. Freud talked of the self as being made up of three components: the id, the ego, and the superego. Does Freud's model cast any light on the voices of "The Waste Land?" Do any lines or parts of the poems seem to be the "voice" of id, ego, or superego?

5. While Eliot later in life denied that "The Waste Land" was a social commentary, it was read at the time of its publication as an indictment of the post-World War 1 cultural landscape. What do you see as being some of the specific criticisms that the poem levels against twentieth-century society?

6. Contrast the sea and the desert as represented in various parts of the poem. What does each landscape seem to represent? Are the two landscapes necessary to each other?

7. What seems to be the attitude toward love and sex in the poem? Are the romantic and sexual impulses complementary or opposed? Are there parallels between the poem's images of nature-flowers, gardens, the desert, dust, the river, the sea, the rain-and its images of romantic or sexual stirrings?

8. Many of the authors and passages that Eliot quotes in "The Waste Land" recur in his critical essays. The poem gathers some of the authors and works of literature that were most important to him. Create your own list of favorite quotations from books, movies, and songs. How do some of these quotations combine to create a meaning that is more than the sum of its parts? Can you draw some conclusions about yourself and your worldview based on these quotes?

9. Discuss the three seers of "The Waste Land": the sibyl, Madame Sosostris, and Tiresias. What connections can you draw among the three? What seems to be the nature of foresight in the world of "The Waste Land"? Are there any other seer-figures in this poem?

10. In his notes to the poem, Eliot seems to offer, at different points, the figure of Tiresias, the legend of the fisher king, and the search for the grail chapel as overarching narratives uniting the disparate parts of "The Waste Land." Do you see an overarching narrative at work in the poem, and if so, what is it?

Essay Ideas

1. Identify the speakers in any one part of "The Waste Land." How does Eliot transition from one speaker to another? What is the effect of juxtaposing any particular pair or group of speakers?

2. One of the themes that unite the disparate parts of this poem is the notion of archetypes. Discuss any of the following archetypal figures: the sailor, the fortuneteller, the witness to calamity, the dishonored girl, the fallen king.

3. Read one of Eliot's sources, be it Shakespeare's "The Tempest," Ovid's "Metamorphoses," Dante's "Inferno," or a short poem such as Marvell's "To His Coy Mistress." Where and how does Eliot allude to this source? How does his allusion both draw on and subvert the original text? What is the context of the quotation in the original text and how does the line's meaning change in the new context of "The Waste Land?"

4. Eliot eventually expressed regret that his notes to "The Waste Land" sent credulous readers on a "goose chase" ("On Poetry and Poets" 110). Do the notes represent a sincere attempt on Eliot's part to explain his own poem or are they, as Hugh Kenner argues, spoken from behind a mask? Are the notes "narrated" by one character or by many?

5. Read or re-read Eliot's earlier poems, such as "The Love Song of J. Alfred Prufrock," "Portrait of a Lady," "Preludes," or "Gerontion." How does Eliot rework some of his earlier themes, characters, or images into the fabric of "The Waste Land?"

Langston Hughes, pictured above, wrote "The Weary Blues," featured opposite. "I, Too, Sing America," also by Hughes, is featured on page 69 of this volume. Photo: Gordon Parks, photographer, Library of Congress

The Weary Blues

by Langston Hughes

Content Synopsis

"The Weary Blues" is a poem in which the speaker describes his experience listening to blues music in a Harlem nightclub. The poem is written in rhymed couplets that mimic the rhythms of blues music using various literary techniques such as alliteration, "Droning a drowsy…," and onomatopoeia, "thump, thump, thump …." The speaker pays special attention to the actions of the piano player, depicting him "Rocking back and forth to a mellow croon" and doing a "lazy sway" as he played from his "rickety stool." Hughes injects phrases such as "Sweet Blues!" and "O Blues!" into the poem in between descriptions to emphasize the emotion and passion that went into the pianist's performance.

The second half of the poem includes the use of song lyrics written in African American southern dialect to capture the full power and passion of the Blues. Lines such as "Ain't got nobody in all this world" and "I ain't happy no mo' and I wish that I had died" sung as the player made his "old piano moan" help recapture the speaker's experience and illustrate the power of blues music on both the player and the listener.

The poem ends as the speaker suggests that after the performer stops singing and playing the piano, he continues to hear the blues music playing in his head. The last line of the poem states that the piano player then slept like a rock or a man that's dead."

The last line implies the hard life and struggles of the piano player, which are reflected in the blues music he performs.

Symbols & Motifs

Hughes uses repetition, alliteration, assonance, and rhyme in order to replicate the pace and rhythm of blues music as well as the overall melancholy associated with the music. Hughes includes elements of personification in "The Weary Blues" to bring the piano to life. It "moans" as the player sings the blues. The image of a moaning piano accentuates the tone of the music and further enhances the musical effect of the poem. The song lyric included in the song also help to illustrate the nature of the blues as a crying out of sorrow and loneliness.

Historical Context

Langston Hughes' success and the rising popularity of blues music coincided with the Harlem Renaissance, a time when African Americans were thriving in the fields of art, music, and literature ("Langston Hughes and the Blues"). During the 1920s, black artists were achieving wide spread recognition for the first time. Harlem became a cultural hub where writers such as Zora Neale Hurston, Claude McKay, and Langston Hughes moved to immerse themselves in the thriving community of arts and letters ("Langston Hughes and the Blues"). As more and more African Americans moved north, blues music evolved and addressed more urban topics and focused on social injustice. At this time, performers such as Louis Armstrong and Bessie Smith played for black and white audiences alike in Harlem nightclubs ("Langston Hughes and the Blues").

Hughes wrote "The Weary Blues" after listening to the blues in a Harlem nightclub one March night in 1922 (Sime and Wahlgreen 761). Hughes then set out to write a poem that integrated music, speech, and poetry. He used sound devices such as alliteration, assonance, and onomatopoeia to replicate the sounds of blues music. He included song lyrics written in dialect and constructed the poem in rhymed couplets typical of traditional lyric poetry (Sime and Wahlgreen 761). The last line of the poem took Hughes two years to write, but when he completed it, "The Weary Blues" was a success and launched his flourishing literary career (Sime and Wahlgreen 761).

Societal Context

Blues music originated from Negro folk music sung by freed slaves after the Civil War ("Langston Hughes and the Blues"). It depicted the lives of Negroes at the turn of the 20th century and expressed feelings of frustration at the prejudice and poverty that dominated this population at the time ("Langston Hughes and the Blues"). Unlike the old hymns and spirituals sung by Negroes, blues music is designed to be sung as a solo ("Langston Hughes and the Blues"). Blues music always has an element of the improvisational and changes with each individual performer (Sime and Wahlgreen 763). Lines are often repeated and some are borrowed from other songs (Sime and Wahlgreen 763). The lyrics are often ironic and comment on daily life and, of course, love ("Langston Hughes and the Blues"). A famous contemporary blues singer, B.B. King, commented that the blues is always about a man losing a woman (Sime and Wahlgreen 763).

The first blues recordings were made in 1920 and feature singers such as Bessie Smith and Ma Rainey. Most blues music was first performed in northern cities such as Chicago, Detroit, and New York where many Negroes migrated to escape the oppression of the South (Sime and Wahlgreen 763). Many fashionable nightclubs opened in Harlem, the setting of Hughes's poem.

Religious Context

"The Weary Blues" does not have a specific religious context.

Scientific & Technological Context

"The Weary Blues" does not have a specific scientific or technological context.

Biographical Context

Langston Hughes was born in 1902 in Joplin, Missouri to an abolitionist family (Jackson). He started writing poetry in the eighth grade but was encouraged by his father to study engineering (Jackson). He attended Columbia University briefly but dropped out to pursue a career as a writer. He was an avid reader and admired poets such as Walt Whitman, Edgar Lee Masters, and Carl Sandburg (Simes and Wahlgreen 760).

His first poem "The Negro Speaks of Rivers" was published in Brownie's Book—a children's magazine published by the NAACP from 1920-1921 (Jackson). He traveled to Africa, Russia, and Europe on a freighter in 1923, moved to Harlem in 1924, and found inspiration in the clubs where he would listen to jazz and blues music (Jackson). He moved to Washington D.C. for a year in 1925 and met poet Vachel Lindsay at a restaurant where Hughes was bussing tables (Simes and Wahlgreen 760). Hughes left a few of his poems at Lindsay's table and the Lindsay liked them so much that he read them at a public reading that night; an event which made Hughes a minor celebrity for a time (Simes and Wahlgreen 760).

In 1926, Hughes' first book of poetry, "The Weary Blues," was published and he moved back to Harlem. His poetry embraced the African American experience and often imitated jazz and blues music. Later in his life, he wrote poems specifically to be accompanied by jazz music (Simes and Wahlgreen 760). Hughes died from cancer in 1967. He had a successful career for over 40 years and published poetry, short stories, scripts, plays and autobiographies (Jackson). He is the first black person known in the United States to support himself solely through his writing ("Langston Hughes and the Blues").

Jennifer Bouchard

Works Cited

_____. *African American Poetry*. Englewood Cliffs, New Jersey: Globe Book Company, 1993.

Fleishmann Anne and Andy Jones. *Jazz and Literature*. 26 March 2008. http://cai.ucdavis.edu/uccp/jazzandliterature.html.

Hughes, Langston. "The Weary Blues." *Elements of Literature: Fifth Course, Literature of the United States*. Austin: Holt, Rinehart and Winston, 2003. 761-762.

Jackson, Andrew. "Langston Hughes." *Red Hot Jazz*. 26 March 2008. http://www.redhotjazz.com/hughes.html.

"Langston Hughes and the Blues". *The Rock and Roll Hall of Fame*. 2007. 26 March 2008. http://www.rockhall.com/exhibitpast/lesson-langston/.

Sime, Richard, and Bill Wahlgreen, eds. *Elements of Literature: Fifth Course, Literature of the United States*. Austin: Holt, Rinehart and Winston, 2003. 760-763.

Discussion Questions

1. What is the tone of the poem?
2. Identify the sensory details that Hughes includes in the poem.
3. How would you describe the rhythm of the poem?
4. What techniques did Hughes choose to create this rhythm?
5. What troubles might the pianist in the poem be experiencing?
6. Hughes spent two years writing the ending of this poem. Do you think the ending works?
7. What do you know about Blues music? Is there a blues influence in some of the music that is popular today?
8. Why is Langston Hughes considered a great American poet?

Essay Ideas

1. Write your own blues poem.
2. Read more poetry by Langston Hughes and write an essay in which you analyze his poetic style, themes, and structure.
3. Write an essay in which you compare the poetry of Langston Hughes to one of his big influences, Carl Sandburg or Walt Whitman.
4. Listen to some famous examples of blues music and write an essay in which you compare Hughes' poetry to blues music. What are some common elements? How do blues and Hughes' poetry reflect the "Negro soul?"
5. Explore visual art produced during the Harlem Renaissance such as the paintings of Aaron Douglas or the photographs of James Van Der Zee and compare it to the blues poetry of Langston Hughes.

The Writer

by Richard Wilbur

Content Synopsis

This 33-line poem addresses a father's emotions and memories triggered by hearing his young daughter typing in her upstairs bedroom. Eleven three-line stanzas create frequent breaks in the speaker's narration, reflecting the kaleidoscopic range of emotions and the stream-of-consciousness nature of his reactions. Rife with (often conflicting) metaphors, the short poem captures not only the essence of feelings parents harbor over their children's activities, but also reflects the difficulty of expressing oneself via language, which he addresses in terms of his daughter's writing as well as his own.

The first stanza sets the scene in which "my daughter" is in her room writing a story. Possessive pronouns in this stanza interestingly reflect the tension present during childhood and the growing need for autonomy—"her" room, given first line priority, is matched by "my daughter" in the last line of the stanza. The first stanza also provides the initial extended metaphor used by the speaker to describe the situation, comparing the writing process to a storm-tossed ship's voyage. The linden trees lashing against the girl's windows as waves would lash at the prow of a boat enforce the feel of "stormy weather." The linden tree, known for its fragrant flowers and heart-shaped leaves symbolizes the feelings of the parent for the child.

The second stanza continues the ship metaphor by comparing the sound of the typewriter keys to "a chain hauled over a gunwale." This increasingly strained metaphor extends for another stanza ("the stuff of her life is great cargo") before the speaker abandons it for a more apt comparison.

In the lighthearted and even bemused tone of the first three stanzas, which culminate in the rather dismissive "I wish her a lucky passage" line, the speaker fails to truly credit the daughter with experiencing the trauma and drama of the creative process. Ramanen cites the lucky passage line as a "benediction." The initial narrative stance projects the father's assumptions about what he feels his daughter feels about her experience to date, the "great cargo."

In stanza four, the speaker admonishes himself by projecting his own realization of the failed and shallow metaphor (he, who is a writer) onto his daughter. Ramanen suggests the speaker realizes that his initial evaluation was "too simplistic." He imagines that his daughter pauses in her composition "as if to reject my thought and its easy figure." As a result, the "poetic debate" in the poem solidifies, "The poem about his daughter becomes a poem about his capacity to write about his daughter's writing" (Ramanen).

Visual and aural imagery are present in the poem. Sounds are described in such a way that the reader can hear the clamor of an old-fashioned typewriter, the daughter banging away with enthusiastic attention. His next metaphor is both more apt and more complete, including not only his daughter's challenges but also his own. In stanza 6, the speaker recounts an incident in which a starling was trapped in the girl's room and the slow progress that led to its eventual escape out an open window. The starling flies away with the help of the father and daughter who unobtrusively open a window and then retreat rather than actively intervening and "affright[ing] it." The retelling of this event provides vivid images for the reader. The bird metaphor is discussed by Ramenen as "very literary indeed . . .Wilbur was perhaps aware of Sterne's use of it in Sentimental Journey and of Maria Bertram's reference to Sterne's use of it in Mansfield Park, for both instance the idea of confinement."

The "helpless hour" in which "we" stood peeking into the room watching the "iridescent creature" trying to make it through the window, is a much more useful metaphor than the ship example. The starling's challenge encompasses the experiences of both the daughter (as bird) and the father (as watcher). Just as the daughter must learn how to 'fly away' on her own, so too must the parent accept that they must watch over rather than intervene in their child's growth. Ramanen notes that Wilbur, "like his daughter, has been moving from captivity to freedom of the imagination and to the creative jouissance of adequate expression."

The violence and pain experienced by the bird reflect the father's deeper connection with the difficulties his daughter faces in writing. Far from the 'safe passage' he wishes her in the opening, the second metaphor allows him to empathize with his fledgling daughter/writer describing the bird "batter against the brilliance" of the window only to drop "humped and bloody" to the floor, gathering its strength for another pass. The bird's determination and sustained wounds express a kind of admiration for the bird's struggles that reflect his growing admiration for his child's attempt to write.

The heartfelt direct address to his daughter in the last stanza shifts the tone significantly. When he thinks of the bird's peril and the parallel to his daughter, he, rather than wishing her a "safe passage," realizes "It is always a matter, my darling / Of life or death, as I had forgotten. I wish / What I wished you before, but harder." This line not only illustrates the father's attitudinal shift but also allows the reader to contemplate the possible meanings of "harder" in the last line. On the most literal level, the harder refers to newer and deeper understanding of his originally shallow safe passage wish. Harder may also be a reflection of the 'hardness' of the writing process.

The form of the poem is connected to the content. While the poem in unrhymed, there is a clear control of form. Ramanen notes, "The first and third lines of each stanza are shorter than the middle line . . . the absence of rhyme is more than made up for by a strong narrative joining the stanzas together. The plot in this poem is one aspect of its unity, and this plot has its climax in a turning point precisely in the middle of the poem."

Even though this short poem is an example of one of Wilbur's works that "reads so easily that it can dispel close scrutiny . . .the smooth surface of the Wilbur poem can successfully distract us from recognizing how unusual and unexpected are the twists and leaps that structure the poem's narrative" (Modern American Poetry).

Historical Context

Growing up in the 1930's, literature, which reflected historical trends and movements, influenced both Wilbur's activities and the tenor of his poetry. He read about "people who in one way or another glamorized hoboes and the life of the road" (Mariani). Citing Hart Crane and John Dos Pasos for fueling interest in hitchhiking and 'bumming,' which influenced him to spend summers as "a kind of privileged hobo" (Mariani).

Later, the poetry of Marianne Moore, Elizabeth Bishop, and William Carlos Williams were counted as significant influences on Wilbur. Some aspects of D.H. Lawrence's natural descriptions also affected Wilbur's writing in what Wilbur calls the "poetry of close observation of things—however small" (though he discusses his feelings of Lawrence's prose as "full of shapeless blather a good deal of the time") (Mariani). Wilbur's extensive writing career has allowed him to influence and be influenced by many shifts in poetic style and form. He disagreed with William Carlos William's free-verse "revolution." He also warned against the "dangers of formalism" (Mariani). Randall Jarrell cites what he sees as the problem of Wilbur never really dealing with issues of his day in an emphatic manner, while others like John Gery see him as a poet "originally provoked by his disturbing experience in war" ("Richard Wilbur"). Another critic, John Reibetanz, points out that "one must gauge the impact of the war on Wilbur not so much by looking for reflections of it in his poetry as by observing the extent to which it has driven him into a world of his own meaning" ("Richard Wilbur"). Wilbur is also cited as having been influenced by the "beats" (Freed).

Societal Context

The issues of parent child relationships are addressed in this poem, as well as the role and difficulty of being a writer. Wilbur comments on the societal aspect of his poetry: "I felt that attention to 'the other,' whatever nature the other might have, was a kind of preliminary to social concerns, to human concerns" which he developed more clearly through his career (Mariani). Social movements against the war combined with his personal experience as a soldier affected his outlook: "Youthful engagements with leftist causes caught the attention of federal investigators when he was in training as a US Army cryptographer ("Richard Wilbur").

Religious Context

During his wartime duty as a cryptographer, Wilbur was stuck in a trench, unable to move for a week due to enemy fire as the Allied bombers "blew St. Gregory's Benedictine monastery to rubble" (Mariani). At this time, he also read Edgar Allan Poe. One interviewer asked Wilbur if "there [was] an epiphany of some sort there for you, this literal deconstruction of a Christian edifice and the simultaneous discovery of a Gnostic mind, an inturned, self-dwelling, self-immolating, and self-transcending imagination?" (Mariani). While Wilbur denies "such an esemplastic feat as that," he does concede that the juxtaposition of the two events had an effect on him that he later considered in writing (Mariani). In discussing his own faith, Wilbur comments "I'm the sort of Christian animal for whom celebration is the most important thing of all . . . When I go to church, what doesn't particularly interest me is the Creed . . . What I respond to is "lift up your hearts!" (Mariani). Brought up in the Episcopal Church, Wilbur was also exposed to Baptist services that he enjoyed for their rousing songs. After his wartime experience, Wilbur turned more firmly away from religion and into literature as a source of influence (Mariani). Freed notes that Wilbur began to write in order to "confront the fear and the physical and spiritual detachment brought about by a world in upheaval."

Scientific & Technological Context

The poem relies on natural imagery and the basic human functions of a family and writing as a physical and intellectual process. The typewriter, the only technological device available for transcribing thoughts before the prevalence of personal computers, reflects more the time than a conscious choice on the part of the daughter to use a manual typewriter instead of a computer. Wilbur also chooses to have his daughter use a typewriter rather than write in longhand. While this could be perceived as a comment on the noise and passion of writing on a typewriter versus the quiet aspects of writing longhand, it also serves a useful plot point. The father can hear the daughter writing from some distance, whereas if she were writing in longhand he would have to observe her to know she was trying to write.

Biographical Context

The poem itself is autobiographical in nature, addressing a moment in which Wilbur listens to his daughter typing a story. Cited as "one of the world's most highly regarded poets—often considered America's finest poet writing in traditional meters and forms" (Mariani), Wilbur was poet laureate in the United States from 1987 to 1988. Born in New York City, his family moved to a farm in North Caldwell, New Jersey when Wilbur was two years old. He is credited with writing his first poem at the age of eight. Wilbur enjoyed the pastoral life until he was approximately sixteen. Farm living is what Wilbur identifies as his first training in honing the observational talents for which he became famous, as well as his interest in "nature and in farming" (Mariani). Wilbur's travels across the country while he was a student at Amherst (once alone over a summer vacation and once in the company of fellow Amherst students) provided a wealth of images. Wilbur would draw upon these images in the future providing a unique perspective from which to explore American life and values at that time. Wilbur served in World War II as a cryptographer for the U.S. army and began to write poems in the 1940s. After the war, Wilbur attended Harvard, receiving his MA in 1954; his first book was published that same year. According to the poetry critic Randall Jarrell, Wilbur "obsessively sees, and shows, the bright underside of every dark thing." ("Richard Wilbur").

Tracy M. Caldwell, Ph.D.

Works Cited

Freed, Walter B. *Richard Wilbur. Critical Survey of Poetry Second Revised Ed.* 2003. *MagillOnLiteraturePlus.* EBSCO. 24 Aug. 2005

Mariani, Paul. "A Conversation with Richard Wilbur." *Image: A Journal of the Arts and Religion 12* (1995 Winter). 24 Aug. 2005. http://www.imagejournal.org/wilburframe.html.

Modern American Poetry. *Richard Wilbur: Biography and General Commentary.* 24 Aug. 2005. http:///www.english.uiuc.edu/maps/poets/s_z/wilbur/bio/htm.

Ramanen, Mohan. "Wilbur's 'The Writer.'" *The Explicator 50.1.* (1991) Academic Search Premier. EBSCO. 24 Aug. 2005.

Wilbur, Richard. "The Writer." *In Literature: An Introduction to Fiction, Poetry and Drama.* X. J. Kennedy and Dana Gioia, Ed. New York: Pearson/Longman, 2005.

Discussion Questions

1. Do you find writing difficult? Do you like writing fiction? Do you think it is harder or easier than writing non-fiction?
2. To what extent do you think autobiographical experiences should appear in fictional literature? How do you draw the line between fiction and non-fiction?
3. Think about the two metaphors provided in the poem. Why is the first inappropriate? Is there any way in which the ship metaphor could have been adapted and/or expanded to be more useful?
4. There is violence in the starling's 'humped and bloody' body as it attempts escape-how does that relate to the daughter's writing? What do you think Wilbur is saying about the process of writing?
5. In what ways are the father and daughter illustrated as parallel characters?
6. What is the overriding emotional tone of the piece? Do you think the tone or mood shifts from the beginning to the end?
7. How does Wilbur utilize the five senses (imagery) in this poem?
8. What might be counted as a symbol in the poem?
9. What can you establish about the relationship between the father and daughter in the few short lines of the poem? Are they close?
10. What other literary devices appear in the poem to emphasize the main point?

Essay Ideas

1. Explore and analysis the use of metaphor, setting, tone and imagery in developing the poem's meaning
2. Compare this poem with any other poem about the process of writer and each speaker's feelings about the writing process.
3. Write a paper that explores the ways in which Wilbur's life experiences seem to have influenced the content of this poem.
4. Write an essay that explores how various writers and writing trends seem to have influenced this poem.
5. Write an essay exploring this poem in conjunction with any other Wilbur poem, comparing and contrasting tone, content and literary devices.

BIBLIOGRAPHY

Ackroyd, Peter. *T. S. Eliot: A Life*. New York: Simon & Schuster, 1984.

Adams, Richard P. "The Failure of Edwin Arlington Robinson." *TSE: Tulane Studies in English*. Vol. 11 (1961): 97–51.

Alvarez, A. *The Savage God: A Study of Suicide*. Harmondsworth: Penguin, 1974.

Angelou, Maya. "Still I Rise." Poets.org. *The Academy of American Poets*. 4 April 2008. http://www.poets.org.

Augustine. *City of God*. New York: Random House (Modern Library), 1994.

Balakian, Peter. *Theodore Roethke's Far Fields*. Baton Rouge: Louisiana State UP, 1989.

Banjeree, Jacqueline. "Grief and the Modern Writer." English: *The Journal of the College English Association*: 43 (1994). 17–36.

Barbour, Brian M. "Poetic Form in 'Journey of the Magi'." *Renascence: Essays on Values in Literature* 40 (1988): 189–196.

Bartow, Anna. *Autobiography: Maya Angelou*. 2008. Yale New Haven Teachers Institute. 5 April 2008. http://www.yale.edu/ynhti/curriculum/units.

Bassnett, Susan. *Sylvia Plath*. Towata, NJ: Barnes & Noble, 1987.

Becker, Ernest. *The Denial of Death*. New York: Free Press, 1973. Print.

Bedient, Calvin. "Sentencing Eros." *Salmagundi* 97. Winter, 1993. 169–181. Print.

Beers, Kylene and Robert Probst, eds. *Elements of Literature: Fifth Course, Literature of the United States*. Austin: Holt, Rinehart and Winston, 2003. 409–417.

Behr, Caroline. *T. S. Eliot: A Chronology of his Life and Works*. New York: St. Martin's Press, 1983.

Bergson, Henri. *Matter and Memory*. New York: Zone Books, 1991.

Berman, Jeffrey. *Surviving Literary Suicide*. Amherst: U of Massachusetts P, 1999.

Bishop, Elizabeth. *The Complete Poems*. New York: Farrar, Straus, and Giroux, 1993.

———. *"One Art: Letters."* Ed. Robert Giroux. New York: Farrar, Straus, and Giroux, 1994.

Bixler, Francis. *Original Essays on the Poetry of Anne Sexton*. U of Central Arkansas P, 1988.

Blalock, Susan E. *Guide to the Secular Poetry of T. S. Eliot*. New York: G.K. Hall, 1996.

Broe, Mary Lynn. *Protean Poetic: The Poetry of Sylvia Plath*. Columbia: U of Missouri P, 1980.

Bronfen, Elisabeth. *Over her Dead Body: Death, Femininity, and the Aesthetic*. Manchester: Manchester UP, 1992.

Bronfen, Elisabeth. *Sylvia Plath*. Plymouth: Northcote, 1998.

Brooks, Cleanth. "Teaching 'The Love Song of J. Alfred Prufrock.'" *Approaches to Teaching Eliot's Poetry and Plays*. Ed. Jewel Spears Brooker. New York: Modern Language Association, 1988. 78–87.

Brooks, Gwendolyn. "The Mother." *Selected Poems*. New York: HarperCollins, 1963.

Budgen, Frank. *James Joyce and the Making of Ulysses*. Bloomington: Indiana UP, 1960.

Bundtzen, Lynda K. *Plath's Incarnations: Women and the Creative Process*. Ann Arbor: U of Michigan P, 1983.

Burgess, E. F. "T. S. Eliot's 'The Journey of the Magi'." *Explicator* 42 (1984): 36.

Burt, Stephen. "Trauma units: Sharon Olds's poems wrestle with the legacy of childhood abuse." *The New York Times Book Review*: *Literature Resource Center* (2002): 22." Web. "19 Sept. 2010."

Cahill, Audrey. *T. S. Eliot and the Human Predicament*. Natal: U of Natal P, 1967.

Campbell, Katie. "Sharon Olds: Overview." *Contemporary Poets*. Ed. Thomas Riggs. 6th ed. New York: St. James Press, 1995. *Literature Resource Center*. Web. 19 Sept. 2010.

Carson, Warren J. "My House." "Magill's Survey of American Literature". Revised Edition. Pasadena, CA: Salem Press, 2007. EBSCO *Literary Reference Center Plus*. Web. 22 Aug, 2010. <http://search.ebscohost.com/login.aspx?direct=true&db=lkh&AN=MOL9830000806&site=lrc-plus>.

Cecile, Kelly Holland. *Maya Angelou*. 1998. University of North Carolina. Edited by Mark Canada. 5 April 2008. http://www.uncp.edu/home/canada/work/canam/angelou.htm.

Chaucer, Geoffrey. *The Complete Poetry and Prose*. Edited by John H. Fisher. London: Harcourt Brace, 1989.

Chodorow, Nancy. *The Reproduction of Mothering: Psychoanalysis and the Sociology of Gender.* Berkeley. Los Angeles, and London: U of California P, 1978.

Ciardi, John. "Robert Frost: The Way to the Poem." *Saturday Review 40.* (April 12, 1958).13–15, 65.

Clark, James A. "Wallace Stevens: A Portrait of the Artist as a Phenomenologist." *Philosophy in the Contemporary World 4.3* (Fall 1997): 1–5.

Classic Poetry Pages. 2003. *Lemon8 Design & Development.* 29 January 2008. http://poetrypages.lemon8.nl/life/roadnottaken/roadnottaken.htm.

Cook, Martha. "Nikki Giovanni: Place and Sense of Place in Her Poetry." *Southern Women Writers: The New Generation.* Ed. Tonette Bond Inge. Tuscaloosa: U of Alabama P, 1990. 279–300. Print.

Cook, Reginald L., and John McWilliams. "Robert Frost." *Sixteen Modern American Authors. Volume 2: A Survey of Research and Criticism since 1972.* Ed. Jackson R. Breyer. Durham, NC: Duke UP, 1990. 360–403.

Cooper, Wayne F. "Claude McKay: Rebel Sojourner in the Harlem Renaissance." Baton Rouge: Louisiana State UP, 1987.

Costello, Bonnie. *Questions of Mastery.* Cambridge: Harvard UP, 1991.

Cramer, Jeffrey S. *Robert Frost among his Poems: A Literary Companion to the Poet's Own Biographical Contexts and Associations.* Jefferson, North Carolina: McFarland & Company, 1996.

D'Avanzo, Mario L. *A Cloud of Other Poets: Robert Frost and the Romantics.* Lanham, Maryland: UP of America, 1991.

Dillingham, Thomas F. "About Sharon Olds." *The Continuum Encyclopedia of American Literature.* London, New York and Harrisburg: Continuum Publishing, 1999. Rpt.in Nelson. 23 March 2006. <http://www.english.uiuc.edu/maps/poets/m_r/olds/about.htm>.

Dillon, Brian. "'Never having had you, I cannot let you go': Sharon Olds's Poems on a Father-Daughter Relationship." *The Literary Review* 37.1 (1993): 108–118. Print.

Eliot, Charlotte C. *William Greenleaf Eliot: Minister, Educator, Philanthropist.* Boston and New York: Houghton Mifflin, 1904.

Eliot, T. S., *The Collected Poems*: 1909–1962. New York: Harcourt, 1963.

Eliot, T. S. *The Complete Poems and Plays.* New York: Harcourt, Brace & World, 1962.

———. *The Complete Poems and Plays: 1909–1950.* New York: Harcourt, Brace & World, 1962.

———. *Inventions of the March Hare.* Ed. Christopher Ricks. New York: Harcourt Brace, 1996.

Eliot, T. S. *For Lancelot Andrewes.* London: Faber and Faber, 1928.

Eliot, T.S. "The Love Song of J. Alfred Prufrock." *The Norton Anthology of English Literature.* Ed. M.H. Abrams and Stephen Greenblatt. 7th ed. 2 vols. New York: W.W. Norton, 2000. 2: 2364–2367.

Eliot, T. S. *Old Possum's Book of Practical Cats.* New York: Harcourt, Brace, & Jovanovich, 1939, 1972, 1982.

———. *On Poetry and Poets.* London: Faber & Faber, 1957.

Eliot, T. S., *The Sacred Wood, Essays on Poetry and Criticism.* New York: Bartleby.Com, 2000.

———. *Selected Essays.* New York: Harcourt, Brace & Company, 1932.

Eliot, T. S. *Selected Essays: 1917–1932.* New York: Harcourt, Brace and Company,1932.

———. "Selected Essays." *Selected Essays: 1917–1932.* New York: Harcourt, Brace and Company, 1932.

———. *The Waste Land: A Facsimile and Transcript of the Original Drafts including the Annotations of Ezra Pound.* Ed. Valerie Eliot. New York: Harcourt Brace Jovanovich, 1971.

Ellman, Richard and Robert O'Clair, Ed. *The Norton Anthology of Modern Poetry.* 2nd Ed. New York: W.W. Norton and Company, 1988. 210–213.

Feaver, Vicki. "Body and Soul: The Power of Sharon Olds." *Contemporary Women's Poetry: Reading/Writing/Practice.* Eds. Alison Mark and Deryn Rees-Jones. New York: St. Martins, 2000. 140–156.

Fleishmann Anne and Andy Jones. *Jazz and Literature.* 26 March 2008. http://cai.ucdavis.edu/uccp/jazzandliterature.html.

Fong, Bobby. "Roethke's 'My Papa's Waltz.'*College Literature.* 17.1 (1990): 79–82.

Fowler, Virginia C. *Nikki Giovanni.* New York: Twayne, 1992. Print.

Freed, Walter B. *Richard Wilbur. Critical Survey of Poetry Second Revised Ed.* 2003. *MagillOnLiteraturePlus.* EBSCO. 24 Aug. 2005.

Frost, Robert. "Crossing Paths." *Elements of Literature: Third Course.* Austin: Holt, Rinehart and Winston, 2000, p. 603.

Frost, Robert. "The Road Not Taken." *Elements of Literature: Third Course.* Austin: Holt, Rinehart and Winston, 2000, p. 602.

Galvin, Brendan. "Kenneth Burke and Theodore Roethke's 'Lost Son' Poems." In *Theodore Roethke*. Ed. Harold Bloom. New York: Chelsea House, 1988. 85–112.

Gardner, Helen. *African American Poetry*. Englewood Cliffs, New Jersey: Globe Book Company, 1993.

———. *The Composition of Four Quartets*. London: Faber, 1978. Shakespeare, William. The Riverside Shakespeare. Boston: Houghton Mifflin Company, 1974.

Gaudier-Brzeska. *A Memoir*. New York: New Directions, 1970.

———. *Selected Poems*. Edited with an introduction by T.S. Eliot. London: Faber and Faber, 1948.

George, Diana Hume. "Oedipus Anne." *Oedipus Anne: The Poetry of Anne Sexton*. U of Illinois P, 1987. 3–23. Print.

George, Diana Hume. "Oedipus Anne: The Poetry of Anne Sexton." Urbana: U of Illinois P, 1987.

Gilbert, Sandra. Review of "My Mother's Body" by Marge Piercy. *Poetry* 147.3 (December 1985): 159–61. Print.

Gilbert, Sandra M. and Susan Gubar. *The Madwoman in the Attic: The Woman Writer and the Nineteenth-Century Literary Imagination*. New Haven: Yale UP, 1979.

———. *No Man's Land: The Place of the Woman Writer in the Twentieth Century*. New Haven: Yale UP, 1994.

Ginsberg, Allen. *Howl: Original Draft Facsimile*. Ed. Barry Miles. New York: Harper Perennial. 1995.

Ginsberg, Allen. "A Supermarket in California." *Howl and Other Poems*. San Francisco: City Lights Books, 1956. Print.

Gioia, Dana. "From Coterie to Canon." *The New Criterion*. Vol. 22, No. 8. April 2004.

Giovanni, Nikki. "My House." *My House: Poems*. New York: William Morrow, 1972. 67–69. Print.

Gluumlck, Louise. "The Forbidden." *Proofs and Theories: Essays on Poetry*. New York: HarperCollins, 1994. Rpt. in Sontag and Graham. 244–253.

Goldensohn, Lorrie. *Elizabeth Bishop: The Biography of a Poetry*. New York: Columbia UP, 1992.

Gordon, Lyndall. "Eliot's New Life." New York: Farrar Straus Giroux, 1988.

Gordon, Lyndall. *T. S. Eliot: An Imperfect Life*. New York: Norton, 1998.

"Graduate Program Faculty." *Creative Writing Program, New York University*. 27 March 2006. <http://cwp.fas.nyu.edu/page/faculty>.

Greenberg, Robert A., and James G. Hepburn, eds. *Robert Frost: An Introduction*. New York: Holt, Rinehart, and Winston, 1961.

Greene, Sheila. *The Psychological Development of Girls and Women: Rethinking Change in Time*. London and New York: Routledge, 2003.

Gunn, Thom. "Poems and Books of Poems." *Yale Review* 51.1 (Autumn 1963): 140–141. Excerpted in McClatchy, ed. 124–126.

Guy-Sheftall, Beverly. "The Women of Bronzeville." *A Life Distilled: Gwendolyn Brooks, Her Poetry and Fiction*. Ed. Maria K. Mootry and Gary Smith. Urbana: U of Illinois P, 1989. 153–161.

Hamilton, David. *The Echo of Frost's Woods. Roads Not Taken: Rereading Robert Frost*. Ed. Earl J. Wilcox and Jonathan N. Barron. Columbia: U of Missouri P, 2000. 123–31.

Harris, Daniel A. "Language, History, and Text in Eliot's 'Journey of the Magi'." *PMLA*. 95 (1980): 838–856.

Harris, William J. "Sweet Soft Essence of Possibility: The Poetry of Nikki Giovanni." *Black Women Writers (1950–1980): A Critical Evaluation*. Ed. Mari Evans. New York: Doubleday, 1984. 218–28. Print.

"Hector Guimard." *The Museum of Modern Art: The Collection*. 2007. 8 Dec. 2008 <http://www.moma.org/collection/browse_results.php?criteria=O:AD:E:2407&page_number=1&template_id=6&sort_order=1>Pound, Ezra.

Heims, Neil. *Allen Ginsberg Philadelphia*: Chelsea House, 2005. Print.

Henry, Nat. "Frost's 'Stopping by Woods on a Snowy Evening.'" *The Explicator* 32.5 (1974): 69.

Hoagland, Tony. "The Unarrestable Development of Sharon Olds." *American Poetry Review*. 38.1 (2009): 7–9. Print.

Homans, Margaret. *Women Writers and Poetic Identity*. Princeton: Princeton UP, 1980.

Huggins, Nathan Irvin. "Harlem Renaissance." New York: Oxford UP, 1971.

Hughes, Langston. "I, Too, Sing America." *Elements of Literature: Fifth Course, Literature of the United States*. Austin: Holt, Rinehart, and Winston, 2003. 740.

Hughes, Langston. "The Weary Blues." *Elements of Literature: Fifth Course, Literature of the United States*. Austin: Holt, Rinehart and Winston, 2003. 761–762.

Jackson, Andrew. "Langston Hughes." *Red Hot Jazz*. 26 March 2008. <http://www.redhotjazz.com/hughes.html>.

Janssen, Ronald R. "Roethke's 'My Papa's Waltz.'*Explicator* 44.2 (Winter 1986): 43–44.

Johnson, Greg. "The Achievement of Anne Sexton." *The Hollins Critic.* 21.3 (1984): 1–13. Print.

Juhasz, Suzanne. *Naked and Fiery Forms: Modern American Poetry by Women, A New Tradition.* New York: Harper and Row, 1976. Print.

Kahn, Jacque. "About Sharon Olds." In *Nelson.* 23 March 2006. http://www.english.uiuc.edu/maps/poets/m_r/olds/about.htm.

Keller, James R. "'A Chafing Savage, Down the Decent Street': The Politics of Compromise in Claude McKay's Protest Sonnets." "African American Review" 28 (Fall 1994): 447–456. "Academic Search Premier." EBSCO. Gordon Library, Savannah State University.

Kendall, Tom. *Sylvia Plath: A Critical Study.* London: Faber & Faber, 2001.

Kenner, Hugh. *The Mechanic Muse.* New York: Oxford UP, 1987.

Kester-Shelton, Pamela, ed. *Feminist Writers.* Detroit: St. James Press, 1996. Print.

Kumin, Maxine. "How It Was." *Sexton, The Complete Poems.* xix-xxxiv. Houghton Mifflin. New York.

La Belle, Jenijoy. *The Echoing Wood of Theodore Roethke.* Princeton, New Jersey: Princeton UP, 1976.

Lancaster, Ian. "Commentary on Marge Piercy's 'My Mother's Body.' *Representative Poetry Online.* University of Toronto, 2003. Web. 28 Aug. 2010. <https://tspace.library.utoronto.ca/html/1807/4350/poem1613.html>.

"Langston Hughes and the Blues". *The Rock and Roll Hall of Fame.* 2007. 26 March 2008. http://www.rockhall.com/exhibitpast/lesson-langston/.

Lee, Ben. "Howl and Other Poems: Is There an Old Left in the New Beats." *American Literature.* 76.2 (2004) 367–389.

Leggett, B.J. *Early Stevens: The Nietzschean Intertext.* Durham: Duke UP, 1992. 12 September 2008. http://www.english.uiuc.edu/maps/poets/s_z/stevens.

Lombardo, Jeanne Belisle. "Woman as Witch in Anne Sexton's 'Her Kind.'" *Center for Future Consciousness.com.* Center for Future Consciousness, n.d. Web. 12 Sept. 2010. <http://www.centerforfuture-consciousness.com/pdf%5Ffiles/2008%5FEssays/Woman%20as%20Witch%20in%20Anne%20Sexton.pdf>.

MacCallum-Whitcomb, Susan. "Claiming Our Birth-Write: The Poetry of American Mothers." *This Giving Birth: Pregnancy and Childbirth in American Women's Writing.* Eds. Julie Tharp and Susan MacCallum-Whitcomb. Bowling Green, OH: Bowling Green State U Popular P, 2000. 39–54.

Maeder, Beverly. *Wallace Stevens' Experimental Language: The Lion in the Lute.* New York: St. Martin's Press, 1999. 12 September 2008.

Malkoff, Karl. *Theodore Roethke.* New York: Columbia UP, 1966.

Mariani, Paul. "A Conversation with Richard Wilbur." *Image: A Journal of the Arts and Religion 12* (1995 Winter). 24 Aug. 2005. http://www.imagejournal.org/wilburframe.html.

Maxwell, William J. "On 'America.'" "Modern American Poetry." Compiled by William J. Maxwell, University of Illinois at Urbana-Champaign <http://www.english.uiuc.edu/maps/poets/m_r/mckay/america.htm>.

"Maya Angelou." *Encyclopedia Britannica.* 2002. PBS.org. 5 April 20008. http://www.pbs.org/wnet/aaworld/reference/articles/maya_angelou.html.

"Maya Angelou." Poets.org. 4 April 2008. *The Academy of American Poets.* 4 April 2008. http://www.poets.org.

McCabe, Jane. "'A Woman Who Writes,' A Feminist Approach to the Early Poetry of Anne Sexton." McClatchy, ed. 216–243.

McCabe, Jane. "A Woman Who Writes: A Feminist Approach to the Early Poetry of Anne Sexton." *Anne Sexton: The Artist and Her Critics.* Ed. J. D. McClatchy. Bloomington: Indiana UP, 1978. 216–43. Print.

McClatchy, J. D., ed. "Anne Sexton: The Artist and Her Critics." Bloomington and London: Indiana UP, 1978.

———. *Anne Sexton: Somehow to Endure.* McClatchy, ed. 244–290.

McDougal, Stuart Y. "T.S. Eliot." *Sixteen Modern American Authors. Volume 2: A Survey of Research and Criticism since 1972.* Ed. Jackson R. Breyer. Durham, NC: Duke UP, 1990. 154–209.

McDowell, Margaret B. *Groundwork for a More Comprehensive Criticism of Nikki Giovanni." I Belief vs. Theory in Black American Literary Criticism.* Ed. Joe Weixlmann and Chester Fontenot. Vol. 2. Greenwood, FL: Penkeville Publishing Company, 1986. 135–60. Print.

McKay, Claude. "America." "Poet's Corner." Ed. Nelson Miller <http://www.theotherpages.org/poems/mckay01.html>.

———"A Long Way from Home." New York: Lee Furman, 1937. New York: Arno, 1969.

McKenna, John J. "Roethke's Revisions, and the Tone of "My Papa's Waltz." *ANQ* 11.2 (Spring 1998): 34–9.

McLaughlin, Charles A. *Two Views of Poetic Unity.* The University of Kansas City Review 22.3 (1956): 312–15.

McManus, Terry. "Marge Piercy—Biography." *Marge Piercy.* margepiercy.com, 2009. Web. 28 Aug. 2010. <http://www.margepiercy.com/main-pages/biography.htm>.

Menand, Louis. *Discovering Modernism: T. S. Eliot and his Context.* Oxford: Oxford UP, 1987

Meyering, Sheryl L. *Sylvia Plath: A Reference Guide.* Boston: G. K. Hall, 1990.

Meyers, Jeffrey. *Robert Frost: A Biography.* Boston: Houghton Mifflin, 1996. Print.

Middlebrook, Diane Wood. *Anne Sexton: A Biography.* Boston: Houghton Mifflin, 1991.

Middlebrook, Diane Wood. *Anne Sexton: A Biography.* New York: Vintage Books, 1992. Print.

———. "Poets of Weird Abundance." *Parnassus: Poetry in Review.* 12/13.1–2 (1985): 293–315. Print.

Modern American Poetry. http://www.english.upenn.edu/~afilreis/88/stevens-13ways.html.

Modern American Poetry. *Richard Wilbur: Biography and General Commentary.* 24 Aug. 2005. http:///www.english.uiuc.edu/maps/poets/s_z/wilbur/bio/htm.

Modern American Poetry. "Wallace Stevens." 12 September 2008. http://www.english.uiuc.edu/maps/poets/s_z/stevens.

Monte, Steven. "Stopping by Woods on a Snowy Evening." *Poetry for Students.* Detroit: Gale, 1998. 1: 279–281.

Monteiro, George. "To point or not to point: Frost's 'Stopping by Woods.'" *American Notes and Queries 16* (2003): 38–40.

Moore, Marianne. *Complete Prose.* New York: Viking, 1986. 406–7.

Moramarco, Fred, and William Sullivan. "'A Whole New Poetry Beginning Here': The Assertion of Gender." *Containing Multitudes: Poetry in the United States since 1950.* Boston: Twayne, 1998. 163–94. Print.

Moss, Barbara. *How the African American Storyteller Impacts the Black Family and Society."* 2008. Yale New Haven Teachers Institute. 5 April 2008. http://www.yale.edu/ynhti/curriculum/units.

Muske-Dukes, Carol. "Women and Poetry: Some Notes." *After Confession: Poetry as Autobiography.* Eds. Kate Sontag and David Graham. St. Paul: Graywolf Press, 2001. 281–304.

Nelson, Cary, ed. *Modern American Poetry: An Online Journal and Multimedia Companion to the Anthology of Modern American Poetry.* Ed. Cary Nelson. 1999. Department of English, University of Illinois at Urbana-Champaign.

———. "Olds, Sharon." *Merriam-Webster's Encyclopedia of Literature.* Ed. Kathleen Kuiper. Springfield, Mass: Merriam-Webster, 1995. 831.

———. "Question and Answer following Reading, January 29, 1998." *Writers Online 2, no. 3* (summer 1998). New York State Writers' Institute, University at Albany, State University of New York. 27 March 2006. <http://www.albany.edu/writers-inst/olv2n3.html#olds>.

———. *Satan Says.* Pittsburgh: U of Pittsburgh P, 1980.

———. "Sharon Olds." Interview with Laurel Blossom. *Poets & Writers Magazine* (September/ October 1993): 30–32. Rpt. in *Nelson.* 23 March 2006. <http://www.english.uiuc.edu/maps/poets/m_r/olds/excerpt.htm>.

Newman, Charles. H., Ed. *The Art of Sylvia Plath: A Symposium.* Bloomington: Illinois UP, 1970.

Olds, Sharon. "Take the I Out." *Blood, Tin, Straw: Poems.* New York: Knopf, 1999. 43. Print.

Parini, Jay. *Robert Frost: A Life.* New York: H. Holt and Co., 1999. Print.

Parini, Jay. *Theodore Roethke, an American Romantic.* Amherst: U of Massachusetts P, 1979.

Piercy, Marge. "My Mother's Body." *The Art of Blessing the Day: Poems with a Jewish Theme.* New York: Knopf, 1999. 19–25. Print.

Plath, Sylvia. *Ariel.* London: Faber, 1965.

Poe, Edgar Allan. "Alone." *Eris Etext Project.* 1 February 2007. http://www.informations.com/etexts/literature/american/1800-1899/poe-alone-426.htm.

———. "The Philosophy of Composition." *The Norton Anthology of American Literature.* Shorter 6th ed. Ed. Nina Baym. New York: Norton, 2003 (748–56).

Poets.org. 1997. *The American Academy of Poets.* 29 January 2008. http://www.poets.org/poet.php/prmPID/192.

Pollard, Clare. "Her Kind: Anne Sexton, the Cold War, and the Idea of the Housewife." *Critical Quarterly.* 48.3 (Autumn 2006): 1–24. Print.

Ramanen, Mohan. "Wilbur's 'The Writer.'" *The Explicator 50.1.* (1991) Academic Search Premier. EBSCO. 24 Aug. 2005.

"The Raven." *The Norton Anthology of American Literature.* Shorter 6th ed. Ed. Nina Baym. New York: Norton, 2003 (697–700).

———. "Sonnet—To Science." *The Norton Anthology of American Literature.* Shorter 6th ed. Ed. Nina Baym. New York: Norton, 2003 (748–56).

Reagan, Leslie J. *When Abortion Was a Crime: Women, Medicine, and Law in the United States, 1867–1973.* Berkeley: U of California P, 1997.

Robinson, Edwin Arlington. "Luke Havergal." *The Norton Anthology of Modern Poetry.* 2nd Ed. New York: W.W. Norton and Company, 1988. 210–213.

Roethke, Theodore. "My Papa's Waltz."*The Norton Anthology of Modern Poetry.* Eds. Richard Ellmann and Robert O'Clair. 1st Ed. New York: W. W. Norton & Company, 1973: 755.

Rose, Jacqueline. *The Haunting of Sylvia Plath.* London: Virago, 1991.

Sato, Hiroaki. *One Hundred Frogs: From Matsuo Basho to Allen Ginsberg.* New York: Weatherhill: 1995.

Schneider, Elisabeth. *T. S. Eliot: The Pattern in the Carpet.* Berkeley: U of California P, 1975.

Schwartz, Murray M. and Christopher Bollas. "The Absence at the Centre: Sylvia Plath and Suicide." *Sylvia Plath: New Views on the Poetry*, ed. Gary Lane. Baltimore: Johns Hopkins UP, 1979. 179–292.

Seager, Allan. *The Glass House: The Life of Theodore Roethke.* New York: McGraw-Hill, 1968.

Serio, John N. *Wallace Stevens: An Annotated Secondary Bibliography.*" Pittsburgh: U of Pittsburgh P, 1994. Print.

Sexton, Anne. "All My Pretty Ones." 1962. Rpt. in *The Complete Poems.* 47–92.

———. *The Complete Poems.* Boston: Houghton Mifflin, 1981.

Sexton, Anne. "Her Kind." *Selected Poems of Anne Sexton.* Eds. Diane Wood Middlebrook and Diana Hume George. 1988. New York: Mariner Books, 2000. 18. Print.

———. *No Evil Star: Selected Essays, Interviews, and Prose.* Ed. Steven E. Colburn. Ann Arbor: U of Michigan P, 1985.

———. "With Harry Moore." *Talks with Authors.* Ed. Charles F. Madden. Carbondale: Southern Illinois UP, 1968. Rpt. in Sexton, "No Evil Star." 41–69.

Sexton, Linda Gray. *Searching for Mercy Street: My Journey Back to My Mother, Anne Sexton.* Boston: Little, Brown. 1994.

Sharpe, Tony. *T. S. Eliot: A Literary Life.* New York: St. Martin's Press, 1991.

Sime, Richard and Bill Wahlgreen, eds. *Elements of Literature: Fifth Course, Literature of the United States.* Austin: Holt, Rinehart, and Winston, 2003. 760–763.

———. The Poetry Archive. *Langston Hughes.* 2005. 14 April 2008. <http://www.poetryarchive.org/poetryarchive/singlePoem.do?poemId=1552>.

Smith, Carol H. *T. S. Eliot's Dramatic Theory and Practice: From Sweeney Agonistes to The Elder* Statesman. Princeton: Princeton UP, 1963.

Smith, Danny D. "Biography of Edwin Arlington Robinson." Gardiner Public Library. 29 April 2009. <http://www.earobinson.com/pages/HisLife.html>.

Smith, Grover. "'Prufrock' as Key to Eliot's Poetry." *Approaches to Teaching Eliot's Poetry and Plays.* Ed. Jewel Spears Brooker. New York: Modern Language Association, 1988. 88–93.

Sontag, Kate and David Graham, Eds. *After Confession: Poetry as Autobiography.* St. Paul, MN: Graywolf Press, 2001.

Spurr, David. "Eliot, Modern Poetry, and the Romantic Tradition." *Approaches to Teaching Eliot's Poetry and Plays.* Ed. Jewel Spears Brooker. New York: Modern Language Association, 1988. 33–38.

St. John of the Cross. *Dark Night of the Soul.* New York: Doubleday, 1959.

Steiner, George. "Dying Is an Art." *Language and Silence.* London: Faber, 1967. 324–31.

Stevens, Wallace. "Sunday Morning." *Collected Poetry and Prose.* Ed. Frank Kermode and Joan Richardson. 53–56. Print.

Stevens, Wallace. "Thirteen Ways of Looking at a Blackbird." *Modern American Poetry.* 8 August 2008. University of Pennsylvania. 12 September 2008. http://www.english.upenn.edu/~afilreis/88/stevens-13ways.html.

Stone, Carole. "Sharon Olds." *American Poets since World War II": Third Series.* Ed. R. S. Gwynn. Detroit: Gale Research, 1992. *Dictionary of Literary Biography Vol. 120. Literature Resource Center.* Web. 19 Sept. 2010.

Tate, Allen. "Our Cousin, Mr. Poe." *Poe: A Collection of Critical Essays.* Ed. Robert Regan. New Jersey: Prentice Hall, 1967.

Thompson, Carole. "Places and Poetry." *The Friends of Robert Frost*. 29 January 2008. http://www.frostfriends.org.

Thompson, Lawrence. *Fire and Ice*. New York: H. Holt, 1942.

Thompson, Lawrence, and R. H. Winnick. *Robert Frost: A Biography*. New York: Holt, Reinhardt, and Winston, 1981.

Tillery, Tyrone. "Claude McKay: A Black Poet's Struggle for Identity." Amherst: U of Mass. P, 1992.

Timmerman, John H. *T. S. Eliot's Ariel Poems: the Poetics of Recovery*. Lewisburg: Bucknell UP, 1994.

Tytell, John. *African American Poetry*. Englewood Cliffs, New Jersey: Globe Book Company, 1993.

———. *Naked Angels*. New York: Grove Weidenfeld, 1976.

"Understanding the Context of Modern Poetry." *Edsitement: National Endowment for the Humanities*. 16 September 2008. http://edsitement.neh.gov/view_lesson_plan.asp?id=615.

Unger, Leonard, and William Van O'Connor. *Poems for Study: A Critical and Historical Introduction*. New York: Rinehart, 1953.

Vendler, Helen. *On Extended Wings: Wallace Stevens Longer Poems*. Cambridge, MA: Harvard UP, 1969. Print.

Vendler, Helen. "On Extended Wings: Wallace Stevens; Longer Poems." Cambridge: Harvard UP, 1969, 75–77. 15 September 2008. http://www.english.uiuc.edu/maps/poets/s_z/stevens/blackbird.htm.

Wagner, Linda. *Critical Essays on Sylvia Plath*. Boston: G. K. Hall, 1984.

Wagner, Linda W. "Anne Sexton: Overview." *Reference Guide to American Literature*. Ed. Jim Kamp. 3rd ed. Detroit: St. James Press, 1994. Print.

Wagner, Linda W. Critical Essays on Sylvia Plath. Boston: G. K. Hall & Co., 1984.

Wagner-Martin, Linda. "Anne Sexton's Life." *Modern American Poetry*. Department of English, University of Illinois at Urbana-Champaign, Feb. 2000. Web. 21 Sept. 2010. <http://www.english.illinois.edu/maps/poets/s%5Fz/sexton/sexton%5Flife.htm>.

Walker, Sue. "Marge Piercy: An Overview." "Ways of Knowing: Essays on Marge Piercy". Mobile, AL: Negative Capability, 1991. 132–47. Print.

Walker, Ursula Genung. *Notes on Theodore Roethke*. Charlottesville, Virginia: Bibliographical Society of the University of Virginia, 1968.

Wilbur, Richard. "The Writer." *In Literature: An Introduction to Fiction, Poetry and Drama*. X. J. Kennedy and Dana Gioia, Ed. New York: Pearson/Longman, 2005.

Wullschlager, Jackie. *Inventing Wonderland: The Lives and Fantasies of Lewis Carroll, Edward Lear, J. M. Barrie, Kenneth Grahame, and A. A. Milne*. New York: Free Press, 1995.

Young, James E. *Writing and Rewriting the Holocaust: Narrative and the Consequences of Interpretation*. Bloomington: Indiana UP, 1988.

INDEX